THE EMIL AND KATHLEEN SICK LECTURE-BOOK SERIES
IN WESTERN HISTORY AND BIOGRAPHY

THE EMIL AND KATHLEEN SICK LECTURE-BOOK SERIES
IN WESTERN HISTORY AND BIOGRAPHY

Under the provisions of a Fund established by the children of Mr. and Mrs. Emil Sick, whose deep interest in the history and culture of the American West was inspired by their own experience in the region, distinguished scholars are brought to the University of Washington to deliver public lectures based on original research in the fields of Western history and biography. The terms of the gift also provide for the publication by the University of Washington Press of the books resulting from the research upon which the lectures are based. This book is the tenth volume in the series.

The Great Columbia Plain: A Historical Geography, 1805–1910
by Donald W. Meinig

Mills and Markets: A History of the Pacific Coast Lumber Industry to 1900
by Thomas R. Cox

*Radical Heritage: Labor, Socialism, and Reform
in Washington and British Columbia, 1885–1917*
by Carlos A. Schwantes

*The Battle for Butte: Mining and Politics
on the Northern Frontier, 1864–1906*
by Michael P. Malone

*The Forging of a Black Community: Seattle's Central District
from 1870 through the Civil Rights Era*
by Quintard Taylor

Warren G. Magnuson and the Shaping of Twentieth-Century America
by Shelby Scates

The Atomic West
edited by Bruce Hevly and John M. Findlay

Power and Place in the North American West
edited by Richard White and John M. Findlay

Henry M. Jackson: A Life in Politics
by Robert G. Kaufman

Parallel Destinies: Canadian-American Relations West of the Rockies
edited by John M. Findlay and Ken S. Coates

PARALLEL DESTINIES

Canadian-American Relations West of the Rockies

EDITED BY

John M. Findlay and Ken S. Coates

CENTER FOR THE STUDY OF THE PACIFIC NORTHWEST

in association with

UNIVERSITY OF WASHINGTON PRESS

Seattle and London

and

McGILL-QUEEN'S UNIVERSITY PRESS

Montreal and Kingston

This book is published simultaneously in the United States and Canada
by the Center for the Study of the Pacific Northwest, P.O. Box 353587, Seattle,
WA 98195, in association with the University of Washington Press, P.O. Box 50096,
Seattle, WA 98145, and McGill-Queen's University Press, 3430 McTavish Street,
Montreal, Quebec H3A 1X9 Canada.

McGill-Queen's University Press acknowledges the support of the Canada
Council for the Arts for our publishing program. We also acknowledge
the financial support of the Government of Canada through the Book
Publishing Industry Development Program (BPIDP) for our activities.

Library of Congress Cataloging-in-Publication Data
and National Library of Canada Cataloguing in Publication Data
appear at the end of the book.

The paper used in this publication is acid-free and recycled from 10 percent
post-consumer and at least 50 percent pre-consumer waste. It meets the
minimum requirements of American National Standard for Information
Sciences—Permanence of Paper for Printed Library Materials,
ANSI Z39.48—1984. ⊗ ☉

CONTENTS

PREFACE

Scholars and the Forty-ninth Parallel

The authors whose work is assembled in this collection of essays were given a single challenge: to consider the historical significance and impact of the Canadian-American border on the lands and peoples west of the Rocky Mountains. This task is more difficult than it might seem, for most scholarship remains locked within the parameters of the nation-state. In an age of free trade, globalization, internationalism, transboundary migration, and the pervasive impact of popular culture, this assertion may seem odd. And given the academic proclivity for picking up ideas, theoretical perspectives, and new methodologies from people of other nations, the statement appears to border on the absurd. But from a practical perspective, from the world of university courses, funding agencies, research agendas, and the publishing priorities of academic journals and university presses, the point has greater legitimacy.

To a larger degree than is typically recognized, university academics work within relatively insular, national worlds. We attend conferences within our respective countries, and relatively rarely venture beyond our borders. (Canadians travel to U.S. conferences far more often than the reverse, however.) We teach courses that are typically framed by national boundaries, a fact that often limits students' understanding of the extranational history of places. Our journals and presses also tend to operate with a regional or national mandate. Occasionally, Canadian book titles find their way onto the lists of American university presses and, less often, the reverse is true. We apply for grants mostly from national agencies, which in turn set funding priorities in largely national—and often nationalistic—terms. The boundary line, which may have in some respects become less significant in recent years, still exerts considerable academic influence.

The situation is not entirely hopeless, however. There are scholars, some of whose work is assembled in this collection, who are very concerned about transborder developments. Many scholars attempt to keep abreast of the intellectual developments on both sides of the border and regularly attend conferences that draw academics from both Canada and the United States. Some scholars deliberately seek to address the concerns of the region as a whole, and not just one side of the boundary. In recent years university presses have worked cooperatively to develop transboundary markets for their books. Yet these examples of openness to cross-border scholarship and audiences remain the exception rather than the rule.

National boundaries play a vital role in professional and intellectual lives, often in ways that serve to limit and constrain scholarly research. There are important intellectual, conceptual, and practical reasons why this is so. On the most basic level, opting for cross-border study typically involves a substantial expansion in the research enterprise. A historian conducting research on a borderlands topic must visit archives in two countries and, given the dispersal of official and private records in both Canada and the United States, the cost of these expeditions can be considerable. Similarly, a geographer seeking to compare urban development in Seattle with that in Vancouver faces significant additional work and expense, often complicated by fluctuating and unbalanced currencies. To these financial and logistical burdens is added the extra challenge of staying abreast of the literature in at least two national communities (in addition to the literature in academic disciplines at large). These are formidable challenges and help explain why scholars often opt to study only Vancouver instead of Vancouver and Portland, or indigenous rights in British Columbia rather than throughout the Canadian and American Wests, or the development of feminist approaches in Washington state but not north of the forty-ninth parallel.

But there is also a more fundamental explanation for this broad pattern of nationally exclusive scholarship. We remain, as scholars and as citizens, largely fixated on the primacy of the nation-state, both as a stage for analysis and as a primary explanatory device for the patterns and developments we seek to describe. Scholars typically write about Canadian attitudes toward immigrants, U.S. Indian policy, western American assumptions about the environment, and patterns in the evolution of British Columbia's cities.

Running through these studies is the implicit assertion—typically unproven yet rarely challenged—that each nation is different and that national background is of fundamental significance in helping explain who we are, what happened, and why it happened. Nation-states are important—of that there is little doubt. But often we do not really know how many of the phenomena we describe as being "national" in character are truly that—and we have largely overlooked the opportunity to examine borders and border regions as a means of exploring nationalism as well as of making regional and cross-boundary comparisons. In this context, then, the study of borders takes on new significance.

Historians and political scientists have long argued that the establishment and maintenance of borders is one of the modern state's primary functions. The state's ability and determination to create a line of demarcation between one country and another—and to enforce economic, diplomatic, and social regulations governing the movement of people and goods across the border— is one of the fundamental acts of sovereignty and hence a vital symbol of national integrity. As the Finnish scholar Jouni Häkli has observed:

> Whether produced within academia or bureaucracy, official discourses have the important function of providing policy-making with legitimate representations and categories of the social world. In these representations the society most often is a clearly defined, bounded unit which is knowable in an objective and impartial way. However, there is a "political geography of knowledge" involved in the ways in which we represent the social world. Therefore we need to reflect upon these discursive limits and understand that this conception of society is only one possible, albeit firmly established and practically viable discursive formation, which emerged as part of the history of modern government. We should sensitize ourselves to the challenges of opening up alternative ways of conceiving society and space, that is, of crossing and rewriting the boundaries which we have inherited from the history of governmental power.[1]

One way to open up understandings of boundaries is to look for *borderlands* instead of *borders*, to consider the boundary not solely as a dividing line but rather as the backbone of a region in which people on either side of the line have key things in common. However, although the idea of borderlands is well established among those who study the American Southwest and northern Mexico, it is much less well developed among those scholars concerned with the more northwestern reaches of North America. There have been a few attempts to underscore the importance of the border regions between Canada and the United States and to begin the process of exploring their historical and contemporary dimensions. The Borderlands Project of the 1980s, linking a number of Canadian and U.S. universities and scholars and drawing its funding largely from the William H. Donner Foundation, sought to highlight borderlands studies, producing several monographs and related materials on the theme.[2] Two of the leaders of this initiative, Lauren McKinsey and Victor Konrad, have provided a useful definition of the borderlands concept:

> Borderlands is a region jointly shared by two nations that houses people with common social characteristics in spite of the political boundary between them. In a more narrow sense, borderlands can be said to exist when shared characteristics within the region set it apart from the country that contains it: residents share properties of the region, and this gives them more in common with each other than with members of their respective dominant cultures. More broadly, the borderlands is an area in which interaction has a tempering effect on the central tendencies of each society. It is assumed that the ways in which two political communities blend into each other is most clearly revealed in their borderlands.[3]

According to this definition, the study of borderland districts functions in part as the antithesis of scholarship on the nation-state. In many instances, scholars of borderlands have been more interested in documenting local connections and overlap than in explicating national distinctiveness, or they have focused their research on themes that predated the nation-state. Perhaps unexpectedly, however, it is precisely in borderlands regions where there exists an unparalleled opportunity to study the most basic questions of national difference. Most would agree that a substantial portion of Canadian and U.S. scholarship seeks, explicitly or implicitly, to identify what is specific to each nation.[4] The study of borderlands presents an occasion to examine the question of national identity in its most highly focused form. For it is on the edge of the nation, at the physical and psychological boundaries between countries, that one might legitimately expect to find a juxtaposition of "national traits," or to discover the limited distinctions between peoples separated by that intensely political artifact: the international border. Controversial developments, such as visions of the cross-border region of Cascadia, challenge regional residents to consider the prospect of a collective future. Intense rivalries—particularly over fishing, environmental concerns, and economic performance—highlight national differences and potentially exacerbate tensions. Borderlands studies—in this case, investigations of the Canadian and American Wests—afford an opportunity to identify those forces that are national and those that cross boundaries and thus potentially sit closer to the heart of the Euro–North American condition.

A small number of scholars, primarily historians, have turned their attention to cross-border, borderlands, or comparative studies regarding Canada and the United States west of the Continental Divide. Some of this work, including the American historian Carlos Schwantes's book on working-class protest, describes the extensive flow of workers and ideas across the border, picking up on a theme developed earlier by the labor economist Paul Phillips.[5] By contrast, the British Columbian historian Robin Fisher's article on indigenous-European conflict seeks to draw distinctions among national experiences.[6] A small study of the borderlands experience in the Far Northwest (Yukon and Alaska) describes the inner workings of a cross-border society—one of several operating in the Pacific Northwest.[7] The urban historian Norbert MacDonald offers a comparative history of Seattle and Vancouver.[8] And the labor historian Richard Rajala writes about capital and labor in the forest industries of British Columbia and the American Northwest.[9] The chapters that follow in this collection illustrate how the variety of historical inquiry could expand considerably beyond the existing scholarship. The essays draw on fields ranging from intellectual to political history and incorporate such themes as environmental change and immigration. Interest in borderlands need not be limited to historians and historical geographers, of course; anthropologists, legal scholars, and economists have, in relatively limited numbers, also begun to explore the differences and similarities between Canada and the United States west of the Rockies.

The American Northwest and Canadian West may offer especially useful case studies of the borderlands concept because they make up an area where the substantial economic and cultural weight of the United States has been at least partially offset by historical ties and connections with a neighbor. The increasing ties within the transnational region—marked by international rivalries in NBA basketball and minor league hockey, shared fan bases for major league baseball (the Seattle Mariners) and hockey (the Vancouver Canucks) teams, extensive cross-border travel and commerce, growing regional political connections, and considerable cultural transference—suggest a relatively new development: the creation of a postmodern world in which the nation-state is overwhelmed by the forces of internationalization. But even a cursory understanding of the history of the American Northwest and Canadian

West reveals that the contemporary situation is a continuation, or a reestablishment, of past levels of cross-border integration.

Although the border has been profoundly significant, assuming much more than a merely symbolic role in regional history, the forces of connection and interaction have also loomed large over the years. In the lands west of the Rockies, at least four aspects of development appear to have created common bonds that mitigated the power of the nation-state. First, Far Western provinces and states were colonized by concentrated eastern economic and political power, which regarded the territories as a hinterland whose raw materials were to be extracted and exported. Second, partly because of the extractive export economy of the American Northwest and the Canadian West, the hinterlands on both sides of the forty-ninth parallel were characterized by relatively sharp tensions between capital and labor as well as the development of a relatively pronounced tradition of labor radicalism. Third, the western borderlands area—and especially its workforces—contained higher percentages of aboriginal peoples and Asian immigrants than did eastern states and provinces. Fourth, the major cities of British Columbia, Washington, and Oregon, at least before 1920, possessed (compared with cities on the Atlantic Coast) greater economic opportunities for people of European descent, less manufacturing, more white-collar and service employment, fewer unskilled workers, better housing, and greater sprawl.[10]

These four common conditions never overrode national distinctions, but they did encourage both the American Northwest and British Columbia to view themselves as misunderstood, sometimes mistreated, and even rather special. The idea of being different from eastern parts of the continent encouraged the notion of exceptionalism in some instances, and even of separatism in a few cases. The Canadian West and the American Northwest did not generally envision being exceptional or separate together, as united entities, but they did occasionally imagine some mode of setting themselves apart from the rest of their respective nations. Despite the impressive power of both the modern globalizing economy and the modern international boundary, history and historical interactions do matter, and regional cultures and societies and tendencies, which transcend national boundaries, do exist.

The Canada–United States border has meant different things to different people, and those meanings have changed over time. The chapters that make up this volume explore those diverse and shifting meanings of that international boundary, particularly in lands west of the Rockies after 1840. The book got its start at a conference designed to commemorate the 150th anniversary of the Oregon Treaty of 1846, an agreement that fixed most of the border between British North America and the United States west of the Continental Divide.[11] The University of Washington in Seattle hosted a 1996 symposium called "On Brotherly Terms," which was devoted to the historical exploration of Canadian-American relations west of the Rockies. The conference organizers took the title from the words of one British commentator on the 1846 treaty negotiations. With the boundary now seemingly settled from coast to coast, he expressed hope that the Americans and the British would proceed to get along in North America "on brotherly terms."[12] (He meant, one assumes, that the two nations would treat each other in a more respectful and friendly fashion. The commentator probably had no brother himself, for otherwise he might have chosen a different adjective.)

The conference produced numerous valuable sessions and conversations—far more than could be easily captured in this one-volume collection. In deciding which contributions to include herein, as editors we chose those conference papers that seemed the most insightful, original, and provocative and that complemented one another in addressing the themes of border, borderlands, and national distinctions. We then asked the authors to revise their oral presentations for publication, keeping in mind the themes we wanted to illuminate. We added to the mix one previously published scholarly article.

The essays that follow take the measure of the border's ever-changing power to affect people's behavior and the different meanings of the border for different groups of people. Grouped into three parts, the chapters are divided somewhat along chronological lines. Part one, "The Permeable Border," focuses particularly on the nineteenth century, when the power of the international boundary was limited. Part two, "Negotiating the International Boundary," mainly examines the twentieth century, when government and bureaucracy constructed a more meaningful border in response to different events, trends, and crises. Part three, "National Distinctions," backs away from specific eras and places, and considers the extent to which the international border and its various interpreters have helped to create, perpetuate, and perhaps exaggerate the differences between Canada and the United States.

At the 1996 conference, Ken S. Coates provided the keynote address. A revised version of that talk, "Border Crossings: Patterns and Processes along the Canada-United States Boundary West of the Rockies," introduces the volume by laying out many of the multidisciplinary issues that borderlands scholars have raised and introducing the significance of the concepts of *border* and *borderland* for the Canadian and American Wests. Coates sets the stage for later essays by pointing out the broad ways in which the international boundary influenced the Far Western regions of Canada and the United States. Until the late nineteenth century, most occupants of the region, including aboriginal peoples, traders, and settlers, did not regard the border as a powerful force in their lives. The boundary remained rather permeable long after it had been drawn in 1846, until, as Coates writes, "the era of the modern state. . . . Anxious to defend national integrity and to give substance to the superficial authority of formal sovereignty, governments passed a welter of rules, regulations, and laws that gave the border and the agents of enforcement greater power." Although this era of the modern state has lasted from the late nineteenth century to the present, Coates concludes with the thought that "the border may be weakening." Regardless of what most Canadians or Americans wish, he suggests, global capitalism and modern technology may be effacing the boundary that the national governments of Canada and the United States so earnestly maintained for more than a century.

The four essays in part one focus on instances, mostly of the nineteenth century, when the power of the international boundary remained quite limited in the lives of different groups. In "No Parallel: American Miner-Soldiers at War with the Nlaka'pamux of the Canadian West," Daniel P. Marshall traces the activities of U.S. miners during the 1850s who, largely ignoring British sovereignty, imported to the mining districts of southwestern Canada a distinctly Californian, and quite brutal, set of attitudes and practices toward Native peoples. This chapter calls to mind the many instances, from the eighteenth through the twentieth centuries, of American disregard for and insensitivity to the international boundary. John Lutz, in "Work, Sex, and Death on the Great Thoroughfare: Annual Migrations of 'Canadian Indians' to the American Pacific Northwest," examines the significance of a migration that headed the other way, from British Columbia to Washington state. He explains how migrating members of British Columbia's coastal tribes preserved their own cultures while adapting to the opportunities presented by the white economy around Puget Sound. In other words, movement across the border represented for these Native peoples a continuation of older ways, not a sharp break in identity.

In "Borders and Identities among Italian Immigrants in the Pacific Northwest, 1880–1938," Patricia K. Wood looks at a third body of people in motion—immigrants whose primary national point of reference long remained in the Old World. Like American miners and First Nation migrants, Italian immigrants long remained largely indifferent to the border and hesitated to embrace Canadian national citizenship. In "Nationalist Narratives and Regional Realities: The Political Economy of Railway Development in

Southeastern British Columbia, 1895–1905," Jeremy Mouat argues that railway investors and town boosters around the turn of the century were also
in large part indifferent to the meaning of the international boundary. The
logic of finance capital and local development tended—like American miners, Native laborers, and Italian immigrants—to downplay the importance
of the international boundary. In arriving at his findings, Mouat calls into
question the nationalist perspective of those Canadian historians who have
been so influenced by the nation-state paradigm that they may have under-
estimated the transnational character of economic development in the western borderland.

The three essays in part two examine Canadian-American relations west
of the Rockies as the two nation-states grew determined to strengthen and
enforce the border during the twentieth century. In "The Historical Roots of
the Canadian-American Salmon Wars," Joseph E. Taylor III traces a century
of international diplomacy over disputed salmon runs. He finds that although
the United States and Canada managed over the decades to define national
interests and assert their respective sovereignty rather well, they did not succeed at preserving the fish they had set out to protect. This was so in part
because the salmon—like Indians, immigrants, and capital during the nineteenth century—remained indifferent to the international boundary and the
nationalist claims made on either side of it. Some proponents of the cross-
border region known as Cascadia argue for their vision on the basis of shared
ecological traits. Taylor's essay suggests that the nationalism inherent in disputes over the salmon fishery has continually trumped the "nature" that western Canadians and Americans share.

The chapters by Galen Roger Perras and Carl Abbott examine the period
since 1930 or so, when (some scholars suggest) the border's significance diminished. In "Who Will Defend British Columbia? Unity of Command on the
West Coast, 1934–42," Perras points once more to an instance of American
disregard for the importance of the international boundary to Canadians.
Although Canada and the United States were staunch allies during World
War II, Canada zealously guarded the integrity of its borders by refusing to
accept U.S. proposals for a joint, American-dominated defense of the West
Coast in the event of a Japanese attack. Perras concludes his essay by pointing out that Canada's forceful words against U.S. influence in fact masked
a substantial geopolitical weakness. Abbott's essay, "That Long Western
Border: Canada, the United States, and a Century of Economic Change,"
acknowledges the rise of free trade and the appeal of the idea of some kind of
transborder region. Yet Abbott suggests that more than a century of border

entrenchment by two modern nation-states and their bureaucracies, as well as the long-standing urban and economic rivalries across the border, count for more. National distinctions, and the border that helps to preserve them, cannot easily be erased. Indeed, as the two nations have each created "webs of regulations and layers of public bureaucracies" that depend on the international boundary for their existence, Abbott suggests that the lines composing the border have grown thicker rather than thinner.

The three chapters in part three reflect on the national distinctions between Canada and the United States and how they have been constructed over more than 150 years. Chad Reimer, in "Borders of the Past: The Oregon Boundary Dispute and the Beginnings of Northwest Historiography," examines the contributions of U.S. and British historians during the 1840s to their respective governments' claims to the Oregon Country. Studies of the past did not merely respond to "official discourses" concerning relations between competing nations; those initial regional works were actually created as part of the ongoing controversy and they helped to influence its outcome. They offer an example of nation-states shaping the work of historians and vice versa. These early historical accounts, then, not only led to the emergence of two historical traditions concerning the lands once unified as the Columbia Department of the Hudson's Bay Company, but they also helped to define the meaning of the international boundary.

In "Wild, Tame, and Free: Comparing Canadian and U.S. Views of Nature," Donald Worster reflects on another national distinction—the ways in which the two countries have gone about defining and preserving wilderness. Passage of the Wilderness Act of 1964 by the U.S. Congress served to illuminate these differences clearly in the twentieth century, but Worster contends that they had been developing since the eighteenth century. He argues that Americans' willingness to preserve wilderness has been bound up with their preoccupation with "liberty." Canadians, by contrast, have been less preoccupied with "liberty" as a defining trait and perhaps as a result have also been slower to devise policies for wilderness protection—even though Canada possesses more wilderness than the United States does. The international boundary, in Worster's formulation, marks a noticeable difference in how two societies view the world, specifically the natural world.

Whereas Worster emphasizes cultural differences between Canada and the United States, Michael Fellman emphasizes cultural similarities in "Sleeping with the Elephant: Reflections of an American Canadian on Americanization and Anti-Americanism in Canada." Fellman inventories some of the U.S. expressions of "annexationism" that have provoked Canadian anti-Americanism over the years. But by insisting on the importance of the international boundary and all the distinctions that it represents, Fellman argues, Canadians have generally denied the profound similarities that exist between the neighboring nations. Fellman finds those similarities—as expressed over a century and a half in the realms of political movements, demography, racial attitudes, foreign policy, and economic integration—to be much more compelling than the differences that many Canadians emphasize (and that many Americans underestimate). "Sleeping with the Elephant" suggests that the border has meant less than Canadians—and more than Americans—have supposed.

The past 150 years of the Canada–United States boundary have been more complex than is typically assumed. We need to know far more about this past—and about both border and borderlands—if we are to understand our contemporary situation. And, equally, we need to ensure that scholars with diverse interests—economists, geographers, legal specialists, urban studies researchers, environmentalists, and others—challenge and probe the boundary's significance as a major element in the shaping of western states and provinces. If the "On Brotherly Terms" conference proved anything, it was that the American Northwest and the Canadian West share a past, a present, and a future. This does not mean that the region exists as a single unit, a solitary culture, or one economy. Rather, it means that the interactions across the boundary—and the border line itself—have shaped the development of both the Canadian and the U.S. side of the border. Each part of the region, to degrees that remain little known, is in part the creation of the other. Many obstacles remain to the clear understanding of developments along and across the forty-ninth parallel. Yet, as the insights and claims of the chapters in this volume suggest, sizable opportunities await scholars who study Canadian-U.S. borders and borderlands.

KEN S. COATES

JOHN M. FINDLAY

NOTES

1. Jouni Häkli, "Borders in the Political Geography of Knowledge," in Lars-folke Landgren and Maunu Häyryen, eds., *The Dividing Line: Borders and National Peripheries* (Helsinki: Renvall Institute, 1993), p. 14.

2. Robert Lecker, ed., *Borderlands: Essays in Canadian-American Relations*

(Toronto: ECW Press, 1991); Roger Gibbins, *Canada as a Borderlands Society* (Orono, Maine: Borderlands, 1989); Seymour Lipset, *North American Cultures: Values and Institutions in Canada and the United States* (Orono, Maine: Borderlands, 1990).

3. Lauren McKinsey and Victor Konrad, *Borderlands Reflections: The United States and Canada*, Borderlands Monograph Series No. 1 (Orono, Maine: Canadian-American Centre, 1989).

4. This generalization is too broad. A great deal of recent scholarship attempts, instead, to situate local or regional developments amid much larger international or human processes, such as work and labor relations, gender relations, and broader ideas and values. Even within this "new" social history is a strong traditional strain of explaining developments largely by reference to national (or regional) traits and/or policies.

5. Carlos Schwantes, *Radical Heritage: Labor, Socialism, and Reform in Washington and British Columbia* (Seattle: University of Washington Press, 1979); Paul Phillips, *No Power Greater: A Century of Labour in British Columbia* (Vancouver: B.C. Federation of Labour, 1967). Labor historians have been particularly reliable in looking across the border for relationships. See, for example, Jeremy Mouat, *Roaring Days: Rossland's Mines and the History of Mining in British Columbia* (Vancouver: UBC Press, 1995).

6. Robin Fisher, *Contact and Conflict: Indian-European Relations in British Columbia*, 2nd ed. (Vancouver: University of British Columbia Press, 1992); Robin Fisher, "Indian Warfare and Two Frontiers: A Comparison of British Columbia and Washington Territory during the Early Years of Settlement," *Pacific Historical Review* 50 (February 1981): 31–51.

7. Ken S. Coates, David McCrady, and W. R. Morrison, "The Integration and Re-integration of the Yukon River Basin: Reflections on the History of the Yukon-Alaska Boundary," *Locus: An Historical Journal of Regional Perspectives* 5 (fall 1992). Some of the themes in this essay are considered in greater detail in Ken S. Coates and W. R. Morrison, "Transiency in the Far Northwest: The Sinking of the Princess Sophia," in Ken S. Coates and W. R. Morrison, eds., *Interpreting the Canadian North* (Toronto: Copp Clark, 1989); Ken S. Coates and W. R. Morrison, *The Sinking of the Princess Sophia: Taking the North Down with Her* (Toronto: Oxford University Press, 1991); and Ken S. Coates and W. R. Morrison, *The Alaska Highway in World War II: The U.S. Army of Occupation in Canada's Northwest* (Norman: University of Oklahoma Press, 1992).

8. Norbert MacDonald, *Distant Neighbors: A Comparative History of Seattle and Vancouver* (Lincoln: University of Nebraska Press, 1987).

9. Richard Rajala, *Clearcutting the Pacific Rain Forest: Production, Science, and Regulation* (Vancouver: UBC Press, 1998).

10. Regarding cities, we rely on the broad speculations of Lionel Frost, *The New*

Urban Frontier: Urbanisation and City Building in Australasia and the American West (Kensington: New South Wales University Press, 1991); and on the detailed portrait in Robert A. J. McDonald, *Making Vancouver: Class, Status, and Social Boundaries, 1863–1913* (Vancouver: University of British Columbia Press, 1996).

11. The border created in 1846 was not without controversy. Great Britain and the United States disputed the border's path through the San Juan Islands, an issue that was settled in 1872. Moreover, the border established in 1846, running latitudinally, was not the only one beyond the Rockies to set apart the United States from what became Canada. The addition of Alaska to the United States in 1867 created another western, Canadian-American boundary, this one running longitudinally. If the boundary created in 1846 has been relatively neglected by historians, the border created in 1867 has received almost no attention.

12. The quotation is cited in Dorothy O. Johansen and Charles M. Gates, *Empire of the Columbia: A History of the Pacific Northwest*, 2nd ed. (New York: Harper & Row, 1967), p. 208.

ACKNOWLEDGMENTS

B ecause this collection received its start during the 1996 symposium "On Brotherly Terms," it is important to acknowledge the many contributions that made that event a success. The conference was cosponsored by the Center for the Study of the Pacific Northwest, in the Department of History at the University of Washington, and the Canadian Studies Center, in the Henry M. Jackson School of International Studies at the University of Washington. Doug Jackson, then director of the Canadian Studies Center, was an enthusiastic supporter from the start. Michael S. Bittner, then assistant director of the Canadian Studies Center, proved very helpful in organizing the symposium and finding funding support. On behalf of the Department of History, Richard R. Johnson and Cheryl Fisk provided numerous kinds of support. Kim McKaig, administrative assistant for the Center for the Study of the Pacific Northwest, shouldered the heaviest load in organizing and running the conference and keeping tabs on the editors' and authors' contributions to this book.

It is a pleasure to acknowledge the funding support that made the 1996 symposium a much more stimulating and inclusive event than it otherwise might have been. Outside of the University of Washington, we received funds from the Canadian Embassy's Canadian Studies Conference Grant Program for 1995–96. Arthur M. Goddard, Ph.D. and political, economic, and academic affairs officer in the Seattle office of the Canadian Consulate General, offered crucial support on our behalf in applying to the Conference Grant Program. Inside the university, we received support from the Canadian Studies Center and the Henry M. Jackson School of International Studies; the Center for the Study of the Pacific Northwest and the Department of History; and the Emil and Kathleen Sick Fund, administered by the Department of History in conjunction with the University of Washington Press. We remain grateful to Julidta Tarver and Marilyn Trueblood of the Press for steering this volume toward publication and for Julidta's sound judgment (we think) in rejecting our preferred title—Borderline History.

All but one of the chapters within this book (Perras's essay) were initially presented as papers at the 1996 conference. The authors have generously revised them for publication, taking into account the comments of the two editors and three anonymous referees. But these polished versions amount to a small fraction of all the papers and presentations made at the conference, which boasted more than seventy participants on the program. The collection as a whole has been strengthened considerably by the ideas of many of those symposium participants. The "On Brotherly Terms" conference produced exactly the kind of warm intellectual exchange that one hopes for from an academic gathering. In the best tradition of scholarly meetings of minds, many borders were crossed.

Two of the essays within initially appeared in other venues. "Who Will Defend British Columbia?" by Galen Roger Perras was originally published in *Pacific Northwest Quarterly*, and we gratefully acknowledge permission to reprint it here.[1] Michael Fellman's "Sleeping with the Elephant" is a revised and more scholarly version of "Sam I Am," originally published in *Saturday Night*.[2]

NOTES

1. Galen Roger Perras, "Who Will Defend British Columbia," *Pacific Northwest Quarterly* 88 (spring 1997): 59–69.

2. Michael Fellman, "Sam I Am," *Saturday Night* 111 (October 1996): 43–46.

PARALLEL DESTINIES

1 / Border Crossings

*Patterns and Processes along the Canada–United States
Boundary West of the Rockies*

KEN S. COATES

B orders are artificial. Even when lines of national demarcation follow clear geographic features, there is nothing fixed about their location or their function. Borders have been around for hundreds of years and gained new authority with the evolution and development of the modern state. As governments gained greater social, economic, and political prominence, it became imperative that they demonstrate their authority by defending their territory. This often involved the protection of ill-defined frontiers of control and regulation. As the role of states continued to evolve, however, the identification and defense of borders became an increasing priority. And as numerous scholars have argued in recent years, the authority of the nation-state has declined in an era of globalization, and protection of the integrity of borders has been relaxed (but still is far from abandoned).[1] Borders, like the Canada–United States boundary west of the Rocky Mountains, are historical constructs that must be understood not as fixtures or permanent marks on the landscape, but rather as an illustration of the evolving relationships among the region's peoples and cultures. The Canada–United States boundary is a political creation that has had great significance.

Put more bluntly, the Pacific Northwest has not merely been influenced by the Canada–United States border. It would not be an exaggeration to argue that the region's history and character have been determined by the boundary's existence and functioning. As Pauliina Raento, a scholar of Basque borderland cultures, argues: "When all boundaries are considered to be social constructs which reflect human territoriality, especially international boundaries appear as strongly differentiating lines. At the same time, they are lines of contact which create special zones of interaction. In this way, the division actually defines the surrounding region."[2] This is a strong and important idea, for it challenges analysts to turn their attentions from the obvious evidence of differences and to explore instead the connections and continuities that run across borders and that exist precisely because the national boundary is in place.[3]

Scholars have paid considerable attention in recent years to the many boundaries that shape individual lives and societies. These boundaries vary from the evident political lines of demarcation to more subtle borders of culture, nationalism, race, and gender. And the struggle of peoples against these boundaries—and the inability of some peoples to move the borders—has determined the limits and opportunities for social change.[4] The argument seems overstated in the case of the Pacific Northwest, for the many other social, economic, and political influences at play in the region seem, superficially, to have had much more influence than an ill-defended border that until the twentieth century held relatively little practical significance. But an examination of the relationships in the border region suggests that the tensions between the Canadian and the American traditions—typically seen as interesting but minor political matters—played a central role in defining and shaping the region's history.[5]

Regional scholars in both Canada and the United States have paid only passing attention to the border. The United States and Canada take as a given the political, economic, and even historical integrity of their national boundaries. Although the northern border of the continental United States (to say nothing of Alaska and Hawaii, the afterthoughts of American expansionism[6]) belies any notion of the geographic integrity of the North American nation-states, few citizens give more than a passing thought to the artificial nature of their country's borders. Canadians, in contrast, have long been preoccupied with the international boundary, which has protected the nation from the "evils" of republicanism and "Manifest Destiny" and slowed the flow of U.S. ideas and values into the northland. Canadians have devoted enormous intellectual and political energy to peering southward from the boundary marker, fearful that the sleeping giant will awake and once again cast its expansionist eyes toward the subarctic.

First, it is important to define the region under consideration. The standard concept of the Pacific Northwest includes Washington, Oregon, and British Columbia—although many portraits of the region restrict this definition even further to include only the coastal areas. Adjoining jurisdictions, particularly the Yukon Territory and Alaska, are only rarely included

in the Pacific Northwest, even though their histories are very closely inter-
woven with the southern jurisdictions. The difficulty with definitions is, on
one level, a reflection of the limited understanding of the historical inter-
connections. From a different perspective, however, it is worth noting that
many concepts of western history leave out the most westerly province and
states (as is beautifully captured in the provocative title of Jean Barman's history of the British Columbia, *The West beyond the West*[7]). As David Emmons
discovered in his analysis of the "West," "More than a few of the respondents,
however, excluded all or parts of California, Oregon, Washington, Hawaii
and Alaska. These areas were, presumably, 'West of the West,' too new, too
urban and sophisticated, too well-watered and too economically favored. All
of this suggests that the 'true' West must be rural, semi-primitive as well as
semi-arid, and broke."[8] A more inclusive definition of the Pacific Northwest—
Alaska and the Yukon as well as Washington, Oregon, and British Columbia—
is used in this chapter. There is a basic geographic integrity in the Pacific
Northwest, as shown by the evident bonds and barriers established by the
Rocky Mountains and the Pacific Ocean. But there are also elements of social
and cultural integration, particularly among the First Nations, and several
important historical processes that have alternatively linked and separated
the peoples on either side of the Canada–United States boundary.

What follows is an overview of the significance of the Canada–United
States border in Pacific Northwest history. More detailed case studies and
illustrations of the importance of the border and borderlands are provided
in the remaining essays in this volume. This chapter provides an overview
of the pattern and processes in the Pacific Northwest borderlands and supports the argument advanced earlier in the essay. In an era when Canadians
and Americans alike are coming to terms with the sweeping impact of economic and cultural globalization, when the impact of the North American
Free Trade Agreement is yet to be fully understood, and when U.S. popular culture seems increasingly invasive in Canada, it is important for residents on both sides of the boundary to recognize the historical continuity
of contemporary dilemmas.

North American scholars have not completely ignored border regions,
however. The still-limited historiographical investigation of the Canada–
United States boundary is much less than the historical attention granted
to the boundary separating Mexico and the United States. Scholars of the
Pacific Northwest, with a few notable exceptions,[9] have kept their feet on
their side of the border while also largely ignoring the influence that the
boundary line has played in establishing or maintaining national or regional

characteristics.[10] The relative imbalance in the attention granted to the northern borderlands—one of the world's greatest trading zones and a region of considerable social interaction—compared with the United States–Mexico boundary area may be a reflection of scholars' interest in conflict over cooperation and racial tensions as opposed to cross-border integration. It might also reflect the American government's concern about the immigration, economic, and social issues relating to the Mexican borderlands.

The study of borderland districts appears, at first glance, to be the antithesis of national history, more interested in documenting connections and overlaps than in explicating national or regional character. Perhaps unexpectedly, it is precisely in these regions where there exists an unparalleled opportunity to study the most basic questions of national history. Most scholars would agree that a substantial portion of Canadian and U.S. historical works seeks, explicitly or implicitly, to identify what is specific to the nation or a large region.[11] The study of borderlands presents a useful opportunity to examine the question of national (or regional) identity in its most highly focused form. For it is on the nation's edge, at the physical and cultural boundaries between countries, that one might legitimately expect to find a juxtaposition of national characteristics or to discover the limited distinctions between peoples separated by an intensely political artifact: the international border. Historical studies of the borderlands—in this case the Pacific Northwest—afford an opportunity to identify those forces that are national and those that cross boundaries and thus potentially sit closer to the heart of the human, or at least the historical, Euro-North American condition.

But an important new question has emerged: Why, in an age when the role of national boundaries has diminished dramatically, should historians be concerned about the border's significance? On the surface, this appears like a preoccupation with an anachronism. There is little question that social and economic forces have changed the influence and importance of the Canada–United States boundary, although the tensions over fisheries through the later 1990s challenged any sense that boundaries have collapsed into irrelevance. The Canada–U.S. Free Trade Agreement (and its successor, the North American Free Trade Agreement) has significantly increased cross-border commerce. For several years low-cost American retail goods drew tens of thousands of Canadian shoppers across the border each week into U.S. stores; more recently, the fall of the Canadian dollar has turned the southward tide into a trickle in the opposite direction.

On a cultural level the swarming impact of American mass culture—from McDonald's to Oprah to the O. J. Simpson trial and Starbucks coffee shops—

has dulled cultural differences and provided abundant transboundary reference points and commonalties. Not surprisingly, regional politicians have dusted off an old concept—the integration of the Pacific Northwest—and introduced the idea of Cascadia to a largely skeptical audience. Canadians have, for several generations, been preoccupied with the demoralizing influence of U.S. economic and cultural imperialism, spawning exhaustive and stultifying studies of the Canadian "identity" and "national character." Buttressed by their much larger numbers and healthier economy, Americans cast only occasional glances to the north—typically to complain about Canada sending yet another terrifying arctic front into the American heartland. It remains an unequal relationship, where Canadians fear the economic and political wrath of the "giant" to the south and where Americans grant but scant attention to the "gentle child" to the north, maintaining a level of ignorance that infuriates Canadians and bemuses Americans.

The increasing integration of the Pacific Northwest, marked by international rivalries in NBA basketball and minor league hockey,[12] the often touted prospect of a shared baseball team (the Seattle Mariners), extensive cross-border travel and commerce, growing regional political connections, and considerable cultural transference[13] appears on the surface to be a new development—the creation of the postmodern world in which the nation-state is overwhelmed by the forces of internationalization. But even a preliminary understanding of Pacific Northwest history reveals that the contemporary situation is a continuation, or a reestablishment, of past levels of cross-border integration. Borders and boundaries have been significant and have assumed a much greater than merely symbolic role in the region's history. So too have the forces of connection and interaction. Despite the impressive power of the modern globalizing economy, history and historical interactions do matter, and regional cultures and societies that transcend national boundaries do exist. The Pacific Northwest provides a useful case study of an area where the impressive economic and cultural weight of the United States has been at least partially offset by historical ties and connections with a neighbor.

DIVIDING LINES: THE BOUNDARIES OF THE PACIFIC NORTHWEST

Boundaries in the Pacific Northwest, however permeable and flexible they are in contemporary times, were established by nineteenth-century international convention. They are, in cartographic and geographical terms, very straightforward: a single, straight line, running along the forty-ninth parallel and dividing what is now British Columbia from Washington and Idaho.

There is, of course, a slight but controversial jog where the boundary hits the Pacific Ocean. A small spit, Point Roberts, accessible by land only through British Columbia, was left as U.S. territory. Extending the line through the Straight of Juan de Fuca proved problematic. Vancouver Island, clearly identified in the Oregon Boundary settlement as British territory, extends several miles south of the forty-ninth parallel. So too do a number of small Gulf Islands. Diplomatic tempers flared over the precise delineation of the border through the San Juan Islands—peaking in the silly but locally infamous "Pig War." The resulting adjudicated settlement favored the United States.

The northwest boundary—now separating Alaska from the Yukon and British Columbia—ran into even greater difficulties. The line of separation between what was then Russian territory and British-claimed lands to the east was initially set at the 125th meridian. The boundary ran south from the Arctic Ocean until it reached the height of land near the Pacific Ocean. Here, the Russian presence along the Alaskan Panhandle added another complication. The Russians wished to hold onto their prized fur trading, missionary, and administrative posts—Sitka, Wrangell, and other sites—and the British accepted their position. The inland boundary was not definitively set, however. No serious difficulties erupted for more than fifty years, principally because European settlers were not very interested in the vast frozen lands in the Far Northwest. The discovery of gold in the Klondike, though, and a particularly messy contretemps over duties and tariffs on trade goods destined for the goldfields in the Yukon, made the question of the boundary one of prime importance.

The emergence of Canada as a separate dominion in 1867, with all of the assertiveness of a young, new nation but with no diplomatic authority, added to the complications. What followed was the Alaska boundary dispute, an underrated and now largely ignored conflict that drove a hard wedge between Canada and the United States, made Canadians question the integrity and support of the British empire, and resulted in a final settlement of the vexing question of the border along the Alaskan Panhandle. The resolution, very much in favor of the United States, set the border a considerable distance inland—much farther than the Canadians had hoped. Tensions surrounding the boundary faded almost as quickly as the gold ran out in the Klondike— they were very much connected. Early in the twentieth century a group of Canadian and U.S. surveyors set to the difficult task of physically marking the Canada–United States boundary in the region.[14]

A political and diplomatic border, however, is little more than an international convention. It has little meaning unless backed by the state's authority. Canadians and Americans have long lauded (with justification) the existence of the world's longest undefended boundary, although they could also point out that it is nearly indefensible in a practical sense. For decades after the boundaries were formally established, they had relatively little practical significance. People and goods moved with considerable ease back and forth across the boundary—although the absence of roads limited the options and afforded governments the opportunity, when they chose to take it, of regulating access and turning away people and trade items that they did not want circulating in their jurisdiction.[15] In the postwar period most border crossings had formal customs stations, and both Canadian and U.S. governments commenced the process of regulating their boundaries. Before that time, efforts had generally been limited to matters of policing and immigration, with insufficient coverage to prevent the more determined migrants from escaping detection.[16] Alcohol trade, of course, presented a special challenge during the Prohibition era in the United States. More recently, concern about the traffic in drugs and illegal immigrants destined for America has resulted in an increase in border vigilance. The intention here is not to present a history of the boundaries and the regulation of the borders in the Pacific Northwest; rather, the focus is on the general patterns that underlie the historical relationships within this large and important region.

PATTERNS AND PROCESS IN THE BORDERLANDS

Describing the broad strokes of cross-boundary interaction in the Pacific Northwest does, of necessity, force generalizations and leads one to overlook the nuances of social, economic, political, and cultural movements. A preliminary consideration of the patterns in the region, however, suggests that there are four main periods in the history of border crossings; within each period several key characteristics, each with a lasting impact on the development of the Pacific Northwest and with a demonstrable contemporary connection, stand out. These periods are described in capsule form and the salient characteristics are identified for consideration and debate. The four periods include aboriginal occupation, colonial encroachment, the imposition of the modern state, and the postboundary or modern era.

Aboriginal Occupation

The long-standing tendency to conceptualize Pacific Northwest history in strictly European terms has, appropriately, come to an end. Scholars are increasingly including a consideration of the precontact history of the First Nations in their descriptions and analyses of regional development, a belated recognition of the historical and contemporary significance of indigenous peoples. Archeologists continue to debate the origins of the First Nations in the region—the long-standing assumption about the inland migration following the retreat of the Ice Age, competing with more recent arguments about the prospects of coastal settlement—but First Nations have been around for thousands of years. The establishment, entrenchment, and evolution of First Nations cultures in the Pacific Northwest occurred several thousand years before Europeans learned of the area.[17]

The societies that evolved—it goes almost without saying—took no notice of the later international boundary and, in fact, initially paid little heed to the imposed border that followed European settlement. They developed in a series of related but distinctive cultural niches, responding and adapting to their physical setting and to a complex series of trade and social relations with neighboring bands. Although anthropologists have identified a "single basic cultural pattern along the entire Pacific coast of North America, from Baja California to Alaska," they have also identified a remarkable cultural complexity in the region.[18] The Pacific Northwest was one of the most densely settled, nonagricultural regions in the preindustrial world, sustained by the area's abundant fish, mammal, and plant resources, especially the massive and predictable salmon runs. Inland, separated from the coast by mountains and the military might of the coastal Natives, more mobile indigenous peoples, smaller in number and less well endowed with natural riches, moved across the land.

The indigenous peoples of the Pacific Northwest—the Nez Perce, Flathead, Kootenai, Okanagan, Sushwap, Carrier, Sekani, Tutchone, and others of the interior plateaus, coupled with the Chinook, Salish, Kwakwaka'wakw, Haisla, Haida, and Tlingit of the coast—are among the best-known First Nations cultures in North America. The dramatic artwork and ceremonial life, particularly of the coastal tribes, and the history of conflict and interaction with the early Europeans gave these people a special place in the historical memory of the continent. The decades-long practice of collecting artifacts along the coast, many of which can still be found in museums and galleries in North America and Europe, played a major role in bringing these cultures to the attention of the western world.[19]

Several aspects of the lives of the First Nations peoples of the Pacific Northwest are important in the context of this essay. First, although the borders and boundaries between peoples were more permeable and less permanent than later European lines of demarcation, the indigenous peoples had (and have) a sense of territoriality. Land, resources, and culture were intricately intertwined, ensuring that each group maintained a strong identification with their special territory. Cultural maps are, in European terms, vague and imprecise, and considerable overlap existed between tribal territories, but First Nations peoples did have a sense of the land belonging or not belonging to them.

Second, and long predating European arrival, there was a fair degree of interaction up and down the coast and among coastal areas and the interior. In general, the stronger and larger coastal groups dominated the interior tribes and maintained considerable control over the trade of surplus goods (particularly in the district's northern reaches). But interior goods routinely made their way down to the coast, where they were traded for surplus fish and marine resources. There was also extensive trade and travel up and down the coast, as the seagoing canoes of the Tlingit, Haida, and Nuu-chah-nulth moved supplies, travelers, and war parties into rival territories. Although rivalries and cultural tensions limited intermingling, there was a reasonable amount of contact among the area's peoples. The cultures and languages of the individual First Nations did not differ that dramatically from that of their nearest neighbors— with the greatest diversity being between coastal and interior groups—but the range from north to south and from east to west was quite substantial, linked primarily by a dependence on the sea's resources.

Colonial Encroachment

The arrival of European explorers, traders, and settlers in the late eighteenth century quickly shattered the state of affairs throughout the Pacific Northwest. Although the First Nations peoples adapted to the new conditions, the introduction of virgin soil epidemics,[20] the alterations wrought by capitalist trade, and the sociocultural transformations that attended the spread of Christianity and the confrontation with European racism altered centuries-old patterns of life and subsistence. Among their arsenal of tricks and trinkets, the Europeans also brought an important new idea: the concept of borders and fixed colonial territories.

The tale of the struggle for hegemony in the Pacific Northwest has been often told: Russians moving haphazardly from Alaska into the Northwest, Spanish and British ships sailing northward along the coast, British traders crossing the Rockies and establishing overland trade routes into the interior of Caledonia, Americans arriving to compete for the quickly lucrative coastal sea otter trade and moving overland into the Oregon Country. The tug and tussle of colonial expansionism passed through several stages, including Spanish and British rivalry for the entire coast, resolved in Britain's favor; British (actually, Hudson's Bay Company) contests with the Russians for the Alaska Panhandle, which left the Russians in titular control of the region but with British trade rights assured; and, nastiest of all, the long and bitter struggle between the British and the Americans for control of the Oregon Country. The latter contretemps, which saw Britain abandon its commercial claims (again, held by the Hudson's Bay Company) to the area that now comprises Oregon and Washington states in order to avoid further conflict with the increasingly belligerent United States, drove a stake through the heart of British occupation in the region. The Hudson's Bay Company, long a beneficiary of its special status as an agent of the British Crown but now a victim of working on the margins of the British empire, retreated north of the new boundary line and reestablished itself in what is now British Columbia. The final, determining act of this period—the Russian sale of Alaska to the United States in 1867—completed the colonial era. Overextended in Eurasia and no longer profiting from its holdings in North America, Russia walked away from its Alaskan holdings, turning over "Seward's Folly" to the Americans.[21]

Throughout the colonial period the Pacific Northwest suffered through two of the more severe consequences of colonialism: lacking regional control over the development of resources and the related social transformations and being a geographic pawn in the broader workings of the international colonial system. Through the processes previously described, European nations and the United States registered and established claims to Pacific Northwest lands and resources. There were a few moves—by the Hudson's Bay Company and later by the Americans in the Columbia River and Puget Sound areas—to follow up territorial claims with settlement, but these were relatively minor initiatives until the middle of the nineteenth century. Of greater significance was the rapacious and unregulated rush for sea otter pelts, a damaging industry that quickly swept the region nearly barren of the prized furs. Little thought was given to the impact of this trade on the First Nations or to the long-term significance of such a "rush" for furs. Within a few decades, the trade was moribund, the indigenous societies significantly transformed, and colonial governments decidedly less interested.[22]

At the geopolitical level this era proved to be of lasting significance to Pacific Northwest history, for it was in the three-quarters of a century from the explorations of Captain James Cook to the negotiation of the Oregon Treaty of 1846 that the region's permanent boundaries were set.[23] In the diplomatic parlors and political halls of Europe and Washington, D.C., U.S., British, Spanish, and Russian negotiators drew new lines on the map of western North America. The lines had no geographic significance, ignored First Nations territories, ran roughshod over existing patterns of trade and commerce, and paid no heed to the needs and aspirations of the handful of nonindigenous peoples living in the region. In the manner and practice of the age, this was colonialism at its most extreme. Agents in distant lands, often with little or no knowledge of the peoples and places affected, redrafted or created international boundaries.

For the local population these decisions were not necessarily of immediate importance or impact. The Hudson's Bay Company left the Oregon Territory after the boundary settlement, and Russian traders withdrew from Alaska following the U.S. purchase of Alaska. In both instances replacements were quickly on the scene, ushering in a new, more competitive era in fur trade relations. With the passage of time, however, the significance of the boundaries became clearer, as the nation-states involved, particularly the United States, took measures to ensure their control over their territories. Populations were small, the First Nations were already undergoing significant change because of the transformations of the fur trade era, and the new colonial or national masters paid little heed to their distant acquisitions (or lost lands). The comparative absence of a dramatic transition, however, belies the long-term significance of the colonial period. For it was these decisions, taken in the eighteenth and nineteenth centuries, that established the pattern for subsequent development in the region. Colonial judgments and compromises, and the drawing of new lines on the maps of western North America, re-created the Pacific Northwest, giving it contours that remain in existence to today.

The Imposition of the Modern State

The establishment of boundaries did not, in and of itself, set the region on a new course. Until a nation defends or enforces a boundary, the line of division remains meaningless. The colonial authorities had proved uninterested in paying more than passing attention to the newly established borders. The Hudson's Bay Company, for example, operated Fort Youcon, located well inside Russian territory, for almost a quarter century.[24] Similarly, in the early years after the Oregon Treaty of 1846, Americans passed freely across the border into British territory. Within the broader sweep of colonial interests, maintaining and defending an indefensible border on the margins of North America was a very low priority.

The same was not true of the new nation-state, however, or of a colonial power with a valuable resource worth protecting. In the mid-nineteenth century the United States was quite belligerent about its boundaries—established or desired. The belief in Manifest Destiny convinced many Americans that the continent would soon be theirs and worried British Columbians about the region's future. America was, on more than one occasion during this period, prepared and determined to fight to protect or extend its national boundaries, a classic illustration of the importance the United States attached to territorial considerations. In subsequent years the United States, Britain, and (after the extension of the Dominion of Canada to the Pacific Ocean in 1871) Canada paid much greater attention to the symbols of territorial sovereignty and control.

Such symbols were important, of course, for they provided governments with a means of asserting their long-term claims even as they effectively surrendered a considerable amount of short-term control. And so, as Americans flooded over the border into British Columbia in the 1850s and 1860s, eager participants in the B.C. gold rushes, colonial authorities were quick to establish the rudiments of administrative control. For example, in the 1850s Judge Matthew Begbie maintained a strong legal presence in the Cariboo, as did the construction brigades of the Royal Engineers and other government agents that assisted with the smooth operation of the new frontier. The colonial government established a variety of regulations, governing movements in and out of the colony and regulating trade, mining lands, and commerce. Effective control of the regional economy rested with the miners, most of whom were Americans, but the symbolic administrative steps ensured that the colonial government did not permit the mining frontier to collapse in anarchy or to fall under U.S. political control.[25]

The scene was reenacted in the late 1890s in the Far Northwest. The discovery of gold in the Yukon River basin touched off the massive Klondike stampede of 1897–99, drawing tens of thousands, mostly Americans, into the northland. Canadian authorities, only recently alerted to the region's potential, left matters of sovereignty and control in the able hands of the North West Mounted Police, the preeminent symbol of Canadian authority.[26] On the ground Americans and U.S. interests held sway—but Canadian laws and regulations were imposed and enforced, leaving at least a vestige of national control intact. The gold rush, to a greater degree than historians have noted, both united the region and created divisions within it. The bitter rivalry for urban domination of the Klondike trade—initially including Vancouver, Seattle, Victoria, and Portland (plus a dangerously silly challenge from

Edmonton, east of the Rockies) and later reduced to a contest between Seattle and Vancouver—resulted in a spate of regulatory initiatives by the Canadian and U.S. governments and helped precipitate the Alaska boundary dispute.[27]

The two gold rushes, plus a variety of other governmental initiatives— the regulation and administration of indigenous affairs, the management of immigration, particularly from China and Japan, efforts to control the spread of radical ideas and organizations, and the enforcement of rules governing shipping and trade—illustrate the important steps taken by governments to assert and protect their national sovereignty. This was, as suggested earlier, one of the defining characteristics of the nation-state, which took its ability to defend the integrity of its boundaries as a primary determinant of its viability. Within twenty-five years of the establishment of the various borders, these artificial lines had assumed considerable political and socioeconomic importance. Cross-border institutions, such as the International Joint Commission established in 1909, represented a recognition of the need to coordinate affairs along the boundary.

This said, however, the boundaries in the Pacific Northwest proved to be exceptionally permeable. During the gold rushes vast waves of prospectors headed north from the United States into British Columbia and later the Yukon. In the Far Northwest the boundary maintained its symbolic significance but had little practical impact on the movement of people, goods, and commerce until after World War I. To the south the boundary appeared to be only a minor impediment. Laborers flowed freely across the British Columbia–Washington boundary, seeking out work and better conditions. The socialist ideas of the hard-rock miners moved with the workers, often generating an owner-government effort to stymie the flow of radicalism. Capital found a receptive home on either side of the international border, but national contests over economic control also soon entered into the equation. National policies and priorities on the economic front, including the stridently protectionist Canadian tariff regulations, erected an important barrier. Much of the money for British Columbia's post-Confederation development came from central Canada or Britain, just as many of the earlier agricultural settlers in the B.C. interior came from British or Canadian stock, both representing efforts to keep Canada British and to restrict the influence of the United States.

During World War II regional residents seemingly put aside national differences in pursuit of a common cause. The shared threat of Japanese invasion and a determination to fight together as North Americans to drive back a shared enemy united the Pacific Northwest as no previous event or process had done. Beginning in the early months of 1942, major construction projects in the Far Northwest—the Alaska Highway, the CANOL pipeline, the Haines Road, and the Northwest Staging Route—were started to prepare for the region's defense. There were numerous other activities: a joint Canadian-American force to fight off the Japanese invasion of the Aleutian Islands, the American occupation of Prince Rupert, and the construction of defensive positions throughout the area. The largest project—the Alaska Highway—had been touted in the prewar era as a joint economic development strategy, designed to provide a link to Alaska and to encourage the opening of northern British Columbia. But the decision to route the highway through Edmonton and Dawson Creek effectively eliminated the integrative potential of the project. And although the wartime initiatives brought Canadians and Americans together in the Pacific Northwest in a manner not seen since the Klondike Gold Rush, the initiative did as much to convince each side of their differences as it did to create a sense of shared destiny.[28]

In the absence of detailed cross-border studies, it is difficult to do little more than speculate on the authority of the boundary in this era. Although there was considerable movement of people and ideas across the Canada–United States boundary, and although the "Northland" (Alaska and the Yukon) operated as an interconnected region, the lines of division had been clearly established. It was not impossible for American capital to enter the Canadian market (or vice versa), and sizable amounts of investment flowed northward, particularly in the forest sector. Immigrants appear to have moved routinely across the boundary. Many Chinese and Japanese migrants to British Columbia in the early twentieth century pushed on quickly to the United States. Labor historians have documented the close connections, and important differences, between workers and radical movements on both sides of the border, but much more remains to be learned about other population and intellectual movements.

On balance, however, the era of the modern state saw the entrenchment and empowerment of the Canada–United States boundary. Regional and local imperatives could postpone the separation—the Far Northwest being, again, the best example—but the pattern had been clearly set. Anxious to defend national integrity and to give substance to the superficial authority of formal sovereignty, governments passed a welter of rules, regulations, and laws that gave the border and the agents of enforcement greater power. But it would be incorrect to focus too strongly on governments as effective managers of a complex and complicated process.

The peoples of the Canadian and American portions of the Pacific Northwest pushed their governments—for economic, social, or political reasons—along the path of protectionism. New settlers came to Washington, Oregon, and British Columbia, typically from other parts of their respective nations (although many who came to British Columbia in the nineteenth century originated in the United States). As internal migrants, they held a greater loyalty to the nation than to an as yet inchoate regional identity, and hence prodded their governments to reenforce the lines of demarcation. Even more important, personal actions—investment and settlement decisions, voting habits, and ideological choices—reenforced the region's "national" character over time, making the American Northwest increasingly American and British Columbia increasingly Canadian. The major exception—the Far Northwest, the one transboundary community that survived well into the twentieth century—helps to prove the rule. The majority of the nonindigenous settlers in this region were transients, either permanent or seasonal, and had only a short-term, economically based association with the Northwest. They were, in large measure, residents of Vancouver, Victoria, Seattle, Portland, or other southern settlements; the shared identification as members of the "Northland" was a temporary condition, surviving only so long as they remained in the area, and had its roots more in shared circumstances, such as cold and isolation, than any lasting sense of regionalism.

Over time the divisions within the Pacific Northwest intensified. But they gained in strength not because of interregional rivalries or hostilities, but because of the separate national roots from which the dominant populations in each area sprang and to which political and economic elites owed their primary allegiance. Different political systems, core values, attitudes toward race and religion, standards of living, and domestic cultures deepened the divide originally established by the Canada–United States boundary. By the early decades of the twentieth century, the Canadian West and the American Northwest had, by choice more than government fiat, embarked on very different paths. These trails ran roughly parallel to each other, and on occasion they would touch or join (as in the case of World War II). But the regions remained on separate paths, supported and sustained by the cultural, social, and economic choices of residents on both sides of the boundary.

In other lands, Africa being the best example,[29] boundary lines ignored cultural and social realities and created artificial divisions that caused chaos and hardship in the postcolonial period. Not so in the case of the Pacific Northwest. With the important exception of the First Nations, several of which saw their traditional lands divided by the border (forcing the choice of being wards of the Canadian or the American state), few people found themselves dislocated by the imposition of the border.[30] (The Hudson's Bay Company employees were, with few exceptions, temporary workers, so the move hardly created a hardship for them.) For most of the First Nations people involved, there were few restrictions on their cross-border movements (for hunting, fishing, or laboring) and hence little reason to protest about the artificial nature of the boundary. By the time such regulations came into existence, the First Nation peoples' lives were intricately connected with their home governments, and a state of economic and political dependency was emerging.

In contrast to the colonial boundaries established in Africa and elsewhere, the British North America–United States boundary did not divide a large, sedentary, and well-established population. It sat across comparatively unsettled territory, a frail fence on unoccupied land. Each nation, then, had the opportunity to settle the claimed territory, and both made efforts to do so before competing claims could be established. The people who moved into the Pacific Northwest thus settled Canadian or American territory, its international identity firmly set. And most came either as Canadians or Americans, or at least respecting the reality of the situation. Only a few people—Americans in British Columbia before the turn of the twentieth century—thought that the situation remained fluid and believed that there could or would be a redrafting of the existing boundaries. The very act of settlement and development, therefore, was a primary factor in entrenching the reality of national control and ownership.

By the latter half of the twentieth century, cross-border connections were relatively few, and most residents seem to have identified more with their particular political jurisdiction and nation than with the cross-border region described as the Pacific Northwest. Whatever geographic and aboriginal integrity the area possessed had been substantially wiped out by colonial fiat, in the form of boundary decisions, the operations of the Canadian and U.S. governments, and the nationalist identifications of the nonaboriginal settlers on either side of the border. What was an interconnected region and what could have been, save for diplomatic and political decisions in Washington, D.C., and London, an integrated region, had been effectively divided in two. The borders had, in fact, both defined and shaped the region.

The Postboundary or Modern Era

Although the historical pattern is fairly clear, questions remain about the relevance of borders and international boundaries in the contemporary age. The writer Joel Garreau's 1980s bestseller *The Nine Nations of North America* offered a provocative analysis of North American life.[31] The international boundary, he argued, was not the prime determinant of regional culture, and moreover, the differences between nations—Canada, the United States, and Mexico— were becoming less pronounced over time. Instead of the long-standing national allegiances, regional cultures had emerged, oblivious to international boundaries, and taken strong root. He included the Pacific Northwest (or, more accurately, the strip of land along the coast) in Ecotopia, which stretched from Santa Barbara, California, to Southeast Alaska. In this area, Garreau argued, a shared conservationist ethic and a tolerance of alternative lifestyles created a regional society that transcended national differences—and stood in sharp contrast to the other "nations," including the Breadbasket, the Empty Quarter, and French Canada. Although Garreau's analysis skimmed over the strong and entrenched commitments to nation that remain across North America, he had identified a vital element in the continent's contemporary development: borders no longer mattered as much as they had previously. A new, transborder unity appeared to be developing in North America.

Garreau's book predated—and perhaps anticipated—the signing of the Canada–United States Free Trade Agreement and the subsequent expanded integration of the North American economy. There are abundant signs, however, that in the Pacific Northwest if not elsewhere the border may be weakening. Some of the indications are practical, such as the creation of "frequent crossing" permits to facilitate border crossings for Canadians traveling regularly to the United States and vice versa (including a growing number of people who live on a different side of the boundary from where they work). Other indications are more ephemeral: the extension of American popular culture throughout the region, the merging of regional economies (recent developments in the fishery sector illustrate this process, as do the numerous contracts for hydroelectric power that permanently link British Columbia and Washington state), and a declining sense of cultural difference. Although too much has been made of the until now minor political rumblings surrounding Cascadia and regional integration, not enough has been said about the increasing cross-border contact between regional governments (a process with strong roots in the World War II era[32]), which suggests a commonality of purpose and planning that is seldom discussed in public.

It would be folly to argue, as some advocates of regional integration have suggested, that cultural distinctiveness is disappearing. Some very basic differences—the high and growing Asian population in Vancouver and

British Columbia, the substantial African American population in Seattle and environs, and the much touted (by Canadians) gap between the standards of British Columbia's public health care system and the American private health care arrangements—remain in evidence. Scarcely a year goes by without an extensive media analysis of the different attitudes toward gun control and violence on opposite sides of the border. One minor example is the cancellation of preferred status for British Columbian students wishing to study at Washington state universities. These students were previously enrolled as residents, with much lower tuition fees. The failure of B.C. universities to attract an off-setting number of U.S. students convinced the Washington state government to scrap the arrangement. On the economic front there is also the important reality that Canadians and Americans are, first and foremost, competitors. In recent times the Port of Vancouver has taken important container contracts away from Seattle, and thousands of U.S. travelers have shifted their flight plans to include Vancouver departures to capitalize on low fares and more frequent service, particularly to Asia.[33] This is, in turn, a repeat of a competitive victory by Seattle only a short time earlier.

The future of cross-border integration remains uncertain. The continued debate about the future of Canada, precipitated by the separatist movement in Quebec, has caused some British Columbians to question their future within the Confederation.[34] There is little evidence, except in highly select circles, that Americans in the Pacific Northwest are contemplating separation or a regional union with British Columbia. The reintegration of the Far Northwest, Alaska and the Yukon, continues apace, aided in large measure by cross-border relations between First Nations and particularly by the expansion of the regional tourist trade (much of it American dominated through the cruise ship industry). There are almost no supporters, however, save for a noisy but marginal group of Alaska separatists, for a cleavage from their respective nation-states and no serious discussion of a regional union.

What does appear to be clear is that the globalization of trade, the technological assault on boundaries that accompanies the digital revolution, and the North American Free Trade Agreement have greatly weakened the border and continued the process of eroding the cultural differences between Canada and the United States in the Pacific Northwest. Sharp distinctions remain across the boundary—the high level of militarization and heavy industry in Washington state assures this—but the contrasts are certainly not much greater than, say, between British Columbia and Nova Scotia or Washington state and Texas. The continued movement of people, ideas, culture, sport, and trade between the regions will likely further erode the distinctions over time, but this is more a function of global and technological factors than it is of developments unique to the Pacific Northwest. The creation of a global, digitally connected culture is under way, not necessarily the establishment of a regional society and economy.

REFLECTIONS ON THE FUTURE OF A HISTORIC RELATIONSHIP

The gap between Canadian and American sectors of the Pacific Northwest appears to be more one of nations rather than of regions—given similarities of climate, geography, and economy—reflecting the separate histories and national assumptions of Canada and the United States. The answer to those who argue for the imminent collapse of national distinctions in North America seems, at least in part, to exist in borderlands regions like the Pacific Northwest, which provide striking evidence that history and the national ethos built up over generations matter, and matter a great deal.

The Pacific Northwest remains a geographic region with restricted cultural and social unity, and the international boundary is substantially responsible for the gaps that remain. The political artifact that is the border has had considerable historical and contemporary impact. The postboundary history of the region could, on one level, be summarized as a contest between the influential economic, social, and cultural forces of integration and the countervailing power of the modern state to maintain separation and ensure continued sovereignty and the imperatives of nationally focused settler societies to ensure their connection to the larger nation-state. The Canada–United States boundary in the Pacific Northwest has been an influential historical instrument, separating indigenous peoples, establishing and supporting separate political cultures, social systems, and economic regimes. The inherent geographic logic of regional integration—a common economic base (fishing, forestry, tourism), roughly comparable climates, similar struggles with distant national governments, and interconnected histories—has been overwhelmed by the political logic of fixed national boundaries, domestic social and political preferences, inherently protectionist government policies, and the evolving nationalism of the modern state.

The study of border cultures—in this instance, the Pacific Northwest—provides some important lessons for historians. It should reveal, first and foremost, the risk of assuming the inevitability of national boundaries and the dangers of rooting one's studies in national settings, rather than in the shifting historical and geographical contexts out of which modern societies evolved. Further, such an examination illustrates the importance of considering the manner in which the modern state created, imposed, maintained, and empowered boundaries, not just by establishing border crossings and implementing customs duties but also in creating and sustaining a sense of national distinctiveness. Washingtonians did not become Washingtonians simply by happenstance, any more than British Columbians were predestined to place their primary allegiance to Canada and their province.

It is in the borderlands, where country rubs against country, where citizens have regular contact with a different way of governing and living, that one finds the true test of nationalism and nationhood.[35] And despite repeated predictions of the inevitable collapse of the nation-state, the evolution of the Pacific Northwest makes it abundantly clear that shared histories and extensive social and economic connections do not easily override more fundamental loyalties. The Pacific Northwest is animated by regional realities. There has been, and remains, a strong undercurrent of common cause, most evident in recent years on environmental and economic matters, offset just as regularly by national rivalries and disagreements over such issues as fisheries quotas and lumber prices. In the final analysis, however, similarities and commonalties seem to be relatively superficial. National ideologies, given physical expression in the international boundary and political strength through an array of legislative initiatives, remain the most powerful determinants of local identity. The study of borderland cultures, both in their historical development and contemporary manifestations, demonstrates that nations do matter and will, in all likelihood, continue to matter well into the future. By exploring, individually and collectively, the opportunities of borderlands study and the need for greater understanding of the influences that have shaped and determined our histories—shared and separate—scholars will develop a much stronger sense of what is Canadian, what is American, and what is regional in Pacific Northwest history.

It is in the borderlands where we stand to learn a great deal about Canada and the United States, about the relative importance of landscape, setting, resources, and nationhood in determining regional development, and about the degrees of separation that stand between Canadians and Americans in the Pacific Northwest. Until recently, we have allowed the seemingly self-evident imperatives of the nation-state to override the historically evident importance of regional connections and cross-border developments. It is time for historians, driven by the desire to better understand the past and not to simply address contemporary regional developments, to reinvest the Pacific Northwest with its historical substance. The Pacific Northwest, so often presented as the land of tomorrow, is a cross-border region with a vibrant, international history.

NOTES

1. David Elkins, *Beyond Sovereignty: Territory and Political Economy in the Twenty-First Century* (Toronto: University of Toronto Press, 1995).

2. Pauliina Raento, "Together and Apart: The Changing Contexts of Basque Borderland," in Lars-folke Landgren and Maunu Häyrynen, eds., *The Dividing Line: Borders and National Peripheries* (Helsinki: Renvall Institute, 1997), p. 241.

3. This idea is explored further in Julian Minghi, "From Conflict to Harmony in Border Landscapes," in Dennis Rumley and Julian Minghi, eds., *The Geography of Border Landscapes* (London: Routledge, 1991), pp. 15–30.

4. John Welchman, ed., *Rethinking Borders* (Houndsmills, England: Macmillan, 1996); Anssi Paasi, *Territories, Boundaries, and Consciousness: The Changing Geographies of the Finnish-Russian Border* (Chichester, England: J. Wiley and Sons, 1995); Benedict Anderson, *Imagined Communities: Reflections on the Origin and Spread of Nationalism*, rev. ed. (London: Verso, 1991); and Robert Stock, *Human Territoriality: Its Theory and History* (Cambridge: Cambridge University Press, 1986).

5. One recurring theme in contemporary scholarship is that ideological and conceptual boundaries are more significant than political ones. The reality, however, is that political boundaries are often extremely relevant and possess direct consequences. For a passionate analysis of this idea, see Nancy Scheper-Hughes, "The Primacy of the Ethical: Propositions for a Militant Anthropology," *Current Anthropology* 36 (June 1995): 409–20.

6. Interestingly, the excellent new *Oxford History of the American West* includes a chapter on Alaska and Hawaii but offers very little commentary on the significance of the Canadian West to the evolution of the U.S. region. Clyde Milner, Carol O'Connor, and Martha Sandweiss, eds., *The Oxford History of the American West* (New York: Oxford University Press, 1994).

7. Jean Barman, *The West beyond the West: A History of British Columbia*, rev. ed. (Toronto: University of Toronto Press, 1996).

8. David Emmons, "Constructed Province: History and the Making of the Last American West," *Western Historical Quarterly* 25, no. 4 (1994): 437.

9. Two good examples are the nineteenth-century historian Hubert Howe Bancroft, whose studies incorporated the broad sweep of Pacific Northwest history, and Seymour Lipset, an American sociologist who has long been interested in the historical and cultural divisions between Canada and the United States.

10. The standard test of this assessment—an old standby in historiographical analysis—is to refer to the survey histories of the border regions to demonstrate the general point. It works here as well. Recent overviews of the history of the American West, British Columbia, the Yukon, and Alaska make scant mention of borderlands regions and realities, leaving the distinct impression that the border is a historical fixture, without a social, economic, cultural, or political history of its own. There is one important exception to this general point, William G. Robbins, *Colony and Empire: The Capitalist Transformation of the American West* (Lawrence: University Press of Kansas, 1994), which devotes a chapter to "The American and Canadian Wests: Two Nations, Two Cultures." More traditional examples include Richard White, *"It's Your Misfortune and None of My Own": A History of the American West* (Norman: University of Oklahoma Press, 1991); Milner, O'Connor, and Sandweiss, *Oxford History of the American West*, which includes a chapter on comparative frontiers that gives Canada as much attention as New Zealand and Australia; Barman, *West beyond the West*; Claus-M. Naske and Herman E. Slotnick, *Alaska: A History of the Forty-Ninth State* (Norman: University of Oklahoma Press, 1987); Ken S. Coates and William R. Morrison, *Land of the Midnight Sun: A History of the Yukon* (Edmonton, Alberta: Hurtig, 1988). See also Carlos Schwantes, *The Pacific Northwest: An Interpretive History*, rev. ed. (Lincoln: University of Nebraska Press, 1996); David H. Stratton, ed., *Washington Comes of Age: The State in the National Experience* (Pullman: Washington State University Press, 1992); Gordon B. Dodds, *The American Northwest: A History of Oregon and Washington* (Arlington Heights, Ill.: Forum, 1986).

11. This is an overly large generalization. A great deal of recent scholarship attempts, instead, to situate local or regional developments amid much broader international or human processes, such as work and labor relations, gender relations, and broader ideas and values. Even within this "new" social history is a strong traditional strain of explaining developments largely by reference to national (or regional) traits and policies.

12. An interesting illustration—highly symbolic—of the increasing integration of the region is the recent acquisition of the Vancouver Canucks hockey team, the General Motors Place arena, and the Vancouver Grizzlies of the NBA by a reclusive Seattle financier. Lest too much is made of this American takeover, it is useful to recall the recent purchase of the Seattle Mariners baseball team by the Nintendo Corporation and the fact that the Vancouver Canucks were initially owned by U.S. investors.

13. Canadians have assumed, in typically Canadian fashion, that this transference is all in one direction—American culture spreading north into Canada. Although that is substantially true (and witness the strong Canadian support for the Seattle Public Broadcasting System station), it is worth noting that the recent decision by Seattle-area cable operators to remove the Canadian Broadcasting Corporation signal from

the basic cable service was greeted with howls of protest, resulting in a promise to reinstate the channel.

14. This issue is covered in many places. One of the most interesting and detailed investigations can be followed in David Hall, *Clifford Sifton,* 2 vols. (Vancouver: University of British Columbia Press, 1981–85). For an analysis of the working out of the boundary on the ground, see Lewis Green, *The Boundary Hunters: Surveying the 141st Meridian and the Alaska Panhandle* (Vancouver: University of British Columbia Press, 1982).

15. To state the obvious, ports are much easier to regulate, through the work of customs officials, than are myriad inland roads, trails, and river crossings.

16. Several of the boundary points remained, and remain, permeable. The Alaskan settlement of Hyder, for example, is closely integrated with nearby Stewart, British Columbia, and no serious attempt is made to regulate movement between the two communities. Similarly, until the early 1970s, the U.S. Customs Service kept only a casual eye on travelers arriving via the Haines Road, a rough, uncertain stretch of highway. Visitors arriving after hours were asked to report in the next day. The situation was similar on several of the smaller, isolated crossing points on the British Columbia–Washington state boundary.

17. Wayne Suttles, ed., *Northwest Coast,* vol. 7 of *Handbook of North American Indians* (Washington, D.C.: Smithsonian Institution Press, 1990). It is worth noting that the most recent survey of indigenous peoples in Canada—Alan McMillan, *Native Peoples and Cultures of Canada: An Anthropological Overview* (Vancouver, B.C.: Douglas & McIntyre, 1988)—focuses exclusively on the Canadian side of the boundary and does not discuss related developments in what is now U.S. territory.

18. Alice Kehoe, *North American Indians: A Comprehensive Account* (Englewood Cliffs, N.J.: Prentice Hall, 1981), p. 413.

19. There is a substantial literature on this subject. The best source is Douglas Cole, *Captured Heritage: The Scramble for Northwest Coast Artifacts* (Vancouver, B.C.: Douglas & McIntyre, 1985).

20. Cole Harris, "Voices of Disaster: Smallpox around the Strait of Georgia in 1782," *Ethnohistory* 41, no. 4 (fall 1994): 591–626.

21. Barry Gough, *The Northwest Coast: British Navigation, Trade, and Discoveries to 1812* (Vancouver: University of British Columbia Press, 1992), *Gunboat Frontier* (Vancouver: University of British Columbia Press, 1984), and *Distant Dominion: Britain and the Northwest Coast of North America, 1579–1809* (Vancouver: University of British Columbia Press, 1980); James R. Gibson, *Otter Skins, Boston Ships, and China Goods: The Maritime Fur Trade of the Northwest Coast, 1785–1841* (Montreal: McGill-Queen's Press, 1992), and *Farming the Frontier: The Agricultural Opening of the Oregon Country, 1786–1846* (Vancouver: University of British Columbia Press, 1985).

22. And historians, too. After a brief discussion of the history of the boundary dispute, Richard White largely drops British Columbia and the Canadian West from his study. White, *"It's Your Misfortune,"* pp. 67–77.

23. Internal boundaries—for Washington, Oregon, British Columbia, the Yukon, and Alaska—would be set in later years. National and international boundaries were finalized during this period. Norman Nicholson, *The Boundaries of the Canadian Confederation* (Ottawa: Carleton University Press, 1979). On surveying the forty-ninth parallel, see J. Mingh, "The Evolution of a Border Region: The Pacific Coast Section of the Canadian and United States Border," *Scottish Geographical Magazine* 80 (April 1964): 37–52; Herman J. Deutsch, "A Contemporary Report on the 49° Boundary Survey," *Pacific Northwest Quarterly* 53 (January 1962): 17–33.

24. Note that the Americans subsequently changed the spelling of Fort Youcon and the Youcon River to Yukon. The latter has remained as the common spelling.

25. Tina Loo, *Making Law, Order, and Authority in British Columbia, 1821–1871* (Toronto: University of Toronto Press, 1994).

26. The North West Mounted Police actions are described in William R. Morrison, *Showing the Flag: The Mounted Police and Canadian Sovereignty in the North, 1894–1925* (Vancouver: University of British Columbia Press, 1985).

27. The Vancouver-Seattle controversy is documented in Norbert MacDonald, *Distant Neighbors: A Comparative History of Vancouver and Seattle* (Lincoln: University of Nebraska Press, 1987).

28. See Ken S. Coates and W. R. Morrison, *The Alaska Highway in World War II* (Norman: University of Oklahoma Press, 1992); and Ken S. Coates, ed., *The Alaska Highway: Papers of the Fortieth Anniversary Symposium* (Vancouver: University of British Columbia Press, 1985).

29. A. I. Asiwaju, *Partitioned Africans: Ethnic Relations across Africa's International Boundaries, 1884–1984* (London: C. Hurst, 1985). On the contemporary manifestations of these culturally illogical boundaries, see Basil Davidson, *The Black Man's Burden: Africa and the Curse of the Nation-State* (London: James Curry, 1992).

30. David McCrady, "Beyond Boundaries: Aboriginal Peoples and the Prairie West, 1850–1885," M.A. thesis, University of Victoria, 1990.

31. Joel Garreau, *The Nine Nations of North America* (Boston: Houghton Mifflin, 1981).

32. See the discussion in Shelagh Grant, *Sovereignty or Security? Government Policy in the Canadian North, 1936–1950* (Vancouver: University of British Columbia Press, 1988).

33. This is, significantly, the reverse of the situation of only a few years ago, when Canadians flooded down to Bellingham and Seattle (many still do) to gain access to the highly competitive U.S. market and when Seattle "stole" away large container con-

tracts from Vancouver. The recent changes reflect more the alterations of the business cycle than they do a major shift in favor of one country or the other.

34. A recent B.C. poll on support for separation revealed a surprisingly high 12 percent in favor. The absence of a strong political leader who is able and willing to capitalize on this sentiment will, in all likelihood, limit further support for the idea.

35. One might argue as well that other peoples on the margins of the nation—indigenous peoples and ethnic minorities—likewise are most anxious to demonstrate their connection to the nation-state, as through considerably higher than average participation rates in wartime military service.

PART ONE

THE PERMEABLE BORDER

2 / No Parallel

American Miner-Soldiers at War with the Nlaka'pamux of the Canadian West

DANIEL P. MARSHALL

We ware on our march by sunrise. This day we made pease with 4 different Chiefs and camped within seven miles of the Thompson River. Here we was met by Spintlum. The war chief of all the tribes for some distance up & down Frazer River. . . . Here I proceded at once to hold our grand counsil which consisted of Eleven Chiefs and a very large number of other indians that had gathered from above and below. We stated to them that this time we came for pease, but if we had to come againe, that we would not come by hundreds, but by thousands and drive them from the river forever. They ware much supprised and frightened to see so many men with guns & revolvers. For marching along in single file they looked to be three times the number their was. . . . I feel well satisfied that the Treaty was the best that could be made under the circumstances, and think it will be held sacred by the Indians.   —H. M. SNYDER[1]

In 1858 the Native lands along the southern section of the Fraser River corridor below the fifty-first parallel were invaded by large companies of foreign miners organized into armies of conquest that had effectively triggered Indian wars in Washington and Oregon and by extension, the Fraser River War of British Columbia. Abraham Lincoln's future secretary of war, Edwin M. Stanton, who declared, "A marvellous thing is now going on here. . . [that] will prove one of the most important events on the Globe," was not the only

FIG. 2.1. Map of "Frazer's River" and the gold-producing districts of North America. Source: *Frank Leslie's Illustrated Newspaper* (New York, 1858).

American to be swept up by the excitement of the Fraser River gold rush.[2] Stanton, then federal agent for land claims settlement in California, merely observed the effects of the massive rush north. But those for whom the call of gold was irresistible—more than thirty thousand migrants—were soon to invade the lands along the Fraser and Thompson Rivers in search of the elusive metal that had been the sole mining preserve of the Salishan peoples (Figure 2.1).[3]

As the mining frontier moved northward from California, through Oregon and Washington, Native discoveries of gold in British Columbia diverted the Euro-American population north of the forty-ninth parallel, precipitating the Fraser River rush: "Never, perhaps, was there so large an immigration in so short a space of time into so small a place."[4] Those who could afford passage, at least twenty-three thousand miners, dashed north to Victoria, Port Townsend, or Bellingham Bay via sailing ships and larger steam-powered vessels. At least eight thousand others trod overland from such places as Sacramento, Placerville, or Yreka through northern California and Oregon, along the Columbia and Okanagan Rivers of Washington Territory, and across the forty-ninth parallel to the northern fur trade preserve of New Caledonia, the unconstituted territory of Britain. The "Fraser River Fever" was of such consequence that U.S. president James Buchanan took the unprecedented step of appointing an emissary to the region to represent and protect American interests.[5] Contemporary accounts claimed that the flood tide of immigration north carried as many as one hundred thousand people.[6]

The effects of such a massive outpouring of people from the U.S. Pacific Coast states particularly affected the gold rush metropolis of San Francisco. By 1858, California's placer mines were largely played out, leaving many old forty-niners without any serious occupation but to frequent San Francisco's bars, boarding houses, or back alleys.[7] Capital- and labor-intensive hydraulic mining had replaced the halcyon days of picks, pans, and shovels and marginalized the average sourdough or made him a wage laborer at best. At the very depths of a city-wide depression, the Golden State's luster became further tarnished as a huge unemployed class was increasingly desperate for news of a "New Eldorado."[8] These placer miners became the advance guard for the expansion of the California mining frontier throughout the American West and Pacific Slope regions. As the British Columbia historian Frederick Howay asserted, "The metropolis of the Pacific Coast was San Francisco; and Victoria, the capital and chief port of British Columbia, was only its northern outpost . . . part of the great hinterland."[9] The historian Earl Pomeroy also stresses the metropolitan-hinterland relationship of the Pacific Slope. "Whatever the neighboring states were," he claims, "they were in large part because it [California] served as catalyst, banker, and base of operations."[10] Before the repercussion of east-west links realigned the Pacific Slope, it is quite clear that

British Columbia, Washington, Oregon, and California were part of a larger north-south transboundary region.

Much of the cultural mentality that informed the genocidal practices of the California mining frontier was baggage carried north with the requisite pick, pan, and shovel.[11] Indian-white interaction in the fur trade, in contrast, had been comparatively peaceful and therefore had not prepared the Indian nations of New Caledonia for outright war. For many U.S. Western gold seekers, fighting Indians and finding gold became conflated. Terms like "Redskins," "Injuns," or "Diggers," labels commonly used in white Californian parlance, were immediately applied to Native peoples in New Caledonia or any Native nation that resisted the advance of the Californian mining frontier. Mining, the single greatest disruptor of Native lands in the American West, created a frontier defined and segregated by race, a frontier that did not recognize the British-American border and that effectively shaped the Fraser River landscape in its own image.[12] This sudden invasion broke the back of Indian control over access and use of their territories and resources, shaped the aboriginal landscape into a series of foreign, ethnically defined mining enclaves, and precipitated the formation of Indian reserves even before the British proclaimed the Crown Colony of British Columbia in the fall of 1858.[13]

In placing the Fraser River gold rush of 1858 into the larger transboundary perspective of the Pacific Slope, this chapter seeks to establish the predominant influence of the American West on aboriginal peoples in the Fraser River corridor before the full exertion of British colonial power. I maintain that California mining culture, in transcending the forty-ninth parallel into the British and fur trade worlds and the Native territories of New Caledonia, ultimately appropriated "Indian country" during this signal event. During the transformative year of 1858, there was no visible line separating British Columbia from Washington—the forty-ninth parallel was of little consequence at this time, as many Americans hoped that the U.S. Boundary Commission would establish the goldfields south of the international divide. Until such time as the boundary was physically located and diplomatically confirmed, many American miners organized and operated in the goldfields to the point of asserting near-sovereign control. Within Canadian historiography, it is also usually assumed that there is no parallel in Canada to the kinds of Native-white violence that occurred in the American mining West. This chapter explores a most notable and neglected exception.

In many ways the Fraser River gold rush was history repeating itself. After all, the invasion of aboriginal lands in the Americas by transplanted Europeans has occurred continuously from 1492 to the modern day. Within the Pacific

Northwest the Indian wars of Washington and Oregon provide ample evidence of Native resistance to white encroachment and social control.[14] The Fort Colvile gold rush of 1855, as a single example, provided British colonial administrators invaluable evidence of the kind of racism and racial war that quickly penetrated the new British-American divide.[15] This rush was a prophetic warning of things to come to the Fraser goldfields just three years later. Gold seekers in Washington Territory, in pushing through the native lands of the Yakama, set off a series of conflicts supposedly unique to history south of the international border.[16] The Portland store keeper Jonathan T. Kerns recorded the disregard with which his company of miners treated a Native elder they encountered on the trail to the new diggings. Kerns wrote that the "old Chief told us his men would mim-loose us if we went on, but we told him to come on if he wanted all of his tillicums killed and we passed on."[17] Kerns then recorded two weeks later his company's surprise that war had been declared on them despite the chief's forewarning. Their mining prospects having declined "faster than lightning ever went down a stump," these miners next made as their object "to thrash the red devils a little."[18] In military-like fashion they proceeded back to Portland, taking up their line of march along the Palouse River in Spokane territory. Once again Kerns was surprised that "the Indians would not let them over and commenced trying to lead off some of their horses, but the men drew their revolvers and guns and give [*sic*] them to understand that they would kill some of them. . . . They knew we would soon clean them out if they commenced."[19]

California, Oregon, and Washington were not the only U.S. states aflame with instances of extreme violence being leveled against First Nations peoples. William I. "Billy" Ballou, a well-known pioneer express man in both California and British Columbia and a veteran of the Mexican-American War, engaged in similar conflict near the forks of the Owyhee River in Idaho. Ballou recalled, "We had hand grenades, & one thing and another. . . . We killed everything that looked like an Indian, dog, or anything else; young ones, by George— shot them all. Col. Moore said 'kill them all, little as well as big; knits [*sic*] make lice.'"[20] Similar accounts in letters, diaries, government records, and newspapers of this time are replete with instances of white aggression toward the indigenous peoples of the American Pacific Northwest.[21] Just as the Indian world was not confined by the Oregon Boundary Settlement of 1846, neither was the armed conflict that inevitably marched north.[22]

By direct land communication with the Fraser and Thompson Rivers, large numbers of gold seekers, particularly from the Pacific Northwest and northern California, collected into sizable groups for mutual protection and the armed incursion of Eastern Washington and British Columbia.[23] If miners starting out numbered only five or ten men, they simply waited at points along the Hudson's Bay Company brigade trail for additional miners to augment their forces. As company membership increased significantly—exceeding perhaps fifty, one hundred, or even two hundred and fifty[24]—miners organized themselves in the same manner that settler-soldier armies had formed in Washington and Oregon in the Indian wars before 1858. Instilled with popular notions of American frontier democracy and provisional camp government, miners elected their leaders to military office, and ordinary mining companies more closely resembled armies of invasion.[25]

With the defeat of Lieutenant Colonel E. J. Steptoe and the U.S. Army by twelve hundred of the Spokane, Palouse, Coeur d'Alene, Yakama, and other Indian tribes during May 1858, much of Eastern Washington was considered off-limits to civilians.[26] Companies of gold seekers, however, held a very different view. Steptoe, "flying before the Indians," demanded that miners "not go beyond where the Government could give them protection. This they would not consent to do, but pushed on."[27] Perhaps the best-known company to have infiltrated the lands of Eastern Washington, Fraser River bound, were those that mustered at Oregon City under the immediate command of David McLoughlin.[28] Richard G. Willoughby, an Indian fighter from Missouri and later a "Texas Cowboy" in the punitive raids into Mexico, recalled the military-like precision with which the McLoughlin party proceeded in its campaign against Steptoe's wishes:

> The miners fully realized the dangerous undertaking it was to force their passage through numerous warlike Indians and therefore remained for some time at Walla Walla [Washington] awaiting the arrival of other parties so as to organize a larger body for mutual protection. They then organized their party into different companies, commencing with the first letter of the alphabet, etc. In the march they generally took their position in advance according to the letter. If "A" was at the head to-day, they would be in the rear to-morrow, and so on throughout the whole party. They elected a Captain whose supreme command and decision in all matters was final. . . . Probably there was never a party on the Pacific Coast better qualified for Indian warfare than this, the majority of the men having had long years of experience in this venturesome life and who had served the United States Government in the war with Mexico.[29]

Judge Robert Frost of Olympia, Washington, emphasizing that it was "as fresh to me as if it occurred only last year," wrote of his membership in the

McLoughlin company and the skirmishes that happened en route to Fraser, including the significant ambush of their party by Chief Tenasket of the Okanagan Indians at what was later known as McLoughlin's Canyon.[30] Proceeding along the east side of the Okanogan River,[31] using the old Hudson's Bay Company brigade trail, the company departed from the river's natural course because of a large bluff that compelled them to enter the "bloody canyon."[32] Frost maintained that "the object of the Indians was to get us all in the Canyon, & had they succeeded, very few if any, would have gotten out alive." As it was, six men were killed and the party of about one hundred fifty miners was driven back and forced to cross the Okanogan before continuing north.[33] By the time the party crossed the forty-ninth parallel, additional skirmishes occurred, but this largely American force finally concluded a peace agreement at Penticton, British Columbia.[34]

John Callbreath, a New Yorker who had sailed around Cape Horn to San Francisco in 1849, also took this overland route to the Fraser River in 1858. Following a similar procedure, his small company of five men waited on the trail to augment their numbers, elect a captain, "and organise for a hostile country." Their party of 250 miners, and 500 mules and horses, marched up the Columbia River, through the Grand Coulee, and ultimately into McLoughlin's Canyon before crossing the border toward Fort Kamloops. By this time Eastern Washington was aflame with Native-white violence as U.S. Army troops sought retribution for Steptoe's defeat. Once the company crossed the international boundary, Callbreath wrote, "We now considered ourselves past the most dreaded Indian country." Yet other companies recorded that conflict continued on the British side of the line.[35]

H. F. Reinhart, a young German emigrant who grew up in New York and Illinois, in 1851 traveled to California in search of gold. In 1858 he joined Major Mortimer Robertson's party of about 250 miners preparing at The Dalles for the Fraser River. Reinhart wrote that Robertson "said if he could make up a company of 300 men with plenty of arms, ammunition, horses and mules and provisions, he would take us to Fraser River if we had to fight the Indians every day."[36] Robertson's prognostication was not far off the mark. The so-called Yakima Expedition to the northern mines organized into companies "A" through "F" each with its own captain, first and second lieutenants, while Robertson as commander had an adjutant and surgeon as staff officers. Of the Indian people, "most of my men seem eager for a fight with them," claimed Robertson, "and I am disposed to think their desire will be gratified before one week has elapsed."[37] Open hostility and general skirmishes with Native peoples are recorded throughout Reinhart's extensive recounting of the trip north: "The old Californian miners and Indian-fighters were the worst," Reinhart lamented, as they believed "they could travel in small parties and clean out all the Indians in the land."38

Once inside British territory, tensions were certainly no better. At Okanagan Lake these gold seekers helped themselves to large stores of nuts and berries cached in a local Indian village. After taking all they wanted, "the balance they just emptied into the lake, destroying them so that the Indians should not have them for provisions for winter."39 Having lost some members of their company to Native-white aggression south of the border, the advance party decided to make a further and more horrific show of force. While the main body of miners broke camp and continued north, twenty-five members of the advance guard held back, concealed within a gulch, and waited for members of the Okanagan Nation to arrive. "As soon as the Indians saw the whites," stated Reinhart, "they were so frightened that some turned back and ran towards their boat, some fell down on their knees and begged for [them] not to shoot, as they had no arms at all, and they threw up their hands and arms to show that they had nothing. But the whites all commenced to fire and shoot at them, and ran out to the lake after those getting in their canoes, and kept on shooting till the few that got in the [canoes] got out of reach of the guns and rifles. . . . It was a brutal affair, but the perpetrators of the outrage thought they were heroes, and were victors in some well-fought battle."40

The Okanagan sought revenge for the unwarranted killings and followed the mining party to Kamloops.41 Reinhart believed that they also attempted to enlist the Nlaka'pamux42 or Thompson River Indians "to help them kill us all."43 Writing to his father from Victoria, on July 14, 1858, William Nixon stated, "I have heard a great many reports here in relation to the Indians killing off the white men, who are going overland by way of the Dalles. There was one party of seventy-five who got within a few days travel of the Thompson river, and the Indians made an attack on them and chased them four days."44 George Wesley Beam, former captain of the Northern Rangers, the Washington Territorial Volunteers, and a participant in the Indian wars of 1856, heard rumors of these conflicts and the eventual response made by some of his fellow countrymen.45 Writing from Puget Sound Bar on the Fraser River, Beam recorded among the daily entries of his diary, "The Oregonians have got to Thompson River and they clear out the Indians where ever the[y] come across them."46 To his friend Winfield Scott Ebey, brother of the well-known customs collector, Beam further elaborated: "Indian report says that they kill all siwashes that they see."47

While overland parties effectively extended Native-white violence from

Washington and Oregon into British territory, maritime routes of communication through Victoria, Port Townsend, and Bellingham Bay expanded aggression even more directly to the Fraser itself.[48] Because of the multiplicity of sea- and land-based routes gold seekers took, Indian-white conflict became widespread. The First Nations that inhabited the Fraser goldfields were, from the very beginning, a river-oriented people whose culture, trade, transportation, and food—particularly the salmon—all depended on the Fraser River itself.[49] When British fur traders arrived, they too saw the critical importance of the Fraser for their own transportation needs and the extensive salmon resource, which became the Hudson's Bay Company's first nonfur export from New Caledonia.[50] And so, with miners arriving en masse from every conceivable angle, gold mining and salmon fishing became incompatible. Conflict on the Fraser River was inevitable when gold (and the environmental consequences of placer mining) began to rival the salmon (fishing and processing) on these same contested grounds.

As overland companies reached Kamloops, they heard their first direct news of the diggings from gold seekers who had traveled upriver from Puget Sound and the Gulf of Georgia. Not only did they receive credible, firsthand accounts of the "New Eldorado," but they also learned that Indians in the Fraser Canyon were resisting white encroachment.[51] Richard Willoughby "learned from them of the Indian War on the Fraser River which had taken place at the same time as they had their troubles on the Columbia."[52] Likewise, Reinhart, in reaching The Fountain near Lillooet (and later at Boston Bar), recorded: "There had been an Indian War lower down Fraser River and the Indians had cut off the heads of many miners, 'Bostons,' or Americans, until . . . the miners just quit work and organized into companies and went out to fight and kill all the Indians they could find, and found several camps of them, and just killed everything, men, women and children, so that the Indians were at last very glad to make terms of peace and promise not to molest miners any more."[53]

Apparently white miners were not the only ones to receive news of these conflicts north of the border, as the *Yreka Union* reported that Native lines of communication also carried word of these events. The northern California newspaper gave great credence to the early Native reports of war from so far away: "We learn that To-lo, Indian Chief of the Scott Valley tribe, arrived in Yreka on 1st September from the Modoc country, with the intelligence—received from the De Shutes—that a fight had taken place somewhere in the vicinity of Thompson river, between the Indians and whites, in which a large number of the former were killed." The paper recorded: "Tolo did not learn

whether the whites were regulars or volunteers, but said the Indians were surrounded and fired upon from all sides. Very few of the whites if any were
killed. We place considerable reliance upon the information thus received from
Tolo, as he brought in the same manner intelligence of Col. Steptoe's defeat
several days in advance of information gained of the occurrence from any
other source. We will no doubt shortly hear of the fight."[54] The distant sounds
of conflict that Chief To-lo heard were that of the Fraser River War, conflict
intimately tied to events in the Canadian and American Okanogan River valley and the wider Indian wars of Washington and Oregon.[55]

The San Francisco *Bulletin,* in one of its many articles on the Native population of the northern "British possessions," noted that Indian runners from
Washington Territory were in direct communication with Natives along the
Fraser River in an attempt to warn them of what was happening in their lands
and to encourage them to drive the miners out.[56] The paper's regular correspondent attributed this information directly to James Douglas, governor of
the colony of Vancouver Island, who had met with a deputation of miners
whom Douglas had received "very coolly, and informed them . . . that the
Americans in arming themselves and going out against the Indians were guilty
of *treason.*" The field reporter recorded Douglas's warnings such that "the
Indians of Washington Territory have sent couriers all through the Fraser river
territory, calling on the Indians to unite and drive out the whites. In consequence, the Indians heretofore hunting for the Hudson's Bay Company have
applied for early and increased supplies of ammunition, which was refused
them, on account of the known object for which the request was made."[57]

Marie Houghton Brent, the great-granddaughter of N'kwala, chief of the
Okanagan Indians during the gold excitement, recalled the early attempts to
unite against their common foe. "During the Fraser River trouble between
the Thompsons [Nlaka'pamux] and the whites in 1858 and 1859," she stated,
"he advocated peace, although preparing for war had the affair not been
settled. The Thompsons were against the miners and settlers. Although he
was begged by the Spokanes and Thompsons to join them in war against the
whites, he refused to allow his people to join them."[58] Natives in the Fraser
and Thompson River corridors had considerable justification for organizing
resistance to the white incursion as they entered via boats, canoes, steamers,
or any suitable water craft that might carry them.

At the beginning of the gold rush, Californians made their presence
known by their treatment of the Stó:lō peoples similar to earlier practices in
the Sierra Nevada.[59] In an 1858 editorial written by Thomas King of the San
Francisco *Bulletin*, these similar extermination practices were condemned as

"likely to produce serious disturbances." The editor related an early incident on the lower Fraser, in which a California miner had shot an Indian for not offering use of his canoe at what he considered a fair rate of exchange. The editor's summation was perhaps prophetic when he advised accordingly: "One or two such acts of brutality on the part of reckless and abandoned white men, will raise such a burning hatred and spirit of revenge in the breast of the Indians, as will cause indiscriminate massacre of hundreds of innocent whites."[60]

The occurrence of Native-white conflict on both sides of the forty-ninth parallel became almost self-fulfilling as U.S. newspapers elevated the military-like prowess of the Salishan peoples and warned gold seekers that battle was imminent. Of the Fraser River Native peoples, in particular, the *Bulletin* had issued its harsh warning that "powerful tribes of Indians *own* that country and will be jealous of its despoliation. They are unlike the Diggers of California, in comparison being athletes—robust, hardy, brave and warlike, well armed, and by no means a common foe. Man to man, in more than one conflict hereafter, Americans will find them hard to whip. It is reasonable to calculate that in these battles—which will inevitably come—and by the usual casualties of an adventure to such a rugged country, death will overtake at least one out of every five persons who go there during the first twelve months."[61]

With Steptoe's defeat it was imagined that "the hostile feeling against our people will probably extend to the Indians in the British possessions, who, by all accounts, are opposed to 'los Yankees' working in the Fraser River mines."[62] Indeed, Governor Douglas believed that it would require "the nicest tact to avoid a disastrous Indian War."[63] Franklin Matthias, just one of many miners who was prevented from proceeding up the Fraser, made the standard response of waiting until the number of miners increased significantly, "when we will move up above the Falls and do just about as we please without regard to the Indians. . . . but there will be h   ll to pay after a while."[64] By early June 1858, during the height of the rush north, the editor of the *Bulletin* advised that miners must "prepare for a war with the savages. They will have to work with a shovel in one hand and a rifle in the other."[65]

Until significant numbers of Euro-Americans claimed the banks of the Fraser, a sort of unspoken détente existed between whites and Natives. Lucius Edelblute, an experienced gold miner who had been involved in conflict with Native peoples in California and near Pyramid Lake, Nevada, took a cautionary approach in his travels along the Thompson River. Traveling with a small group of miners from Pennsylvania, Kentucky, Virginia, and Illinois,

Edelblute and friends masqueraded as British subjects to escape death.[66] Just
as they were about to help themselves to some local salmon, a large contingent of Natives surrounded them and demanded that the fish be put back in
the river. With the use of a Chinook jargon dictionary, these men interpreted
Native demands such that "the cheaf sed them fish was thar liven and we had
no rite to take them and for us to pout them back. we dun so at once. the
indien ast us if we was boston men or not. we told him that we was king gorge
men and we was sent out to see thare cuntry and we wodent du any harm . . .
the brit amarican indins dident like the amaricans a toll."[67]

Through their alliances with the Hudson's Bay Company, Salishan peoples
had grown accustomed to receiving payment for *all* resources traded in their
country. They were also concerned about the damage that placer mining would
have on their fishery. Of equal consequence was the fact that they were the
controlling agents in the collection of gold before the 1858 rush.[68] Governor
Douglas had warned that the Nlaka'pamux were actively protecting their lucrative gold trade, having "taken the high-handed, though probably not unwise
course, of expelling all parties of gold diggers . . . who had forced an entrance
into their country." He also predicted "that serious affrays may take place
between the natives and the motley adventurers who . . . may probably attempt
to over power the opposition of the natives by force of arms."[69]

By April 1858, Douglas warned London again that Natives, particularly the
Nlaka'pamux, "expressed a determination to reserve the gold for their own
benefit" and that "affrays and collisions with the whites will surely follow the
accession of numbers."[70] As tensions between Natives and non-Natives
increased over the Fraser's limited resources and lands, H. M. Snyder, a regular correspondent to the San Francisco *Bulletin*, was one of the first to report
the outbreak of violence near the big canyon. "We have just been attacked by
a party of Indians," announced Snyder. "Their chief led them. They all come
with their guns and knives in their hands, and wished us to leave immediately.
But as soon as we got our pistols and knives ready, they began to quiet down. . . .
The band have driven every miner from this bar who attempted to locate on
it."[71] Although miners, like Snyder, nevertheless continued to remain on the
Fraser's gold-producing bars in opposition to mounting Native pressure, elsewhere First Nations were in all-out war against the combined militaries of
the U.S. Army and miners' militias that sought to ramrod a feasible route
to the Fraser mines through the Pacific Coast interior.

As many as a thousand well-armed miners were reported waiting at The
Dalles for an appropriate moment to enter Eastern Washington, Fraser River
bound.[72] At the same time it was also reported that First Nations from north-

ern California were heading to the Columbia River in support of First Nations in Washington Territory who opposed the trespass of Fraser River gold seekers. "The Indians in the neighborhood of Yreka, Pitt river, and other localities in that direction," claimed the *Pioneer & Democrat*, "have all left for the Columbia river, by way of Klamath lake, east of the Cascades, for the purpose of joining with the Yakimas, to prevent miners from passing through the Indian country, towards the northern gold region by way of the Columbia River."[73] It was also reported in the Portland *Standard* that an express man by the name of Tom Hughes was sent to Thompson River to provide an advance field reconnaissance for miners. Traveling without difficulty to the Okanogan River, Hughes was subsequently met by a party of Natives who ordered him to return. As reported in the *Bulletin*:

> He was told he would not be allowed to go to Thompson river. He proceeded on to Colville and when on the opposite bank of the Columbia, not more than a mile and a half from the fort, the Indians stripped him of his arms, and took from him his horses and every article of value he had about his person, and threatened to kill him. . . . [Hughes] reports all the tribes north as hostile to the advance of U.S. troops into their country, and says that they threaten to fight them as soon as they cross the Snake river, and if they get routed by the troops, then they will burn the grass and flee to the mountains, and fight the troops there if pursued, until the last man of them is killed.[74]

One must necessarily question many of these press reports, however. Certainly there is evidence that newspaper journalists had fueled or even created Indian wars at varying times and in different regions of the American West.[75] The motives associated with inventing such scares were numerous and most often contrived for personal gain. The threat of war might advance a governor's political career, while merchants could profit by supplying the needs of an enlarged military presence. Likewise, rumors of war with Native peoples could promote newspaper circulation, stall immigration, or at the very least, give volunteer militias the excuse to prospect for gold in Indian-controlled lands. Nevertheless, comparable rumors associated with the Fraser River gold rush appear to have been resolved quickly, although the motives for starting them appear less clear. Certainly the extension of the California mining frontier did not operate in a vacuum north of the forty-ninth parallel. The presence of the Hudson's Bay Company and the Royal Navy, in addition to the deployment of British civil authority, though marginal, provided a perspective on Native-white violence not found in the American West, a

perspective that tended to confirm or deny the reports of Native-white violence in prompt fashion. With the possible exception of fueling increased
newspaper circulation or checking the tide of emigration from California,
reports of Native-white violence, in this instance, seem largely confirmed by
non-newspaper sources.

U.S. Brigadier General N.S. Clarke, in command of the Department of
the Pacific, ordered Colonel Wright and his men to the region to counter the
Native threat.[76] Meanwhile, John Owen, superintendent of Indian affairs at
Fort Colville, claimed that the First Nations had obtained "all the powder
and ball they want from the Hudson's Bay Company at their new post called
Fort 49 [Fort Sheppard] . . . in the British possessions."[77] Within the American
consciousness there was always the suspicion that the Hudson's Bay Company
quietly supported Native opposition to the advance of the U.S. citizens. As
the First Nations prepared to battle once again with the U.S. military in
Washington Territory, Natives along the Fraser River also began to make more
concerted efforts to thwart any further entrance of white miners into their
country.[78] The Nlaka'pamux, aware of the extreme events transpiring against
the First Nations south of the border, began to mount greater opposition to
the presence of white gold seekers in protection of their land and resources.
Speaking of miners' camps beyond the forks of the Fraser and Thompson
Rivers, the special correspondent for the *Bulletin* offered a lengthy synopsis
of reasons for such Native opposition:

> Indians, of whom there were great numbers, would walk into tents and with
> their paint on, muskets cocked, take all that they desired. One party of Indians
> came down to French Bar, four miles above the Forks, and on approaching
> him, one of them demanded tobacco "quick!"—and in the same manner the
> whole party of miners were treated. The Indians told him that the whites were
> afraid of them, and they were going to kill them all in a short time. They said
> the "Bostons" and their steamboats had stopped the Salmon, and their were
> going to make friends with the Indians below at Fort Yale, and then make war
> with the whites. In corroboration of this, I will mention, that I know, that on
> the day yesterday, there was a large Indian council at Spuzzen [Spuzzum], 12
> miles above here, at which there were a number of "Fork" Indians, who have
> hitherto been at enmity with the Indians down here, and something in rela-
> tion to the whites was concocted amongst them. Indians have been noticed
> removing their provisions away from fishing stations above here. . . . On last
> Monday, 9th August, two Frenchmen, who were on their way up from here,
> while walking along the trail, were fired at, and both shot. One died instantly;

the other received the ball through his hand, which at the time was across his breast, and it (the ball) went clear through his body. . . . the Indians have evinced a growing disposition to provoke a collision with the whites.[79]

The Victoria *Gazette* concurred, reporting that "some two thousand Indians fifteen miles above Fort Yale are assembled, evidently for no friendly purpose."[80] The deaths of two French miners at the height of foreign occupation of the Fraser River corridor was akin to a match lighting the tinder-dry lands of the river corridors.[81] A fuse was thus lit, and the canyons set ablaze. With non-Native gold seekers numbering in the tens of thousands, punitive action was taken by companies of white miners who organized for the express purpose of making war with the aboriginal peoples along the Fraser and Thompson Rivers.

The tentative détente was shattered as the First Nations began to expel miners from their territories in advance of the concerted military-like campaign of gold seekers to clear the path of resistance through the Fraser River corridor. One such case was that of Edward Stout. The forty-niner from Eldorado County, California, had left San Francisco in 1858 with a party of twenty-six miners headed for the Fraser River. After prospecting at Fort Yale Bar, Emory Bar, and New York Bar for about two weeks, they decided to climb the river in search of the source of the fine flour gold that had been found throughout the bars and bench lands of the lower Fraser. Traveling over the Douglas Portage that skirted around the lower canyon to Spuzzum, Stout's party of miners took A. C. Anderson's 1848 brigade trail, which ascended the mountains of the big canyon to Boston Bar. They next hiked further north to the forks of the Thompson and Fraser Rivers, before testing the auriferous grounds near the confluence of the Nicoamen and Thompson Rivers, the approximate location where Governor Douglas had suggested that gold was first discovered by a Nlaka'pamux Native. They set up their base camp in mid-June at Thompson's Siding, near the spectacular Nicoamen Falls, where a Nlaka'pamux prophet is said to have foreseen the coming of the white man.[82] Although the party had located gold in paying quantities, the Thompson was in flood, thus submerging the most profitable mining areas. Like every other gold seeker along the Fraser and Thompson Rivers, they would have to wait patiently for water levels to recede as hot summer temperatures continued to thaw the surrounding snow-crested mountains.

While waiting, Stout recollected, a Native woman approached their camp one morning with the alarming news that a number of white miners had been "massacred" further down the river "and warned us to get out of the country as they were coming after us."[83] The gold seekers quickly gathered their provisions and headed back down the Thompson River toward China Bar. "We had to fight our way through and we burned every rancherie and every salmon box that we could get a hold of," claimed Stout. "They shot at us when ever they got a chance and we did the same. They did their best to cut us off and we had a very hard trip as we had to keep clear of the river as much as possible. I was shot in the arm and breast and a number of our men were killed and wounded. On the way down we came across an Indian who stood on a rock and waved defiance at us. He was shot by one of our men. . . . I do not know just how many white men were killed during these fights, but there were thirty six at least. The first notice which came of the trouble was one morning when nine dead bodies drifted down the river past Yale. The heads were severed and the bodies horribly mutilated."[84]

The truce among Natives and whites was further shattered as miners' militias practiced a scorched-earth policy typical of the kind of exterminationist campaigns that had been waged against Natives south of the international border.[85] As the historian Richard Maxwell Brown succinctly expressed, "The vigilante tradition, in the classic sense, refers to organized, extralegal movements, the members of which take the law into their own hands."[86] American miners, by practicing vigilantism, and forming militias north of the border, had in this instance not only taken the law into their own hands, but they had done so in a foreign land. As Jason O. Allard, son of Chief Trader Ovid Allard in charge of Fort Yale at the time, put it: "Agitations were started to clean up the Indians. . . . The irregular troops started for vengeance, in military formation, the stars and stripes at their head."[87]

As miners evacuated the upper river country and returned to Yale for safety, the Victoria *Gazette* reported on the first in a series of armed companies that were bent on making war. Captain Charles Rouse, an old Texas Ranger, with the assistance of his volunteer soldiers "route[d] the Indians [near Spuzzum], who took refuge in the mountains; they then burnt *three* of their rancheries, destroying all of their provisions, which consisted of salmon and dried berries. The miners found quite a number of packages of powder and lead in the different camps. There have been, in all, five of their rancheries burnt; three above the Big Canon, and two below."[88] Rouse returned to Yale, just twelve miles from the action, "having in custody an Indian Chief [Kowpelst[89]] . . . and the crowd were for lynching the Indian first and inquiring what he had done afterward."[90] Although white miners claimed that they had killed nine Natives, including a chief during the conflict, it was later confirmed "from the Indians themselves" that in fact thirty-one Natives and an additional five chiefs had been massacred.[91] The general excitement among white miners grew to crisis level as all-out war appeared to be imminent.

Tom G. Todd, writing from Fort Yale on August 18, 1858, to his friend Charlie M. Dewey of Placer County, California, expressed everyone's shared fear:

> It was reported yesterday that the Indians was coming down in thousands from Fraser & Thompson, they did come down as far as the Big Canon killing all they met so consequently we had to bury our provisions and come to this place. There now is not one white man above the Big Canon which is 20 miles above this place, there was about 100 men left here this morning armed & equiped to fight the Indians, also a host left yesterday, killing 15 Indians & wounding several whites. At the time of the affray, there was several men and one woman jumped into a canoe and started down the river, in the excitement they upset the canoe and all was drowned. There is scarcely a day passes but some person looses their lives & boats. The boys say that the Indians was so bad above that they would come right into the tents and gratify a call of nature in one corner and then take one corner of your blanket or towell and wipe their posterior, But I swear by all the Saints in Christendom if one does such a trick in my ranch he is a dead Injun and no Tom-foolery. . . . I think I shall go along if we can raise arms, guns and ammunition is very scarce—I do not think it much honor to be shot by an Indian, But if stern necessity says so, I am ready.[92]

Before news reached Yale of Rouse's campaign of reprisal, a mass meeting of several thousand miners was held to organize against the Indians. Captain George Wesley Beam, writing from Puget Sound Bar, recorded in his diary on August 18, 1858 that "some of the White men are frightened to death. They think there [*sic*] day has come and they are not ready to go."[93] Just three days later Beam penned in his diary that "at Union Bar they got five men out of the River that was shot by the Indians. They had their heads cut off."[94] Although the prominent ethnographer for this area, James Alexander Teit, believed that "beheading was not much practised by the Thompson Indians," he nevertheless noted that "they occasionally resorted to . . . [scalping], and would bring home for display the head of some distinguished enemy slain, after which it was thrown into the river."[95] Certain reminiscences have tended to sensationalize the number of white miners who were found decapitated, but there is considerable evidence among contemporary letters, diaries, and newspaper accounts that numbers of such instances occurred.[96] (This point is worth making because the academic community has tended to discount these reports.) Suffice it to say, as the English miner Radcliffe Quine wrote of the conflict to his brother, that they "declared war aginst the whites but we some put and [*sic*] end to it, but many Hundred lives lost."[97]

The San Francisco *Bulletin*'s special correspondent, in one of his lengthiest articles on the Fraser River mines, announced, as if reporting the fulfillment of the *Bulletin*'s own prophesy, that an Indian war had finally broken out in the northern British possessions. Writing from Fort Yale on August 16, 1858, the correspondent outlined the dramatic events as they were unfolding. "The War has commenced at last," he stated, "the Indians will find to their cost that the 'Bostons,' if slow to be aroused, will prove terrible to them when they do act."[98] White miners were being driven from the upper reaches of the Fraser and Thompson diggings, beaten back to Spuzzum, where they briefly congregated, hurriedly burying their canoes filled with provisions, before scrambling over the Douglas Portage to the safe haven of Fort Yale. With the arrival of so many hapless miners beating a retreat to Forts Hope and Yale, public meetings were called that served to incite the miners to further arm and organize against Native peoples. Locally, retribution was immediate, with non-Natives disarming at gunpoint the Native village next to Fort Yale, appropriating the weapons for their own use in the war.[99]

Rumors began to fly that significant numbers of white miners were being killed by the First Nations, especially with the increasing paranoia over the potential threat of massive numbers of Natives that were presumed to sweep down on the lower Fraser. In late August, Beam recorded the rumors of forty-three white miners having been killed on the upper Fraser and an additional one hundred and fifty murdered by Natives on Harrison River.[100] Neither of these two reports proved true, but the general panic that ensued caused Euro-Americans to obtain, by force, all the arms and ammunition available from the Hudson's Bay Company at Forts Yale and Hope. Typical of miner camp-style government, a meeting was called at Fort Hope on August 21, 1858, to vote on resolutions and frame an address to Governor Douglas "on the alarming character of the gathering of Indian difficulties."[101] A committee of six from among the mining population of Fort Yale had been sent down to Fort Hope, "representing the necessity for succor and ammunition, forthwith," as the excitement among the miners was described as intense "and the determination fixed to exterminate the red man."[102] The assembled miners again looked for scapegoats to help explain the concerted Native action to expel them from First Nations territory. If it was not whiskey or the Chinese, then once again the Hudson's Bay Company was suspect as white miners gave voice to assumed conspiracies. J. L. Morton, the agent for Kent & Smith's Express in Fort Hope, accused: "Should the authorities [Hudson's Bay Company] be found in anyway conniving at the bloody deeds of the savages, this will result not only in the sacking and burning of all their stockades and storehouses, but stripping this territory of every Vestige of British rule. I trust, however, that these suspicions are groundless."[103] A committee of four were subsequently selected to wait on the "commandant" of Fort Hope to determine the amount of arms and ammunition the Hudson's Bay Company held that the miners might access.[104]

The committee delivered its assessment within the hour. They had ascertained that the intention of the fort's officers was to cooperate cordially in the whites' defense. There were at Fort Hope at this time 25 guns, 125 pounds of powder, and 175 pounds of lead. The committee recommended the immediate forwarding of this ammunition by the Fort Yale Committee to Fort Yale, and the retention of the muskets for the defense of Fort Hope. They further recommended that a deputation of two Fort Hope citizens be sent to Fort Langley, instantly, with a certified copy of the meeting proceedings and introductory letters from the chief officers at Fort Hope, to solicit such aid in the premises as may be at the bestowal of the officers in command at Fort Langley.[105]

On the motion of S. W. Daggett, the report was received and adopted and the two members of the Fort Langley deputation selected.[106] The chairman next instructed all assembled "that at the ringing of the bell it was expected that every adult male would report himself at the Fort, with his arms, that he be enrolled and his arms inspected and a military organization effected for the defense of the place."[107] A collection was then made among the miners to help defray expenses before the meeting was officially adjourned. An urgent communication was also sent to Governor Douglas by Daggett on August 21, 1858, on behalf of Fort Hope miners and residents.

Dear Sir:—at a meeting of the immigrants and miners held previous to the departure of the steamer *Umatilla* from Fort Hope, I was selected to apprize your Excellency of the deplorable condition of affairs existing above this point, arising from the hostile attitude assumed by the Indians in this territory towards the white population. The fact is patent to all impartial observe[r]s, that a spirit of conciliation and fairness have characterized, on the part of the whites, hitherto, their deportment towards the Indians. Whether, from the *prestige* given to the red man by inaccurate representations made by newspaper correspondents, of their numerical strength and superiority over the more southern aborigines, and the general distribution among them of firearms, the whites have been more forbearing and lenient than was to be expected; or whether a too firm reliance has been placed upon the local authorities, it is not our province to determine; but, certain is it, the forbearance of the miner has been carried to a degree which has ceased to be a virtue, and the Indian, in his insolence and outrages, has progressed steadily from bad to worse, until isolated bodies of prospectors have been murdered and robbed by them, and the indignation and vengeance of the whiteman have burst forth in a fearful retribution.

Decapitated, denuded corpses of unfortunate adventurers are daily picked up on the river, while reports have reached us of the progress of retaliatory measures on the part of whites, involving indiscriminate slaughter of every age and sex. The brief moments allotted to me will not allow of details. It has been deemed advisable by the residents of Fort Hope to apprize your Excellency of the existing state of affairs, that your Excellency may inaugurate and enforce such a series of measures as will check the further effusion of blood, and restore tranquillity and order to this territory.[108]

Captain George Wesley Beam, writing upriver at Puget Sound Bar, confirmed the results of the Fort Hope meeting and the vigilante behavior of the gold-seeking community. "The miners have went to Forts Yale and Hope," he wrote, "and made them give all of the arms and ammunition they had. Mr. Walker of Hope did not want to do it but they shoved him one side and told the gentleman they would look for them selves. The miners have sent Governor Douglass some strong talk about there protection from the Indians but the Governor cant do any thing he has not the Power."[109] Subsequently, in the case of Fort Hope, white miners decided to store all their weaponry inside the outpost in the event that Natives descended the river that far. Beam jotted in his diary, "The men there think it Best to put their arms and ammunition in the Fort so if the Indians kill all they can't get them. They stand guard all the time."[110] Historians can be thankful that the miners were so organized, for a paper trail of these events is nowhere to be found in the official records of either the colonies of Vancouver Island or British Columbia. The California miners' penchant for the rules, regulations, and written records of camp government—especially the great tendency to publish them in newspapers for all to see—has left a decidedly different view of events when compared with the gaping silence of the colonial government's record.

By late August 1858 the American Pacific Northwest and southern British Columbia were on a war footing. Brigadier General Clarke, in charge of U.S.

Pacific Slope military operations, landed additional troops for engagement with First Nations in Washington Territory, the total command reportedly amounting to upwards of fifteen hundred men. At the urging of Isaac Stevens, former governor and congressional representative of Washington Territory, the U.S. War Department transferred a regiment from Utah and made preparations for sending an additional four hundred recruits from New York.[111] A special correspondent for the *Bulletin*, writing on August 27, 1858, happened to be traveling with four hundred reinforcements being shipped up the coast from California "to subdue sundry hostile Indian tribes." The Natives were "very desperate," he said, "forseeing [*sic*], as they do, certain expulsion from their hunting-grounds at an early day, if they permit the white-man to push eastward of the Cascades in search of gold."[112]

By this time, practically all of California's U.S. Army troops had been shifted to the Pacific Northwest for a final massive battle that would inundate Native peoples in the Columbia Plateau region with professional soldiers and weaponry, and all provoked by the Fraser River-bound gold seekers. In early September the Portland *Standard* reported that Okanagan Natives south of the forty-ninth parallel had "retreated to the British Possessions or the Blackfeet country."[113] Although the Okanagan peoples had moved to safe ground, the Coeur d'Alene, Spokane, and Yakama, in addition to members of the Palouse, Walla Walla, and Cayuse tribes, stood firm to defend their lands at the Battle of Four Lakes in what has been called the final phase of the Yakima War.[114] Colonel George Wright, commanding the Ninth Infantry and equipped with howitzers, inflicted on the tribes a "secure defeat."[115] The number of warriors killed was reported to be at least seventeen men, including one chief, but other opinions suggested substantially greater numbers of Native deaths at the hands of the U.S. Army.[116]

Although newspapers continued to report the existence of considerable quantities of gold along the Fraser River, these articles were more frequently mixed with news of Wright's military success at "carrying devastation and ruin wherever he went."[117] In one engagement, after Wright's soldiers had defeated the Natives in Coeur d'Alene country, Wright instructed his men to round up eight hundred or nine hundred horses and assorted livestock belonging to First Nations, which were subsequently destroyed. His campaign of destruction also included the torching of the Natives' grain fields and winter provisions so that they would be "reduced to the last stage of starvation and suffering." Although it was reported that Native peoples attempted, at this point, to broker a peace, Wright refused any and all terms and demanded their unconditional surrender.[118] With the First Nations of Eastern Washington having been totally overwhelmed by the enormous numbers of white soldiers and weaponry, Brigadier General Clark realized there would be no need for General William Harney's contingent to be sent out from New York. The U.S. military concluded that it had effected a wholesale defeat of its enemies. Peace treaties were subsequently forced on First Nations that would have as their primary directive that all white men, whether trappers, settlers, or gold miners, should thereafter pass through the Native lands of Eastern Washington unmolested.[119] The interior route to the Fraser River mines was thus cleared of all "impediments," and white miners henceforth were assured complete and unfettered access to communication routes east of the Cascade Mountains.

In anticipation of victory, Oregon resident General Joel Palmer had already begun traveling to the Fraser River with a train of no fewer than twelve supply-filled wagons. Regardless of the fact that Stevens had urged miners to wait for more "definite and peaceable" conditions,[120] Palmer, the former Oregon superintendent of Indian affairs, pushed through to Fort Okanogan two days in advance of the U.S. Army, such that "the worthy pioneer . . . [had] opened a wagon road from the great valley of the Columbia to the northern gold fields."[121]

While U.S. Army troops were engaged in Eastern Washington, volunteer miners' militias on the Fraser River were also busy clearing the path of all resistance. As previously noted, within the general vicinity of Yale, all Natives were apparently disarmed by white miners and required to suffer a variety of abuses. Ovid Allard, the Hudson's Bay Company trader in charge of Fort Yale, wrote to Governor Douglas "that the Miners have abused the Indians in many instances particularly at what is called New York Bar by insulting there women after they had voluntarily given up there arms. I understand that the same thing has also occurred at 'Quayome.' From what I can learn I have reason to believe that some 15 or 20 Indians have lost there lives and three or four whites. Also as many wounded during the excitement and many are leaving for Victoria and other places."[122] The Victoria *Gazette* reported from Yale, "Canoes arrived from New York, Hill's and Texas Bars loaded with armed men, who mostly joined in some of the companies formed here, and served to keep alive the excitement."[123] In all, at least five companies ascended the river in August 1858, each with differing views on how to reopen the upper diggings.[124] Some were for exterminating all Native peoples encountered, while others offered to broker a peace settlement supported by a large demonstration of armed force. One such company was the Pike Guards commanded by Captain H. M. Snyder, a regular correspondent to the San Francisco *Bulletin*.

With the newspaper's correspondent as "Commander of the Company," the *Bulletin* provided its readership with detailed field reports of Snyder's campaign, laced with a certain degree of bravado typical of the nineteenth-century Californian press.

This morning [18 August], at sunrise, three companies, armed with rifles and shot-guns, left for the upper cañons, and as far as Thompson river. One was under the command of Henry Snyder, who is well known in San Francisco. They carried a white flag, on which was inscribed, "PIKE GUARDS." One of the others was a company of French men, who have already shown themselves countrymen of Chasseur de Vincennes [a massive French fortress] and the Zouaves [well-known Papal guards], in their activity and agility in pursuing the Indians in their cañons. One party of eleven men last week went off by themselves, and succeeded in instilling a wholesome dread in the minds of the Indians. I have just learned that the name of one of the two French men shot, a few days ago, is John Le Croise, who died instantly. The other was Pierre Sargosse, who has been brought down here to-day. . . . The Justice of the Peace from Hill's Bar came up this morning, and took charge of the Indian chief "Suseechus," removing him to Hill's Bar. It was with some difficulty, however, that he accomplished it, as the miners were inclined to try him summarily here. . . . This morning [19 August], news arrived that some more Indians had been shot, above the rancheria [Spuzzum], by the men who went up from here.[125]

William Yates, the Hudson's Bay Company trader that assisted Ovid Allard during the gold excitement, remembered the tumultuous scene that developed when a Native was hauled into Fort Yale by white miners bent on interrogating their prisoner. Because Allard and Yates were the only whites familiar with some of the Native languages spoken, miners often brought their victims to the company's fort and demanded an immediate character assessment. One afternoon, perhaps the day that Copals [Kowpelst] or "Suseechus" was brought in, a party of about fifty white miners could be seen in the distance headed for the company's store. Yates recalled: "The miners said 'You are a Hudson's Bay man?' I said yes. 'What kind of an Indian is this—what kind of an Indian is this,' they yelled. I said I did not know—he was good as far as I knew. A party from the outside called me a liar and they dragged me and the Indian off from the Hudson's Bay store into the crowd. . . . I went to Hill's Bar that night and stopped all night with Judge Perry [Perrier]. The

Judge took me over so as to stop the trouble."[126] Allard claimed that the Indian prisoner "was pretty near Hung by the miners through Excitement & Liquor."[127] Stories such as this illustrate the extremely precarious position in which employees of the Hudson's Bay Company were often placed between warring whites and Natives.

During the mass meeting in Yale in August, preparations were made for the ultimate contest over the land and resources of the Fraser and Thompson Rivers. In a lengthy letter to Governor Douglas, Captain Snyder told of his ten-day military-like campaign, which concluded with a number of peace treaties with Native chiefs from above Yale to the forks of the Fraser and Thompson Rivers at present-day Lytton. On August 16, 1858, "a company was formed to procede at once up the river," penned Snyder. "And by a unanimous vote I was elected their Captain. . . . When I stated the object I had in view, and the manner in which I intended to procede, which was to take an interpreter and make pease with the Indians by peasible means if we could, and by force if we must, on those terms I would consent to be their commander and on no others. On taking the vote an unanimous consent was given. We then elected our other officers and took up our line of march for the river below Saylor's Bar."[128]

The language of democratically elected officers and mustering under arms is reminiscent of the settler-soldiers that organized in Washington and Oregon to fight in the Indian wars of the 1850s. For placing the future colony of British Columbia in the context of the transboundary West, this unexplored document is both remarkable and exceptional in that a foreign mining population had effectively taken matters into its own hands. As the Pike Guards marched along the Fraser, they were subsequently joined by a large company of French miners who shared Snyder's view that peace treaties would expend less time and resources than all-out war. The main object, of course, was merely to clear the path of resistance so that miners could continue extracting gold. Of the other companies encountered along the way, however, one—known as the Whatcom Guards—called for a campaign of wholesale extermination. Snyder related to Douglas:

We proceded to the Indian Rancherie [Spuzzum] above some five miles further up. There we found two other companys and quite a large number of miners that had been driven from their claims above. We camped here for the night and held a counsil of war with some sixty Indians, and pease was made with them at this place. I had a consultation with the 2 captains [Graham and Martin Gallagher[129]] that we found at this place as their views were different from mine and the Austrain [French] Company. They wished to procede and kill every man, woman & child they saw that had Indian blood in them. To such an arrangement I could not consent to. My heart revolted at the idea of killing a helpless woman, or an innocent child was too horrible to think of. They requested me to state my views to the crowd which consisted of six to seven hundred. I consented to do so and after I was through, and on taking the vote, I found that they were almost unanimous in supporting my course.[130]

Snyder's interpreter was none other than Hudson's Bay Company trader William Yates, who had accompanied the Pike Guards as far as Chapman's Bar near present-day Alexandra Bridge, between Fort Yale and Boston Bar. Apparently, the miners had written to James Murray Yale at Fort Langley, asking whether Ovid Allard might accompany the militias. Because Allard was getting on in age, it was suggested that Yates go instead. Allard wrote to Douglas, "A party of armed men requested me to send Yates with them. I thought it would be as well for him to go with them & try to stop as many murder[s] and robery by this said party as possible."[131]

Yates's account of the campaign appears to approximate Snyder's own report in the press and to Douglas. Yates noted that about 150 men accompanied them "with a white flag to give to each of the Indian Chiefs along the river, as a guarantee not to bother the whites in any shape or form."[132] He does not say whether the white flag was generally interpreted by the gold seekers as a truce with Indians or, as it has been historically viewed in the American West, as surrender. As for the Nlaka'pamux, the ethnologist Andrea Laforet has suggested that the color white would not have symbolized peace for them, but death—"specifically ghosts, the spirit world, dead people, skeletons, bones, and sickness coming from the dead."[133] Considering what would unfold in the post-gold rush world of British Columbia, the omen of sickness and death proved more correct than the symbolism of a peace, truce, or surrender.

As Snyder's men approached Spuzzum (a large Native settlement above Fort Yale at the confluence of Spuzzum Creek and the Fraser River) from Yale, their forces were estimated to have reached 250 men. Yates's account gives significantly more attention to the disagreement that occurred between Captains Snyder and Graham while at Spuzzum than do the few other remaining accounts. In Yates's words:

Cap[tain] Snyder learned then that an opposition party had gone by the old trail [Douglas Portage] over the mountain and they were going to go to the lodges to kill the indians and wipe them out, as they went through. He then rushed me ahead of the parties with 25 men to the Indian village [Spuzzum] where Captain Graham was with a party of about 50. They were going to attack the Indians. We told Captain Graham that we were sent from Captain Sneider to tell him that there was to be no attack made on the indians. We told him to hold on until Captain Sneider and his men came up and then talk to him. He said that he would but that he was going through to wipe the indians out if he could. The head of our party told him that he was not doing the right thing—that he had better wait until Captain Sneider came up and that they would then have an understanding about the matter. Before they got through talking Captain Sneider had come up. It was nearly dusk then. Cap[tain] Sneider got Captain Graham calmed down and told him to wait and not to be so rash as he was endangering the lives of white men by doing so. They stacked their arms there and lay down for the night.[134]

The next morning Graham and Snyder apparently consulted each other again; it was agreed that Graham and the Whatcom Guards would remain behind and continue forth only in the event that Snyder's companies ran into trouble while passing through the big canyon.

Snyder then commenced with the original peace plan endorsed by the mass meeting held at Fort Yale. The miner-cum-commander instructed that two canoes be taken two miles upriver in advance of his men, who would make their crossing to the other side of the Fraser in the vicinity of Alexandra Bridge. Snyder did not realize at the time that, while the Pike Guards and the French Company under the leadership of John Centras made their way to the canoe crossing, Graham and his men were surreptitiously crossing Spuzzum Creek, near its confluence with the Fraser, and proceeding up the opposite side of the canyon. Just as Snyder and his men were about to make their canoe crossings, they were alarmed to see that Graham's party had broken its promise and was advancing further upriver. Although Snyder called to Graham to halt, the war party paid no heed and continued to advance.

Yates was again pressed into service to chase after the Whatcom Guards.[135] Snyder attempted to reason with Graham once more and "againe solicited him to joine us, but he would not." As a last resort, Snyder threatened that if Graham persisted in his plan of extermination and did not remain put as agreed, Snyder and the Pike Guards would head back to Yale. Graham finally agreed to allow Snyder the opportunity of brokering a peace settlement with Native peoples and to wait until the Pike Guards had reached the head of the big canyon: "And if I could make pease with the indians & send a white flag through the canion, that he would return to this place [Fort Yale] on those conditions and understanding."[136]

With Graham and company remaining on the Fraser's west side, Snyder, Centras, and their companies finally took up their line of march on the river's east side to take advantage of the Hudson's Bay Company's brigade trail that climbed the mountain, near present-day Alexandra Lodge, and bypassed the canyon until descending the Anderson River to Boston Bar.[137] Yates claimed that Snyder's party continued to watch Graham's movements from their side of the river, but as the day was coming to an end, the Whatcom Guards made camp "on a large shelving rock" opposite the vicinity of Chapman's Bar, being careful to place guards at either end for protection while the majority of the men slept.

During the night pandemonium erupted among Graham's volunteer troops. Yates, whose own small party had remained to watch the Whatcom Guards at some little distance, recalled the frantic scene. "Some of Captain Grahams men rushed right through where our men were lying," said Yates, "and some of them were around us and said that the indians had been shooting at them . . . we found two dead bodies in the morning. We thought it was not indians but that it was their own party that got in a panic some way and started shooting in the night. Some of the men were drowned in the river and some were shot and killed or wounded by dragoon pistols and five shooters—not indian guns at all."[138] Although Yates did not realize it at the time, both Graham and his first lieutenant Shaw were the ones shot dead. Although the little that has been written on this mysterious episode has tended to accept the idea that Graham's own men were the cause of the deaths that night, there is yet another, more compelling explanation for the deaths of the Whatcom Guards' two highest-ranking officers. Snyder's own words to Douglas suggest that there was good reason why Native peoples might assassinate these individuals beyond the quite obvious reasons already recounted here.

After Snyder had climbed the canyon to the next Native settlement, another peace treaty was established with three chiefs and symbolic white flags issued: "They appeared to rejoice to think that pease was to be restored." Of course, Snyder had also stated that a white flag would be sent to Graham if the Yale-endorsed peace plan was succeeding. Snyder related to Douglas how his men were received by the intransigent Graham upon seeing the white flag of peace. Graham apparently had "order[ed] his men to take the white flag that I had sent to him and throw it away, which was done," outlined Snyder. "One of my men went and picked it up and slept on it the balance of the night. They then layed down, my men some two or three rods from the rest. He says, if Grayham had any guard posted that they must of been a sleep. About twelve o'clock they ware aroused from their sleep by the firing of some guns. Grayham was shot through the back at the first [fire] and died some two hours afterwards. He thinks that the Indians had watched him, if it was Indians, and had scene the treatment he gave the white flag. His firs[t] Lieutenant was also killed in the first firing. Had he done as he promised to do he would now be alive."[139]

The fact that a chief's son from China Bar had accompanied Snyder's men downriver to deliver the message of peace lends even greater credence to the idea that the Nlaka'pamux would not have been pleased to see Graham's response; they most certainly would have seen how he reacted. Snyder's credibility and success in confirming peace treaties was aided immeasurably by Native peoples having their own emissaries accompany him from village to village. As Andrea Laforet has suggested, "The demonstrated support of the chiefs whom he had met was of critical importance to his success in each new locality."[140] In such a case, even with Native peoples having removed themselves to the safer precincts of the mountains, reconnaissance of white miners' movement would have continued throughout.

As Snyder pursued his campaign upriver, he achieved additional peace agreements with the assistance of chiefs who accompanied him on his mission. By August 21, 1858, Snyder confirmed peace with four more chiefs before coming within seven miles of the Thompson River. It was here that he first met Spintlum, "the war chief of all the tribes for some distance up & down Frazer River." The Nlaka'pamux at the "Forks," or present-day Lytton, had heard that the miners' militias were traveling upriver and sent a runner after Spintlum, who had been some seventy-five miles up the Thompson. He came down quickly to meet them, and Snyder continued his practice of peace-making in his presence. "Then the War Chief made a speech to the Indians that had collected together," continued Snyder. "He is a very cool calculating man and spoke to them for at leas[t] [a] half hour. . . . Here I proceded at once to hold our grand counsil which consisted of Eleven Chiefs and a very large number of other indians that had gathered from above and below. We stated to them that this time we came for pease, but if we had to come againe, that we would not come by hundreds, but by thousands and drive them from

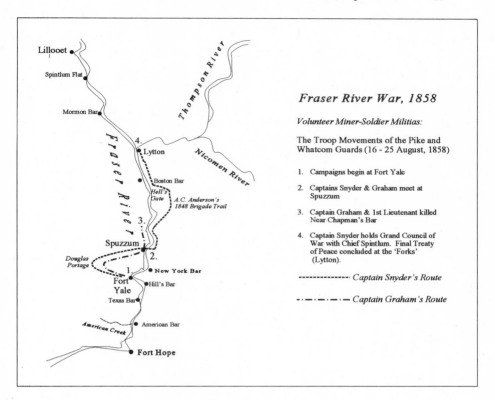

FIG. 2.2. Military campaign routes taken by militias from Yale to Lytton, Fraser River War, 1858. Copyright © 1996 by Daniel P. Marshall. Source: Daniel P. Marshall, "Claiming the Land: Indians, Goldseekers, and the Rush to British Columbia" (Ph.D. diss., University of British Columbia, 2000), p. 234.

the river forever. They ware much supprised & frightened to see so many men with guns & revolvers. For marching along in single file they looked to be three times the number there was" (Figure 2.2).[141]

It is difficult to say, of course, whether this bravado was intended solely for Governor Douglas, or whether Snyder actually had the audacity to state it to eleven Nlaka'pamux chiefs in the very center of their homeland. One thing is for certain, though: the Nlaka'pamux would have been well aware of the circumstances in which First Nations found themselves south of the border. If Snyder threatened the possibility of thousands more to drive them from the river forever, it certainly would not have appeared as an idle threat, considering that upwards of fifteen hundred U.S. Army troops waged a full-scale assault against the First Nations in that region.

Spintlum certainly had much to reflect on. The ethnographer James Teit perhaps captured the dilemma these people faced when he recorded, some forty years later, the different stances of individual chiefs for and against war.

Hundreds of warriors from all parts of the upper Thompson country had assembled at Lytton with the intention of blocking the progress of the whites beyond that point [he stated], and, if possible, of driving them back down the river. The Okanagan had sent word, promising aid, and it was expected that the Shuswap would also render help. In fact the Bonaparte, Savona, and Kamloops bands had initiated their desire to assist if war was declared. For a number of days there was much excitement at Lytton, and many fiery speeches were made. CuxcuxesqEt, the Lytton war-chief, a large, active man of great courage, talked incessantly for war. He put on his headdress of eagle feathers, and, painted, decked and armed for battle, advised the people to drive out the whites. At the end of his speeches he would dance as in a war dance, or imitate the grisly bear, his chief guardian spirit. Cunamitsa, the Spences Bridge chief, and several other leading men, were also in favor of war. CexpentlEm [Spintlum], with his great powers of oratory, talked continually for peace, and showed strongly its advantages. The people were thus divided as to the best course to pursue, and finally most of them favoured CexpentEms proposals.[142]

Snyder may not have realized it, but it almost seems that the Nlaka'pamux had already decided for peace among themselves before the commander of the company's ultimatum. Snyder, Centras, and their volunteer militias had reached the forks where the Fraser and Thompson Rivers meet, and further peace treaties were established with a final total of twenty-seven different chiefs,[143] "a letter stating their proceedings" given to each and white flags to show other possibly more hostile companies of miners.[144] Incidentally, Snyder was also pleased to have received "some beautiful specimums of gold" from various chiefs he met while climbing the river toward Lytton.[145]

From Fort Hope on August 23, 1858, the *Bulletin*'s correspondent reported that a letter had been received from Snyder to S. W. Daggett via Ballou's Express stating that peace had been restored, and miners could return to their abandoned claims between the lower canyon and Foster's Bar above Lytton. Snyder asked of the white mining population "circumspection and forbearance towards the Indians" and expressed "his conviction that the desire of the Indian is sincere for peace."[146] Snyder's white flags of peace were subsequently seen flying at all the Indian villages that had been visited by the Pike Guards.[147] Snyder estimated that during the course of his campaign, he had "entered into treaty" with at least two thousand Native peoples.[148]

Mary Williams, an Nlaka'pamux elder, later told a story passed down from previous generations that appears to approximate the extraordinary meeting of the Pike Guards with the Thompson peoples at Lytton. From the Nlaka'pamux perspective, "They arrived with one of their headmen, and told the Lytton people to gather at the place where the Canadian National Railways station is now situated. That was where they were all to be shot," Williams remembered. "Every one of the White men had loaded rifles, ready to shoot the people of Lytton." The Native elder then recalled that Spintlum entered the fray to halt any further bloodshed.

> Chief Sexpínlhemx spoke up, asking, "What are you going to do?" The Whites said that all the old people were going to be killed off—only the young woman were to be kept. "Stop right there!" commanded Chief Sexpínlhemx. "End that talk right there! I am going to give you some land!" Chief Sexpínlhemx stood up and stretched out his arms to the sundown and the sunrise, saying, "This side will be yours and this side will be my people's. You are not to kill anyone. . ." This is what Chief Sexpínlhemx said. The White people agreed. They put down all their guns and shook hands with the Indian people and went back to where they came from, back to Yale.[149]

In the immediate aftermath of the ten-day march, Snyder explained his "conciliatory" approach to ending violence in the canyons. "The Indians held possession of the Big or Upper Canon," he claimed, "and if war was made on them, they had it in their power to prevent all canoes from ascending the river, as well as preventing any men from going over the trail. . . . True, they *could* be driven out—but it would take time and money to effect it. The mining season was just commencing, and the object to be gained *now* was, to enable men to go up the river as soon as possible."[150] In reading Snyder's words, it would appear that "road blocks," whether of rivers, trails, or the modern highways of today, have been an established fact in Canada's westernmost province since 1858.[151] During the 1990s the most recent road blockades have occurred at such places as Gustafson Lake, Douglas Lake, and Apex Developments near Penticton, to name but a few, and continue to be militant expressions of Native determination to protect their land and sovereignty. Clearly, the roots of British Columbia's current impasse in resolving Native land claims can be found in the events of the Fraser River gold rush of 1858.

In the immediate aftermath of the Fraser River War, on August 30, 1858, Douglas—along with the Crown Solicitor George Pearkes, thirty-five non-commissioned officers from both HMS *Satellite* and Her Majesty's Boundary Commission, and other government officials—sailed for Fort Hope "for the purpose of making treaties of peace with the Indians."[152] Douglas was spurred to travel specifically to Fort Hope in acknowledgment of miners' urgent pleas regarding large numbers of whites having been killed, especially the communiqué written by S. W. Daggett and endorsed at a mass meeting.[153] Arriving on the evening of September 3, via the *Umatilla*, Douglas entered in his diary an extremely brief synopsis of the terrible conflict that had just occurred: "It appears from the reports of miners who have lately returned from the upper country that the Indians are thievish and without being positively hostile plunder the miners in the most shameless manner. Drew up a proclamation prohibiting the sale or gift of intoxicating drinks to Indians, to be published immediately, and also a plan for the administration of justice; and otherwise establishing order & government in Fraser's river."[154]

The Fraser River War had just occurred. It was widely reported throughout the press of the Pacific Northwest and California. Hudson's Bay Company servants such as Ovid Allard and William Yates were involved and supplied reports to the governor. Captain J. C. Prevost of the Royal Navy filed a lengthy description with Rear Admiral Robert Baynes.[155] White miners such as George Wesley Beam, Thomas Spence, Billy Ballou, H. F. Reinhart, and many others had recorded the conflict in their diaries, letters, and reminiscences. Miners' meetings had been called to vote on defense plans and approve communications to the governor. And, of course, Douglas himself had cautioned the imperial government of Great Britain that an all-out war would likely occur. So how was it that the governor of the colony of Vancouver Island could simply whitewash events in this way? Just how could this same man, as chief factor of the Hudson's Bay Company, suggest for a moment that alcohol was the primary reason for the terrible conflict of the preceding weeks?

For all of the complaints and distress that Douglas undoubtedly heard, he chose not to record the particulars of extreme Native-white conflict in his official dispatches to London, dispatches that were ultimately published as

Parliamentary Papers. The governor's only response was the formal *Proclamation* "prohibiting the gift or sale of intoxicating drinks to the Native Indians of Fraser's River," a decree that might equally have been leveled against the white mining population of Fort Yale, but one that nevertheless provided convenient closure to a most tumultuous and inauspicious beginning to the fledgling British colony that was shortly to be proclaimed. Although Douglas informed the secretary of state for the colonies that he witnessed lamentable "fatal accidents that were daily occuring to miners" who had capsized their boats and canoes attempting to navigate the Fraser's higher reaches, he never reported the significantly greater number of deaths of the Fraser River War. In short, it would have been viewed as a major embarrassment to British and Hudson's Bay Company policy toward Native peoples. One need not wonder how Sir Edward Bulwer Lytton would have viewed a report in which the foreign mining population was found to have taken the law into its own hands, massacring enormous numbers of Native peoples, in the absence of any significant British colonial presence. Especially so, considering that the powerful and influential Aborigines Protection Society had just made representations to Lytton earnestly imploring that the genocidal history of the California goldfields not be repeated in British Columbia.

If one compares Douglas's early dispatches through 1857 and early 1858 with his reports in the aftermath of the Fraser River War, his tone, once overwhelmingly pro-Native, becomes decidedly dismissive of Native rights. It is important to remember that Douglas's early dispatches were subsequently published, and therefore groups like the Aborigines Protection Society were given access to Douglas's views and precolonial policy as they were taking shape. Specifically, Douglas had earlier sounded the warning bell with regard to future conflict between Americans and First Nations, and though the British government was less inclined to act, pressure from the Aborigines Protection Society forced the Colonial Office to acknowledge Douglas's concerns. The governor's later silence with respect to the Fraser River War, undoubtedly, was in part due to the realization that whatever he wrote would not only be seen by Lytton and other members of the Colonial Office, but that other outside interests might use the dispatches to discredit the British government.

The general absence within the goldfields of any significant civil administration meant that white miners quite happily operated according to their own customs, rules, and regulations until the overwhelming threat of war with Native peoples caused them to embrace colonial rule: "The necessity which has for some time existed for the appointment of peace-officers, and the establishment of some kind of government . . . has been apparent to every one."[156] While Douglas was on the Fraser, miners continued to report that his presence was particularly for the purposes of making peace with First Nations.[157] It also appears that many chiefs accompanied Snyder back to Fort Yale and eventually attempted to meet personally with the governor.[158] Nowhere are these meetings recorded or the nature of the discussions held between the representative of Her Majesty Queen Victoria and the Native peoples of the Fraser River corridor.

Likewise, upon reaching Yale on September 20, 1858, and establishing a camp on the opposite river bench from the town site, Douglas was to grant an audience with Captain H. M. Snyder. The old San Franciscan, since the war, had become a leader of the white mining community and in essence Spintlum's counterpart. "I had quite a long conversation with him," stated Snyder. "I was much pleased with his course, which he says will be pursued in regard to the miners. He will not interfere with any rules and regulations that the miners may have adopted. He complimented me highly for the course I had adopted in restoring peace with the Indians; and also tendered me any assistance I might wish in the way of an office."[159] Douglas's reported words to Snyder only make sense if we consider the tenuous position of British authority on the Fraser in 1858. Like First Nations, colonial author-ity was also overwhelmed by the huge number of miners and weaponry. Just as Douglas had written that it was "prudent to pursue a conciliatory policy" with respect to First Nations such as the Nlaka'pamux, so too may one be forgiven for assuming that this strategy was equally applicable to the intransigent white mining population that had taken the law into its own hands.[160]

In the contest over land and resources the Native peoples of the Fraser River corridor were finally overwhelmed by enormous numbers of miners and weaponry, their monopoly control of gold forfeited, their claim to the land marginalized through modern day. Douglas, in advance of any author-ity from London, took immediate action in the war's aftermath and estab-lished the basis for colonial administration through appointment of gold commissioners and justices of the peace.[161] Yet his message to the "citizens of that great republic which like the mustard seed has grown into a mighty tree . . . that offshoot of England of which England is still proud" spoke more of ingratiating oneself to a foreign army of occupation than any attempt to arrest the illegal practices of miners.[162] Douglas in his official communiqués to London did little to mention that British sovereignty had been undermined by a foreign population that took the law into its own hands. Neither did he comment on the degree to which massacres had occurred. In the final analysis Douglas's fledgling, unconstituted colonial authority, consisting of a handful of officials, was terribly dwarfed by the tens of thousands of foreign adventurers who claimed the land.

The Fraser River War may have ultimately precipitated the institution of full British sovereignty, but it also broke the back of full-scale Native resistance. Within British Columbia the number of Native deaths at the hands of white miners also appears to have been much larger than previously suspected (as is, perhaps, the number of deaths of white miners at Native hands). Once these military-like actions were complete, the Fraser River corridor was further appropriated and ordered into a typical California landscape segregated by race and ethnicity, an extension of the American West, and one in which Native peoples were quickly compartmentalized and reduced to a matrix of Indian reserves. In fact, the entire transboundary region of southern British Columbia and northern Washington Territory was affected. The American Indian wars in the Pacific Northwest during 1858, like the Fraser River War, were devastating contests that dispossessed Native peoples on either side of the forty-ninth parallel of much of their traditional landscape, with some further evidence suggesting an extended effect on Native peoples within the larger Pacific Slope region.

The fact that it has taken 140 years to tell this story suggests that, if the forty-ninth parallel has played a role in shaping the Pacific Slope, its influence has been most dramatic within the written histories of the United States and Canada. Before the repercussion of East-West links realigned the Pacific Slope, British Columbia, Washington, Oregon, and California were part of a larger North-South transboundary region. For Native peoples, fur trappers, gold miners, and others during the nineteenth century, the forty-ninth parallel was little more than a paper demarcation with no parallel in physical space. For both Canada and the United States the historical exploration of borderland regions such as the Fraser River has been largely undermined by preoccupations with national history and the blinding influence of a political divide. Although the events of the 1858 gold rush were centered north of the border, key aspects of the rush, and indeed much of the paper trail, are found to the south. By recontextualizing the Pacific Coast region, it becomes obvious that the dominant, defining influence in mainland British Columbia during its formative year was not that of Britain or Canada, but the extended reach of the American West. That there is no parallel in Canadian history to the kinds of violence leveled against Native peoples, such as that which occurred in the Western states, is an oft-repeated rule that in this instance is quite unfounded.

Clearly, the forty-ninth parallel's greatest influence at this time was not so much the physical reality of a dividing line, but the persuasive force lent to national myths—myths that have failed to recognize these important north-south links within a shared region that had previously experienced a period of joint British-American sovereignty and the rapacious expanse of the Californian mining frontier.

NOTES

1. H. M. Snyder, captain of the Pike Guards and Commander of Company, to James Douglas, governor of Vancouver Island, Fraser River, Fort Yale, August 28, 1858, Colonial Correspondence (hereafter referred to as CC), British Columbia Archives, Victoria, B.C. This letter is published in Daniel P. Marshall, "Document. Introduction: The Fraser River War," *Native Studies Review* 11, no. 1 (1997): 140–45.

2. Edwin M. Stanton to P. H. Watson, San Francisco, California, June 19, 1858, Beinecke Rare Book and Manuscript Library, Yale University, New Haven, Conn.

3. For the role of Native miners in this rush, see Daniel P. Marshall, "Rickard Revisited: Native 'Participation' in the Gold Discoveries of British Columbia," *Native Studies Review* 11, no. 1 (1997): 91–108.

4. Alfred Waddington, *The Fraser Mines Vindicated* (Victoria, B.C.: P. de Garro, 1858), pp. 16–17.

5. Special Agent John Nugent was the former editor of the *San Francisco Herald*.

6. See John Nugent, special agent appointed to the Fraser River by U.S. president James Buchanan, *Message from the President of the United States* (Ex. Doc. No. 111) 35th Cong., 2d sess., House of Representatives, February 28, 1859, p. 2. The American historian Clinton A. Snowden estimated that between seventy-five thousand and one hundred thousand people entered British Columbia and Washington Territory in the summer of 1858. See Lelah Jackson Edson, *The Fourth Corner: Highlights from the Early Northwest* (Bellingham, Wash.: Whatcom Museum of History and Art, 1968), chap. 10.

7. Rodman W. Paul, *California Gold: The Beginning of Mining in the Far West* (Lincoln: University of Nebraska Press, 1947), pp. 171–96.

8. (San Francisco) *Bulletin*, February 9, 1858, p. 3.

9. F. W. Howay, W. N. Sage, and H. F. Angus, *British Columbia and the United States: The North Pacific Slope from Fur Trade to Aviation*, ed. H. F. Angus (Toronto: Ryerson Press, 1942), pp. v, 184.

10. Earl Pomeroy, *The Pacific Slope: A History of California, Oregon, Washington, Idaho, Utah, and Nevada* (New York: Alfred A. Knopf, 1965), pp. vi, 264.

11. It is supposed that between 1848 (marking the discovery of gold in California) and 1870, about fifty thousand California Indians died as a result of disease, starva-, tion, and "simple and direct homicide." See Robert F. Heizer, ed., *The Destruction of California Indians: A Collection of Documents from the Period 1847 to 1865* (1974; reprint, Lincoln: University of Nebraska Press, 1993), p. vi. Elsewhere, the population decline of California's Indians is deemed even greater—from approximately one hundred fifty thousand in 1845 to thirty-five thousand in 1860, as noted in John M. Findlay, "An Elusive Institution: The Birth of Indian Reservations in Gold Rush California," in George Pierre Castile and Robert L. Bee, eds., *State and Reservation: New Perspectives on Federal Indian Policy* (Tucson: University of Arizona Press, 1992), p. 16.

12. "No industry had a greater impact on Western history than did mining," writes Patricia Nelson Limerick in *The Legacy of Conquest: The Unbroken Past of the American West* (New York: W. W. Norton, 1987), p. 99.

13. The Crown Colony of British Columbia was proclaimed on November 19, 1858, at Fort Langley, British Columbia.

14. For a detailed record of volunteer troops mustering with U.S. Army forces in the Indian wars of the 1850s, see Charles M. Gates, ed., *Messages of the Governors of the Territory of Washington to the Legislative Assembly, 1854–1889*, vol. 12 (Seattle: University of Washington Press, 1940). Also Clifford E. Trafzer and Richard D. Scheuerman, *Renegade Tribe: The Palouse Indians and the Invasion of the Inland Pacific Northwest* (Pullman: Washington State University Press, 1993).

15. The Oregon Boundary Settlement of 1846 established the forty-ninth parallel west of the Rockies as the border.

16. For rather dated accounts of these conflicts, see Ray Hoard Glassley, *Pacific Northwest Indian Wars* (Portland, Oreg.: Binfords & Mort, 1953); and A. J. Splawn, *Ka-mi-akin: Last Hero of the Yakimas*, 3d ed. (Yakima, Wash.: Caxton Printers, 1958). For a much more recent view on these conflicts and others, see Richard White, *"It's Your Misfortune and None of My Own": A History of the American West* (Norman: University of Oklahoma Press, 1991), pp. 92–108.

17. "Trip to the Colvile Mines, 1855," Journal of Jonathan T. Kerns, August 11, 1855, Oregon Historical Society (OHS) Library, Portland, Oregon. In Chinook Jargon *mim-loose* means "to kill" and *tillicums* are friends.

18. Ibid., August 15–25, 1855.

19. Ibid., September 7–9, 1855.

20. "Adventures of William I. Ballou," Seattle: 1878. P-B/1, Bancroft Library, University of California, Berkeley.

21. Ibid.

22. "Editor's Table," *Hutching's Illustrated California Magazine* 16 (August 1858): 92–93. Californians "were never guilty of neglecting a region simply because it did

not fly the Stars and Stripes." Rodman W. Paul, "'Old Californians' in British Gold Fields," *Huntington Library Quarterly* 17, no. 2 (1953–54): 161.

23. Joel Palmer, "The Si-mil-ka-meen and Frazer River Gold Fields: Advantages of the Columbia River Route over Others for Travel and Commerce," January 28, 1860, Howay Reid Collection, Box 46:5, University of British Columbia Special Collections.

24. Some more romanticized, jingoistic accounts inflate their numbers to as many as eight hundred miners forming a single armed company. William Shannon, "Richard G. Willoughby," unpublished manuscript, British Columbia Archives.

25. For a detailed example of volunteer troops mustered in this manner for waging war with Indians, see William N. Bischoff, *We Were Not Summer Soldiers: The Indian War Diary of Plympton J. Kelly, 1855–1856* (Tacoma: Washington Historical Society, 1976). For an example of the large numbers and muster roll listings of volunteer veterans in Oregon's Native-white conflicts, see Frances Fuller Victor, *The Early Indian Wars of Oregon from the Oregon Archives and Other Original Sources* (Salem, Oreg.: Frank C. Baker, 1894). In the case of Washington Territory, see *Washington Territorial Volunteers' Papers: Indian War Muster Rolls, 1855–1856* (Olympia, Wash.: Office of the Secretary of State, Archives & Records Management, 1990).

26. For an accounting of these battles by the commanding general of the U.S. Army, see Thomas W. Prosch, "The Indian War of 1858," *Washington Historical Quarterly* 2–3 (October 1907–July 1908): 233–40; and T. C. Elliott, "Steptoe Butte and Steptoe Battle-field," *Washington Historical Quarterly* 18 (October 1927): 243–53. See also "Later from Oregon: The Frazer River and Fort Colvile Mines," (San Francisco) *Bulletin*, May 22, 1858, p.3.

27. Shannon, "Richard G. Willoughby," p. 11.

28. David McLoughlin was the son of Dr. John McLoughlin, governor of the Hudson's Bay Company west of the mountains and considered the "Father of Oregon."

29. Shannon, "Richard G. Willoughby," pp. 11–12.

30. Robert Frost to George H. Hines, Olympia, Washington, February 28, 1907, Reminiscences, OHS Library. See also Robert Frost, "Fraser River Gold Rush Adventures," *Washington Historical Quarterly* 22 (July 1931): 203–9.

31. "Okanagan" is the accepted spelling in Canada, while "Okanogan" is used south of the border.

32. The bluff at the entrance to McLoughlin Canyon, although largely reduced by later railway construction along the Okanogan River, still bears many ancient rock-writings of these Native peoples; their signs of ownership are clearly visible today, as they were undoubtedly in 1858. The canyon, near present-day Tenasket, is an incred-

ible natural corridor that was used by Hudson's Bay Company trappers and thousands upon thousands of miners making their way to the Fraser goldfields.

33. Frost's views are representative of the Oregon contingent in the McLoughlin party and state that there were approximately 150 men, whereas Willoughby was a member of the California contingent that joined them. Willoughby's memory glorifies and embellishes the McLoughlin Canyon event, evident in the fact that he claimed 800 men participated accompanied by 2,000 pack animals.

34. Shannon, "Richard G. Willoughby," p. 13.

35. John Callbreath to mother, Bridge River, British Columbia, January 24, 1859. Bancroft Library.

36. Doyce B. Nunis Jr., ed., *The Golden Frontier: The Recollections of Herman Francis Reinhart, 1851–1869* (Austin: University of Texas Press, 1962), p. 115.

37. "The Yakima Expedition," *Weekly Oregonian*, August 14, 1858. For the Robertson party's hostile encounter with Natives on the Columbia River, where twenty Indians were apparently either killed or wounded, see "The New Northern Mines," (San Francisco) *Bulletin,* July 19, 1858, p. 2. The *Oregonian* suggested that Reinhart's party was indeed led by Captain Robertson, not Robinson as Doyce Nunis, editor of *The Golden Frontier*, had suggested.

38. Reinhart, *Golden Frontier,* p. 120.

39. Ibid., p. 126.

40. Reinhart thought that ten or twelve Natives must have been killed and a similar number wounded, "a deed Californians should ever be ashamed of, without counting the consequences." Ibid., pp. 126–27.

41. James Teit noted these attacks. See Teit, *The Salishan Tribes of the Western Plateaus,* vol. 45, *Annual Report of the Bureau of Ethnology,* ed. Franz Boas (Washington, D.C.: Smithsonian Institution, 1930), pp. 198–294.

42. Former usage by scholars and the public was "Thompson Indians," denoting the fact that these people lived along the Thompson River. The modern transliteration used in this chapter is Nlaka'pamux, meaning "people of the canyon," and is the current spelling accepted by the Nlaka'pamux Nation Tribal Council of Lytton, British Columbia.

43. Reinhart, *Golden Frontier,* p. 130.

44. William Nixon to Robert Nixon, "Letter from Victoria," (San Francisco) *Bulletin* 20 (July 1858): 2. References to numerous parties of miners that were confronted with Native resistance during 1858 can be found in Ted Van Arsdol, "Trail North—1858," part 1 in *Okanogan County Heritage* (March 1969): 19–25, and part 2 (June 1969): 13–27.

45. For Beam's membership in the Washington Territorial Volunteers and participation in the Indian wars south of the border, see *The Official History of the*

Washington National Guard, vol. 2: *Washington Territorial Militia in the Indian Wars of 1855–56* (Tacoma, Wash.: Office of the Adjutant General, n.d.), Washington State Archives, Olympia.

46. The Fraser River Gold Rush Diary of George Wesley Beam, August 22, 1858, in Beam Papers, 1858–1866, vol. 1. University of Washington Library. Manuscripts & University Archives Division, Seattle. Hereafter cited as UWL Archives.

47. Beam to Winfield Scott Ebey, August 20, 1858, Puget Sound Bar, Fraser River. Winfield Scott Ebey Papers, Incoming Correspondence, UWL Archives.

48. "This flooding of the country with strangers may have a tendency to rouse the whole northern Indians to an active spirit of hostility, the consequences of which will be truly disastrous to the Whites; as much blood will be spilt before an opening can be affected to the [Fraser] mines." See James Beith, Letter Book (1854–1867), July 10, 1858, pp. 27–29, Bancroft Library.

49. Wayne Suttles, "Central Coast Salish," in *Handbook of North American Indians,* vol. 7, *Northwest Coast,* ed. Wayne Suttles (Washington, D.C.: Smithsonian Institution Press, 1990), pp. 453–75. See "The Importance of Salmon," in Dianne Newell, *Tangled Webs of History: Indians and the Law in Canada's Pacific Coast Fisheries* (Vancouver: UBC Press, 1993), pp. 29–32.

50. Richard Somerset Mackie, *Trading beyond the Mountains: The British Fur Trade on the Pacific, 1793–1843* (Vancouver: UBC Press, 1998), pp. 221–30.

51. British Columbia was termed the "New Eldorado" in newspapers, private letters, and in an early published work by Kinahan Cornwallis, *The New El Dorado; or British Columbia* (London: Thomas Cautley Newby, 1858).

52. Shannon, "Richard G. Willoughby," p. 14.

53. Reinhart, *Golden Frontier,* pp. 130 and 135. Yale Bar is at the site of present-day Yale, British Columbia, the location of Fort Yale, a Hudson's Bay Company post established in 1848.

54. "Reported Bloody Fight with the Indians on Thompson River," (San Francisco) *Bulletin,* September 7, 1858, p. 3. As found in *Yreka Union,* September 2, 1858.

55. Elsewhere Chief Tolo is noted as the tribal head in the country around Yreka, in northern California, although he certainly seems to have had connections to the Scott Valley Tribe too. See "The Rogue River War," in Glassley, *Pacific Northwest Indian Wars,* pp. 62–63.

56. "Later from Washington Territory and the British Possession," (San Francisco) *Bulletin,* May 3, 1858, p. 3. There is much evidence, to state the obvious, that Natives on either side of the border were in communication with each other. For instance, see Gates, *Messages of the Governors of the Territory of Washington,* pp. 20, 43, and 50–51.

57. "Indian Difficulties on Fraser River," (San Francisco) *Bulletin,* September 1, 1858, p. 3.

58. Marie Houghton Brent, "The Memories of Marie Houghton Brent." Republic, Washington. Transcript (n.d.). British Columbia Archives.

59. The Stó:lō peoples live along the lower reaches of the Fraser River and are neighbors to the Yale First Nation and the Nlaka'pamux who live beyond. The cultural dividing line between these two peoples occurs approximately in the vicinity of Spuzzum, which is situated at the confluence of Spuzzum Creek and the Fraser River.

60. [Thomas King], "The Federal Government and the Northern Indians," (San Francisco) *Bulletin,* May 20, 1858, p. 2.

61. "Something New of the Northern Goldfields," (San Francisco) *Bulletin,* June 18, 1858, p. 2.

62. "Indian Troubles on the Columbia—Great Loss of U.S. Soldiers," (San Francisco) *Bulletin,* May 31, 1858, p. 2. This paper reported that fifty men and three officers were killed in the battle. See also "Letter from Fort Hope, Fraser River," (San Francisco) *Bulletin,* May 31, 1858, p. 2.

63. *Papers Relative to the Affairs of British Columbia,* part 1 (London: Eyre and Spottiswoode, 1859), p. 16.

64. "Later from Puget Sound and Frazer River," Letter of Franklin Matthias, (San Francisco) *Bulletin,* May 31, 1858, p. 3.

65. [Editorial], "Take It Coolly," (San Francisco) *Bulletin,* June 7, 1858, p. 2.

66. The practice of masquerading as non-Americans was quite common in both Eastern Washington territory and British Columbia. See Roderick Finlayson, "The History of Vancouver Island and the Northwest Coast," Reminiscences (1878). Bancroft Library.

67. Reminiscences of Lucius Samuel Edelblute, British Columbia Archives. "Boston Men" and "King George's Men" were Chinook jargon terms used by Native peoples to describe the American and English sea otter traders respectively during the eighteenth century, terms still used by the 1858 gold rush.

68. T. A. Rickard, "Indian Participation in the Gold Discoveries," *British Columbia Historical Quarterly* 2 (January 1938): 3–18.

69. Douglas to Henry Labouchere, July 15, 1857 (No. 5), in *Correspondence Relative to the Discovery of Gold in the Fraser's River District, in British North America* (London: George Edward Eyre & William Spottiswoode, 1858), pp. 7–8.

70. Douglas to Labouchere, April 6, 1858 (No. 8), *Correspondence Relative to the Discovery of Gold,* p. 10.

71. "Editor of the San Francisco Bulletin," (San Francisco) *Bulletin,* August 2, 1858, p. 2. Also H. M. Snyder, "Letter from Fraser River," (San Francisco) *Bulletin,* August 18, 1858, p. 3.

72. "Army Movements in the North—The Hostile Indians," (San Francisco) *Bulletin,* August 19, 1858, p. 2.

73. "Reported Mustering on the Columbia, the Northern California Indians," (Olympia) *Pioneer & Democrat,* July 23, 1858, and reprinted in the (San Francisco) *Bulletin,* August 2, 1858, p. 3.

74. "The Gold Mines and the Hostile Indians in Washington Territory," (San Francisco) *Bulletin,* August 19, 1858, p. 3.

75. An excellent example of an unfounded rumor fueled by newspapers occurred in the Dakota Territory in 1867. This particular Indian "massacre" of white settlers received national coverage for almost a month before it was finally viewed as a hoax. Robert G. Athearn, "The Fort Buford 'Massacre,'" *Mississippi Valley Historical Review* 41 (March 1955): 675–84. Also see James L. Thane Jr., "The Montana 'Indian War' of 1867," *Arizona and the West* 10 (summer 1968): 153–70. My thanks to Professor Brian Dippie, University of Victoria, for drawing my attention to the above articles.

76. "Army Movements in the North," (San Francisco) *Bulletin,* August 19, 1858, p. 3. Clark was appointed to the Department of the Pacific in 1857. William F. Strobridge, *Regulars in the Redwoods: The U.S. Army in Northern Californian, 1852–1861* (Spokane, Wash.: Arthur H. Clarke, 1994), p. 146.

77. Reported in the *Salem Statesman,* August 3, 1858. Reprinted in the (San Francisco) *Bulletin,* August 19, 1858, p. 3.

78. "Letters from Fraser River," (San Francisco) *Bulletin,* August 24, 1858, p. 2.

79. Ibid. With respect to the deaths of the two Frenchmen, the correspondent credited the information to two other members of the mining party, Messieurs A. Camels and Francois Moran.

80. "Indian Difficulties," (Victoria) *Gazette.* Reprinted in (San Francisco) *Bulletin,* August 24, 1858, p.3.

81. James Douglas noted the deaths of the two Frenchmen by Nlaka'pamux Natives, July 14, 1858. See "Diary of Gold Discovery on Fraser's River in 1858," British Columbia Archives. Ovid Allard, the Hudson's Bay Company trader at Fort Yale, wrote to Douglas about the conflict. Allard to Douglas, August 20, 1858, CC, British Columbia Archives.

82. Cheryl Coull, *A Traveller's Guide to Aboriginal B.C.* (Vancouver, B.C.: Whitecap Books, 1996), p. 118.

83. Unless otherwise noted, most of the information found here is in "Taken from Edward Stout at Yale, British Columbia," May 14, 1908, E/E/St71, British Columbia Archives.

84. A more detailed, perhaps embellished version of Ned Stout's account is found in "Reminiscences by Edward Stout of Yale, B.C," E/E/St71, British Columbia Archives. See also W. W. Walkem, *Stories of Early British Columbia* (Vancouver, B.C.: New Advertiser, 1914). Stout claimed that he and his party sought refuge from Native attack in a cave somewhere on the Fraser River above Boston Bar. He also stated that many of his party were killed at this place, Stout being one of the few survivors. This por-

tion of Stout's story may be plausible if Francis Wolff's recollections are examined. Wolff apparently joined in with volunteer forces at Yale during the Fraser War. "On arriving there," he stated, "we joined the volunteers and assisted in cleaning out the Indians, seeing at one place in a cave 16 dead miners mutilated." Francis Wolff, "Ambush at McLaughlin Canyon and Other Adventures of Francis Wolff," *Okanogan County Heritage* 2 (June 1964): 11.

85. The genocidal treatment by white miners of California's indigenous peoples set a precedent that was to accompany the expansion of the California mining frontier throughout the Far West and British Columbia. In particular, see James J. Rawls, *Indians of California: The Changing Image* (Norman: University of Oklahoma Press, 1984), pp. 109–33. Also see White, *"It's Your Misfortune and None of my Own,"* pp. 85–118; and Heizer, *Destruction of the California Indians.*

86. See Richard Maxwell Brown, *Strain of Violence: Historical Studies of American Violence and Vigilantism* (New York: Oxford University Press, 1975), pp. 95–133.

87. Jason O. Allard, "White Miners Saved Lives of B.C.'s First Chinese—Some Stories of Yale in the Gold Rush," Reminiscences, Howay-Reid Collection, Box 21:4, UBC Special Collections.

88. Letter from Captain Snyder, "The Indian Difficulties," (Victoria) *Gazette,* August 24, 1858, p. 3. Note: *rancheries* or *rancherias* was a Spanish term used in California to describe Native village sites.

89. Kowpelst, or Copals as he was referred to in press reports, was a chief of the Spuzzum peoples. See Andrea Laforet and Annie York, *Spuzzum: Fraser Canyon Histories, 1808–1939* (Vancouver: UBC Press, 1998), p. 51.

90. "From the Mines: Letter from Fort Yale," (Victoria) *Gazette,* August 24, 1858, p. 2.

91. (Victoria) *Gazette,* August 24, 1858, p. 2. Captain Rouse's company "killed, in all, some thirty-one Indians—as reported by the Indians themselves." See "Letter from Fort Yale," (Victoria) *Gazette,* September 1, 1858, p. 2. Also see "Another Letter from Fort Yale," (Victoria) *Gazette,* September 1, 1858, where it states: "The chief says that 31 warriors and 5 chiefs have been killed; he does not know how many whites." On p. 3 of the same issue Captain Snyder reported that Rouse had "indiscriminately killed some 31 Indians, the most of whom had always been friendly to the whites." The historian Robin Fisher mistakenly referred to this period of conflict as "a potentially ugly situation. . . . The miners at Yale formed themselves into volunteer companies to take reprisals against Indians up river. There was wild talk about exterminating the Indians, but these militia units involved themselves more in bravado than in action." This suggests that there was much more than bravado occurring along the Fraser River in 1858. Fisher, *Contact and Conflict: Indian-European Relations in British Columbia, 1774–1890* (Vancouver: University of British Columbia Press, 1977), p. 99.

92. Tom G. Todd, Fort Yale, to Charlie M. Dewey, Placer County, California, August 18, 1858. My sincere thanks to Robert Chandler, Historical Services, Wells Fargo Bank Archives, San Francisco, for this very pertinent and telling letter that he discovered in their private collections.

93. Beam Diary, August 18, 1858.

94. Ibid., August 21, 1858.

95. James Alexander Teit, *The Thompson Indians of British Columbia*, part 4 of *The Jesup North Pacific Expedition*, vol. 1, Memoir of the American Museum of Natural History, ed. Franz Boas (1900; reprint, Merritt, B.C.: Nicola Valley Museum Archives, 1997), p. 268.

96. In addition to articles found throughout the San Francisco *Bulletin* and the Victoria *Gazette*, as well as many other Pacific Northwest newspapers that note instances of beheaded miners being pulled from the Fraser River, there are also the diary and letters of Captain George Wesley Beam, and the reminiscences of Billy Ballou, Edward Stout, William Yates, H. F. Reinhart, Frank Tarbell, Edward McGowan, Thomas Spence, and many others. In the case of Thomas Spence, a veteran of a filibustering campaign in Sonora, Mexico, and later immortalized in the town today known as Spence's Bridge, he claimed that there were upwards of two hundred decapitated bodies taken from the river, but nowhere have I found this extreme number confirmed. See Arthur Wellesley Vowell and Thomas Spence, "Mining Districts of British Columbia," 1878. Reminiscences. PC/28. Bancroft Library.

97. Radcliffe Quine to his brother John, March 22, 1878, Seattle, Oregon Historical Society (OHS) Library.

98. "An Indian War Broken Out," (San Francisco) *Bulletin*, September 1, 1858, p. 2.

99. Ovid Allard stated to Chief Trader James M. Yale that the salmon trade at Fort Yale was effectively suspended as the "Indians are so much afraid" because of the warring action of white miners. At the same time, Allard also noted that some four hundred miners had left the Fraser in the previous four days, presumably because of the heightened conflict. Allard to Yale, August 20, 1858, Fort Langley, Correspondence In, 1844–1870, Hudson's Bay Company Archives. Provincial Archives of Manitoba. Hereafter referred to as HBCA.

100. Beam Diary, August 22 and 25, 1858.

101. "Miners Meeting at Fort Hope," (San Francisco) *Bulletin*, September 1, 1858, p. 3.

102. "Letter from Fort Hope, Fraser River: The Indian Hostilities—Proceedings of the Miners," (San Francisco) *Bulletin*, September 2, 1858, p. 3.

103. Ibid.

104. Ibid. The committee included J. D. Galbraith, J. C. Rice, W. T. Knox, A. J. Weaver, and Dr. R. W. Murphy.

105. Ibid.

106. Ibid. A Mr. Burch and [J. C.] Rice were selected to go to Fort Langley. Richard Hicks, the lone British gold commissioner, wrote to Chief Trader James Yale, "to my great surprise and sorrow have been informed that you have been sent to for Arms, &c, to fight the poor indians. . . . [I] trust you will not forward any arms whatever should any thing of the sort be wanted I will immediately make the application to you myself with every particular." Hicks to Yale, August 22, 1858. Fort Langley, Correspondence In, 1844–1870, HBCA.

107. Ibid.

108. "To His Excellency Jas. Douglas, Governor of Vancouver Island," (San Francisco) *Bulletin,* September 2, 1858, p. 3.

109. Beam to Ebey, Puget Sound Bar, August 20, 1858, Ebey Papers.

110. Beam Diary, August 23, 1858. Beam noted on August 24, "Two more men picked up with their heads off," and on August 27, "Picke[d] up a man at Hill's Bar [and] supposed he had drowned."

111. Kent D. Richards, *Isaac I. Stevens: Young Man in a Hurry* (1979; reprint, Pullman: Washington State University Press, 1993), p. 332.

112. "Narrative of a Voyage to Victoria, V.I.," (San Francisco) *Bulletin,* September 7, 1858, p. 1. Major Mortimer Robertson's party of 350 miners headed for the Fraser River is mentioned in this article. Also see "Overland Travel of Miners through Northern California and Oregon, to Thompson River," (San Francisco) *Bulletin,* September 7, 1858, p. 3. In this letter a miners' militia with 150 members is mentioned.

113. "Latest News from the Indian Country," (Portland) *Standard,* September 8, 1858. Reprinted in (San Francisco) *Bulletin,* September 13, 1858, p. 1. Also, "Indian Hostilities in the Northern Counties—Something for Kibbe to Do," (San Francisco) *Bulletin,* September 8, 1858, p. 3; and "Further Particulars on the late Indian Fight," (San Francisco) *Bulletin,* September 9, 1858, where it notes U.S. troops battling First Nations while Major Mortimer Robertson's miners' militia pushed through to the Fraser River.

114. For a detailed account of Colonel George Wright's campaigns in the Yakama and Coeur d'Alene Wars, see Glassley, *Pacific Northwest Indian Wars,* pp. 143–50.

115. "Later from Oregon: A Victory over the Indians," (San Francisco) *Bulletin,* September 25, 1858, p. 2.

116. Glassley, *Pacific Northwest Indian Wars,* pp. 143–50.

117. "Letter from the Dalles, O.T.," (San Francisco) *Bulletin,* October 16, 1858, p. 3.

118. "To Our Eastern Readers," (San Francisco) *Bulletin,* October 14, 1858, p. 2.

119. "Letter from Camp in Washington Territory," (San Francisco) *Bulletin,* October 16, 1858, p. 2. Also see "Official Report of the Indian War in the North," (San Francisco) *Bulletin,* October 16, 1858, p. 2.

120. Richards, *Isaac I. Stevens: Young Man in a Hurry*, p. 330.

121. "General Palmer's Command—The Columbia Valley Open to Fraser River," (San Francisco) *Bulletin*, October 16, 1858, p. 3. See Joel Palmer, "The Si-mil-ka-meen and Frazer River Gold Fields: Advantages of the Columbia River Route over Others for Travel and Commerce," January 28, 1860, Howay-Reid Collection, Box 46:5 (Transcript), UBC Special Collections. Also Joel Palmer, Diary 1860–61, OHS Library.

122. Allard to Douglas, August 20, 1858, CC, British Columbia Archives. Captain George Beam confirmed the disarming of the Yale First Nation: "They have taken the arms from the Indians at Fort Yale so they would not join the hostiles." See Beam to Ebey, August 20, 1858.

123. "From the Mines," (Victoria) *Gazette*, August 24, 1858, p. 2. One of the greatest indications of the American presence on the Fraser River is the large number of California-like gold rush bar place names that existed. Here is a sampling of those that reflect American nationality: Fifty-Four Forty Bar, Santa Clara Bar, American Bar, Yankee Doodle Bar, Eagle Bar, Sacramento Bar, Texas Bar, Ohio Bar, New York Bar, Washington Bar, and Boston Bar.

124. Ibid.

125. "An Indian War Broken Out," (San Francisco) *Bulletin*, September 1, 1858, p. 2, and found under "Armed Companies Proceeding up the River." The Chasseur de Vincennes was a massive French fortress and the Zouaves were well-known Papal Guards. My thanks to the historian Mark Cox, Victoria, B.C., for this clarification.

126. "Reminiscences of William Yates," Hope, B.C., undated, E/E/y2, British Columbia Archives.

127. Allard to Douglas, August 20, 1858, CC, British Columbia Archives.

128. Snyder to Douglas, August 28, 1858. The campaign lasted from August 16 through August 26, and the other officers elected were John Gordon, first lieutenant; P. M. Warner, second lieutenant; D. McEachern, orderly sergeant; and P. Gascoigne, quartermaster.

129. Edward McGowan stated that his close friend Martin Gallagher was in command of one of the companies that went up the Fraser. His jingoistic recollections suggested that "two companies, of one hundred men each, were organized to proceed up the river and teach these Indians a lesson. Martin Gallagher was placed in command of one of the companies, and a man by the name of Snyder, an old San Franciscan, of the other." Edward McGowan, "Reminiscences: Unpublished Incidents in the Life of the 'Ubiquitous,' *The Argonaut*," June 1, 1878, M/454, British Columbia Archives.

130. Snyder to Douglas, August 18, 1858. The result of Snyder's speech is that an additional thirty-one miners joined the Pike Guards for a total of eighty-two men.

This occurred near present-day Spuzzum (meaning "little Flat") at the south side of the confluence of the Spuzzum and Fraser Rivers.

131. Allard to Douglas, August 20, 1858, CC, British Columbia Archives.

132. "Reminiscences of William Yates," British Columbia Archives.

133. Laforet and York, *Spuzzum: Fraser Canyon Histories,* p. 55.

134. "Reminiscences of William Yates," British Columbia Archives.

135. Ibid.

136. Snyder to Douglas, August 28, 1858, CC, British Columbia Archives.

137. The Hudson's Bay Company Brigade Trail was located by A. C. Anderson in 1848. It climbs the mountain, which is to say, out of the canyon at present-day Alexandra Lodge, where portions of this historic route may still be traversed.

138. "Reminiscences of William Yates," British Columbia Archives.

139. Snyder to Douglas, August 28, 1858.

140. My thanks to Andrea Laforet for having shared this important point with me some years ago before the recent publication of her book. See Laforet and York, *Spuzzum: Fraser Canyon Histories,* pp. 55–56. At the same time, I can not agree with her assessment that the killing of Graham and his first lieutenant looked "suspiciously like a garden-variety homicide by one of Graham's companions." I believe that Snyder's words to Douglas combined with Laforet's own insight into the important role played by Nlaka'pamux emissaries suggests otherwise, especially in terms of the larger and, until now, untold context of this chapter.

141. Snyder to Douglas, August 28, 1858.

142. Teit, *Mythology of the Thompson Indians,* part 2, vol. 8, *The Jesup North Pacific Expedition.* American Museum of Natural History Memoir 12 (Leiden: E. J. Brill, 1912), p. 412. Also quoted in Laforet and York, *Spuzzum: Fraser Canyon Histories,* pp. 54–55.

143. H. M. Snyder, "Letter from Fort Yale, Fraser River," (San Francisco) *Bulletin,* September 25, 1858, p. 2.

144. Snyder to Douglas, August 28, 1858. The letter of proceedings is recorded in "Massacre of Forty-Five Miners by Indians," (Victoria) *Gazette,* August 25, 1858, p. 2. The "treaty" was subsequently shown to Graham of the Whatcom Guards. "The Story of the Massacre of the Forty-Three White Men Untrue," (Victoria) *Gazette,* August 26, 1858, p. 2.

145. "Letter from Fort Yale, Fraser River," (San Francisco) *Bulletin,* September 25, 1858, p. 2.

146. "Latest News from the Fraser River: Indian Hostilities—Prospects of the Diggings," *Bulletin,* September 2, 1858, p. 3. The same article noted an additional five corpses picked up from the river about Fort Yale, apparently increasing the number to thirteen.

147. "Letter from Fort Yale, Fraser River," (San Francisco) *Bulletin,* September 25, 1858, p. 2.

148. Snyder to Douglas, August 28, 1858. "Account of Capt. Snyder's Expedition," (Victoria) *Gazette,* September 1, 1858, p. 3. Snyder's peace-making process is roughly similar to the councils held in Washington Territory. See Richards, *Isaac I. Stevens: Young Man in a Hurry,* and also Terence O' Donnell, *An Arrow in the Earth: General Joel Palmer and the Indians of Oregon* (Portland: Oregon Historical Society Press, 1991).

149. "The Coming of the White Man" as told by Mary Williams (translated by Mamie Henry) in Darwin Hanna and Mamie Henry, eds. *Our Tellings: Interior Salish Stories of the Nlha7kápmx People* (Vancouver: UBC Press, 1996), pp. 130–31.

150. For thousands of miners who had been waiting months for the Fraser to fall in order to gain access to the gravel bars, Snyder's expeditious plan to conclude peace instead of costly war was most welcome. See the special correspondent's "Account of Capt. Snyder's Expedition," (Victoria) *Gazette,* September 1, 1858, p. 3.

151. Marshall, "Rickard Revisited."

152. "Later from the Northern Waters: Departure of Governor Douglas for Fraser River," (San Francisco) *Bulletin,* September 6, 1858, p. 3. See also Douglas to Lytton, October 12, 1858, No. 3, CO 60/1, p. 213. Public Record Office, London, UK. Hereafter cited as PRO.

153. Douglas wrote, "An alarming report reached this place of the murder of 42 miners by the Indians of Fraser's River. . . . That alarming report has since been con-tradicted. . . . I am nevertheless preparing for an excursion to Fraser's River, with a small military force of 35 men . . . for the maintenance of peace and good order among the motely [*sic*] population of foreigners. . . . The military force is absurdly small for such an occasion, but I shall use every exertion in my power to accomplish the great object in view, and to assert the rights of my Country, in hopes that early measures will be taken by Her Majesty's Government to relieve the country from its present perilous state." Douglas to Lord Stanley, August 27, 1858, CO 60/1, p. 129, PRO.

154. James Douglas, "Diary of Gold Discovery on Fraser's River in 1858," September 3–4, 1858, British Columbia Archives.

155. J. C. Prevost, captain of HMS *Satellite,* to Rear Admiral Robert Lambert Baynes, commander-in-chief of the Pacific Station, August 31, 1858. Enclosure in William G. Romaine, secretary to the admiralty, to Herman Merivale, under-secretary of state for the colonies, October 15, 1858. CO 60/2. PRO.

156. "From Oregon: Progress of Indian War," (San Francisco) *Bulletin,* September 6, 1858, p. 3.

157. "Saw at Hope Governor Douglass and some thirty soldiers on there [*sic*] way up the River to make peace with the Indians." George Wesley Beam, September 5, 1858, Beam Diary, UW Archives.

158. "Latest News Direct from Fraser River," (San Francisco) *Bulletin,* September 25, 1858, p. 2. Captain H. M. Snyder noted, "The chief from the head of the Big Cañon, where all the trouble was, came down here [Fort Yale] this morning to see Governor Douglas."

159. Ibid.

160. Douglas to Lytton, September 9, 1858, No. 39, CO 60/1, PRO.

161. Frederic W. Howay, *The Early History of the Fraser River Mines* (Victoria, B.C.: Charles F. Banfield, 1926). Only a very few appointments were made as early as June and these were formalized in September.

162. "Address of His Excellency the Governor to the Inhabitants at Fort Yale," September 12, 1858, CC, British Columbia Archives.

3 / Work, Sex, and Death on the Great Thoroughfare

Annual Migrations of "Canadian Indians" to the American Pacific Northwest

JOHN LUTZ

A dramatic reorientation of the Pacific Northwest's many worlds took place between 1841 and 1871, forcing the territory's aboriginal inhabitants to reformulate their lives and economies. This chapter looks at one aspect of the reorientation of these North Coast peoples as they came face to face, for the first time, with towns and cities of immigrants, and more specifically, as they encountered capitalist wage work and assimilated it into their long-standing practices of slave-raiding, taking heads as trophies, and potlatching.

The extent of the reordering of the Pacific Northwest is visible in the demographics of this era. Within these thirty years the nonaboriginal population in the vast expanse from the northern California border to the Russian territory in Alaska grew from fewer than 1,000 to 125,000.[1] This reorientation affected all aboriginal people along the Pacific Coast, but not at the same time or with the same force. By 1860, south of the forty-ninth parallel, Euro-Americans overwhelmed aboriginal populations along the more densely populated coastline and banks of the major rivers. Aboriginal lives were disrupted by disease, treaties, a series of "wars," removal to reservations, and the settlement of their former lands. North of the forty-ninth parallel, however, aboriginal people still outnumbered Euro-Canadians, who were then only slightly more numerous outside a half-dozen small urban centers than they had been twenty years earlier. Here aboriginal people had more space and time to adjust to the pressures and opportunities the burgeoning settler society created.[2]

Aside from a series of trading posts, each staffed by a handful of non-aboriginals, Euro-American and Canadian communities did not come to the North Coast until the 1880s and even then only in a limited way. In the intervening years, aboriginal peoples from the top of the Alaskan Panhandle to Vancouver Island went south to investigate for themselves. For more than a century, from the 1850s to the 1950s, aboriginal men, women, and children from all along the Canadian West Coast joined an annual migration to Victoria, the Fraser Valley, and in Washington Territory (later, state), Puget Sound. At its peak around 1885 some six thousand aboriginal people from British Columbia, more than 20 percent of the province's aboriginal population, made a seasonal migration to Washington.[3]

In part, this chapter suggests the permeability of the national boundary between Canada and the United States and its lack of impact on aboriginal people. However, the main focus is on the set of borders connecting and dividing an elaborate, sophisticated, and long-standing aboriginal economy and a recently arrived industrial, capitalist economy. This chapter focuses on fifteen years of migrations—from 1854 to 1869—during which aboriginal northerners first incorporated annual visits to Victoria, Vancouver Island, and Puget Sound into their own cultural patterns and priorities.

This little-known migration owes its obscurity to two factors. First, it is a difficult topic to research. The workers themselves—the aboriginal migrants—left precious few written records, and their oral history, transcribed by ethnologists, has been noticeably silent on their postcontact work patterns.[4] Moreover, the kind of work that they did—seasonal agricultural labor, work in sawmills, and, for want of a better term, sex-trade labor—generated few records in these early years of state formation.[5] Second, and more important, is the set of historical images that have affected how we as researchers have historically seen aboriginal people. Important studies have highlighted the long-term history of assimilation and dispossession of aboriginal people. On the one hand, the historian Robin Fisher argues that aboriginal people were excluded from the capitalist labor force; on the other hand, works like Rolf Knight's *Indians at Work* have argued that aboriginal people went to work for the same reasons as did nonaboriginal people. A more recent view has seen the same history as a period of resistance and protection of culture.[6] But none of these approaches captures the period's complexity, when some actions were simultaneously assimilative and assertive of a distinct aboriginal culture. A "stereoscopic" vision that brings these two different perspectives together better explains a time when aboriginal people combined industrial wage labor with the long-standing practice of raiding, taking heads as trophies, and taking captives as slaves. These labor migrants-cum-slave raiders illustrate that the borders between "savage" and "civilized," between "marauder" and "laborer," between "aboriginal" and "settler" are as porous as the forty-ninth parallel itself, and even less effective as historical boundaries.[7]

The 1846 establishment of the forty-ninth parallel as the boundary between British and American territory coincided with the arrival of Puget Sound's first sawmill and ushered in a new era of industrial capitalism. By 1855 no fewer than sixteen mills were operating on the Sound. A few of them, like the Port Gamble Mill, were among the largest in the United States, cutting twenty thousand board feet of lumber a day.[8] These mills were steam-powered factories that required a large labor force not readily available among the settler population. As early as 1851, the superintendent of Indians affairs remarked that aboriginal people from around Puget Sound filled this gap, "render[ing] themselves useful in many ways as laborers and servants." Local aboriginal people were drawn into these enterprises, but still more labor was needed.[9] The aboriginal people in British territory, immediately to the north of Puget Sound, were drawn to Victoria, the capital of the colony of Vancouver Island, which was also developing as a commercial center. In addition to those aboriginal groups in close proximity to Victoria, other clusters from the northern end of Vancouver Island and north into the Alaskan Panhandle (nominally Russian but leased by the British Hudson's Bay Company from 1839 to 1867[10]) began making seasonal visits to Victoria to trade and work. From Victoria it was a short hop to the labor-short shores of Puget Sound. In the early 1850s these so-called Northern Indians began to extend their existing seasonal economy to include a season of wage work, far to the south of their ordinary migratory range (Figure 3.1).[11]

Visits by some northern aboriginal people to Puget Sound were not entirely new. When Europeans first arrived in Puget Sound in the 1790s, they noticed that many of the villages were fortified. The aboriginal people told them that the main danger was from the Kwakwaka'wakw group the Lekwiltok (also called Yaculta and Euclataw—the name translates as "unkillable things"), which periodically sent raiding parties.[12] The Kwakwaka'wakw, located on the northern end of Vancouver Island, had direct contact with European traders during the sea otter trade of the late eighteenth century and so acquired iron blades and muskets before their southern neighbors. The new technology emboldened them, and they extended their traditional raids on immediate neighbors more than three hundred miles south into Puget Sound.[13]

After 1853 more Kwakwaka'wakw than ever were heading south on seasonal trips, but the increased number was a result of a completely new component. The Kwakwaka'wakw added seasonal wage work in the Vancouver

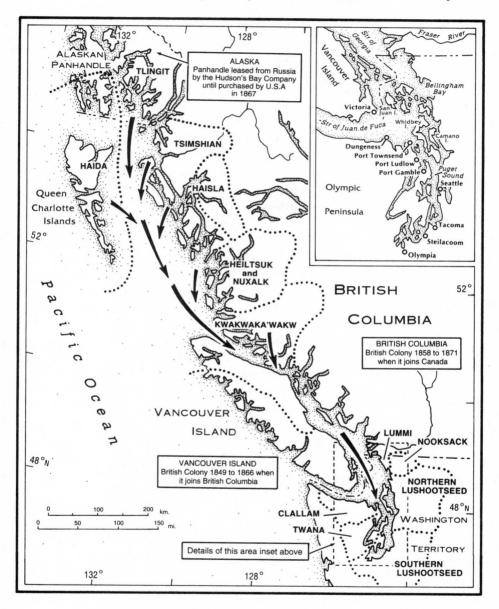

FIG. 3.1. The Northwest Pacific, showing southward migrations of "Northern Indians" along the "Great Thoroughfare" in the 1850s-1860s. Insert: Puget Sound and adjacent communities at the same time. Used with permission of the author.

Island towns of Nanaimo and Victoria to their earlier pattern of raiding. Their raids into Puget Sound and the lower Straits of Georgia seemed to have dwindled though not stopped by this time.[14] Also an entirely new phenomenon was that their northern neighbors, the Tsimshian, the Haida, and the Tlingit—who had never, according to the ethnographic evidence, traveled so far south— also began visiting Victoria and Puget Sound to raid and obtain work. Although there is now a small historiography that has begun to chart aboriginal involvement in the wage labor force, there has been no attention to this period when aboriginal people began accepting wage labor. Very little is known about why aboriginal people joined the immigrants' wage labor force and how they integrated this work into their own economic and social networks.[15] We ought to suspect that the reasons varied among aboriginal groups according to their concepts of wealth, ownership, and subordination required by wage labor.

Along the coastal Pacific Northwest there were distinct concepts of wealth and cultural practices that predisposed these groups to involvement in the capitalist economy.[16] Although different in many ways, including linguistically, the North Coast cultures were characterized at this time by two distinct economies. Food circulated in a subsistence economy, where individual gatherers and heads of families had some but not full control over its distribution. Most other goods circulated in a "wealth" or "prestige" economy. Wealth goods—such as canoes, blankets, regalia, tools, and slaves—circulated in the prestige economy, where the purpose was to ensure status, not sustenance. The central feature of the prestige economy, and the most important reason for accumulating goods in Northwest Coast society, was the potlatch complex.[17]

Potlatches were usually hosted by a family or a group of families, who invited their community as well as kin and dignitaries from communities with which they had close connections. The event, which lasted anywhere from several days to two or more weeks, involved feasting, speeches, gambling, games, as well as song and dance performances by the hosts and guests. The defining characteristic of the potlatch, however, was the giveaway. In the process of any potlatch, the hosts gave away most, if not all, of their accumulated material wealth and sometimes also their "spiritual possessions." The larger the gathering, the higher status the guests; the more valuable the gifts, the more the host family enhanced its social status, so there was an element of competition and inflation involved in the process.[18] A family knew that its peers were accumulating property in an attempt to give away still greater amounts, so it had a powerful incentive to begin accumulating immediately for its next potlatch. Inherent in the North Coast prestige economy was this incentive to acquire possessions.

Before the arrival of Europeans, there were three ways to acquire possessions. First, such goods as canoes, tools, and blankets could be made by household members. Second, goods could be acquired by trading with neighboring communities, but this avenue was limited by the overlap in resources between nearby groups, or those not far away, resulting in few unique items to trade.[19] Third, goods and particularly slaves could be acquired through raiding.[20] All three routes to wealth were either time-consuming or risky and so limited the inflationary one-upmanship.

When Europeans arrived, they introduced tools that increased domestic production. The European economy also offered the possibility of earning wealth through the sale of labor, and many aboriginal groups grafted this onto their traditional means of acquiring goods to give away at potlatches. The imperatives of their own economy drew aboriginal people from the north to participate in Puget Sound's expanding capitalist economy. Instead of substituting their culture for the capitalist economy, however, aboriginal people added wage labor to their existing economy, without giving up their long-standing roads to riches, including raiding one's aboriginal neighbors.

The incorporation of wage labor was accomplished through these decades without major disruption because the seasonal rounds of the aboriginal economy meant that there was surplus labor in the spring and summer— the same seasons when there was a high demand for labor in the capitalist economy. The resources that had traditionally been harvested in the spring and summer—bulbs and berries—were less important to the northern coastal economies than those in the south, and could be maintained at a reduced level by the young and the elderly, who did not participate in the migrations. In some cases the access to flour and other prepared foods that could be purchased by wages likely substituted for the reduced gathering effort.[21] The earliest documentary account of aboriginal people from north of Vancouver Island working in Puget Sound is Theodore Winthrop's 1853 account of hiring "Haida" to transport him to Victoria.[22] That same year witnessed the start of annual mass migrations of two thousand to four thousand so-called Northern Indians to Victoria. Thereafter, a spring and summer visit to Victoria became a part of the seasonal cycle for many Northwest Coast people from as far away as Russian America. They came to work and trade. Those who could not find work in Victoria in the 1850s continued south into American territory.[23]

Employment records from this era have not survived, so reconstructing the work patterns of these migrant laborers is difficult. Most references to Northern people are not about work but about the apparent threat they posed to white settlers, so information about the timing and extent of work has to be gleaned from incidental references. Although details of these migrations remain obscured, the general pattern emerges quite vividly. According to the governor of Vancouver Island, from 1853 on, aboriginal people from "all parts of the mainland coast south of Cape Spencer, in north latitude 59 degrees" began making annual visits to Victoria and Puget Sound to find work.[24] A settler in Puget Sound during this period, Robert C. Hill, described the pattern in his reminiscences: "Often a party of these Indians would stop at one of the mill towns. The bucks would hire out their squaws for housework or any other employment, and the men themselves would go to work in the mills, remaining through the summer."[25]

There are also brief, tantalizing accounts of these migrations from aboriginal people. John Fornsby, a Salish from Puget Sound, first saw Northern Indians up close around 1865, when he came to work at a Puget Sound sawmill that employed forty to fifty of them. One of these Northern Indians, William Pierce, remarked that in the mid-1870s his coworkers at the Port Ludlow Mill on Puget Sound were "several hundreds of Indians," including Haida from the Queen Charlottes, fellow Tsimshians from the North Coast, Nisga'a from the Nass River, as well as Haisla, Heiltsuk, Nuxalk, and Kwakwaka'wakw from the Central Coast and Tlingit from the Alaskan Panhandle. The Kwakwaka'wakw Charles Nowell also mentioned his trip to Puget Sound in his reminiscences. The best documented account of one of these workers is contained in the diary of Arthur Wellington Clah, a Tsimshian.[26] Clah, however, only came as far south as Victoria. The term "Northern Indians" usually referred to the groups enumerated by Pierce, those aboriginal people living along the coast north of the Strait of Georgia, including those in the Alaskan Panhandle.[27]

James Gilchrist Swan, a sometime Indian Department employee, justice of the peace, and ethnographer based in the American town of Port Townsend at the mouth of Puget Sound, noted that "hundreds and sometimes thousands of the Northern Indians" come yearly to work in the mills or for farmers; he described them as "faithful and efficient." There were also reasons for women to make the trip: "The women, by their cleanly habits, their bright dresses and hoop skirts (for they have learned the fashions), winning the hearts or purses of white bachelors."[28] Women found work as domestic help and farm labor in Puget Sound but were also in demand as sexual and marital partners. Sexual relations between immigrant men and aboriginal women date back to the earliest days of the fur trade on Puget Sound, if not back to the earliest expeditions by European explorers. What was new about these relations in the 1850s, however, is that they increasingly involved northern rather than local aboriginal women. Northern aboriginal women were considered superior to the local aboriginal women for several reasons: they did not flatten their foreheads, a mark of nobility for women in the south; northern women were taller and in the eyes of many Euro-Americans "paler" than the local aboriginal women and so were considered more beautiful; and the northern tribes were considered superior in terms of ability and bravery than the people of Puget Sound.[29] Quite a number formed longer lasting relationships and married or lived common-law with male settlers.[30]

The numbers of canoes containing only, or largely, northern women mentioned in settler accounts suggest that this trade in sexual favors was well under way by 1855. By 1859 an American soldier stationed on San Juan Island, just off the mouth of Puget Sound, noted that there were two hundred aboriginal women on the island, "almost all of them prostitutes," thanks to the presence of U.S. and British military garrisons. As late as 1873 the Indian commissioner for Washington Territory lamented that "the British Columbia Indians, from Vancouver and other islands and the mainland, come in their canoes in swarms around our logging camps and towns around the sound, get all the whiskey they want, and their women engage in prostitution. A number of brothels at different points on the sound are filled with their women."[31]

In some regards the behavior of these aboriginal migrants was assimilative in that it paralleled white mill workers and prostitutes. The mill workers were subject to industrial work discipline, learned to work with advanced technology, and undoubtedly picked up some of the concepts and terminology of wage labor. As for after-work activities, the Tsimshian mill worker Pierce recalled that "all hands were paid every Saturday, and as saloons were open to the Indians without any restriction, they spent most of their money at those places, with the result that there was drunkenness and fighting all day on Sunday, and when Monday morning came nobody was in a fit state to begin work, or if they turned up at their post, nothing was satisfactory."[32]

In three important respects, however, the aboriginal workers were quite different from their white coworkers. First, many aboriginal people accumulated their wages over the summer, and when they returned home they used their saving to host a potlatch and gave their newfound wealth away. The anthropologist Helen Codere, who has made an intensive study of the Kwakwaka'wakw, one of the northern peoples who migrated to Puget Sound, noted that although fur trade wealth increased the frequency of potlatches, wage labor made them still more ostentatious, with more guests and more wealth distributed. She calls 1849–1921 "the potlatch period."[33] This is borne out by the Kwawkewlth (Kwakwaka'wakw) district Indian agent George Blenkinsop's 1881 observation that potlatches "of late years, increased to a very great extent." He explained that among the Kwakwaka'wakw, "the custom was formerly almost entirely confined to the recognised chiefs, but that of late years it has extended to the people generally, and become very much commoner than before. . . . [The potlatch] has spread to all classes of the community and became the recognised mode of attaining social rank and respect."[34] Other sources confirm this pattern for the Tlingit, Haida and Tsimshian, and Puget Sound peoples.[35] Contemporary Euro-American commentators wondered at what they called the "lunacy" of giving away all this money, but that was because they understood aboriginal wage work from a capitalist viewpoint. Part of the wage work experience was undoubtedly assimilative, but the main motivation for engaging in the process at all was to expand the potlatch complex and enhance the laborer's status in aboriginal society.[36]

The second difference concerned the sex-for-pay exchange. Although the settlers considered this prostitution, there is ethnographic evidence that the aboriginal women involved put the exchange of sex for gifts in a completely different cultural context. Some of the early exchange was likely the forced use of slaves, hired out by their owners—if the experience in nearby Victoria is a guide. However, most women involved in this exchange seemed to have been involved on their own behalf or that of their families. The Canadian Indian commissioner I. W. Powell remarked that the Haida "women annually flock[ed] to the ports of Puget Sound for the purpose of prostitution." But he also noted that, in contrast to the place of a prostitute in white society, "their social condition at home however, is above average." Among the Kwakwaka'wakw, Tsimshian, and Haida, the earnings from the sex-for-pay exchange were also used to enhance women's position as holders of potlatches.[37]

From his mission among the Tsimshian, William Duncan wrote in 1858 that annually, in mid-February, about two hundred Tsimshian go to Victoria or to "American parts," a distance of about five hundred miles: "At the latter part of the year the Indians who went south return bringing great quantities of rum and various kinds of property most of which is got by prostitution. Then feasting and house building commence and a great many young people of both sexes are admitted into the mysterious craft they call 'Allied.'. . . Property also now is given away or changes hands and a great quantity is torn up."[38]

The third striking difference in the behavior of aboriginal workers that confirms that these migrations were incorporated into an aboriginal economy and worldview was that, in the words of James Swan: "Regularly, when fall approaches, and they wish to go to their homes in the North, they commit some murder or depredation." On their way home from their jobs these seasonal laborers raided, robbed, enslaved, or beheaded aboriginal strangers.[39] Raiding was a long-standing part of interrelationships among aboriginal groups on the Northwest Coast. Oral histories, many of them now transcribed, exist for almost every aboriginal group describing both raiding and being raided. Archaeological work suggests that villages began to be fortified about a thousand years ago. Some of the raiding was prompted by the desire to acquire slaves, which were valuable economically, and for prestige purposes among the stratified Northwest Coast societies.[40] What was new about these raids is that they were between people brought into contact by the desire on the part of the Northern Indians to engage in wage work and the sex trade, and the aboriginal groups involved had never been at war with each other (the exception being the Kwakwaka'wakw and the people of Puget Sound).

The accounts of these attacks come largely from white sources who were not overly concerned about what they viewed as internecine battles. They are fragmentary, but from them a pattern of attack and revenge emerges. The Tlingit are first mentioned as a threat in 1854 when a party of sixty attacked the Bellingham Bay Indians. Stikine Tlingit are again mentioned as having raided the Nisqually village near Steilacoom in 1856, robbing the houses and taking fifty to seventy-five bushels of potatoes. A few days later when a canoe of some "British-Russian" Indians tried to land at the village, the Nisquallys attacked them, killing two men and a boy. The newspaper the *Pioneer and Democrat* reported that the Puget Sound Indians "declare their determination to kill all these foreign intruders wherever and whenever opportunities present themselves."[41]

In 1857 the Indian agent assigned to Bellingham Bay noted that the Samish people near there now numbered only two hundred, where a decade ago there were twelve hundred. He alleged that like other tribes living contiguous to the "great thoroughfare," as he called the Strait of Georgia, "they have been nearly annihilated by the hordes of northern savages that infested, and do now, even at the present day," Puget Sound and neighboring waters.[42] Some aboriginal villages consolidated in locations that were less vulnerable to attack.

Similar encounters were reported between the Clallam and Northern Indians in May 1857, Northern Indians and the Lummi in 1858, between Haida and the Suquamish in 1859 on Bainbridge Island, and between the Haida and the Snohomish on May 25, 1860.[43] The battles between the northern and local aboriginal people usually resulted in the loss of a few lives on each side, the main goal being the taking of slaves. The aftermath of one attack was witnessed by a reporter in 1864: "One day last week two large war canoes put into Comox filled with Fort Rupert Indians [Kwakwaka'wakw] returning from a raid against their hereditary foes the Lummis. One of the canoes contained three heads, a man's a woman's and a child's. The other was filled with a large number of captives taken as slaves. Our informant examined the decapitated heads, and says they seems to have been taken off in a most artistic manner, being free from distortion or scars and quite bloodless. The heads were cut off at the jaw and were set upright in the bow of the canoe where they presented an almost life-like but horrible appearance."[44] Several of Fort Rupert people were severely injured and stayed with their Comox neighbors to recuperate.

The work migrations were complicated by the fact that the Northern Indians were actually members of many different aboriginal nations, most of which were on hostile terms with each other. Not only did they have to be on their guard against attack in Puget Sound by the victims of their raids, they also had to watch out for the other northern raiders. Moreover, on their journeys to and from work, ranging from three hundred to nine hundred miles each way, they were largely passing through waters inhabited by aboriginal groups ready to attack and enslave the passersby. Every trip involved running the gauntlet along what is now called the Inside Passage, a passage that at its narrowest, the top of Georgia Strait, was controlled by the aggressive Lekwiltok. William Duncan observed that "nearly every tribe between here and Victoria are now at war with these Indians [Tsimshians] and are ever on the alert to kill or enslave them."[45] A Tlingit woman, Matilda Paul, returning to Russian America from Victoria in the 1860s, described how her party managed their six-hundred-mile trip: "They travelled from even-tide to early dawn and, for safety, they stashed their canoe in the woods and built their fires of the driest wood to minimize the smoke while awaiting the covering darkness of approaching night."[46]

Ironically, the arrival of Euro-Americans that drew aboriginal people into wage labor—one element of what Euro-Americans considered "civilized society"—also accelerated the traditional raiding and slave-taking economy. The anthropologists Donald Mitchell and Leland Donald have argued that the arrival of the fur traders increased the value of slaves in the aboriginal economy because the fur traders provided a new market for foods and furs, the processing of which was accelerated by slave labor. Slaves could also be hired out as laborers or sexual partners to the traders, and this made them suddenly more valuable. The result was increased slave raids.[47]

When a settler economy based on agriculture and industry supplanted the fur trade, the use of slaves to their aboriginal owners increased again. The new economy demanded still more food, labor, and sexual services; slave labor was an efficient means to capitalize on this. The long-distance migrations to work and slave-taking missions were directly linked to Euro-American immigration, just as both were also extensions of the long-standing West Coast prestige economy. Although slaves were incorporated into the early trips to Victoria and Puget Sound as paddlers and as laborers and prostitutes to be hired out by their owners, increasingly such trips gave slaves a chance to escape. As the presence of missionaries and government officials grew, slaves had people with whom they could take refuge. Moreover, enslaved women forced into the sex trade may have found it possible to take refuge with nonaboriginal men seeking a partner. After the early 1860s it appears that slaves were left at home, where they continued to contribute to the new economy.[48]

Although the data are admittedly thin, it seems likely that slave-taking and slaveholding peaked between the mid-1840s and early 1860s. Hudson's Bay Company censuses of 1845 found that many of the northern groups had populations that were a quarter slave. James Simpson, the governor of the company, thought "fully one-third of the entire population of this region were slaves," although this estimate was off-the-cuff and may have been high. A reliable 1861 census of the Kaigani Haida, one of the groups regularly frequenting Puget Sound, put the slave population at 198, or 26 percent of the total population.[49]

The targets of the slave raids were aboriginal villages, but Euro-American settlers occasionally got caught in the crossfire.[50] Wanting to avoid trouble with the whites when they were in Puget Sound in 1860, Northern Indians told the white settlers not to worry: "They say they are not here to trouble Bostons but to attack Clallams" and that they "do not have any grudge against the Bostons."[51] Still, the presence of large numbers of well-armed aboriginal people in canoes that could outrun all the vessels ordinarily available in Puget Sound was disturbing to white settlers who were accustomed to holding the upper hand when it came to dealing with aboriginal people: "It was known that there were many of the northern men at work at different places on the sound. As many of their women were living with white men, it was feared they were acting but the part of spies, and could at any time induce their friends, if so disposed, to make a sudden attack on the white settlements."[52]

The American settlers also felt that their inability to defend American Indians from attacks by foreigners diminished their stature with the local aboriginal population, who accused the settlers of "having no strong hearts" (i.e., being afraid of the northerners).[53] There was also a fear that an alliance might be struck between the local and the northern aboriginal people against the immigrants.[54] When Governor Stevens traveled around Puget Sound making treaties in 1854 and 1855, he made it a requirement of the treaties that Puget Sound Indians not trade with "Foreign Indians" or let them live on Puget Sound.[55] Weighing the pros and cons of their valuable labor with the threat they posed to the physical and the supposed moral well-being of the territory, on January 20, 1857, the territorial legislature passed a bill outlawing the employment of, or cohabitation with, Northern Indians by a vote of twenty to two.[56]

The bill, "An Act to Prohibit the Employment of, and Trade with Northern Indians," was an attempt to use the border as a line to exclude what the legislators considered as undesirables. The act imposed a fine of $100 and thirty days for violators.[57] There were three problems, however. The first was that the employers and the male workers of Puget Sound took a view opposite to the legislators about the desirability of the Northern Indians and continued to employ them and live with them as usual. Second, the law, in the opinion of many, including Justice of the Peace Swan, was unconstitutional and could not be enforced. "So long as we are at peace, we cannot refuse any nation, kindred or tongue on the face of the earth from coming to free America, and particularly 'Native Americans.'"[58] Third, when the American state did try to intercept these canoe-borne workers, it found that the presence of small detachments of soldiers at Steilacoom, Port Townsend, and after 1859, San Juan Island, did nothing to dissuade these nautical migrants who could travel faster than the soldiers. Only the navy's fastest steamships, none of which was permanently stationed in Puget Sound, offered a match for sleek northern canoes.

The indignation of the Puget Sound nonaboriginal population was stirred up against the Northern Indians later that year when a party of Kake Tlingit killed and beheaded Colonel Isaac Ebey, customs collector for Puget Sound, in retaliation for a U.S. naval attack on their encampment at Port Gamble, which had killed twenty-seven. After this event the acting governor of Washington Territory wrote the governor of Vancouver Island, saying that it had been fully determined "to allow none of these tribes to visit our waters and such as do venture, render themselves liable to the punishment of death."[59]

It would seem as though these threats had only a short-term effect, however. The missionary William Duncan, who worked among the Tsimshian at Fort Simpson, observed, "Because of the murder of an American officer by some Northern Indians all belonging to these tribes have been glad to get away and are forbidden to return on the American side." He expected this, combined with the fact that "during the last few months so many of the Northern Indians have been murdered in the sound" to limit the trips south.[60] Yet two summers later, the continuing migration of Northern Indians and the cohabitation of northern women with settlers prompted the citizens of Port Townsend to hold a public meeting calling for enforcement of the law. Settlers employing Northern Indians were urged to send them away. A resolution required "that all men having northern women be notified that if they do not on or before the first day of June next, send the same out of the country that legal action will be commenced against them."[61] The law continued to be a dead letter, but that did not stop Governor Richard D. Gholson from issuing a proclamation the next year, drawing attention to the law: "It would seem that there are some who are not aware of this fact, or else scruple little to violate it." The *Pioneer and Democrat* added that "it has lately come to the attention of the Governor that Numbers are employed and that their number is again increasing."[62]

The employment of the Northern Indians actually continued to increase into the 1870s and 1880s, but by the late 1860s their visits had become less of a threat to settlers. Through this decade the settlers' numbers had themselves increased dramatically, so they felt more secure. After the end of the Civil War in 1865, the U.S. government had more military resources available to control its northern border. The United States took control of Alaska after 1867, where the Tlingits resided, and put it under military governorship. In 1869 the U.S. military torched the Tlingit village at Kake, where Ebey's murderers had come from. Moreover, aboriginal patterns were changing for reasons independent of Washington's antihiring law.

One of the reasons for the dwindling of the combination of work and raiding was the increasing presence and power of state agents on both sides of the border to inhibit the slave trade. The treaties made by Governor Stevens in 1855 stipulated that the Puget Sound Indians free their slaves. When the Puget Sound Snohomish attacked a party of Haida in 1860, killing two men and one women and enslaving the remaining seven women, the American Indian agents forced them to surrender the slaves, who were returned to British territory.[63] The British sent Royal Navy ships to visit the northern villages in the early 1860s, threatening those groups who continued to raid their neighbors. Increasingly in the 1860s slaves were emancipated by government agents and missionaries; thus they became less secure and less desirable as

property. Emancipation of slaves in the potlatch also was becoming an acceptable way of demonstrating wealth. The implication was that the owner had
so much wealth he could afford to give it away.

State officials on both sides of the border also began acting as if those
crimes committed between aboriginal parties were a concern for the justice
system.[64] One of the last documented of the reciprocal attacks began with
the murder of four Clallam women from the Strait of Juan de Fuca, adjacent
to Puget Sound, and the enslavement of four others by the northern Tsimshians in 1864. The next year the Tsimshians attacked a party of ten Clallams,
killing six and enslaving four. The Clallams had to wait until September 1868,
when they found a party of nineteen Tsimshians camped near Dungeness
Spit. Attacking the party at night while they slept, the Clallams killed all but
one Tsimshian. As punishment the American officials arrested twenty
Clallams and held them. The Clallam agreed to restore all the property stolen
from the Tsimshian and the offenders were sentenced to six months hard
labor.[65]

Aboriginal people were apparently also deciding that an end to hostilities
would be to their own advantage. The wars made mobility hazardous and
made every trip to work or to trade a life-and-death test of stealth and strength
as canoes tried to avoid their enemies. As early as 1860, the Haida chief "Konyi"
told the captain of a Royal Navy ship that he was anxious to live at peace with
all "in order that they can make their annual visit to Victoria unmolested."
He offered to return all the slaves he had taken from Vancouver Island if other
tribes would do the same. The HMS *Alert* heard the same story from the
Kwakwaka'wakw at Fort Rupert that year.[66]

The dwindling and ultimate demise of aboriginal slavery removed one of
the main reasons why aboriginal people fought with each other.[67] By the late
1860s the raiding element had disappeared from the work migrations.
Intertribal rivalries found an outlet in expanded potlatch competition, as many
formerly hostile peoples reconciled and found themselves as coworkers in
the expanding industries of Puget Sound. The annual migrations expanded
until the 1880s and continued until the 1950s, when automation and the competition from foreign migrant laborers, Mexican and Filipino, finally succeeded
in keeping the Northern Indians out of Puget Sound.

The century-long migration of aboriginal workers from British Columbia
down to Puget Sound reveals something of the character of the border between
Canada and the United States. The border was not always undefended—it was
just poorly defended. The border of 1846 was a permeable one with northern aboriginal people defying law, army, and navy to work, raid, and cohab-

itate with the people of Puget Sound, with relative impunity. American employers needed labor and northern aboriginal people wanted wealth; together they demonstrated in the 1850s what the Mexico–United States border does today. Under these circumstances the state can harass and slow laborers crossing its frontiers, but it cannot stop them.

The failure to block the border migrations also challenges our understanding of the boundaries between aboriginal people and immigrants, historically characterized according to the savage-civilized dichotomy. When the northern migrants to Puget Sound are mentioned in the press or by historians, they have been typically described not as migrant laborers but as savage raiders who were threats to the settlers.[68] The evidence of savagery is their slave-taking, but it is not usually acknowledged in these same sources that until 1865 the United States also allowed slavery. Their practice of taking the heads of their victims as trophies is cited without noting that in the wars against aboriginal people in Washington and elsewhere, the U.S. government encouraged its soldiers and allies to take the heads of its enemies, paying a bounty for them, or that U.S. troops were guilty of many other kinds of mutilation beyond decapitation.[69]

The distinction between "settler" and "savage" also collapses as it becomes apparent that many northern aboriginal people were also settlers. They married or had long-term relationships with Euro-American men, had families, and over time became integrated into settler societies. The best documented examples of this are on the San Juan Islands, but scattered throughout the journals, newspapers, and contemporary reports are mentions of significant populations of northern women married to immigrants at Fort Nisqually, Steilacoom, Port Townsend, Port Gamble, and the farms in between.[70] Although the rhetoric of the newspapers and government officials characterized the Northern Indians as fiends who "delight in war, rapine and murder," it seems clear that most settlers knew some of the thousands of Northern Indians who visited and lived in Puget Sound either as coworkers, employees, neighbors, or partners in sexual, common-law, or marital relationships.

An examination of these canoe-borne migrants from the North also shows the permeability of another border—the one between capitalist and aboriginal economies—and the continuing need for stereoscopic vision. Aboriginal people were able to use the new wage-work and sex-for-pay economy of the settlers to expand their long-standing prestige economy. Individual aboriginal men and women used the opportunities in settler society to raise their status in their own societies, and so wove the two economies together. In their demand for resources, labor, and for sexual partners, the settlers' economy was also linked to the aboriginal slave-raiding economy. This pattern reinforced the aboriginal prestige economy as it siphoned aboriginal people off for increasing periods into a capitalist economy.

As the historian Sarah Deutsch points out, capitalism is a social as well as an economic system that stands for private property, individualism, Protestantism, and Anglo-Saxonism.[71] Participation in this social system was also transformative, as aboriginal people were offered choices that undermined their own cultural economy and were constantly judged negatively by the measures of capitalism. By the late nineteenth century the continuing expansion of the capitalist system along with laws and regulations banning the potlatch, plus concerted attempts by missionaries and government agents, did undermine the prestige economy but never entirely supplanted it. In the communities of the so-called Northern Indians the prestige economy remained intertwined with the immigrant economy through the remainder of the nineteenth and throughout the twentieth centuries.

NOTES

1. The 1871 nonaboriginal population of British Columbia was approximately 10,000, while Washington and Oregon had a combined population of 115,000. British Columbia, Blue Books, reprinted in *Census of Canada, 1881*; U.S. Bureau of Census, *Historical Statistics of the United States* (Washington, D.C.: Government Printing Office, 1976).

2. This was particularly true of those peoples who lived north of Nanaimo, the most northerly of the coastal immigrant urban centers, one-third of the way up Vancouver Island. Beyond this, the Euro-Canadian and Russian presence was limited to a handful of trading posts and a few missions.

3. Canadian Parliament, *Sessional Papers*, 1886, vol. 4, pp. 81, 84.

4. The problems of sources are discussed in Leland Donald, *Aboriginal Slavery on the Northwest Coast of America* (Berkeley: University of California Press, 1997), p. 121; and in John Lutz, "Work, Wages, and Welfare in Aboriginal—Non-Aboriginal Relations in British Columbia, 1849–1970," Ph.D. dissertation, University of Ottawa, 1994, chapter 1.

5. Moreover, the few Euro-American records that capture migrant movement are scattered in archives across an international border that has proved to be more of an obstacle to researchers than to the aboriginal migrants themselves.

6. Robin Fisher, *Contact and Conflict: Indian-European Relations in British Columbia, 1774–1890* (Vancouver: UBC Press, 1992); Rolf Knight, *Indians at Work: An*

Informal History of Native Labour in British Columbia, 1858–1930 (Vancouver, B.C.: New Star Books, 1996); Robert Ruby and John Brown, *The Chinook Indians: Traders of the Lower Columbia River* (Norman: University of Oklahoma Press, 1976). More recent work stressing resistance includes Paul Tennant, *Aboriginal Peoples and Politics: The Indian Land Question in British Columbia, 1849–1989* (Vancouver: UBC Press, 1992); Joanne Drake Terry, *The Same as Yesterday: The Lillooet Chronicle the Theft of Their Lands and Resources* (Lillooet, B.C.: Lillooet Tribal Council, 1989).

7. A recent book that takes a nuanced look at this period and challenges the conventional terms separating *Indian* and *settler* is Alexandra Harmon, *Indians in the Making: Ethnic Relations and Indian Identities around Puget Sound* (Berkeley: University of California Press, 1998); see also Jean Barman, "What a Difference a Border Makes: Aboriginal Racial Intermixture in the Pacific Northwest," *Journal of the West* 38 (July 1999): 14–20.

8. I. L. Buchanan, "Lumbering and Logging in the Puget Sound Region in Territorial Days," *Pacific Northwest Quarterly* 27 (January 1936): 35–37.

9. U.S. Senate Exec. Doc., 32d Cong., 1st sess., No. 613, Report of the Commissioner of Indian Affairs, 1851, p. 265; Henry Yesler employed them in his sawmill at Seattle; the Bellingham Bay mines employed other aboriginal people. A settlement called "Boston" grew up on the spit opposite the Pope and Talbot Mill at Port Gamble to house the local aboriginal employees. For Port Gamble, see E. E. Liddel in Pope and Talbot Papers, University of Washington Archives Acc. 1744, File: v f 715; for the Yesler mill, see J. A. Eckrom, *Remembered Drums: A History of the Puget Sound Indian War* (Walla Walla, Wash.: Pioneer Press Books, 1989), p. 86.

10. See James Gibson, "The Russian Contract: The Agreement of 1838 between the Hudson's Bay and Russian American Companies," in Richard A. Pierce, ed., *Russia in North America* (Kingston, Ont.: Limestone Press, 1990), pp. 157–80.

11. For a fuller description, see Lutz, "Work, Wages, and Welfare," chapter 3.

12. The forts were still in use in the 1840s, when the Reverend Jean B. Z. Bolduc described examples at Cadboro Bay near where Fort Victoria was built, and on Whidbey Island where Charles Wilkes described a Skagit fort. When the raids into Puget Sound commenced is uncertain. Charles Wilkes, *Narrative of the United States Exploring Expedition, during the Years 1838–42* (Philadelphia: Lea and Blanchard, 1845), p. 481; Jean B. Z. Bolduc, *Mission of the Columbia*, trans. Edward J. Kowrich (1843; reprint, Fairfield, Wash.: Ye Galleon Press, 1979), p. 107; for more on aboriginal forts, see Madonna Moss and Jon Erlandson, "Forts, Refuge Rocks, and Defensive Sites: The Antiquity of Warfare along the North Pacific Coast of America," *Arctic Anthropology* 29, no. 2 (1992): 73–90.

13. The Lekwiltok also may have escaped the smallpox epidemic of the 1780s that debilitated their southern neighbors. See Robert Galois, *Kwakwaka'wakw Settlements,*

1775–1920 (Vancouver: UBC Press, 1994), pp. 55, 223, 234–35; William Elmendorf, *Twana Narratives: Native Historical Accounts of Coast Salish Culture* (Seattle: University of Washington Press; Vancouver: UBC Press, 1993), pp. 145–53; Report of E. C. Fitzhugh, Special Indian Agent, Bellingham Bay, in U.S. Department of the Interior, *Annual Report of the Commissioner of Indian Affairs, November 30, 1857* (Washington, D.C.: Government Printing Office, 1858).

14. See, for example, the Kwakwaka'wakw raid on the Lummis recounted in the *Victoria Colonist*, April 23, 1864.

15. Knight, *Indians at Work*; Alice Littlefield and Martha Knack, *Native Americans and Wage Labor: Ethnohistorical Perspectives* (Norman: University of Oklahoma Press, 1996); John Lutz, "After the Fur Trade: The Aboriginal Labouring Class of British Columbia, 1849–1890," *Journal of the Canadian Historical Association*, n.s. 2 (1992): 69–94; Victoria Wyatt, "Alaskan Indian Wage Earners in the Nineteenth Century: Economic Choices and Ethnic Identity on Southeast Alaska's Frontier," *Pacific Northwest Quarterly* 78 (January–April 1987): 43–49.

16. Harmon, *Indians in the Making*, p. 35.

17. "Potlatch" is a Chinook jargon word for a variety of ceremonies among West Coast aboriginal people. Although all the West Coast nations held potlatches, the nature of the events that comprised a potlatch and the occasions when they were held varied widely. For the Straits Salish, for example, potlatches were held periodically to mark significant events, particularly marriage. Among the Tlingit, Tsimshian, and Haida memorial potlatches to honor the dead and pass on their wealth were the most important. Potlatches might also be held to wipe away shame brought on by oneself or one's family.

18. There is an enormous ethnographic literature on the potlatch; a good bibliography can be found in Douglas Cole and Ira Chaikin, *An Iron Hand upon the People: The Law against the Potlatch on the Northwest Coast* (Vancouver, B.C.: Douglas and McIntyre, 1990), pp. 213–23.

19. Some items like dentalia shells (*haiqua*) and obsidian blades traveled great distances through trading networks, but the numbers of such items were small compared with the postcontact period.

20. The fullest description of this is in Donald, *Aboriginal Slavery*. See also Ruby and Brown, *Indian Slavery*.

21. A concise and recent description of the coastal rounds of the Tsimshian and the incorporation of wage labor into these rounds can be found in Robert Galois, "Colonial Encounters: The Worlds of Arthur Wellington Clah, 1855–1881," *BC Studies* 115–16 (autumn–winter 1997–98): 105–47.

22. Theodore Winthrop, *The Canoe and Saddle, or Klalam and Klickatat: To Which Are Now First Added His Western Letters and Journals* (Tacoma, Wash.: John H.

Williams, 1913), p. 207. Winthrop notes that all Northern Indians were called Haida by whites at this time.

23. Colonial Office, Original Correspondence, Vancouver Island, 1846–1867, (CO) 305/7, James Douglas to Sir George Grey, March 1, 1856, 3969, CO 305/7, p. 5, and April 10, 1856, 5814, p. 25. Governor James Douglas occasionally mentions individual nations like the Haida and the Tsimshian but generally refers to them in his dispatches as Northern Indians. For a fuller description of this migration, see Lutz, "Work, Wages, and Welfare," chapters 3–4.

24. James Douglas to Duke of Newcastle, October 24, 1853, CO 305/4, 12345.

25. Robert C. Hill, "The Murder of Colonel Ebey," in U.S. Public Works Administration, *Told by the Pioneers*, vol. 2 (Olympia, Wash.: Public Works Administration, 1938), pp. 15–17.

26. J. P. Hicks, ed., *From Potlatch to Pulpit, Being the Autobiography of the Rev. William Henry Pierce* (Vancouver, B.C.: Vancouver Bindery, 1933), p. 15; June Collins, "John Fornsby: The Personal Document of a Coast Salish Indian," in Marian Smith, ed., *Indians of the Urban Northwest* (New York: Columbia University Press, 1949), p. 301; Clellan Ford, *Smoke from Their Fires: The Life of a Kwakiutl Chief* (1941; reprint, Hamden, Conn.: Archon Books, 1968), p. 134; Galois, "Colonial Encounters."

27. In rare circumstances it was used by Americans to refer to all Indians living north of the forty-ninth parallel; see Governor Fayette McMullin to President James Buchanan, October 20, 1857, cited in "Defending Puget Sound against the Northern Indians," *Pacific Northwest Quarterly* 36 (January 1945): 75.

28. James Gilchrist Swan, *Almost Out of This World* (Tacoma: Washington State Historical Society, 1971), p. 98; Swan, "The Haidah Indians of Queen Charlottes Islands, British Columbia," *Smithsonian Contributions to Knowledge* 21 (1876): 14.

29. James G. Swan, "The Northern Indians," *San Francisco Evening Bulletin*, October 4, 1860; *Puget Sound Courier*, May 31, November 11, and December 7, 1855; (Olympia) *Pioneer and Democrat*, June 24, 1854.

30. For more on the fur trade, see Sylvia Van Kirk, *"Many Tender Ties": Women in Fur-Trade Society in Western Canada, 1670–1870* (Winnipeg, Man.: Watson & Dwyer, 1980); for the settler period, see Alexandra Harmon, "Lines in the Sand: Shifting Boundaries between Indians and Non-Indians in the Puget Sound Region," *Western Historical Quarterly* 26 (winter 1995): 429–53; and Karen Jones-Lamb, *Native American Wives of San Juan Settlers* (Decatur Island, Wash.: Bryn Tirion Publishing, 1994). Jean Barman estimates that in British Columbia one in ten aboriginal women married or cohabitated with nonaboriginal men in "Taming Aboriginal Sexuality: Gender, Power, and Race in BC," *BC Studies* 115–16 (autumn–winter 1997–98): 248, and "What a Difference a Border Makes"; from the 1840s through the 1860s I would judge the percentage to be much higher in Puget Sound.

31. William A. Peck, *The Pig War*, ed. C. B. Coulter and B. Webber (Medford, Oreg.: Webb Research Group, 1993), p. 105; U.S. Department of the Interior, *Annual Report of the Commissioner of Indian Affairs*, R.H. Milroy, Superintendent of Indian Affairs, Washington Territory, 1873.

32. Hicks, *From Potlatch to Pulpit*, p. 15; repelled by the drinking, Pierce started holding a service on Sunday and founded a temperance society. For conditions of work in a similar mill at a similar time, see Morley Roberts, *The Western Avernus; or, Toil and Travel in Further North America* (London: Smith, Elder, and Company, 1887), pp. 181–82.

33. "The Kwakiutl had a potential demand for European goods in excess of any practical utility the goods might have possessed. This can be seen both as a stimulus to the Kwakiutl integration in their new economy and as a direct stimulus to the potlatch." Helen Codere, *Fighting with Property: A Study of Kwakiutl Potlatching and Warfare* (Seattle, Wash.: University of Washington Press, 1972), p. 126.

34. George Blenkinsop, Indian agent, and Rev. A. J. Hall, cited in George Mercer Dawson, "Notes and Observations on the Kwakiool People of Vancouver Island and Adjacent Coasts made during the Summer of 1885," *Transactions of the Royal Society of Canada*, Section 2 (1887), p. 17; another reason for the increase in potlatching was the many deaths from disease and raiding, which required memorial potlatches.

35. Albert P. Niblack, *The Coast Indians of Southern Alaska and Northern British Columbia* (1888; reprint, New York: Johnson Reprint Corporation, 1970), pp. 338, 346–47; NAC, CMS c.2./o Appendix C, Reel A-105; William Duncan, First Report Fort Simpson, February 1858; J. A. Jacobsen, *Alaskan Voyage, 1881–83: An Expedition to the Northwest Coast of America,* translated from the German text of Adrian Woldt by Erna Gunther (Chicago: University of Chicago Press, 1977), pp. 8–9; Harmon, *Indians in the Making,* p. 101.

36. An 1892 account of an aboriginal sawmill worker in Puget Sound holding a potlatch and giving away all of his earnings of several years can be found in F. I. Vassault, "Patsy's Potlatch," *Overland Monthly*, ser. 2, vol. 19 (May 1892): 461–64; see also Lutz, "Work, Wages, and Welfare," chapter 3.

37. Rev. C. M. Tate, "Thrilling Story of Missionary Adventure and Success: An Autobiographical Sketch of Nearly Sixty Years Labor among Indian Tribes of B.C.," *The Western Recorder* 5 (September 1929); I. W. Powell, National Archives of Canada, RG 10, vol. 11213; Jacobsen, *Alaskan Voyage*, pp. 18–19, 23.

38. Church Missionary Society, William Duncan to Rev. H. Venn, Secretary of the Committee of the C.M.S. February 1858, c.2./o Appendix C. Micro A 105.

39. Swan, *San Francisco Evening Bulletin*, October 4, 1860.

40. Moss and Erlandson, "Forts, Rock Refuges. . . ."; for Haida stories about their raiding, see Carol Eastman and Elizabeth Edwards, *Gyaehlingaay: Traditions, Tales,*

and Images of the Kaigani Haida (Seattle: Burke Museum of Natural History and Culture, 1991), pp. 19, 67–77; for Tsimshian stories of Tlingit and Tsimshian raiding, see George MacDonald and John Cove, eds., *Tsimshian Narratives 2* (Ottawa: National Museums of Canada, 1987); for Kwakwaka'wakw, see Galois, *Kwakwaka'wakw Settlement,* pp. 45, 58–59.

41. *Pioneer and Democrat,* December 10, 17, 24, 1854; and December 12, 1856, p. 2.

42. Report of the Commissioner of Indian Affairs, "Report of E. C. Fitzhugh, Special Indian Agent," November 11, 1857, p. 327; there were other reasons for population decline, see Robert Boyd, "Demographic History, 1774–1874," *Handbook of North American Indians,* vol. 7, *The Northwest Coast,* ed. Wayne Suttles (Washington, D.C.: Smithsonian Institution Press, 1990), pp. 135–48.

43. *Pioneer and Democrat,* May 15, and July 24, 1857; *Puget Sound Herald,* March 19 and June 18, 1858; Robert H. Ruby and John A. Brown, *A Guide to Indian Tribes of the Pacific Northwest* (Norman: University of Oklahoma, 1992), p 228; *Port Townsend Register,* May 30, 1860.

44. (Victoria) *Colonist,* April 23, 1864.

45. Church Missionary Society, William Duncan to Rev. H. Venn, Secretary of the Committee of the c.m.s., October 6, 1857, c.2./o Appendix c. Micro A 105.

46. Nora Marks Dauenhauer and Richard Dauenhauer, eds., *Haa Kusteeyi, Our Culture: Tlingit Life Stories* (Seattle: University of Washington Press, 1994), pp. 469–70.

47. Donald Mitchell and Leland Donald, "Some Economic Aspects of Tlingit, Haida, and Tsimshian Slavery," *Research in Economic Anthropology 7* (1985): 19–35.

48. Donald, in *Aboriginal Slavery,* p. 237, reports the persistence of slavery into the 1880s.

49. Mitchell and Donald, "Some Economic Aspects," pp. 22–23.

50. There were violent attacks on whites, which involved the death of nineteen whites between 1846 and 1866, but all were specific retaliatory attacks for earlier murders by whites of Northern Indians. See John Lutz, "When Is an 'Indian War' Not a War? Canadian Indians and American Settlers in the Pacific Northwest, 1850s-1860s," *Journal of the West* 38 (July 1998): 7–13.

51. *Port Townsend Register,* July 26, 1860; *Pioneer and Democrat,* August 3, 1860.

52. James Swan, "Smith's Lighthouse Excitement," *San Francisco Bulletin,* October 4, 1860.

53. R. C. Fay to I. I. Stevens, April 31, 1877, *Records of the Washington Superintendency of Indian Affairs,* Mic, A -171, No. 10, Roll 22; thanks to Alexandra Harmon for this reference.

54. *Puget Sound Courier,* December 11, 1855; M. T. Simmons to I. I. Stevens, May 1, 1857, *Records of the Washington Superintendency of Indian Affairs,* Mic, A-171, Roll 9, Reel 17; thanks to Alexandra Harmon for this reference.

55. Articles XII and XIII, "Point No Point Treaty," published in Gerry Gorsline, ed., *Shadows of Our Ancestors* (Port Townsend, Wash.: Empty Bowl, 1992), p. 50.

56. *Pioneer and Democrat*, January 23, 1857.

57. Washington Territory, *Laws of Washington Territory* (Olympia, 1866), p. 26.

58. James Swan, *San Francisco Evening Bulletin*, October 4, 1860. Although it was not raised, the law was also in violation of Jay's Treaty between the United States and Great Britain; see Elizabeth C. Duran and James Duran Jr., "Indian Rights in the Jay Treaty," *Indian Historian* 6 (winter 1973): 33–37.

59. For more details on Ebey's death and the settlers' fears, see Lutz, "When Is an 'Indian War' Not a War?," pp. 7–13.

60. Church Missionary Society, William Duncan to Rev. H. Venn, secretary of the Committee of the C.M.S. October 6, 1857, C.2./0 Appendix C. Micro A 105.

61. *Pioneer and Democrat*, June 10, 1859, p. 2.

62. *Pioneer and Democrat*, May 18, 1860, p. 2.

63. (Port Townsend) *Register*, May 30, 1860.

64. Barry Gough, *Gunboat Frontier: British Maritime Authority and Northwest Coast Indians, 1846–90* (Vancouver: University of British Columbia Press, 1984); Donald, *Aboriginal Slavery*, pp. 238–45; R. C. Mayne, *Four Years in British Columbia and Vancouver Island* (London: John Murray, 1862), pp. 208–10.

65. (Port Townsend) *Register*, May 30, 1860; Diary of James Swan, University of Washington Archives, Seattle, May 27 and 29, 1860; C. S. King, Indian Agent to T. J. McKenney, Wash. Supt. Indian Affairs, October 7, 1868, Records of the Washington Superintendency of Indian Affairs, No. 5, Roll 13; British Columbia Archives, Colonial Correspondence; File: F347 26a, James Cooper to James Douglas, October 10, 1860; United States, *Report of the Commissioner of Indian Affairs*, Report of T. J. McKenney, Superintendent, W. T., 1869.

66. Cooper to Douglas, October 10, 1860; Mayne, *Four Years in British Columbia*, pp. 208–10.

67. See, for example, in October 27, 1858, George Moffat at Fort Rupert noting that "Quacquilths have made war on several tribes lately. . . . their wish to obtain slaves to sell to the Southern Indians is the cause." Moffat to Board of Management, in Fort Rupert Correspondence Out, British Columbia Archives, A/B/20/ R2.

68. More recent works, including that by Harmon, "Lines in the Sand," and her *Indians in the Making*, as well as that by Drew W. Crooks, "Murder at Butler Cove: The Death of Tsus-sy-uch and Its Violent Consequences," *Occurrences* 14 (winter 1996–97): 3–12, take a more sophisticated look.

69. See Richard White, *"It's Your Misfortune and None of My Own": A History of*

the *American West* (Norman: University of Oklahoma Press, 1993), p. 101; H. H. Jackson, *A Little War of Destiny: The First Regiment of Oregon Mounted Volunteers and the Yakima Indian War of 1855–56* (Fairfield, Wash.: Ye Galleon Press, 1996); H. H. Bancroft, *History of Washington, Idaho, and Montana* (San Francisco: History Company, 1890), p. 134.

70. For intermarriage at Nisqually, see Crooks, "Murder at Butler Cove"; on the San Juan Islands, see Jones-Lamb, *Native American Wives*; for Steilacoom, see "Report of M. T. Simmons, Indian Agent Puget Sound," *Report of the Commissioner of Indian Affairs,* November 30, 1857; for Port Townsend, see *Pioneer and Democrat,* June 10, 1859, p. 2; for the southern Puget Sound area, see June Collins, "John Fornsby: The Personal Document of a Coast Salish Indian," in Marian Smith, ed., *Indians of the Urban Northwest* (New York: Columbia University Press, 1949), pp. 287–341.

71. Sarah Deutsch, "Landscape of Enclaves: Race Relations in the American West," in William Cronon, Jay Gitlin, and George Miles, eds., *Under an Open Sky: Rethinking America's Western Past* (New York: W. W. Norton, 1992), p. 113.

4 / Borders and Identities among Italian Immigrants in the Pacific Northwest, 1880–1938

PATRICIA K. WOOD

When we discuss Canadian-American relations, we make several assumptions: we recognize the existence of two political nation-states, Canada and the United States, whose governments and citizens "relate" or "related" to each other and thus recognized each other as "Canadians" and "Americans." We also assume the existence and recognition of a border that separates the nations and the peoples, that they relate to each other from specific and different places that are divided by an important line. Such assumptions are quite basic and we make them comfortably, but they are located in a specific understanding of North American political geography, one that was not shared by all those living in the Pacific Northwest around the turn of the century. My research into the development of national and ethnic identities among Italian immigrants in western Canada led me to new considerations of the border and its implications in identity formation. The American border was not a meaningful line to Italian immigrants nor, I suspect, to other immigrant groups and perhaps Natives as well, for reasons I shall make clear in this chapter.

It is and has been principally English Canadians who have viewed the border as significant and indicative of difference. In his work *A Border Within: National Identity, Cultural Plurality, and Wilderness*, the sociologist Ian Angus argues that "the philosophical theme of the border" is "the core of the issue of English Canadian identity."[1] Indeed, Angus theorizes that other distinctions in English-Canadian thought are rooted in the preoccupation with the forty-ninth parallel. He writes: "All concern with English Canadian identity, formulated abstractly, is engaged in maintaining a *border* between us and the United States. I thus take the border as the leading metaphor for this work and suggest that it can also be seen as a border between self and other and between humanity and nature."[2] Frequently described as simply "Canadian," the Anglo-Canadian image of the United States has been central to the creation of the dominant nationalist ideology. Historically, politicians, scholars, and citizens alike have underscored those characteristics that distinguish two nations and emphasized tensions between them.

The scholarship on Canadian-American relations has largely been predicated on the understanding of Canada and the border that Angus describes. In the introduction and chapter overviews of his collection *Partners Nevertheless: Canadian-American Relations in the Twentieth Century*, Norman Hillmer frequently employs blanket statements such as "A legacy of distrust and suspicion of the United States was every Canadian's inheritance," asserting even that "history has made Canada and the United States anything but friends." Hillmer's concern with power relationships begins and ends with the discrepancy between the two nations' governments in relation to one another.[3] Similarly, in J. L. Granatstein and Robert Cuff's *The Ties That Bind: Canadian-American Relations from the Great War to the Cold War* and Granatstein and Hillmer's *For Better or For Worse: Canada and the United States to the 1990s*, the emphasis is placed on the tensions between the two governments over boundaries, trade, fishing rights, and the like, and the ways in which Canadian government and business have been disadvantaged by their more powerful U.S. counterparts.[4]

The historians John Herd Thompson and Stephen J. Randall's recent *Canada and the United States: Ambivalent Allies* is more nuanced, however. The authors attempt to look beyond the large-scale political and economic relations and to incorporate other aspects and levels of Canadian-American relations, such as the cultural and the local. In particular, these two scholars do the best job of addressing the constructed nature of nations and their degrees of relevance to different people. In their discussion of the West in the late nineteenth century, Thompson and Randall make the point clearly that there were different ways of understanding the border: "But this western boundary [between Canada and the United States] existed only in a diplomatic sense; in terms of human and economic geography, national perimeters remained undefined. The Great Plains and the mountain ranges were oblivious to the political ambitions of men and women."[5] Unfortunately for my purposes here, Thompson and Randall stop at this point, providing no details of these women and men nor their perceptions of the border and the nations it delineated.

There is now a strong consensus regarding the constructed nature of nations: there is no such thing as an objective "Canada" that exists independently of our imposition of meaning into that geographic space. The importance of political geography and its ability to create and enforce the meaning and integrity of national borders notwithstanding, such borders have not held the same relevance to everyone. By looking at one group's experience of the Canadian-American border, I argue that one's perspective of the border changes with one's position of power. Even international borders, with which everyone encountering them must reckon, are most important to those whose power relies in some way on these borders.

What political geography delineates is *territory*; this is not the only way in which to understand the physical or the human landscape, however. Territory is to land what race is to human beings: it is a way of categorizing that presupposes ownership or control. Those who are able to view land as territory are situated in a position of power whereby they feel able to defend their ability to maintain their current relationship to that land. The borders that demarcate territory thus mark the limits of power. The same borders also indicate an "other" whose territory implicitly prevents the extension of one's power. It was with such an imperialist mind-set that the Canadian and U.S. governments "settled" the western half of the North American continent, expanding their nations' borders. The land was seen as territory: to be bought, traded, or conquered and brought under the control of what were in practice empires but were called nations. The competition between the governments and businesses of the United States and Canada was fierce, and both sides associated territorial expansion with an enhancement of their power.

We study international relations, such as those between Canada and the United States, from a similar perspective. We recognize nations as territories with states that wield power. In particular, we do not properly divorce the state from the nation or, more specifically, the citizenry, as evidenced in Hillmer's assertions about "every Canadian's inheritance." Although we are occasionally able to acknowledge the exclusion of a particular group or groups from power within a study of the nation, such details are marginalized or erased in international relations. Our discussions of nations as actors accord the political geography legitimacy, especially legitimacy of representation. Here the state equals the nation, thereby creating a public national identity representing only those in power and their interests. The concern is not merely the workings of politics, but the reproduction of political and social hierarchies in academic literature.

So my question remains: What about people on the margins? What about people who inhabit a place without the ability to impose their will on it? It follows that without a social, political, or financial investment in territory, such persons will attach themselves to their place of residence in a different way. They will identify themselves with the symbols and rhetoric of the dominant national identity to varying degrees—or not at all. While not diminishing their capacity to recognize and understand the practical aspects of national borders, they may not find those political borders to be meaningful cultural borders. For these people the border is not an encroachment on their power; it represents instead the power of others with whom they are unlikely to identify. They may live in Canada or the United States, may even be citizens of those places, yet not identify themselves as "Canadians" or "Americans." Or they may in fact take up those identities, but in a manner quite distinct from the dominant ideology, in a way that also does not accord great significance to the border.

Italian immigrants who came to western Canada in the late nineteenth and early twentieth centuries rarely ascended to the top of social, economic, or political hierarchies. Their experience of Canada was one of marginality. These people were marginalized in terms of class, ethnicity/race, religion, and language from the moment they set foot in Canada. Their journey to the country's westernmost reaches led them to areas that were at best in the process of urbanization but were more commonly remote with few services. Their connections to the society around them were immediately hindered by their inability to communicate well in English and by the discrimination they faced as Southern Europeans, as Catholics, and as physical laborers with no job security or insurance. Their places of residence were segregated from other class and ethnic/racial groups, even in the smallest of mining towns. They were people with few or no resources outside of the Italian (or, even more narrow, regional) community. They were people who fled desperate places for those that were only slightly less desperate.

Italian immigrants in the nineteenth century, like many other immigrants of the same period, came to North America looking for work. Most were agricultural peasants or small-town working-class people and possessed few industrial skills. They came from many *paesi* (regions), north and south, and began immigrating to western Canada in the late nineteenth century. Some Italian immigrants hoped for gold in the Fraser Valley, but most made their fortunes much more slowly working in the mines or on the Canadian Pacific Railway.

Throughout the twentieth century, Italians found work and settled all over Alberta and British Columbia, with significant populations in Edmonton, Calgary, Coleman, Nordegg, Drumheller, Lethbridge, and Barrhead in Alberta; and in Vancouver, Trail, Rossland, Kamloops, Revelstoke, Powell River, Duncan, Port Alberni, and Nanaimo in British Columbia. Italians followed many different paths to the West: some came directly; others first spent time in eastern Canada or the United States.[6]

The Italians' initial perception of Canada was partly shaped by their expectations and motivations for emigrating. More than twenty years of violence had created the modern nation-state of Italy, pitting classes and cultures against one another as the urban middle class and the rural landowners of the north gained more political power and the former landholdings of the church, while southerners and peasants of all regions were ignored or forcefully suppressed.[7] Opportunities dwindled both in the forgotten South and in the North, where peasants were pressured off their land to become an industrial labor pool. Despite any legal or political status Italy may have had at this time, it was not a nation in any meaningful sense that these people left behind them. It was home, but it no longer had much to offer them.

By contrast, the New World—from Australia to Argentina to America—held the promise of opportunity. And in the nineteenth century the New World was simply the New World. Prospective Italian migrants made few distinctions between Canada and the United States.[8] Despite the high politicization of the border by Canadian and U.S. politicians, there was little difference to Italians. Both Canada and the United States were *"l'America."* Where there was work was home. Even on a legal document drawn up at the Italian Royal Consulate in San Francisco in 1884, a deceased miner was described as living *"nella Colombia, America del Nord."*[9] The specifics of one nation as opposed to the other were immaterial to any person or state who had few investments in that difference. What did it matter, to immigrants or their governments, which part of North America it was, as long as they could find who or what they were looking for? The political geography of the New World was important to the extent that it served as a device for location.

The region these immigrants came to was undergoing a rapid transformation at the turn of the century. In the space of a generation, small-scale agriculture and remote trading posts gave way to industrial capitalism and booming cities. Alberta and British Columbia were expanding resource-based economies and most of the available employment was in mining or city and railway construction.[10] The conditions and locations of employment, in the broader ideological context of Anglo-Canadian empire building, created an experience and a related image of Canada that came to define both the ethnic and national identities of Italians in the earliest days of settlement. As the context of their settlement is central to my argument, a brief description of the places Italians settled and the formation of communities from very small numbers is warranted here.

Italians began arriving in Victoria on Vancouver Island in the 1860s, venturing from there to the interior along the Fraser Valley in search of gold. Before Confederation, much of the region had been administered by the Hudson's Bay Company, which discouraged settlement, only opening its doors under duress for the gold rush in 1858. In the 1870s coal mining was under way all over the island, and many Italians accepted the offer of a regular paycheck. By 1910 there were only thirty or forty Italians in Victoria, mostly merchants, but there were more than ten times that number in the mines at Wellington and Extension, near Nanaimo, plus a "'strong nucleus' of Piedmontese" mining in nearby Ladysmith.[11] There was also a significant community sixty miles up the coast from Nanaimo in Cumberland, where the Dunsmuirs' Canadian Collieries had additional shafts.[12]

Before the turn of the century, few Italians settled in the Vancouver area. At that time, of a total population of around twenty-seven thousand, there were only about one hundred Italians, "engaged mainly as artisans."[13] The city itself got off to a rocky start. Originally a sawmill camp, it was incorporated as a city in 1886 and "blossomed from village to city within a few months." A good portion of it was destroyed by fire that same year, but the Canadian Pacific Railway was within moments of reaching the Pacific and the city expanded in anticipation. In the 1890s Victoria was hard-hit by depression and began deindustrializing, but Vancouver met the new century in full force. By 1911, Vancouver's population had risen to 100,401, more than a 270 percent increase over the previous decade.[14] Italian immigration to the city more than matched that pace. By the time the traveler Amy Bernardy visited in 1910, fifteen hundred Italians, mostly Calabrese and Venetian, were employed in manual labor in Vancouver. By the following year, the population of this Italian community may have been as high as five thousand or six thousand, including sojourners. The community was even large enough to merit the services of an Italian vice consul, Augustino Ferrera.[15] Italians were also finding work, mainly "brute labour," a little further up the coast, in the pulp and paper mills at the company town of Powell River, established in 1909.

The Italians, like other working-class immigrants, tended to gather in the East End of Vancouver, along Burrard Inlet. A 1913 survey, which did not count the Japanese or the Chinese, found "forty-two different peoples," fewer than

half of whom had been born in Canada. The more transient stayed in room-
ing houses; those with families and more stable employment lived in over-
crowded, "dirty but sanitary" houses in what Bernardy described as the "most
rundown [area] of the city." As three-quarters of these Italians were single
men on their own, they often boarded with other families.[16] Public life in most
cities and towns in the West was multicultural, especially for the working
class.[17] Although their closest friends were likely Italian, as miners, navvies,
and construction workers they mixed with coworkers of all backgrounds, picking up English and sometimes other languages. For example, when Mario
Grassi arrived in Calgary in 1910, a young black man who worked with his
cousins met Grassi at the station and greeted him in his own dialect.[18] As much
as immigrant groups settled with fellow countrymen, they also had to share
the poorer areas of town with other recent arrivals.

Trail, in southeast British Columbia, was another popular destination for
early Italian migrants who came to work for the Consolidated Mining and
Smelting Company of Canada (Cominco), of whose shares the Canadian
Pacific Railway held better than 50 percent. With an agreement with the Crow's
Nest Pass Coal Company for a supply of coal, Cominco emerged as the area's
largest employer in mining and smelting. The company attracted a large number of Italians, which made it a relatively comfortable place for them to live
and work. On the job there were usually many other Italians in the gang; in
1919, Cominco even had one night shift of fifty men composed entirely of
Italians.[19]

Other smaller towns in British Columbia's Kootenay Mountains also provided employment for Italians. There was mining in nearby Rossland (six miles
from Trail), as well as in Revelstoke, about two hundred miles north into the
interior, and Fernie to the east, near the Alberta border. By 1910, according
to Bernardy, there were between six hundred and one thousand Italians in
Fernie, and according to the 1911 census, they were 10 percent of the town's
population of 8,645. Just across the Alberta border, there were an additional
682 Italians in the mining towns and camps of the Crowsnest Pass region,
comprising 13.5 percent of those communities, 14.5 percent by 1919.[20]

What would immigrants have known of Canada or the United States before
arriving? What might their first impressions have been? Compared with Italy's
overpopulation (nearly three hundred people per square mile[21]), Canada must
have seemed not only the other end of the earth—and Vancouver its furthest
reaches—but also vast and empty beyond imagination. Italians traveled by
ship and then by train, gaining through such disorientation a real appreciation for how far away and how enormous Canada truly is. Leaving his native

Antrodoco in the mountains of central Italy at age 12, Mario Grassi spent fifteen days with his father on a freighter, which dropped them off in New York on April 15, 1910. After four days on a train, they stopped in Winnipeg, Manitoba, where the high piles of snow frightened the young Grassi. He was relieved a few days later by the milder climate of Calgary and no longer believed he would freeze to death.[22]

Some of the emigrants' journeys were more harrowing than others, no doubt contributing to the trauma and disorientation of the migration process. Henry Butti, coming in the midst of World War I from Milan, sailed with his mother and sister for twenty-four days aboard a small ship, the *Giuseppe Verdi*, from Genoa to New York. They could travel only during the day; at night, for fear of German submarines, all of the lights were turned out, the port-holes closed, and the engines stopped, "and you'd drift God-knows-where." Once ashore they journeyed an additional five or six days by train to western Canada to join Butti's father; during this time it was difficult even to get something to eat, as none of them spoke a word of English.[23] Not all immigrants were fortunate enough to have someone waiting for them, however. In June 1898, for example, Nicholas Palidore and thirty-one other Italians came to Montreal from Boston in response to advertisements by R. J. Eelbeck to work on the Crow's Nest Railway. They were given rail tickets, only to arrive in southeastern British Columbia to find no work for them anywhere. They walked for many miles, inquiring at all the camps. Hungry, the immigrants were finally given food and shelter at Fort Steele.[24]

What was most salient about this place to Italians, whatever their welcoming committee, was that it was *terra straniera*—foreign ground. Their consciousness of being immigrants initially overrode other attachments and identities.[25] Their neighborhoods, organizations, and socializing, even their charity work, were oriented toward making the adjustment to a new society. Even after many years in their new home, some immigrants still felt their most rewarded efforts were within the immigrant community and that the larger society would not welcome them. The differences between Canadian and U.S. societies were minute compared with the cultural barriers, especially linguistic, between the New and the Old Worlds.

This is not to say that the Italian immigrants did not know where they were. There were many ways in which Italians expressed their sense of location. However, these expressions emphasized the borders of their neighborhoods and communities, or explicitly acknowledged the New World, rather than focusing on Canada or the United States. Italians migrated to several different areas of the Canadian West and thus adjusted to a variety of cli-

mates, both physical and social. There were also differences in origin, as well
as destination, and all of these affected the subsequent ethnic community
organization. The communities with significant Italian populations organized themselves in some fashion to maintain their ethnic culture as they relocated themselves in new landscapes. The first way they did this was through
the development and enrichment of Italian neighborhoods.

A combination of language difficulties, chain migration, and employment
circumstances (income and location) led many Italians to live close together.
This was true for even the smallest of mining towns. Like Vancouver's East
End, like Powell River's "other side of the dam," towns in the Crowsnest Pass
area had their "Dagotowns." Coleman, Alberta, was only a couple of streets
and a mess of shacks with only five or six houses, and not more than five or
six married women, but by 1913 immigrant Angelo Tappano ran a grocery
store in the part of town called "Italiantown."[26] In Trail the residential arrangements were similar to the working conditions in which Italians were frequently
grouped together. There the Italian community was large enough, with
enough families, to maintain its Italian language even publicly for more than
one generation. Italian was heard on the streets, where some Italians established small shops. For them British Columbia was not Italian, but their little corner was well-established and secure.[27] Communities developed beyond
casual social exchanges through the establishment of various associations and
institutions. The Italian community in the Nanaimo area, on Vancouver
Island, was the first in western Canada to establish a society of some kind,
the Italian Cavallotti Lodge, on November 4, 1900.[28] By 1905 the Vancouver
community had established a mutual aid organization, the Società Mutuo
Soccorso Figli d'Italia. In 1906 the Italians of Coleman's Italiantown organized a mutual aid society, Società Operaio di Mutuo Soccorso, to compensate for the fact that the mine provided no insurance of any kind.

By 1911 the Italians of Vancouver read an Italian-language newspaper,
L'Italia nel Canada. They had also founded a second club, the Società Veneta,
and that same year the Roman Catholic archbishop wrote to the Apostolic
Delegate in Ottawa to request an Italian parish in Vancouver.[29] The formation of a separate organization for Venetians suggests that the Figli d'Italia
was formed by the Calabrese, and that the two groups did not overlap. This
was the beginning of a phenomenon that would dominate Italian organization in Vancouver to the present day. Whereas in Toronto, as the historian John E. Zucchi has observed, an overarching identity as "Italians"
managed in some ways to supersede the regional identities, this was not the

case for Vancouver.[30] In Vancouver circumstances made the cultural and linguistic gap too large, and it has still not been bridged by other factors.

In 1918 the Italian families in Calgary formed the John Cabot Lodge, as part of the order that was headquartered in Fernie and had eight branches in British Columbia and Alberta (Calgary was the eighth). To "keep families together," the lodge held picnics and dances and brought in speakers, "prominent people from Calgary," such as the mayor.[31] Powell River established its benevolent society in 1924, later than the other communities, but its membership of three hundred reflected the growth of a "flourishing Italian enclave."[32] The Calgary community's organization honored Giovanni Caboto, the Italian explorer in the service of England, who was believed to be the first European to set foot on Canada in 1497. The Cristoforo Colombo Society of Trail recognized another explorer perhaps even more responsible for the opportunity of Italians to come to *l'America*. These two wanderers have little if anything to do with the actual political and constitutional (or even cultural) founding of either nation, however. The names of these lodges do not celebrate the specific nation that houses them. Nor have I discovered any societies in either country from this time that honored the likes of Sir John A. Macdonald or George Washington. Rather, the names acknowledge a more general recognition of being in the New World. These immigrants knew where they were, but the relevance of that "where" varied with circumstances.

In general, in the late nineteenth and early twentieth centuries the forty-ninth parallel was not a meaningful line for immigrants. Movement from one country to the other was common. For example, when Alfredo Montalbetti of Fernie died in 1924 and left his widow with three small children, she moved south to Eureka, California.[33] By the time a couple's children grew up and married, it was not unusual to find family members in each country, such as the Corsinis of Extension, British Columbia, whose three sons stayed in Extension, along with one daughter, while another daughter married and went to San Francisco and two others moved to Seattle.[34] When Giovanni Cavallero died in Fernie, three of his five brothers lived in the area. Of his remaining two brothers, one was still in Italy and the last was somewhere in the United States. In the early 1920s Frank Carosella mined in Fernie, his daughter married and moved to nearby Coleman, Alberta, but his oldest son enlisted in the U.S. Army.[35] It was the norm, rather than the exception, for these immigrant families to extend over the border. Obstacles to Italians' migration were related to cost and opportunity, not political beliefs.[36]

This view of the border as somewhat irrelevant was not a uniquely Italian perspective. Before the First World War migrant workers from many European countries crossed the Canada–United States border from coast to coast looking for work.[37] These foreign-born migrants were joined by the native-born, including aboriginal peoples: in 1910 there were 1,204,637 Canadian-born persons living in the United States, 115,781 of them in Montana, Idaho, and the states along the Pacific Coast.[38] These statistics confirm the observations of Thompson and Randall, among other scholars, that "in terms of human and economic geography, national perimeters remained undefined."[39] Certainly, national affinities were no more able to hold residents in search of better employment opportunities than they are today.

Italian immigrant workers, like many other immigrant workers, were a mobile group. Although mining companies frequently had bad years that threw many people temporarily out of work, immigrants themselves sometimes made the choice to leave. Those who had families with them and were looking for services such as churches and schools, often grew tired of the mining camps and moved on to small towns or cities. The turn of the century was a period of growth for western towns and cities, and migrant workers moved frequently in search of the next project. Despite their frequent changes of workplace, these laborers tended to specialize themselves and look for employment similar to what they had held before. For example, the pulp and paper mill town of Powell River, just up the coast from Vancouver, was established in 1909. Migrant construction workers helped to build the mill, but others came to take up the jobs inside the mill and settle their families in the area.

Italians were often pushed into moving on by the occasional economic distress that hit parts of the West. Unemployment due to shutdown or strike could move workers, as could more generalized depression or deindustrialization. For example, "one-quarter of Greater Vancouver's population" left the area after the "economic collapse" of 1913 through 1916.[40] Even workers with steady employment did not remain in one spot, given the nature of their work: many who lived in the cities of Vancouver, Calgary, and Edmonton, for example, only spent the winters there.[41] The other seasons were spent out on mining, railway construction, and farm work. Mobility stretched beyond provincial borders. As evidenced in the family networks mentioned earlier, Italian immigrants went south for work too. Going to the United States was no more of a foreign experience than wandering to other parts of the Canadian West. In fact, with the right connections, it could even be easier.

In addition to family networks, community networks extended into the United States as well. The mutual aid societies for Italian immigrants mentioned earlier are one such example. Mutual aid societies had a history in Italy, particularly in the South, where alienation from the government helped produce local societies to serve the communities.[42] A similar alienation from the government and other societal institutions was at work in the West. After 1916 the Coleman lodge joined the Federation of Columbia, which was headquartered in Pennsylvania, and later joined the Figli d'Italia, whose Grand Lodge was in New York City. These American associations had branches all over the United States and Canada, and before World War I the connections across the border were often stronger than across a country. Sometime after the war, after a larger Italian community had planted roots in the region, the Coleman lodge linked itself with its counterpart in nearby Fernie.

Migrant Italians also had cross-border connections in their labor unions. The United Mine Workers, to which many Italians belonged, was a transborder organization.[43] Unions did not replace mutual aid societies; rather, they were seen by the immigrants who joined as a complement to their community support. Such international organizations enabled workers to cross the border more easily without being taken advantage of as nonunionized employees. As one miner from British Columbia asserted, "There is no 49th parallel of latitude in Unionism. The Canadian and American workingmen have joined hands across the Boundary line for a common cause against a common enemy."[44] Despite a few exceptions that were not binational, such as the Western Federation of Miners, this phenomenon extended across Canada: in 1911 approximately 90 percent of Canadian unionized workers were members of international unions.[45]

Around the time of World War I, a more distinct sense of "Canadian-ness" emerged from the relatively general awareness of North America. There are many aspects to this, but I emphasize two points: first, that there were nevertheless some real obstacles for Italians to imagine themselves as Canadian or to publicly claim or participate in such an identity; and second, that the construction of a Canadian identity was not as preoccupied with the U.S. border as English-Canadian constructions were. In many ways this Canadian identity was North American Canadian, with a different understanding of the continent's political geography. The exclusionary nationalist strategies of the Anglo-Canadians from the earliest days of Italian immigration helped produce immigrant communities that were isolated both spatially and culturally. The opposition to Southern European immigrants, especially Catholics, rose significantly in the interwar period, particularly during the Depression. The most extreme manifestation of this discrimination would come with World War II. After Italy's alliance with the Axis Powers, the Canadian gov-

ernment interned approximately seven hundred Italian Canadians from coast to coast, and other community members were required to surrender firearms and report regularly to the RCMP. The RCMP also began a thorough surveillance of suspected fascist activities in the community.[46]

Following the turn of the century, Canada received record numbers of immigrants, culminating in 1913, with the arrival of 382,841 persons (a figure unsurpassed to this day).[47] What was especially significant about those years is that fewer residents, both Canadian-born and foreign-born, were leaving for the United States. With the end of World War I, the Canadian identity became a hot political issue, stoked by concern about immigration. The biggest concern for both those opposed to and those in favor of immigration was the number of immigrants who were not from the preferred Britain, United States, or Scandinavia. Alfred Fitzpatrick, founder and Principal of Frontier College, was one of the more outspoken citizens on this issue.[48] "The influx of non-English-speaking peoples into Canada is very large in proportion to the population," he wrote in 1919. "We allow new-comers to live in settlements on the prairies or, what is worse, to form colonies in large urban and industrial centres." Fitzpatrick was concerned about the existence of separate "colonies," because when they did not integrate into society, immigrants' "racial characteristics are continued and encouraged by native societies and leagues, forming unassimilated groups, which are a menace to Canadian unity."[49] Alan W. Neill, an independent Member of Parliament from Comox-Alberni on Vancouver Island, had reminded the House of Canada's need for agriculturalists and insisted that prospective farmers were not to be found among Southern Europeans. "It is a phantasy," he said, "the belief that we can bring labourers in from southern Europe, from the sunny towns of Italy, to work the farms in western Canada."[50] Neill's objections to lower classes of immigrants were also racially motivated. An outspoken opponent of Asian immigration, he was on the record as a supporter of "a white Canadian citizenship, a citizenship all white, and all Canadian."[51]

Italians facing opposition to their presence were not able—indeed, were not allowed—to present themselves publicly as Canadians according to a British-Canadian model. From their isolated position, and rooted in their own experiences of Canada, Italian immigrants in western Canada created their own attachment to their new home in a distinct fashion. The notion of two founding nations, England and France, that was more popular in central and eastern Canada, found little resonance among western Canadian Italians. The physical distance from Quebec and its concerns, coupled with their own need to accommodate Italian ethnicity to a Canadian nationality left the two-founding-nations theory unappealing. Most important for the purposes of this chapter, these Italians did not share the resentment or fear of the United States that was considered the root of English-Canadian nationalism. To do so would have entailed an understanding of the border as a line that demarcated territory and power impinged by the encroachment of the neighbors to the south. Italian immigrants did not focus on the United States, nor Canadian-American relations, in the negotiation of their Canadian identity.

Although Anglo-Canadians have nurtured an ambivalent relationship with the United States since the American Revolution, formulating and institutionalizing a Canadian identity that was centered on loyalty to Britain and antipathy toward the United States,[52] Italians have not been similarly preoccupied. Their axis of cultural identity has been an immigrant/nonimmigrant or perhaps an Italian/British-Canadian one, rather than a Canadian/American one. Even in the 1960s and 1970s, when there was a resurgence of anti-Americanism among many Canadians, Italians did not relate or participate. Their history and struggle for survival revolved around the immigration experience and the clash of cultures in their new home that reverberated for generations. Without roots in the competitive relationship Canada had with its southern neighbor, Italians were less attentive to alleged threats of cultural or economic dominance. As a minority, Italians were too concerned with the hegemony of the Anglo-Canadian elite to worry about enemies outside Canada. The space they occupied within Canada, and within the New World in general, was a marginal one.

Scholars have successfully questioned the central role and the supposedly objective nature of political, economic, and military studies. It has been suggested that such history is male, middle class, white, and so on. In this case we have privileged a certain perspective, which to a certain extent is specific to one ethnic group. British Canadians who viewed Canada as a British dependency, even after Confederation, were more inclined to feel anti-American because strong ties to the United States seemed to parallel weaker ties with Britain. They convinced themselves that Americans were the antithesis of Canadians, that they had chosen to behave differently by violently leaving the empire, and that those who wished to remain British had fled north to begin the real settlement of Canada. The image of the United States was thus always central to British Canadians' image of themselves. Other ethnic groups, such as the Italians, would not immediately jump to these arenas as the focus of their own Canadian identity or Canadian-American relations.

The Italian immigrant's experience of Canada was generally not as comfortable as that of the Anglo-Canadian, immigrant or otherwise. There was little sense of entitlement that might lead to a territoriality, particularly toward the United States. Instead, there was the constant awareness that one was on foreign ground, and that only in certain spaces could one feel at home. Moreover, those places, such as Italian neighborhoods, while distinct, were not exclusive. Italians shared their residential areas with other members of the working class, frequently immigrants as well. In this way their earliest experiences of Canada were multicultural and probably locally competitive. Borders of ethnic identity, from families to neighborhoods to mutual aid societies, marked "territory" that was significant to these groups. These spaces regularly crossed the Canadian-American border, a delineation that was much less important to their identities and their perception of their space.

A final but important point: Having emphasized the constructed nature of nations and national identities, I emphasize that I am not, in turn, asserting the "naturalness" of areas that cross political borders, such as the Pacific Northwest, or as it is sometimes called, "Cascadia." These too are created by the economic, social, and cultural connections that are made by the inhabitants of any given area. Ultimately any argument for the existence of Cascadia would have to be balanced against the political history—and subsequent social, economic, and cultural history—of Canada and the United States. There is no "natural" geographical feature, such as a mountain chain or an island, that will inherently bind the people who share it. Perceptions of international borders can be political, economic, and military constructions; they can also be intellectual, social, and cultural. In the end they are all products of our imaginations, reflections of our interests and experiences. The example of the Italians in western Canada indicates that, as we consider more broadly the history of Canadian-American relations, we need to appreciate alternate meanings of the border and the ways in which Canada and the United States do not exist, as much as the ways that they do.

NOTES

1. Ian Angus, *A Border Within: National Identity, Cultural Plurality, and Wilderness* (Montreal: McGill-Queen's University Press, 1997), p. 111.

2. Ibid., p. 47.

3. Norman Hillmer, ed., *Partners Nevertheless: Canadian-American Relations in the Twentieth Century* (Toronto: Copp Clark Pitman, 1989), pp. 1, 6.

4. J. L. Granatstein and Robert Cuff, *Ties That Bind: Canadian-American Relations*

from the Great War to the Cold War (Toronto: A. M. Hakkert, 1977); Granatstein and Norman Hillmer, *For Better or For Worse: Canada and the United States to the 1990s* (Toronto: Copp Clark Pitman, 1991).

5. John Herd Thompson and Stephen J. Randall, *Canada and the United States: Ambivalent Allies* (Athens: University of Georgia Press, 1994), p. 47.

6. Gabriele P. Scardellato, "Beyond the Frozen Wastes: Italian Sojourners and Settlers in British Columbia," in Roberto Perin and Franc Sturino, eds., *Arrangiarsi: The Italian Immigration Experience in Canada* (Montreal: Guernica, 1989).

7. Rafael Zariski, *Italy: The Politics of Uneven Development* (Hinsdale, Ill.: Dryden Press, 1972), pp. 15–20.

8. Scardellato, "Beyond the Frozen Wastes"; Robert Harney, *Italians in Canada*, Occasional Papers on Ethnic and Immigration Studies (Toronto: Multicultural History Society of Ontario, 1978).

9. British Columbia Supreme Court (Nanaimo), Probate/Estate Files, 1881–1948, box 2, file 16B/1890, British Columbia Archives and Records Services (BCARS).

10. Gerald Friesen, *The Canadian Prairies: A History* (Lincoln: University of Nebraska Press, 1984), pp. 274–300; Jean Barman, *The West beyond the West: A History of British Columbia* (Toronto: University of Toronto Press, 1991), pp. 129–50, 176–201.

11. D. M. LeBourdais, *Metals and Men: The Story of Canadian Mining* (Toronto: McClelland and Stewart, 1957), chapter 1; Scardellato, "Beyond the Frozen Wastes," pp. 147–49.

12. Coal Tyee Society, Coal Tyee History Project, #4051:43, interview with Abbondio Franchesini; Coal Tyee History Project Part II, #4343:7, interview with Dorothy Maxwell Graham, Marie Bono Conti, and John Marocchi, BCARS.

13. Scardellato, "Beyond the Frozen Wastes," p. 141.

14. Robert A. J. McDonald, "Working Class Vancouver, 1886–1914: Urbanism and Class in British Columbia," in Robert A. J. McDonald and Jean Barman, eds., *Vancouver Past: Essays in Social History* (Vancouver: University of British Columbia Press, 1986), pp. 35–36; Barman, *West beyond the West*, pp. 110–11.

15. Scardellato, "Beyond the Frozen Wastes"; McDonald, "Working Class Vancouver," p. 39; Vancouver Directory, 1906.

16. Jean Barman, "'Knowledge Is Essential for Universal Progress but Fatal to Class Privilege': Working People and the Schools in Vancouver during the 1920s," *Labour/Le Travail* 22 (fall 1988): 9–86; McDonald, "Working Class Vancouver," p. 40; Scardellato, "Beyond the Frozen Wastes," pp. 148–49.

17. Papers of Giovanni Mamini, Glenbow Archives, Alberta (GAA); Barman, *West beyond the West*, p. 66; Barman, "'Knowledge Is Essential,'" p. 17; David Bercuson, "Labour Radicalism and the Western Industrial Frontier, 1897–1919," *Canadian Historical Review* 58 (June 1977): 157, 165.

18. Interview with Abbondio Franchesini, BCARS, Coal Tyee History Project; PAA, Interviews, Mario Grassi.

19. Papers of Cominco Ltd., Reel A1516, file 346, Personnel, 1898–1939, and Oral History Project Recordings, #4245:47–48, interview with Mike Landucci, BCARS.

20. The 1911 Crowsnest Pass region figures include Coleman, Blairmore, Frank, Lille, Bellevue, Hillcrest, and Passburg; see the census table in Allen Seager, "Socialists and Workers: The Western Canadian Coal Miners, 1900–21," *Labour/Le Travail* 16 (fall 1985): 23–59; Howard Palmer with Tamara Palmer, *Alberta: A New History* (Edmonton, Alb.: Hurtig, 1990), p. 155; Scardellato, "Beyond the Frozen Wastes," p. 148. Unfortunately, Bernardy may not have known where she was, as she identified Fernie as located on Vancouver Island.

21. This is assuming a population of roughly thirty-five million in the late nineteenth and early twentieth centuries; it was the figure estimated in 1914. It is difficult to establish the exact population as the emigration rate was known to be high but was not officially counted until 1932. It is asserted that "by 1876 a hundred thousand people were leaving Italy a year, by 1901 half a million, and in the single year of 1913, 872,000 people left the country, that is to say one person in every forty." Denis Mack Smith, *Italy: A Modern History* (Ann Arbor: University of Michigan Press, 1959), p. 239.

22. Interviews, Phonotape #74.106/9, Mario Grassi, Calgary, August 14, 1973, by C. Grelli, Provincial Archives of Alberta (PAA).

23. Interviews, Phonotape #74.106/5, Mr. and Mrs. Henry Butti, August 10, 1973, by S. Roncucci, PAA.

24. Scardellato, "Beyond the Frozen Wastes," pp. 145–46; Robert Harney, "Montreal's King of Italian Labour: A Case Study of Padronism," *Labour/Le Travailleur* 4 (1979): 57–84; Donald Avery, *"Dangerous Foreigners": European Immigrant Workers and Labour Radicalism in Canada, 1896–1932* (Toronto: McClelland and Stewart, 1979), p. 34; British Columbia Attorney General, Correspondence inward, 1872–1937, box 4, file 2:1247/98, BCARS.

25. This is still true, to some extent, today. A recent article by a journalist in a Toronto newspaper echoes these sentiments. A woman born in Toronto to Italian immigrant parents did not realize she was Canadian, rather than American, until she was six. As she remembers: "We came to *America*. [My parents] made no distinction between the United States and Canada, or maybe I just didn't grasp it." Rosie DiManno, "Growing up on Grace," *Toronto Star,* June 28, 1997.

26. Interviews, Phonotape #74.106/17, Angelo Tappano, August 18, 1973 by C. Grelli, PAA.

27. Barman, *West beyond the West,* p. 143.

28. Commemorative Plaque, near Maffeo-Sutton Park, Nanaimo, British Columbia; photo in author's collection. Little else is known about this lodge; the only other

reference I have seen is in Barman, *West beyond the West*, p. 143, who mentions a self-help society among miners in the area but not by name.

29. Scardellato, "Beyond the Frozen Wastes," pp. 149–51.

30. John E. Zucchi, *Italians in Toronto: Development of a National Identity, 1875–1935* (Kingston, Ont.: McGill-Queen's University Press, 1988).

31. Interviews, Mario Grassi, PAA.

32. Scardellato, "Beyond the Frozen Wastes," p. 154.

33. British Columbia Supreme Court (Fernie), Probate/Estate Files, 1907–1940, box 3, file 11/24, BCARS.

34. British Columbia Supreme Court (Nanaimo), Probate/Estate Files, 1881–1948, box 73, file 7/36, BCARS.

35. British Columbia Supreme Court (Fernie), Probate/Estate Files, 1907–1940, box 3, file 16/24, BCARS.

36. One group for whom the political ideology of each nation may have mattered in the nineteenth century was the Irish. Some scholars have argued that Catholic Irish Republicans were far more comfortable with the independent United States than with the British colony, Canada. See David A. Wilson, *The Irish in Canada* (Ottawa: Canadian Historical Association, 1989), pp. 11–12.

37. Avery, *"Dangerous Foreigners,"* p. 11.

38. Leon E. Truesdell, *The Canadian Born in the United States: An Analysis of the Statistics of the Canadian Element in the Population of the United States, 1850–1930* (New Haven, Conn.: Yale University Press, 1943), p. 26.

39. Thompson and Randall, *Canada and the United States: Ambivalent Allies*, p. 47.

40. Scardellato, "Beyond the Frozen Wastes," pp. 153–54; Barman, *West beyond the West*, pp. 142–42, 197; McDonald, "Working Class Vancouver," p. 68.

41. Howard Palmer, *Patterns of Prejudice: A History of Nativism in Alberta* (Toronto: McClelland and Stewart, 1982), p. 20; Interviews, Mario Grassi, PAA.

42. The basic work on mutual aid as an idea and as a social reality is Petr Kropotkin's *Mutual Aid: A Factor of Evolution* (1902; reprint, Montreal: Black Rose Books, 1988). For details of collective property and mutual aid societies in Italy, see Alberto Cencelli, *La Proprietà Collettiva in Italia*, 2d ed. (Milano: Ulrico Hoepli, 1920); E. A. Lloyd, *The Co-operative Movement in Italy with Special Reference to Agriculture, Labour, and Production* (Westminster: Fabian Society and George Allen and Unwin, 1925); John W. Briggs, *An Italian Passage: Immigrants to Three American Cities, 1890–1930* (New Haven, Conn.: Yale University Press, 1978), pp. 15–36; Filippo Sabetti, *Political Authority in a Sicilian Village* (New Brunswick, N.J.: Rutgers University Press, 1984), pp. 6–13, 88–94. See also Zucchi's discussion of Italian mutual aid societies in Toronto in his *Italians in Toronto*, pp. 157–62.

43. Interviews, Angelo Tappano, PAA. Coleman had one of the larger concentrations of Italians in the Crowsnest Pass area; by 1913 its lodge had some two hundred members, all of whom were miners.

44. Bryan Palmer, *Working-Class Experience: The Rise and Reconstitution of Canadian Labour, 1800–1980* (Toronto: Butterworth, 1983), p. 149. Thanks to John Thompson for the reference.

45. Thompson and Randall, *Canada and the United States: Ambivalent Allies,* pp. 84, 141.

46. In the United States, 250 Americans of Italian descent were also interned and 10,000 others were forcibly relocated from the West Coast. See Franca Iacovetta, Roberto Perin, and Angelo Principe, eds., *Enemies Within: Italian and Other Internees in Canada and Abroad* (Toronto: University of Toronto Press, 2000).

47. Canada, Department of Citizenship and Immigration, *Report of the Department of Citizenship and Immigration Fiscal Year Ended March 31, 1954* (Ottawa: Queen's Printer, 1954), p. 30.

48. George L. Cook with Marjorie Robinson, "'The Fight of My Life': Alfred Fitzpatrick and Frontier College's Extramural Degree for Working People," *Histoire Sociale—Social History* 23, no. 45 (May 1990): 81–112.

49. Alfred Fitzpatrick, *Handbook for New Canadians* (Toronto: Ryerson Press, 1919), p. 1.

50. Canada, House of Commons (HOC), *Debates,* March 5, 1928, p. 1,018.

51. Canada, HOC, *Debates,* April 15, 1924, p. 1,391.

52. See Carl Berger, *The Sense of Power: Studies in the Ideas of Canadian Imperialism, 1869–1914* (Toronto: University of Toronto Press, 1970); R. Craig Brown, "The Nationalism of the National Policy," in Peter Russell, ed., for the University League for Social Reform, *Nationalism in Canada* (Toronto and New York: McGraw Hill, 1966); and Patricia K. Wood, "'Under Which Flag, Canadian?': Anti-Americanism and the Election of 1891," M.A. thesis, Queen's University, 1991.

5 / Nationalist Narratives and Regional Realities

The Political Economy of Railway Development
in Southeastern British Columbia, 1895–1905

JEREMY MOUAT

The forty-ninth parallel, which divides British Columbia and Washington state, is an invisible line. Unlike "real" boundaries—rivers, oceans, or the height of land—this parallel is geographically meaningless. It is an imagined border, legitimized by an agreement made in 1846 between two states far removed from the region. Over the next fifty years the forty-ninth parallel acquired new significance and its purpose was defined in different ways. This process reflected other changes that were taking place across North America. The years around the end of the nineteenth century have been described as "the directly formative birth-time of basic institutions, social relations, and political divisions of United States society as it evolved toward and beyond the mid-twentieth century," and these years were equally important in Canada for many of the same reasons.[1] Such writers as Alfred Dupont Chandler and Martin J. Sklar have described the consolidation of capitalism then under way, a process linked to the emerging transcontinental economy. Railways were largely responsible for creating this new economy: their importance in the late nineteenth and early twentieth centuries cannot be overstated. Not only were they the largest corporate entities on either side of the border, they also exercised enormous political and economic influence.[2] And railway companies were very interested in the ways in which the border affected their operations.

In southeastern British Columbia the meaning attached to the forty-ninth parallel was inextricably linked to debates over economic development, nationality, and the public good. This chapter revisits those debates and con-

cludes that earlier Canadian scholars have imposed a nationalist gloss on events
in the region. Their work tends to see railway construction as a metaphor for
nation-building and subsumes the realities of the region's development
within a linear narrative of progress. The result is a misleading interpretation of the region's history that fails to acknowledge the complex nuances of
the time. In particular, the activities of railway companies are described in
ways that discount their quest for profits and market control.

This chapter offers a different approach, one that emphasizes the usefulness of a critical materialist analysis as a way to understanding events in southeastern British Columbia. Space does not permit an extensive account here,
so the focus is on the competition between the Canadian Pacific Railway (CPR)
and the Great Northern Railroad in the late 1890s and early 1900s. The larger
aim is to rehabilitate a particular way of seeing the history of British Columbia,
to rescue political economy from the margins of historical inquiry—at least,
historical inquiry in British Columbia. Although it may seem platitudinous
to claim that capitalism has shaped British Columbia's economic and political development in profound ways—as well as defining, and more recently
redefining, the forty-ninth parallel—the proposition is not one that has
received much attention in the province's historiography.[3]

The competition that began in the late 1890s between the CPR and the Great
Northern Railroad in southeastern British Columbia was a culmination of
events that dated back a dozen years or more. North America's first transcontinental railway came in 1869, but because its route was well to the south of
the forty-ninth parallel, it had little direct impact on the Pacific Northwest
or British Columbia. (At this time British Columbia was not part of Canada;
it did not join the Confederation until 1871.) Much more significant for the
region was the completion of the Northern Pacific in 1883; it ran through Idaho
and Spokane in eastern Washington before dipping south to reach Portland.
Steamboats on the region's rivers and lakes complemented and extended the
rail system, making many once-isolated valleys relatively accessible. And the
trip across the continent was no longer an arduous and time-consuming journey: people and goods could move many hundreds of miles quickly and safely.

The railway's arrival created numerous opportunities in the resource-rich
West. Industries that needed access to bulk transportation to reach distant
markets—such as agriculture, forestry, mining, and fishing—responded to
the new possibilities opened up by the railway. The quickening pace of economic activity in turn attracted more and more migrants. In particular, the

transcontinental railway helped to fuel mining booms, first in the Coeur d'Alenes and then in southeastern British Columbia. The region's mineral wealth had long been recognized, but lack of transportation facilities had prevented the exploitation of any but the richest deposits. With the completion of the Northern Pacific, however, all that changed.[4]

Government officials and business people in British Columbia looked on jealously as the Northern Pacific brought economic benefits to areas within its reach. They were impatiently waiting for their own railway: the federal government had promised that one would connect the province with central Canada within ten years of British Columbia joining the Confederation, that is, by 1881. (The CPR's first through train did not reach tidewater until 1885.) In an effort to reap some benefit from the American transcontinental, the provincial government approved a railway proposal for southeastern British Columbia in 1883. The Columbia and Kootenay would be a portage line, connecting the west arm of Kootenay Lake to the Columbia River near present-day Castlegar; it would also connect with the Northern Pacific via steamboats. This latter prospect was not greeted with enthusiasm by Ottawa, however. The federal government disallowed the provincial railway charter, pointing out that "the company consists almost wholly of American capitalists, and . . . notwithstanding the representations made that the proposed railway will connect by steamer with the Canadian Pacific Railway, and thus bring traffic to that road and to the Canadian seaboard, . . . the road under consideration would in all probability eventually become a feeder to the Northern Pacific Railway."[5] Ottawa's action angered the provincial government, but it could do little other than express its indignation.

The federal government prevented the Columbia and Kootenay from going ahead in 1883, but it could not alter geography. The easiest way to reach southeastern British Columbia was from eastern Washington or northern Idaho, even after the completion of the CPR in 1885. By this time mining had begun in earnest in the Kootenays and the first ore shipments were being prepared. The CPR's tracks were too far north to attract much of this ore traffic, however. Mine operators in the Kootenays and the Slocan needed straightforward transportation links: too much loading and unloading, from rail car to barge and then back to rail car again, rendered the operation uneconomical. Smelters in Butte, Helena, and other points in the western United States treated the bulk of the area's ore until the turn of the century (Figure 5.1).

As the mines began to ship ore, railway construction in the Kootenays boomed. The CPR acquired several branch lines in the region in the early 1890s,

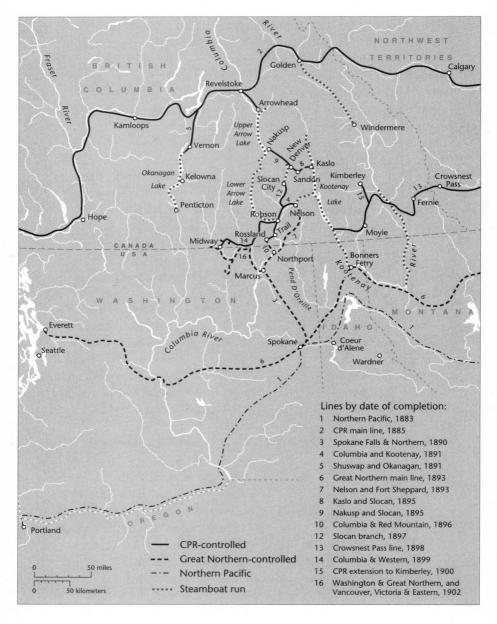

FIG. 5.1. Rail lines into southeastern British Columbia, c. 1905. Map by Eric Leinberger.

and then in 1896 it opened a line from Revelstoke south to Arrowhead, to improve its connections between Upper Arrow Lake and the CPR main line. The following year it purchased the Columbia and Kootenay Steam Navigation Company, owner of the major group of river boats connecting the area's various rail lines. Such moves were clearly meant to facilitate traffic from the CPR's main line at Revelstoke south into the mining region. However, the CPR finally concluded that this spur line into the Kootenays simply did not provide adequate access. To compete successfully with the American lines, the company had to have a more direct link with the region. That was the purpose of the Crowsnest Pass railway, a project that dated from 1893. The CPR acquired Galt's Lethbridge line in southern Alberta that year as a prelude to building directly through the Rockies into the Kootenays.[6] The company assured its shareholders that such moves would stimulate mining in southern British Columbia. The rationale was straightforward: the company's annual report explained that the new acquisitions were "certain to add largely to the earnings of the Company."[7]

While the CPR was working to establish connections from its main line down into southeastern British Columbia from the north, Americans were building into the region from the south. D. C. Corbin, who had earlier built a very successful line from Spokane into the Coeur d'Alenes, constructed several lines into the Kootenays in the early 1890s. By 1896 his trains ran from Spokane to both Rossland and Nelson. The completion of James J. Hill's Great Northern Railroad in 1893 meant that the city boasted two transcontinentals. Whether one was traveling from Montreal or Toronto, from Vancouver or Seattle, the easiest and most convenient route to the Kootenays was through Spokane and then north on one of Corbin's trains.

Corbin was not the only railroader south of the border with an interest in the Kootenays. For some time Hill, from his base in St. Paul, Minnesota, had followed events there closely. In light of the comments of later historians, it must be emphasized that this reflected the determined efforts of entrepreneurs in southeastern British Columbia to attract Hill's attention as much as it did any sinister desire on Hill's part to dominate the region's trade.[8] In 1891, for example, the ubiquitous Colonel James Baker, a provincial politician and entrepreneur with an eye for the main chance, tried to sell his interest in the Crow's Nest Coal and Mineral Company Limited and the British Columbia Southern Railway to Hill. Baker cautioned Hill that "we shall have to keep things very quiet & get everything settled this fall otherwise we shall have the CPR interest working against us." (The conspiratorial tone was more than a little disingenuous because Baker had earlier attempted to interest both the

federal government and the CPR in his project.)[9] To Baker's chagrin, however, Hill declined the offer.

At about the same time, Hill was looking at mining properties in the
Kootenays, and in 1892 he contemplated advancing $200,000 to have a mine
there developed.[10] Three years later he built a short narrow-gauge rail line
from Kootenay Lake west into the booming Slocan mining area around
Sandon. Steamers on the lake connected the railhead at Kaslo with the Great
Northern at Bonner's Ferry, Idaho. In late 1895 the CPR was building a similar line into Sandon from the other direction, from Nakusp on Upper Arrow
Lake. Sandon was at the head of a narrow valley with little space for two rail
lines, leading to a rather comic-opera confrontation between the two construction crews. First on the scene, the CPR crew quickly positioned its station on the right-of-way of the (Great Northern-backed) Kaslo & Slocan
Railway, blocking the latter's access into town. Hill's crew rose to the challenge: the workers arrived early one morning, strapped cables around the
station, and—with the help of a locomotive—yarded the offending building out of the way.[11] The competition between the two companies had begun
in earnest.

Two events in the late 1890s provide a useful focus for looking more closely
at the competition between the CPR and Hill's Great Northern. The first came
some months after the skirmish in the Slocan, when the newly elected Liberal
government in Ottawa had to determine which company should be encouraged to construct a line through the Crowsnest Pass from the east into southeastern British Columbia.[12] The issue was hotly debated in public meetings
and newspaper editorials of the day, and focused public attention on such
matters as the role of railways in economic development, public versus private ownership, and the power of the CPR. The British Columbia election
campaign of 1898 kept these issues before the public, because the power of
large companies generally, and the influence of the CPR in particular, was
used by the provincial opposition to attack the government in the run-up to
the vote.

The southeastern corner of British Columbia attracted a great deal of pub-
licity during the summer and autumn of 1896. A speculative fever gripped
Ontario: two Toronto papers brought out special issues on mining, traveling sales people took to handling gold stocks along with their other wares,
and the *Canadian Mining Review* wrote disparagingly of "the wave of partial
insanity, which has broken loose in Toronto."[13] The newly elected Liberal government in Ottawa followed events in the Kootenays closely, forming a very
high estimate of its potential economic significance. At one point the prime

minister told the House of Commons that the region was "the hope of this country."[14] The fact that transportation between the Kootenays and other Canadian centers was poor and that the easiest access point was from south of the border became a sore point with many people who felt that this explained why the economic benefit from a rich Canadian natural resource was draining south to Spokane, with American entrepreneurs and businesses the main beneficiaries of the boom. A railway from southern Alberta through the Crowsnest Pass into the Kootenays seemed—at least to people in central Canada—the obvious way to stem this outflow of wealth.

The debate over a railway through the Crowsnest Pass followed from the earlier one over the federal government's tardiness in fulfilling the terms of British Columbia's entry into Confederation, with the promise of a railway connection with central Canada, as well as Ottawa's disallowance of the Columbia and Kootenay bill in 1883. What was new in the Crowsnest Pass debate was the unequivocal assertion of the needs of the regional economy. Few people on the Pacific Coast saw a railway linking the Kootenays with central Canada, while neglecting the needs of the coast to tap the same area, as an adequate measure. The popular Vancouver Member of Parliament George Maxwell made a special trip to Toronto to publicize this point. "Speaking of the building of the Crow's Nest Pass Railway," Maxwell explained,

> The residents on the coast are favorable to the project and recognize the benefit it will be to the Province if it is constructed as it should be, right through to New Westminster and Vancouver. He points out that the people in those two cities and in the districts adjoining as well as the residents on the Island contend very justly that it would be unfair to build a line of railway by the route suggested and not connect it with that portion of the Province which contains almost the entire white population of British Columbia. Simply to build the road through the pass to Rossland would be to exclude the coast cities from any share of the benefit in the resources of the Province, of which they are the chief commercial centres. This point of view is keenly appreciated in Vancouver and Victoria.[15]

A month earlier, in November 1896, the Boards of Trade of the coastal cities met and passed resolutions urging the speedy construction of a coast-to-Kootenay rail link. Even Vancouver's Trades and Labor Council was prepared to compromise its belief in the efficacy of state ownership and to endorse the railway: "While this Council favors the Government ownership of all railways, they are of the opinion that the proposed Vancouver, Victoria and

Eastern railway should be built at as early a date as possible, believing that the undertaking will greatly benefit this Province."[16] When it became clear that the CPR was likely to receive the federal government's blessing to construct a line through the Crowsnest Pass from the east, ending in Nelson, the company's unwillingness to continue through to the coast drew the ire of many coastal residents. A Victoria paper noted tartly that "the Canadian Pacific Railway is doubtless anxious to make its way into the Kootenay district from the East, but as for furthering the trade interests of the western part of the province, that does not seem to come within the bounds of its ambition. We must have an independent short route into the mineral bearing district if we are to profit as we should by its development."[17] When a writer claimed in the *Globe* that "the quick construction of the Crow's Nest Pass railway has won enthusiastic approval from the people of the entire Province of British Columbia," a Kootenay paper angrily dismissed the statement as "disgraceful misrepresentation."[18] Perhaps a better indication of the local estimate of the CPR came from the pen of a Toronto journalist who traveled through the Kootenays a few months earlier. He needed seven columns of print to chronicle the litany of complaints against the CPR. "The stranger may travel from Revelstoke through the Slocan to Rossland and back again," he noted with some surprise, "and in all his journeyings find no man who is the friend of the C.P.R."[19]

The CPR was able to take advantage of the growing interest and concern in central Canada about developments in the Kootenays to assert its claim for government assistance to construct the railway through the Crowsnest Pass. (The company was less vocal about the fact that it had been planning to build such a line for some time.) CPR vice president T. G. Shaughnessy was quick to identify the company's interests with those of the country, and in September 1896 he wrote to Wilfrid Laurier, the newly elected prime minister, to outline what he felt should be the government's priorities:

> To my mind the most important railway work if not indeed the most important work of any kind now requiring the attention of Government is the construction of a railway from Lethbridge or Fort McLeod through Crows Nest pass, East Kootenay and part of West Kootenay to Nelson, B.C. . . . To answer the purpose for which it is intended, viz., to preserve for Canada the business incident to the mining of the precious metals copper and coal in that section of Canada by building up smelting enterprises and smelting towns, it is essen-

tial that the railway be an integral part of the Canadian system without any
interest South of the International Boundary.[20]

Shaughnessy's memo made it clear that his company intended to be the
one to build the line through the Crowsnest Pass, and a month later CPR president William Van Horne underlined the point in newspaper interviews.[21]
The *Globe*, one of Toronto's leading newspapers and a partisan journal of the
governing Liberals, was a firm supporter not only of the general need for a
railway into the Kootenays but also of the CPR as the company that ought to
control the line. Opposition papers seized on the *Globe*'s editorial posture as
an example of supreme hypocrisy, because the paper had been a sworn enemy
of the CPR and monopoly throughout the 1880s.[22] Even greater indignation
was generated in March 1897, when journalists discovered that two prominent Liberals who were co-owners of the *Globe* (Robert Jaffray and George A.
Cox) also had a substantial interest in a company with coal deposits in the
Crowsnest Pass and thus stood to benefit from a railway through the district.[23]
"Quite a furious controversy is raging among the Toronto papers over who
should construct the Crow's Nest Pass railway," noted the Victoria *Daily Times*,
before reiterating the common theme of newspapers on the Pacific Coast:
"Western British Columbia will be 'in the soup' unless [an] independent con-
nection is furnished from this side."[24]

Despite critical comments from various quarters, in June 1897 the Liberals
formally introduced a motion in the House of Commons that would subsi-
dize the CPR to build the Crowsnest Pass railway. The federal government
justified this by repeating the argument about the need to exploit the
Kootenays' mineral wealth in such a way as to provide maximum benefit to
Canada. The continued diversion of trade from the region into the United
States was seen as an unfortunate loss that had to be prevented if at all possible; only a direct rail line could establish a viable Canadian presence in the
region.[25] Politicians claimed that this would have an immediate impact on
development. For example, Sir Richard Cartwright, minister of trade and commerce, argued that the proposed railway would create ten dividend-paying
mines in the region for every one that existed at present. He went on to claim
that "no one thing is more likely to aid Canada and bring immigrants to the
North-west than the opening up . . . of large and well developed gold fields,"
citing the experience of the Australian colonies as proof of this.[26] The proposed agreement met with little opposition in the Commons because the
Conservatives had agreed to support the CPR's proposal before their defeat

in the 1896 election. The CPR was content; as another scholar has pointed out, "the company plainly obtained pretty much the agreement it wanted."[27]

The CPR's efforts to control the rail traffic of the Kootenays did not end with its successful bid for the Crowsnest Pass railway. It then turned its sights on Rossland, the center of the mining excitement in 1896 and 1897. The Crowsnest Pass railway would end in Nelson, and an American entrepreneur, Fritz Heinze, already held a railway charter to build from that city into Rossland. Heinze—one of Butte's Copper Kings—had also built a smelter in Trail in 1895 and 1896. After considerable negotiation, accompanied by much public posturing, the CPR and Heinze finally agreed in early 1898 that the company would acquire his railway rights and the Trail smelter.

The CPR's role in British Columbia was hotly debated in the province, as a brief discussion of the election of 1898 makes clear. By this time many were alarmed at the company's growing power, which was frequently associated in the public mind with the much-disliked Dunsmuir family on Vancouver Island. Both symbolized wealth and power; a number of people in British Columbia believed that railways generally, and the CPR in particular, were becoming too powerful. The dominant refrain during the 1898 campaign was that corporate influence was out of control in the province. This theme emerged even before the campaign was under way, when—in a dramatic gesture in March 1898—the Speaker of the House resigned. By way of explanation, D. W. Higgins attacked the government of Premier J. H. Turner and its policies of deficit financing and generous railway subsidies. "He found the Government," the ex-Speaker told his colleagues in the legislature,

> Giving railway franchises in every quarter of the Province to men whose only object is to sell the charters for the best price they can get. He related a story of meeting a man on the summit of Red Mountain [in Rossland] who indicated by a sweep of his arm the holdings of Heinze, Corbin and the C.P.R. to show that there was nothing left for the people, or the Government in that vicinity except the blue vault of heaven. . . . He believed that it was necessary for the preservation of the country that there should be a change of Government. He had severed political ties that had bound him to the Government party for 25 or 30 years, and he intended to do all in his power to bring about a change. . . . the interests of the Province demanded that the present oligarchy and reign of syndicates be put down.[28]

Once the campaign began, opposition candidates stressed that they did not want to prevent development but claimed that Turner had been responsible for a massive sellout of the province's resources. Charles Semlin—ultimately the victor and the province's next premier—explained to a crowd that he "agreed with all that [Premier Turner] said as to the wisdom of the policy of opening up the country by means of railways and kindred public works, [Semlin's] argument—and the argument of the party that he had the honour to lead—being not against these works, but that bargains not the best for British Columbia had been made in the bringing in of the various railways—undue advantage having been given to promoters and monopolies."[29] At another meeting an oppositionist reduced the debate to a simple choice, asking the crowd "whether it was anxious for its children to grow up as slaves and servants of rich monopolies or as free independent sons of the soil."[30] London's *Pall Mall Gazette* echoed this analysis in an article on the provincial election, explaining to its readers that "since Mr. Turner personally took the helm, [the government] has fallen victim to the wiles of the charter hunter and the big monopoly corporations, which have wound Mr. Turner in any sort of ball they liked. . . . People of England could hardly understand how many of the poor electors of this fair province are under the heel of powerful corporations. The curse of monopoly, bred by the Turner Government, is over all this fertile country."[31]

Few people in British Columbia wanted a government that would privilege corporate power; the suggestion that monopoly capitalism was acting as a brake on individual enterprise met with widespread disapproval. The CPR was the focus of voter anger and on election day, the Turner government went down in defeat. This defeat in the 1898 election was a key political divide in the history of the province. It symbolized the final eclipse of the Victoria-based merchant elite that had held power for more than a decade and had dominated provincial politics since Confederation. Social and business links held this group together, rather than any ideological commitment or party loyalty. The five years that followed Turner's defeat were stormy ones, but public condemnation of the CPR and its influence on the provincial government continued. The most notable moments came in 1901 and 1902. On the former occasion, E. V. Bodwell (a prominent Victoria lawyer) denounced the CPR's influence at a public meeting, provoking an angry response from the premier on the floor of the legislature.[32] In 1902, Smith Curtis, a member of the legislature and former cabinet minister, charged Premier Dunsmuir as well as various cabinet ministers with giving preferential treatment to railway companies and called for a public inquiry.[33]

The election of a Conservative government headed by Richard McBride in 1903 signaled the beginning of the modern era of party politics in British

Columbia.[34] A congratulatory letter sent to the new British Columbia premier shortly after his election victory sheds considerable light on the contemporary political scene. T. Mayne Daly, a former federal Conservative cabinet minister who had been active as a lawyer and mining promoter in the Kootenays following the federal Liberals' victory in 1896, began by engaging in some rhetorical hand-wringing over the province's recent turbulent past—"Unhappy British Columbia! What a turmoil things have been in since 1897!"—and then offered McBride some advice. "There are three things you want in my opinion especially to avoid," Daly wrote. He cautioned the new premier against "any 'entanglement' with Dunsmuir," with the Western Federation of Miners or its affiliates, and with "*any* railway interests." Daly felt that this last "entanglement" had been one of "the disturbing factors in B.C. politics."[35] This volatile milieu was the context in which the CPR's efforts to secure a competitive advantage over its rival in southeastern British Columbia, the Great Northern, took place.

Hill never enjoyed the same intimacy with Canadian prime ministers that characterized CPR executives such as Van Horne and Shaughnessy, and he could not capitalize on the nationalist mood of late nineteenth-century Canada as the CPR was able to do.[36] Nor was this his style: Hill had always been more concerned with business and making money than currying favor with politicians. His retirement from the Great Northern was one of the few occasions when he reflected publicly on his career, and he summed up his working life with characteristic brevity: "Most men who have really lived have had, in some shape, their great adventure. This railway is mine."[37] Hill's railway career had begun in the 1870s, when he had built the St. Paul, Minneapolis, and Manitoba Railroad, along with Donald Smith (later Lord Strathcona), George Stephen (later Lord Mount Stephen), and Norman Kittson. The group's windfall profits were such that the Canadian government approached the four men in 1880 to see if they would consider building the proposed transcontinental railway that was to become the Canadian Pacific Railway.[38] They accepted the challenge, although Hill left the CPR syndicate after three years, preoccupied with his own business centered in St. Paul. Nonetheless, he remained on close terms with his former colleagues, and a number of the individuals who secured the financing for the CPR were later to help Hill with his own transcontinental, the Great Northern Railroad.[39] George Stephen—the chief architect and financier of the Canadian Pacific Railway—was a particularly heavy investor in the Great Northern. It was he who urged Hill to turn his St. Paul–based railway into a transcontinental.[40]

Hill's Great Northern line enjoyed some significant advantages over the

CPR in the contest to secure Kootenay rail traffic. This certainly was the view of M. P. Jordan, a French mining engineer who spent the summers of 1896 and 1897 in the area. "Between these two rival companies," he explained, "the fight is far from equal. The Great Northern holds the upper hand, for various reasons." Jordan felt that the American flavor of southeastern British Columbia gave a significant advantage to Hill: "The population of the Kootenays is largely American; the capital invested in the mines is mostly American; quite apart from anything else, this explains the close ties between the Kootenays and the States."[41] Jordan went on to note that most of the Kootenays' mining equipment came from either the Chicago workshops of Fraser & Chalmers, or Portland, Oregon, and that much of its ore went south across the border to U.S. smelters. Even Montreal shippers, he pointed out, preferred to send goods with the Grand Trunk Railway and then link with the Great Northern: "By doing this, they're able to ship directly to Rossland or Nelson without trans-shipment. On the CPR there are three trans-shipments."[42] But in 1898 such advantages seemed to be slipping away. The Crowsnest Pass railway addressed the problem of access from eastern Canada. At the same time leading business people from central Canada began to purchase some of the principal mining properties in the Kootenays. For example, Toronto's Gooderham-Blackstock group bought two of the most well-known mines in Rossland, while L. J. Forget and other Montreal business people acquired the Payne mine, the richest of the Slocan mines. Hill was never one to quit when challenged, however.

Shortly after the CPR acquired the Trail smelter and the Nelson-Rossland railway charter from Heinze, Hill decided to purchase Corbin's two rail lines that linked Rossland and Nelson with Spokane. Hill's son, who was now playing an active role in Great Northern affairs, explained to an acquaintance that the railway "will be a valuable feeder to the system, as the country it reaches is a very rich new mining district and may possibly develop some such mines as they have in Butte. If they should, it would, of course, very materially increase our tonnage and revenue."[43] But the move also raised the prospect of tensions between the Great Northern and the CPR; others found this a worrying possibility. One of Hill's key contacts in London, Gaspard Farrer, cautioned Louis Hill of impending trouble: "You may take it as certain as anything in this world can be that the C.P.R. is not going to sit still and allow . . . the G.N. [Great Northern] to Kootenay & Rossland without retaliation; & though that may do the C.P.R. no good it will assuredly work harm to G.N. besides entailing on you all anxiety & irritation."[44] Despite such concern, the two companies did not come to any arrangement to share the Kootenay traffic.

As already noted, Colonel Baker had been unable to interest Hill in his coal property in the Crowsnest Pass in the early 1890s, but he had eventually succeeded in selling it to a group of Toronto business people, which included Robert Jaffray and George Cox of the *Globe*.[45] With a rail line in place, this group began to develop the pass's enormous coal deposits. (Both the CPR and Hill had serious misgivings about the company's management, harboring suspicions that it was more interested in short-term stock manipulation than in successful coal mining.[46]) In 1901, Hill decided to purchase a majority share in the company, an investment he maintained until his death.[47] He then became interested in mining west of the Kootenays, in the Boundary region. The Boundary's abundant copper deposits drove a booming industry in the decade before World War I, including both mines and smelters in the area around Grand Forks, Phoenix, and Greenwood. In the summer of 1904, Hill invested heavily in the leading Boundary company, the Granby Consolidated Mining and Smelting Company. "C.P.R. Is Outwitted," ran the headline in the Victoria *Daily Colonist*, "J. J. Hill Grabs Vast Mining Interests in the Boundary Country."[48] Hill's ability to carry the bulk of the Boundary's freight on his Great Northern irked CPR management, who had pushed rails into the district in 1899 and had hoped that the company's Trail smelter would treat all of southeastern British Columbia's ore.[49]

The CPR had been disappointed by the vagaries of mining generally, and the rather indifferent success of its Trail smelter in particular. By the early 1900s Rossland mines—the principal feeders of the Trail smelter—were proving to be less rich than anticipated. In an effort to rationalize the mines and protect its investment, the CPR pushed to consolidate the various Rossland mining properties with its smelter. The original idea seems to have come from people involved with Rossland's Le Roi mine, a famous property owned by a disparate group of British investors. The CPR's smelter manager, W. H. Aldridge, met one of the Le Roi's directors in the fall of 1904, later advising Shaughnessy that this person was "anxious to make a large consolidation of Rossland and Boundary interests, . . . and I told him that such a consolidation would certainly receive the encouragement of the [Canadian Pacific] Railway so long as they were sure that they would receive the haulage."[50] Negotiations went on fitfully for another twelve months, involving Aldridge as the representative of the CPR's interests, as well as the owners and managers of the Le Roi, War Eagle, and Centre Star mines. (These last two properties were both owned by the Gooderham/Blackstock liquor interests of Toronto.) The British owners of the Le Roi eventually opted not to participate in the consolidation, but the CPR secured the other two properties, the

War Eagle and the Centre Star. "c.p.r. Frightened By J.J. Hill Into Buying Rossland Mines," proclaimed a Toronto newspaper's headline. The journal posed a rhetorical question:

> Does the absorption of the Gooderham and Blackstock mining interests in British Columbia by the crowd that has been identified with the c. p. r. smelters at Trail mean that it is a continuation of the fight that has been waged against J. J. Hill . . . in that Province? Those who have closely followed the changes in ownership are of the belief that it [is] but another move in the diplomatic war of commerce.
>
> . . . . it would seem that a strategic move was made on the part of the c.p.r. people, and by this they acquired the stock that they needed to preserve their smelting trade and also their haulage to the east.
>
> . . . . Under such conditions as have been detailed in the foregoing it does not seem possible that other than amalgamation, or at least the pooling of interests will follow.[51]

The author of the story was well informed, for the cpr did subsequently merge the two Rossland mines with its smelter, thereby creating the Consolidated Mining and Smelting Company of Canada (more commonly known as Cominco).[52]

The Le Roi's reluctance to join with the other properties reflected behind-the-scenes maneuvering by Hill and his associates. Hill outlined his strategy in a confidential letter to a friend: "For some time past," he explained, "there has been a plan between some Canadian mine owners at Rossland and the Canadian Pacific Railway to consolidate the Rossland mines and the smelter at Trail." He continued: "To carry this into effect all depends upon their acquisition of the LeRoi mines [sic] and the Northport smelter. By buying LeRoi shares, as outlined in letter attached, we will be able to prevent the consummation of the scheme and hold control of the LeRoi property, which really controls the Rossland camp, and prevent practically the wiping out of the business of our Red Mountain and Northport line which represents the main business of the Spokane Falls & Northern Railway."[53]

When Aldridge went to London in the winter of 1905, hoping to persuade Le Roi shareholders to assent to the amalgamation project, he discovered that Hill had preempted him: "The Great Northern . . . spent large sums of money in purchasing LeRoi stock and perfecting an organization throughout England in collecting proxies."[54] The company meeting that considered his proposal voted it down. Aldridge was undaunted by the setback, however: "We are going right ahead to form our Canadian Company comprising Centre Star, War Eagle, St. Eugene and the Trail Smelter."[55] Cominco was launched several months later and proved to be an exceptionally successful company. But the episode also reveals very clearly the convoluted backroom dealings in which both CPR and Great Northern executives were prepared to engage in their efforts to thwart each other's goals.

It is hoped that the earlier discussion of the debate surrounding the Crowsnest Pass railway and the provincial election in 1898 made the point that the CPR was not universally acclaimed as the savior of western Canada, whatever its reputation among later historians. Not only were some newspapers inclined to dismiss the CPR as "a hidebound monopoly"; they also could portray Hill as benevolent, or at least without ulterior motive: "Mr. Hill purposes coming into British Columbia upon precisely the same terms as he came to the coast through Minnesota, Montana and Washington. He asks for no assistance from Dominion, province or municipality. . . . He has viewed the situation in British Columbia, marked our potentialities and resources, and has decided that profits can be made upon capital investment in railway construction."[56] People were also aware that the same capitalists controlled both lines and recognized that the competition between the CPR and Hill's alternative rail route just south of the United States–Canada border was an economic struggle.[57] Nor did journalists shrink from exposing the CPR's appeals to nationalist sentiment as self-interested hypocrisy. In a biting editorial on the "Qualms of Patriots," the Victoria *Daily Times* sarcastically evaluated Hill's critics in 1905:

> It is all but intolerable for a capitalist and the representative of capitalists to offer to construct a railway in Canada, and especially in British Columbia, without asking for a bonus from the Dominion or from the province. Such an idea is subversive of all the principles that have guided the courses of promoters in the past. It is establishing a precedent that may have extraordinary effects in the future. It is no wonder chartermongers and promoters stand aghast and are all but incapable of proving to the railway committee of Parliament that such revolutionary suggestions should not be considered for a moment.
>
> As it would obviously be ridiculous to refuse consideration of the proposition, the representatives of the old-line operators have graciously permitted the advocates of the Hill scheme to lay their case before the committee. It would not be politic to take the bill in hand and tear it up before the eyes of the country. There is a more excellent way. Rend the life out of it by tacking

on prohibitive conditions under the guise of "protecting the interests of the country.". . .

Mr. Hill should have his horns sawed off ere he comes over here in the guise of a ministering capitalistic angel, and offers to build us railways for nothing. The whole thing is unnatural and incomprehensible. But the opposition to the Great Northern is not. The very fact of that opposition, persistent and inflexible, should be sufficient to convince everybody, even the guardians of our frontiers at Ottawa, that the construction and the competition of the Great Northern are very much to be desired by the people of British Columbia.[58]

During the 1890s and the 1900s the CPR and the Great Northern both sought to control the freight and passenger traffic in the Kootenays. The area seemed destined for a prosperous future, and each company wanted to carry fuel and supplies to the region's mines and smelters, and to transport the ore, concentrates, and matte to the wider world. To secure this business, they established— through purchase and construction—new transportation routes. But at least as important as the provision of infrastructure were long-term contracts with corporate customers, guaranteeing regular and ongoing traffic. The CPR and the Great Northern went even further, acquiring mining properties and smelters with this goal in mind. The two mining and smelting conglomerates owned by the respective companies—Cominco and Granby—grew to become very large enterprises in their own right, of far greater importance to the province's history than the jostling egos of Hill and Van Horne.[59]

Some of Canada's most well-known writers—the popular historian Pierre Berton, the poet E. J. Pratt, the singer Gordon Lightfoot—have produced works on the country's first transcontinental, the Canadian Pacific Railway.[60] This is hardly surprising: the railway bridged vast distances, facilitated European settlement across western Canada, embodied the much discussed dream of a famous politician, and acted as a counterbalance to the strong north-south networks linking the country with the more populous United States. The railway's obvious importance has encouraged people to see its construction as a metaphor for the nation's coming of age. The tale becomes an epic in which the company/country surmounts the opposition of shortsighted politicians, sceptical financiers, and of course nature itself (in the form of a hostile northern climate as well as daunting geographical obstacles). The completion of the railway through to the Pacific Coast is a moment of triumph, tangible evidence of an emerging transcontinental nation, the justification of a particular national vision (that of the Conservative Party), and so on. Few people have regarded the railway's completion as an index of industrialization or as the agent of metropolitan capital, although this perspective makes a good deal more sense than those that view steel rails and locomotives as mystical symbols of national destiny.[61]

Western Canadian historians who have described the construction of the CPR have tended to adopt a whiggish approach, that is, to assume the inevitability of the railway. Such an approach is problematic, however, for it becomes all too easy to describe the CPR in triumphalist terms, applauding its success and scorning its opponents. Hill and the Great Northern, in particular, are frequently cast in the role of the menacing American "other." All too often the literature juxtaposes in stark terms the motives and influence of the people who constructed and ran the two transcontinental railways. Hill is the sinister and devious (Canadian-born) American; his company looms as a threatening presence just south of the border. The managers of the CPR, on the other hand, are dynamic and forceful (American-born) entrepreneurs, preserving Canadian sovereignty against all odds. In his *History of the Canadian Pacific Railway*, for example, W. Kaye Lamb describes "Hill's invasion of southern British Columbia" and refers to the way in which "Hill had insinuated his line into the territory between the Northern Pacific and the international boundary."[62] Similarly, John Eagle's chapter on the Crow's Nest Pass agreement in *The Canadian Pacific Railway and the Development of Western Canada, 1896–1914* is titled "Canadianizing the Kootenays," and he too refers to the "invasion of the Kootenays by an American railway."[63] In his biography of Clifford Sifton, David Hall reiterates the point, with a reference to "preserving the trade of the mining districts of southeastern British Columbia from the greedy clutches of the Americans."[64] Such widely held views are simplistic and misleading.

The competition between the CPR and the Great Northern Railroad did not take place in a vacuum. As the companies sought maximum advantage in the Kootenays, they also were active in other arenas. They were, after all, two of the largest companies in North America. Hill's economic power and corporate profile were such that at the same time that he was building into the Boundary district and following the CPR's moves in Rossland, he was also trying to fight off the U.S. federal government and its determined prosecutors who had identified the Hill interests as the obvious choice to tackle in a landmark antitrust case, which went all the way to the U.S. Supreme Court.[65] For its part, the CPR increasingly became associated with the business elite of central Canada, a group that by the end of the nineteenth century controlled much of the country's economy.[66] A tariff fence stretched from the Atlantic to Pacific Coasts, and American branch plants were emerging as a key feature of the central Canadian economy. But the most important economic development of the century's closing decades was the construction of the CPR's transcontinental railway, moving people and freight both east and west. The railway—accompanied by the National Policy's protectionist tariff—fixed the center of economic activity firmly in Ontario and Quebec. Efforts to diversify the economy of other regions were actively discouraged.[67] The debate over reciprocity in 1910 and 1911 reveals the self-interested motives of the CPR, and many other businesses in central Canada, who fought fiercely to uphold the status quo.[68]

The fact that the business elite of central Canada shaped national economic development to maximize its position—and thus its profits—is unremarkable. This was simply rational capitalist behavior. Unfortunately such behavior is rarely regarded as a topic worthy of serious historical study. As William G. Robbins has argued, historians "have been reluctant to pursue lines of inquiry focusing on the broader influence of capitalism on the country's historical development. The failure to reckon with capitalism indicates, in part, an unwillingness to confront significant power and influence in our culture, a tendency that is widespread, especially so in the study of the American West. Most historians do assume the existence of capitalism; the problem rests in the inclination to disregard its imperatives, its broader implications for society, the nature of the economy, and politics."[69] The tendency to view the behavior of Canada's business elite as a heroic struggle to fashion a new country, an epic contest against geography and Jim Hill, is particularly deceptive. However comforting such a view might be to shareholders in the Canadian Pacific Railway, it is hardly an accurate characterization of railway development in western Canada.

NOTES

My sincere thanks to Athabasca University's Academic Research Committee and to the James Jerome Hill Reference Library of Saint Paul, Minnesota, for their generous support of the research on which this chapter is based.

1. Martin J. Sklar, *The Corporate Reconstruction of American Capitalism, 1890–1916: The Market, the Law, and Politics* (New York: Cambridge University Press, 1988), p. 1; cf. Alfred Dupont Chandler, *The Visible Hand: The Managerial Revolution in American Business* (Cambridge, Mass.: Belknap Press, 1977), passim. For an overview of the

Canadian context, see Robert Craig Brown and Ramsay Cook, *Canada 1896–1921: A Nation Transformed* (Toronto: McClelland and Stewart, 1974); Kenneth Norrie and Douglas Owram, *A History of the Canadian Economy*, 2d ed. (Toronto: Harcourt Brace Canada, 1996), pp. 217–90; and Christopher Armstrong and H. V. Nelles, *Monopoly's Moment: The Organization and Regulation of Canadian Utilities, 1830–1930* (Philadelphia: Temple University Press, 1986), a very useful analysis despite the narrow focus the title suggests.

2. The fact that railways were able unilaterally to redefine standard timekeeping for the continent in 1883 suggests their impact and influence on North American society. See Stephen Kern, *The Culture of Time and Space, 1880–1918* (Cambridge: Harvard University Press, 1983), p. 12; David Landes, *Revolution in Time: Clocks and the Making of the Modern World* (Cambridge: Harvard University Press, 1983), especially pp. 285–89; Derek Howse, *Greenwich Time and the Discovery of the Longitude* (Oxford: Oxford University Press, 1980), especially pp. 81–115; and Wolfgang Schivelbusch, *The Railway Journey: The Industrialization of Time and Space in the Nineteenth Century* (Leamington Spa, England: Berg Publishers, 1986), pp. 42–44. In addition, of course, railways were powerful and complex symbols of industrialization. Leo Marx lists some of the salient points: "the railroad as a system incorporated most of the essential features of the emerging industrial order: the substitution of metal for wood construction; mechanized motive power; vastly enlarged geographical scale; speed, rationality, impersonality, and a spirit of efficiency that included an unprecedented emphasis on precise timing." See Marx, "Closely Watched Trains," *New York Review of Books*, March 15, 1984, p. 28.

3. Naturally, there are exceptions. Historians of British Columbia's resource industries—in forestry, Richard Rajala and Gordon Hak as well as the sociologist Patricia Marchak, and in fishing, Keith Ralston—have produced fine studies, while Robert A. J. McDonald's *Making Vancouver: Class, Status, and Social Boundaries, 1863–1913* (Vancouver: University of British Columbia Press, 1996), is in part a fine materialist study. It remains the case, however, that the major surveys of the province's history fail to explore its political economy in any detail. Martin Robin's *The Rush for Spoils: The Company Province, 1871–1933* (Toronto: McClelland and Stewart, 1972), did confront such issues, but his work was marred by sloppy scholarship and swiftly condemned by the conservative gatekeepers of the academic establishment.

4. See the discussion in Jeremy Mouat, *Roaring Days: Rossland's Mines and the History of British Columbia* (Vancouver: University of British Columbia Press, 1995), pp. 5–16; for the Coeur d'Alenes boom, see John Fahey, *The Ballyhoo Bonanza: Charles Sweeny and the Idaho Mines* (Seattle: University of Washington Press, 1971), passim.

5. "Report of a Committee of the Privy Council," June 14, 1883, reprinted in *British Columbia Sessional Papers*, 1884, p. 175. For discussions of this episode, see Patricia E.

Roy, "Railways, Politicians, and the Development of the City of Vancouver as a Metropolitan Centre 1886–1929," M.A. thesis, University of Toronto, 1963; and Ronald Howard Meyer, "The Evolution of Railways in the Kootenays," M.A. thesis, University of British Columbia, 1970.

6. See A. A. den Otter, *Civilizing the West: The Galts and the Development of Western Canada* (Edmonton: University of Alberta Press, 1982), pp. 156–57.

7. *Annual Report of the Canadian Pacific Railway Company, for the Fiscal Year Ending December 31st, 1897,* p. 6.

8. As late as 1909, efforts were still being made to persuade Jim Hill to come north. That year the secretary of the Kelowna Board of Trade penned the following letter to Louis W. Hill (James J. Hill's son and a senior official with the Great Northern Railroad): "I am instructed by the Board of Trade here to write to you, and ask you to give your most serious consideration to the question of building a branch line from Oroville, Wash., to Penticton, B.C. . . . the Okanagan is the only valley in South-eastern B.C. which you have thus far overlooked. You have lines to East Kootenay, West Kootenay, and Boundary; then you skip the Okanagan and go into the Similkameen. Surely so rich a valley as the Okanagan is not a thing to be overlooked." (R. B. Kerr to Louis W. Hill, October 23, 1909, "Canadian Railway Matters, 1903–1915," File #4015, Box 71, President's Office—Subject Files, Great Northern Railway Papers, Minnesota Historical Society, St. Paul, Minnesota.)

9. The quotation is from James Baker to James J. Hill, July 30, 1891, in Folder 2, Box 1, Kootenay Railway and Navigation Company Papers, James J. Hill Papers, James Jerome Hill Reference Library, St. Paul, Minnesota [hereafter Hill Papers]. Similarly: "A Col. Baker here a few days since interviewed me on the subject of coal N.W. of Great Falls [Montana]; it is called Crows Nest in Kootenay, B.C. He brought me specimens of this coal which looked well, and told me that he had some interviews with you and was now going out to see you." (J. B. Haggin to James J. Hill, May 17, 1892, in Hill Papers—General Correspondence by Date). There are strong hints in Baker's letters to Hill that he would be willing to use his political influence to aid in the sale. (Baker represented East Kootenay in the provincial legislature from 1886 to 1900, and until 1898 was associated with the governing group.) Baker had tried to sell the coal properties to Sir George Stephen in the late 1880s; see Heather Gilbert, *The Life of Lord Mount Stephen,* vol. 2, *The End of the Road, 1891–1921* (Aberdeen, Scotland: Aberdeen University Press, 1977), pp. 16–17; and A. A. den Otter, "Bondage of Steam: The CPR and Western Canadian Coal," in Hugh A. Dempsey, ed., *The CPR West: The Iron Road and the Making of a Nation* (Vancouver, B.C.: Douglas & McIntyre, 1984), especially pp. 194–98.

10. E. T. Nichols to Hill, February 17, 1893, to James J. Hill, in Hill Papers—General Correspondence by Date.

11. See "The Railway War at Sandon," *The Miner* (Nelson), December 21, 1895, p. 1; "Fun at Sandon," *Kaslo Claim*, December 21, 1895, p. 1. Robert Turner provides a very good account of this episode in Turner and David S. Wilkie, *The Skyline Limited: The Kaslo and Slocan Railway* (Victoria, B.C.: Sono Nis Press, 1994), pp. 61–65.

12. "Crowsnest Pass" is the contemporary term for the area, although in the 1890s and early 1900s "Crow's Nest Pass" was more common. Throughout this chapter I follow contemporary usage in the text but reproduce the earlier phrase when it is used in quotations or as part of a company's name, and so on.

13. For the theme issues on British Columbia mines, see *Evening Star*, January 19, 1897, and *Saturday Globe*, February 6, 1897; more generally, "Truth vs. Exaggeration," *Canadian Mining Review* 15 (December 1896): 248; "Notes on Canada's Mines," *Globe*, December 24, 1896, p. 9; "The Mines of Canada," *Globe*, February 9, 1897, p. 5; "Mining Development," *Globe*, February 15, 1897, p. 12.

14. "In the Commons," *Daily World*, September 23, 1896, p. 2.

15. George Maxwell quoted in "Crow's Nest Pass Railway," *Globe*, December 28, 1896, p. 7.

16. "Endorse the Railway," *Daily World*, November 7, 1896, p. 4. The Trades and Labor Council's endorsement, however, was conditional and hedged by a racist caveat, as the complete motion suggests: "That while this Council favors the Government ownership of all railways, they are of the opinion that the proposed Vancouver, Victoria and Eastern railway should be built at as early a date as possible, believing that the undertaking will greatly benefit this Province, and that Mr. Maxwell, M.P., be requested to give the scheme his assistance, providing that the people's interests are carefully guarded in the matter of regulation of rates, and that no Chinamen be employed." For coverage of the meeting of the Boards of Trade, see "On to Kootenay," *Daily World*, November 7, 1896, p. 4; "Kootenay Trade," (Victoria) *Daily Colonist*, November 8, 1896, p. 1; "Kootenay Railway," (Victoria) *Daily Times*, November 9, 1896, p. 3.

17. "An Unbeliever," (Victoria) *Daily Times*, November 7, 1896, p. 4; this was the lead editorial.

18. "The Crow's Nest Pass Railway," *Mining Review* (Rossland), May 1, 1897, p. 2.

19. "Want No C.P.R. Control," *Evening Telegram*, December 21, 1896, p. 3. This article was subtitled "Mining Owes Nothing to the C.P.R"; "Canada Pacific [*sic*] Apathy Crippled the Industry Which Its Greed Would Crush"; "Grievances Many and Great."

20. T. G. Shaughnessy to Wilfrid Laurier, September 12, 1896, #6990, quoting an earlier memorandum to Sir Charles Tupper, April 15, 1896; reproduced on microfilm, "Papers Relating to British Columbia from the Laurier Collection in the Public Archives of Canada," reel 1 (copy in University of British Columbia Library).

21. See, for example, his comments in "Vancouver to Rossland," *Weekly News-*

Advertiser (Vancouver), October 21, 1896, p. 8. (The article is an interview with William Van Horne, concerning the construction of the Crowsnest Pass railway and its possible extension to the coast from the Kootenays.)

22. See especially "Eating Its Own Words," *Toronto World*, March 1, 1897, pp. 1–4; "The Globe and The Crow's Nest," *Toronto World*, March 1, 1897, p. 4; "What the Papers Say," *Toronto World*, March 1, 1897, p. 4; "What the Papers Say," *Toronto World*, March 2, 1897, p. 4; "That Railway Deal," *Evening News* (Toronto), March 1, 1897, p. 4; "Effective Fighting," *Evening News,* March 2, 1897, p. 4.

23. In addition to the references in the previous note, see the account of the Crowsnest affair in Hector Charlesworth, *More Candid Chronicles: Further Leaves from the Note Book of a Canadian Journalist* (Toronto: Macmillan, 1928), p. 162. More generally—on the *Globe*'s history and links with Robert Jaffray and George A. Cox—see W. T. R. Preston, *My Generation of Politics and Politicians* (Toronto: D. A. Rose, 1927), p. 135; also Richard Thomas George Clippingdale, "J. S. Willison, Political Journalist: From Liberalism to Independence, 1881–1905," Ph.D. dissertation, University of Toronto, 1970, especially pp. 351–80. For a discussion of the larger context, see Brian P. N. Beaven, "Partisanship, Patronage, and the Press in Ontario, 1880–1914: Myths and Realities," *Canadian Historical Review* 64 (September 1983): 317–51.

24. "Crow's Nest Talk," (Victoria) *Daily Times*, March 5, 1897, p. 4.

25. See, for example, the comments of Andrew Blair, minister of railways, and Richard Cartwright, minister of trade and commerce, in *Canada Parliamentary Debates*, June 18, 1897, pp. 4,519, 4,541–42.

26. *Canada Parliamentary Debates*, June 18, 1897, p. 4542.

27. D. J. Hall, *Clifford Sifton*, vol. 1, *The Young Napoleon, 1861–1900* (Vancouver: University of British Columbia Press, 1981), p. 155.

28. "Provincial Parliament," *Daily News Advertiser*, April 8, 1898, p. 2. D. W. Higgins was not alone in this analysis: cf. the report of a speech by a former Member of Legislature, "Macpherson Talks Figures," (Vancouver) *Daily Province*, April 11, 1901, pp. 3 and 7. More generally, see the close analysis of the 1898 campaign in John Tupper Saywell, "The McInnes Incident in British Columbia, 1897–1900," B.A. essay, University of British Columbia, 1950, pp. 37–52.

29. (Victoria) *Daily Colonist*, June 25, 1898, p. 7. In a similar vein several other prominent oppositionists accused the government of "Dunsmuirism," that is, of being simply a tool in the hands of the powerful Vancouver Island coal barons. See, for example, the comments of Joe Martin and Ralph Smith, quoted in the *Daily News Advertiser*, July 8, 1898, pp. 1 and 2; also the *Daily News Advertiser*, July 1, 1898, p. 2 (quoting the [Nelson] *Tribune*), where the Turner government is charged with "being controlled absolutely by one family—the Dunsmuirs."

30. *Daily News Advertiser*, June 29, 1898, p. 2.

31. "British Columbia General Election," *Pall Mall Gazette*, July 29, 1898, p. 6.

32. For an account of the public meeting and E. V. Bodwell's speech, see "Endorsed The Road," (Victoria) *Daily Times*, March 20, 1901, p. 6; for Premier Dunsmuir's response to Bodwell, see "Provincial Parliament," (Victoria) *Daily Times*, March 21, 1901, p. 3. Note also the editorial on the affair, "The Railway Question," (Victoria) *Daily Times*, March 21, 1901, p. 4, which is very supportive of Bodwell.

33. See "Charges and Defence," (Victoria) *Daily Times*, March 20, 1902, p. 4 (editorial); "Proceedings of the Legislature," (Victoria) *Daily Times*, March 20, 1902, pp. 3 and 6. For the subsequent inquiry, see "The Commission on Railway Deal," (Victoria) *Daily Times*, March 27, 1902, pp. 1 and 8; "Royal Commission Hears Evidence," (Victoria) *Daily Times*, March 29, 1902, pp. 3 and 8.

34. See the description in R. E. Gosnell and E. O. S. Scholefield, *A History of British Columbia*, part 2 (written by Gosnell) (Vancouver and Victoria, B.C.: British Columbia Historical Association, 1913), especially p. 149; the analysis of the 1903 election result in "The Prospects of British Columbia and the North-West," *Mining Journal* (London), November 28, 1903, pp. 613–14; and John Belshaw's perceptive comments in "Provincial Politics, 1871–1916," in Hugh J. M. Johnston, ed., *The Pacific Province: A History of British Columbia* (Vancouver, B.C.: Douglas & McIntyre, 1996), especially pp. 148–51.

35. All quotations are from T. Mayne Daly to Richard McBride, June 3, 1903, Winnipeg: Letter 68, File 2, Box 76, Correspondence Inward (Private), 1903, Premiers Papers, GR 441, British Columbia Archives [hereafter BCA]. Emphasis in original.

36. The relationship of the CPR with the federal government deserves far greater critical scrutiny than it has received thus far. Previous scholars have recognized the close association but most have been silent about its possible implications. Many examples of the intimate relationship of senior CPR executives with members of Laurier's government could be cited. Shaughnessy's letter to Laurier of September 12, 1896, quoted earlier in this chapter, was marked "personal," and its tone demonstrates that Shaughnessy was on familiar terms with the prime minister. (The letter opens, "Referring to our conversation when I had the pleasure of meeting you in Ottawa a few days ago.") See also Shaughnessy's account of his meetings with several Liberal cabinet ministers in his letter to William Van Horne, October 6, 1897, Van Horne Papers, RG 1, #82689, Canadian Pacific Archives, Windsor Station, Montreal. Similarly, key figures in the provincial arena were on close terms with the CPR's senior executives. See, for example, Van Horne's letter to Premier Turner, November 28, 1896, Van Horne Papers, RG 1, #82016, Canadian Pacific Archives, and Van Horne's letter to Lieutenant-Governor Edgar Dewdney, February 28, 1896, Edgar Dewdney fonds (M320), Glenbow Archives, Calgary. There are good discussions of the public mood in Canada during this period in Brown and Cook, *Canada 1896–1921*, especially pp. 28–33;

and Carl Berger, *The Sense of Power: Studies in the Ideas of Canadian Imperialism, 1867–1914* (Toronto: University of Toronto Press, 1970), passim.

37. James J. Hill, "The Great Northern and the Northwest," in Stuart Bruchey, ed., *Memoirs of Three Railroad Pioneers* (New York: Arno Press, 1981) ["James J. Hill's letter to the stockholders on retiring from the chairmanship of the Board of Directors, July 1 1912"]. Twenty years earlier Hill offered this analysis to a Vancouver journalist: "The sole and prime aim of all railway managers was to get business and to run lines to such places as would supply this, the only essential to successful railroading." ("President J. J. Hill," [Vancouver] *Daily World*, September 14, 1891, p. 5.)

38. See the account in Heather Gilbert, *Awakening Continent: The Life of Lord Mount Stephen*, vol. 1, *1829–91* (Aberdeen, Scotland: Aberdeen University Press, 1965), pp. 63–73.

39. For a valuable discussion of railway financing, particularly useful for its exploration of the informal links of friendship between politicians, bankers, and railway builders, see Dolores Greenberg, "A Study of Capital Alliances: The St. Paul & Pacific," *Canadian Historical Review* 57 (March 1976): 25–39. (The St. Paul & Pacific railway became the St. Paul, Minneapolis, and Manitoba Railroad described in the chapter, and ran from St. Paul, Minnesota, northwest to the Red River valley and Manitoba.) Other important studies that shed light on western railway financing during this period include Albro Martin, *James J. Hill and the Opening of the Northwest* (1976; reprint, St. Paul: Minnesota Historical Society, 1991); and Heather Gilbert's two volumes on George Stephen, *Awakening Continent* and *The End of the Road*.

40. Hill was thinking of buying the troubled Northern Pacific, but in a letter to Hill in the summer of 1889 Stephen tried to change his mind: "I am not clear in my own mind as to our ability to capture the control of the Northern Pacific. That is, I do not see so clearly how it is to be done as I do our ability to build a new line of our own. Of that I have no doubt, and think I can see my way to finance an extension to the Coast on very economical terms so far as the finding of the money is concerned." (Quoted in Gilbert's *The End of the Road*, p. 23.)

41. M. P. Jordan, "Notes sur la Colombie Britannique," *Annales des Mines*, ou Recueil de Mémoires sur l'exploitation des Mines et sur les sciences et les arts qui s'y rattachent, Neuvième Série, Mémoires—Tome XVII (1900), p. 226. I have translated the passage from the French original.

42. Ibid., p. 227. Again, I have translated the passage from the original French.

43. Louis W. Hill to Edward Tuck, July 28, 1898, Personal Papers, General Correspondence, 1898–March 1901, Louis W. Hill Papers, James Jerome Hill Reference Library.

44. Gaspard Farrer to Louis W. Hill, September 9, 1899, Personal Papers, General Correspondence, 1898–March 1901, Louis W. Hill Papers. On Farrer, see Martin, *James J.*

Hill and the Opening of the Northwest, p. 414; on Louis Hill's position, see ibid., pp. 421–24.

45. See the comments in John A. Eagle, *The Canadian Pacific Railway and the Development of Western Canada, 1896–1914* (Kingston, Montreal, London: McGill-Queen's University Press, 1989), pp. 115–16.

46. "Their mixture of coal interests, railway schemes, and politics gives the Coal Company a complexion that differs substantially from that of an ordinary commercial enterprise," grumbled Shaughnessy in a letter to the prime minister (Shaughnessy to Laurier, January 14, 1901, #52446–52453, in the Laurier Papers Relating to British Columbia, microfilm held in the University of British Columbia Library). Shaughnessy appended a five-page typed memo on the company's history to the letter. For his part, Hill—in a letter to the son of the former Liberal cabinet minister Sir Richard Cartwright—noted that "the Crows Nest Company, unfortunately, was largely run more as a stock exchange matter than a coal mine and while the property is of itself a valuable one the manner in which it was handled resulted as all companies do that are handled at arms' length by people who are inclined to speculate. I invested a large sum of money in the property at a high rate for the stock but found I had to either lose the investment or invest more." (James J. Hill to A. D. Cartwright, Secretary, Board of Railway Commissioners, Ottawa, January 6, 1916, James J. Hill Letterpress Books, Vol. P 22, p. 939, Hill Papers.) Cartwright had sought Hill's advice on whether to hang on to his late father's shares in the company. Hill urged him to keep the shares, adding, "If at any time you desire to sell the Company's shares, my confidence in the property is so great that I would be inclined to buy them at a fair price and will be glad to hear from you." See also John Fahey, *Shaping Spokane: Jay P. Graves and His Times* (Seattle: University of Washington Press, 1994), p. 75.

47. Martin, *James J. Hill and the Opening of the Northwest*, p. 593.

48. "C.P.R. Is Outwitted," (Victoria) *Daily Colonist*, July 15, 1904, p. 1; cf. "Reported Control of Granby Mines," (Victoria) *Daily Colonist*, July 14, 1904, p. 6.

49. John Fahey points out that "the Great Northern between 1904 and 1910 [carried] three-fifths of the freight of the Boundary" (*Shaping Spokane*, p. 80). For the CPR's interest in the Boundary, see *Shaping Spokane*, pp. 10, 15, and 81.

50. W. H. Aldridge to Sir Thomas Shaughnessy, November 1, 1904, Cominco Historical Files, Microfilm Reel #8, Add. Mss. 2500, BCA.

51. (Toronto) *World*, June 26, 1905, p. 1.

52. For a description of these events, see Mouat, *Roaring Days*, pp. 130–43.

53. James J. Hill to E. T. Nichols (Confidential), June 7, 1905, James J. Hill Letterbook, Hill Papers. A. J. Macmillan worked on Hill's behalf in Britain, and one can follow his activities through correspondence held in a file titled "Merger of the

Le Roi Mining Company et al., 1905–1906" (File 172, Box 12, in the papers of Crowsnest Resources Limited, M1561, Glenbow Archives).

54. Aldridge to C. A. Molson, January 4, 1906, Cominco Historical Files, Microfilm Reel #8, Add. Mss. 2500, BCA.

55. Ibid. The St. Eugene mine was a silver lead property in Moyie, in East Kootenay.

56. "Audacious Mr. Hill," (Victoria) *Daily Times*, May 9, 1905, p. 4. The earlier quotation in the text is from "Selwyn on the Crow's Nest Pass," *Mining Review* (Rossland), April 24, 1897, p. 2.

57. For example: "Mr. J. J. Hill, the well-known Canadian-American railway king of the north-west . . . reached this city on Friday evening . . . accompanied by Lords Mount Stephen and Elphinstone, Messrs. J. W. Sterling, of New York and Wm. Stephen, all of whom are largely interested in the Great Northern as well as in the Canadian Pacific. . . . The capital represented by the few gentlemen present on that occasion would aggregate a sum close upon $450,000,000–an amount larger than was ever before represented at any one meeting on this coast." ("President J. J. Hill," [Vancouver] *Daily World*, September 14, 1891, p. 5)

58. "Qualms of Patriots," (Victoria) *Daily Times*, May 12, 1905, p. 4.

59. For an introduction to Cominco's history, see Jeremy Mouat, "Creating a New Staple: Capital, Technology, and Monopoly in B.C.'s Resource Sector, 1901–1925," *Journal of the Canadian Historical Association*, n.s., 1 (1990): 215–37. Something of Granby's importance may be gleaned from L. E. Carter's "Granby: Seventy-Five Years of British Columbia Copper Mining," B.A. honor's essay, Simon Fraser University, 1979.

60. Pierre Berton's two-volume account of the railway is the most significant of the many popular works on the CPR (*The National Dream: The Great Railway, 1871–1881* [Toronto: McClelland and Stewart, 1970], and *The Last Spike: The Great Railway, 1881–1885* [Toronto: McClelland and Stewart, 1971]). It remains one of the most successful historical works ever published in Canada and was reissued in several other formats (a condensed single volume, an illustrated volume); it was also being turned into a major television production. Although Berton's work is well researched and eminently readable, it did little more than chronicle the railway's conception and construction, seeing its completion as symbolic of the national project. (Viv Nelles provides a thoughtful critique in "The Ties That Bind: Berton's C.P.R.," *Canadian Forum* [November-December 1970]: 271.) For the poem mentioned in the text, see E. J. Pratt, *Towards the Last Spike* (Toronto: Macmillan, 1952). Subtitled "A verse-panorama of the struggle to build the first Canadian transcontinental from the time of the proposed Terms of Union with British Columbia (1870) to the hammering of the last spike in the Eagle Pass (1885)," the poem has been reprinted numerous times and has

provoked a rejoinder from F. R. Scott, "All the Spikes but the Last" (1954), reprinted in *The Collected Poems of F. R. Scott* (Toronto: McClelland and Stewart, 1981), p. 194. Gordon Lightfoot's "Canadian Railroad Trilogy" was very popular during the late 1960s and early 1970s; the song appeared first on the album "The Way I Feel" (United Artists, 1967), was reissued on the live album "Sunday Concert" (United Artists, 1969), and again on "Gord's Gold" (Warner Brothers/Reprise Records, 1975). For thoughtful reflection on the ways in which the CPR's construction has been used for nationalist purposes, see Maurice Charland's "Technological Nationalism," *Canadian Journal of Political and Social Theory (Revue canadienne de théorie politique et sociale)* 10, nos. 1–2 (1986): 196–220; and A. A. den Otter's *The Philosophy of Railways: The Transcontinental Railway Idea in British North America* (Toronto: University of Toronto Press, 1997), which appeared after this chapter was written.

61. For works that take a critical look at the railway's significance, see Norbert MacDonald, "The Canadian Pacific Railway and Vancouver's Development to 1900," in W. Peter Ward and Robert A. J. McDonald, eds., *British Columbia: Historical Readings* (Vancouver, B.C.: Douglas & McIntyre, 1981), pp. 396–425; Robert A. J. McDonald, "Victoria, Vancouver, and the Economic Development of British Columbia, 1886–1914," reprinted in Ward and McDonald, eds., *British Columbia: Historical Readings*, pp. 369–95; and A. A. den Otter's work, especially *The Philosophy of Railways*; "Bondage of Steam: Transportation, Trade, and Regional Identity in the Southwestern Prairies," *Prairie Forum* 15 (spring 1990): 1–23; and "Railway Technology, the Canadian Northwest, and the Continental Economy," *Railroad History*, Bulletin 162 (spring 1990): 5–19.

62. W. Kaye Lamb, *History of the Canadian Pacific Railway* (New York: Macmillan, 1977), pp. 199, 196.

63. Eagle, "Canadianizing the Kootenays," in *The Canadian Pacific Railway and the Development of Western Canada, 1896–1914*, pp. 23, 25.

64. Hall, *Clifford Sifton*, vol. 1, p. 150.

65. See Martin, *James J. Hill and the Opening of the Northwest*, pp. 494–523; and Chandler, *The Visible Hand*, pp. 171–75.

66. For various perspectives on this (enormous) topic, see Ronald Radosh, "American Manufacturers, Canadian Reciprocity, and the Origins of the Branch Factory System," *CAAS* Bulletin 3, no. 1 (1967): 19–54; Michael Bliss, "Canadianizing American Business: The Roots of the Branch Plant," in Ian Lumsden, ed., *Close the Forty-Ninth Parallel Etc.: The Americanization of Canada* (Toronto: University of Toronto Press, 1970), pp. 26–42; Thomas William Acheson, "The Social Origins of Canadian Industrialism: A Study in the Structure of Entrepreneurship," Ph.D. dissertation, University of Toronto, 1971; and Craig Heron, "The Second Industrial Revolution in Canada, 1890–1930," in Deian R. Hopkin and Gregory S. Kealey, eds.,

Class, Community, and the Labour Movement: Wales and Canada, 1850–1930 (Aberystwyth, Wales: Llafur, 1989), pp. 48–66.

67. Scholars in eastern Canada have produced a rich historiography, analyzing the process of deindustrialization and decline. Useful introductions to this work include Eric Sager, "Dependency, Underdevelopment, and the Economic History of the Atlantic Provinces," *Acadiensis* 17 (fall 1987): 117–23; various essays in P. A. Buckner and David Frank, eds., *The Acadiensis Reader*, vol. 2, *Atlantic Canada after Confederation*, 2d ed. (Fredericton, New Brunswick: Acadiensis Press, 1988); and Phillip J. Wood, "'Barriers' to Capitalist Development in Maritime Canada, 1870–1930: A Comparative Perspective," in Peter Baskerville, ed., *Canadian Papers in Business History* (Victoria, B.C.: Public History Group, 1989), vol. 1, pp. 33–57. Little comparable work has been done in western Canada, but see John Lutz, "Losing Steam: The Boiler and Engine Industry as an Index of British Columbia's Deindustrialization, 1880–1915," Canadian Historical Association, *Historical Papers/Communications historiques*, 1988, pp. 168–208; and Mouat, "Creating a New Staple."

68. See Stephen Scheinberg, "Invitation to Empire: Tariffs and American Economic Expansion in Canada," *Business History Review* 47 (summer 1973): 218–38; Robert E. Hannigan, "Reciprocity 1911: Continentalism and American Weltpolitik," *Diplomatic History* 4 (winter 1980): 1–18; and Gordon T. Stewart, *The American Response to Canada since 1776* (East Lansing: Michigan State University Press, 1992), pp. 101–26.

69. William G. Robbins, *Colony and Empire: The Capitalist Transformation of the American West* (Lawrence: University Press of Kansas, 1994), p. 8. In the quotation Robbins is speaking of the American West, but I would argue that these comments apply equally well to western Canada. He has recently restated his thesis with considerable vigor; see "In Pursuit of Historical Explanation: Capitalism as a Conceptual Tool for Knowing the American West," *Western Historical Quarterly* 30 (fall 1999): 277–93.

PART TWO

NEGOTIATING THE
INTERNATIONAL BOUNDARY

6 / The Historical Roots

of the Canadian-American Salmon Wars

JOSEPH E. TAYLOR III

Salmon, the foundation of a rich industry and heart of a culture, is the
subject of a jealous tug-of-war between two otherwise friendly neighbors.
—THOMAS C. JENSEN

In the past few years Canada and the United States have clashed in remarkably vitriolic fashion over the fate of Pacific salmon. In 1994, Canada tried
to leverage changes in international harvest allocations by imposing fees on
American vessels bound for Alaska through British Columbia waters. American
officials responded by threatening to raise duties on ships traveling to Canadian
ports through Juan de Fuca Strait. The following year, Indian tribes and the
governments of Oregon, Washington, and Canada sued Alaska over its salmon
management policy. The problems continued in 1996, when Canada criticized
Alaska's quota on chinook salmon, and in 1997, when British Columbia once
again impounded American vessels en route to Alaska and unilaterally set
fishing quotas on Pacific salmon stocks. American managers replied by
unleashing a free-for-all harvest on Fraser River sockeye (*Oncorhynchus
nerka*), and in retaliation Canadian fishers blockaded an American ferry in
Prince Rupert harbor. To the uninitiated it might appear as though salmon
fishing had devolved into a state of near anarchy, but close observers have
understood these conflicts differently.[1]

These contests reveal not a lack of order but the flawed way order has
evolved throughout the past century. Many of the fishery's recent problems
are the by-products of solutions to fishing disputes arrived at during the 1970s
and 1980s. Those conflicts, in turn, erupted from the failings of treaties dating back all the way to the 1890s. In other words international fishery man-

agers are struggling against a chain of mounting failure. They are caught in a downward spiral that began with an event that comes as close as anything does in fishery management to original sin: the estrangement of fishing from discrete runs of salmon; that is, the moment when fishers abandoned rivers and their genetically distinct runs to prey on homogenous schools of fish in the larger and less-regulated ocean. The problem emerged first in the Puget Sound and Gulf of Georgia in the 1890s, where rival fishers began to harvest Fraser River sockeye at alarming rates. The United States and Canada searched for a solution by focusing solely on the allocation of Fraser sockeye, but their inability to contain or sustain that fishery snowballed into additional treaties acknowledging the complexity of the forces involved and extending regulation over an ever-expanding area and array of fisheries. Unfortunately, none of these solutions met with much success.

The reasons for failure were manifold. Early treaties were often behind the times, addressing outmoded conditions and covering insufficient areas, and negotiators usually lacked the foresight and power to effect conservation. Even worse, later treaties rested on a diplomatic foundation that had already hopelessly confused the biological coherence of management. Diplomats had reached agreements by engaging a strategy of abstraction that conceptualized salmon populations as national claims. This subordinated the fate of any individual run, such as Fraser River sockeye or Columbia River chinook (*O. tshawytscha*), to parity between Canadian and U.S. shares of overall harvests. To maintain this sense of balance, parties agreed to trade fish like blocks of stock, reallocating some fisheries to compensate for imbalances in others. This created a fiction of international equity through biological bookkeeping. National quotas were sustained via deliberate constructions of regional inequalities: American fishers in Puget Sound and Alaska maintained access to Fraser and Skeena River runs by allowing Canadian trollers on Vancouver Island to prey on Columbia River and coastal stocks. This was an expedient way to forge international comity, but it was also (and remains today) an irrational way to manage salmon. It validated the same ocean fisheries that fishery scientists had tried to throttle during the 1920s because of trolling's tendency to undermine managers' ability to know which runs were being harvested, and how intensely, until it was far too late. Treaties thus fostered a process that distanced harvest from natal streams and made saving salmon increasingly difficult.

To understand how fishery management devolved into this irrational mode, we must look at the historical roots of Canadian-American fish fights. This chapter examines the paradoxical evolution of salmon fishing, its environmental and industrial contours, the many interests and tensions that shaped diplomatic negotiations and scientific research, and the managerial consequences of international policy. Salmon talks began in the 1890s, and in 1937 the U.S. Senate finally ratified an agreement. Unfortunately, this reconciliation created as many conflicts as it resolved. By abstracting a complex fishery into national quotas, negotiators concocted an image of international parity that masked severe imbalances among fisheries. Thus the 1937 treaty alleviated immediate political tensions but did not anticipate the changing face of a dynamic industry. More seriously, as recent events demonstrate, it failed to solve any of the fishery's more fundamental problems.

The initial conflict between Canadian and American fishers is a classic case of unregulated fishing gone awry. Unchecked industrial participation led to cutthroat competition as fishers leapfrogged across fishing space to intercept salmon before their competitors. To comprehend the underlying significance of this contest, we first need to consider the other salient element of this story: biological space. Pacific salmon (*Oncorhynchus spp.*) are anadromous; they use the relative security of freshwater environments to reproduce but migrate to sea early in life to exploit the ocean's greater abundance. After one to five years of maturing (depending on the species), salmon return to their natal streams to spawn. Salmon thus move *through* many environments during their lives, creating in the process a biological space that extends thousands of miles from the gravel of inland lakes and streams to the far reaches of the Gulf of Alaska. The rhythms of salmon produce a magnificent fish, but they also pose problems for humans because salmon's natural spaces have never been fully conterminous with the social spaces of the people who have depended on them.

Indians were the first to try and reconcile the incongruities between natural and social space in the salmon fisheries. As salmon proceeded up the Fraser River, they traversed the territories of many groups and villages while other Indians arrived from as far away as the northern Strait of Georgia to consume the great runs of sockeye and pink salmon (*O. gorbuscha*). Many people depended on salmon for subsistence, and all fished intensively using methods ranging from spears, leisters, and harpoons to seines, trawl nets, traps, and weirs. The latter implements were particularly effective—and potentially devastating—but unlike the later industrial fishery, Indians ended netting operations and disassembled weirs once they had sufficient stores for winter. They also limited access to fishing sites through kinship networks that further restricted fishing pressure at any given location. The biological movement of salmon and the economic dependence of Indians created the potential for serious intergroup conflict, but aboriginal strategies of accommodation had effectively ameliorated these tensions before the arrival of Euro-Americans.[2]

In the early nineteenth century, Indians along the lower Fraser River began to fish for commercial purposes. They initially sold salmon to the North West Company and Hudson's Bay Company (HBC) to feed resident trappers and traders, but in 1830 the HBC began to purchase much larger quantities. To supplement the income from fur trapping and undermine the efforts of rival American fishers, the HBC salted, barreled, and shipped salmon to the Sandwich Islands, Mexico, Chile, China, Australia, and England. The harvest actually declined during this period because European pathogens were killing Indians at catastrophic rates, but consumption rebounded during the 1850s and 1860s, as salmon fed hungry miners during the Caraboo gold rush. The number of salmon involved in these exchanges was relatively small compared with that of later years, but these exchanges introduced Pacific salmon to a vast and diverse market. Thus, by the time entrepreneurs built the first cannery on the Fraser in 1871, the world was primed to consume its product in almost unlimited quantities.[3]

The Euro-American way of fishing initially concentrated the spaces of the fishery. Instead of harvesting runs throughout the river system as Indians had done, gillnetters and trap owners focused their efforts in the river delta. They did so for three reasons: first, salmon stopped feeding once they began their spawning runs, so they were freshest and fattest as they entered the river; second, the meat degraded rapidly after capture, so it was essential for fishing operations to be located near processing facilities; and third, before railroads arrived, the only viable way to transport canned salmon was by ship, so canneries had to be accessible to ocean-going vessels. By concentrating catching at the mouth of the river, however, fishers tended to homogenize a previously diversified harvest. What had once been a series of localized fisheries not only in the lower river but also in the Pitt, Chilliwack, Lillooet, Thompson, Chilicotin, Quesnel, and Nechako watersheds had become a fishery of the river as a whole. From its very inception the industrial fishery began to blur the distinctions of discrete runs.[4]

The introduction of industrial methods of fishing and food preservation after 1871 intensified harvest to unprecedented levels. Aboriginal methods were highly effective, but they paled before the size and scale of capitalistic efficiency. Indian nets were a fraction of the size of industrial gillnets and seines, and Indian weirs, although impassable obstacles, were ephemeral constructions when compared with the larger, more permanent traps and pound nets that proliferated beginning in the 1870s. Canning was another important innovation. Aboriginal techniques could preserve salmon for about six months, but canned salmon could keep almost indefinitely. Expatriate New England fishers first used canning procedures on the Sacramento River in 1864. Two years later, following a drastic decline in Sacramento runs, they moved north to the Columbia River. Competitors soon followed, and by 1871 they had established the first cannery on the Fraser, which packed 7,247 cases of sockeye that year. Salmon fishing was becoming a high-stakes game. Most of the capital for operations came from San Francisco or the East, as did supplies. To equip themselves, canners had to make significant outlays for supplies without any guarantee that they would recoup expenses; they tried to offset risks by maximizing profits through frenetic harvesting. In one instance a large run of Fraser salmon exhausted the supply of tin plate at a cannery, all of which had been imported from Bolivia, before the season was half over. The profits from such boom runs encouraged additional investors, and by 1901 forty-nine canneries packed almost a million cases of salmon on the lower Fraser River.[5]

After 1901, however, the number of canneries on the Fraser quickly dwindled. The reduction resulted partly from industry consolidation as firms drove out or bought up weaker competitors, but falling harvests also discouraged participation. The diminishing catches stemmed from three separate causes. First, a natural fluctuation in runs, peaking every four years, caused a cyclical decline. Thus the exceptionally good years of 1893, 1897, and 1901 preceded three rather indifferent years before the next big run. Producers familiar with this rhythm were reluctant to expend resources in off years. Second was a suspicion that runs overall were beginning to decline. The 1905 season was far less spectacular than predecessor big years, and some observers feared that unrestrained harvest and development were undermining the future of the fishery. Third, American fishers were beginning to intercept sockeye runs before they reached the Fraser River (Figure 6.1).[6]

This third factor revealed a potentially fatal idiosyncrasy of Fraser runs. Most salmon do not come close to shore until they reach their natal streams, but geography and biology combined to make Fraser sockeye uniquely vulnerable to numerous fisheries. Because Vancouver Island lies between the Fraser and the open ocean, salmon have to swim a circuitous path around the island when they return to spawn. And because salmon depend on scent to find their natal stream, they also gravitate toward stronger currents. Therefore the majority of Fraser runs returned not from the north via the weak currents of Johnstone Strait but around the southern end of the island through Juan de Fuca Strait and the San Juan Islands. This route, driven by geology and

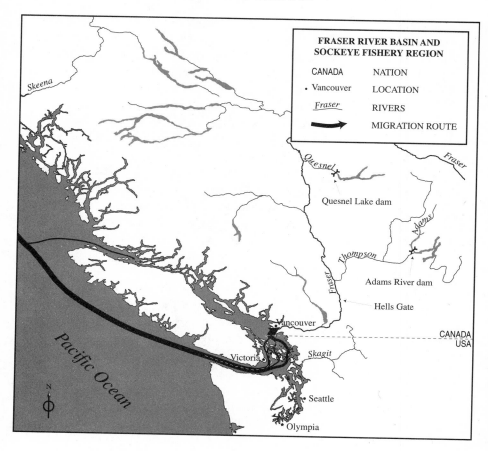

FIG. 6.1. Fraser River Basin and sockeye fishery region.

evolution, drew salmon into close proximity to land and fishers at numerous points before they reached the Fraser. The most important of these landmarks was Point Roberts, a spit of land that juts into the Gulf of Georgia only a few miles south of the Fraser River delta. The base of the spit was in British Columbia, but the point extended south of the forty-ninth parallel and thus became available to opportunistic U.S. fishers. By the turn of the century Point Roberts had become ground zero of an exploding controversy.[7]

The growing contention over Fraser sockeye stemmed from the intersection of three contingencies of nature and history: the Fraser sockeye's unique migration route; the United States's claim to Point Roberts; and the trans-

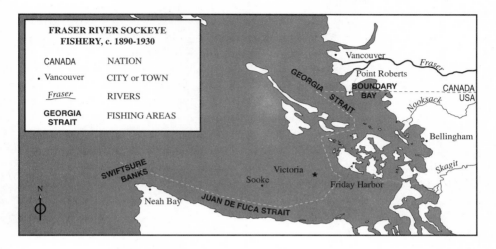

FIG. 6.2. Fraser River sockeye fishery, c. 1890–1930.

formation of fishing by market capitalism. The interception of sockeye before they reached the Fraser delta was not new. For centuries Salish Indians had used reef nets in shallow locations around Point Roberts and among the San Juan Islands to capture migrating salmon, but the scarcity of locations suitable to this technology severely limited the amount of salmon Indians could catch. Fraser runs suffered little from this fishery, but in 1880 a local canner named John Waller mimicked Indians by erecting a trap on the eastern edge of Point Roberts. Waller's initial experiment disappointed, but further experimentation taught him and other Americans about the superiority of locations on the western edge of the Point and the necessity of constructing weirs able to withstand the Strait of Georgia's strong currents and sudden storms. By 1894 there were three canneries profitably using traps south of the border at Point Roberts, on the Washington shore at Semiahmoo, and at Friday Harbor on San Juan Island. As the design and reach of traps and weirs improved, the American fishery grew astonishingly. By 1900 nineteen American canneries were canning 57 percent of the Fraser sockeye before they reached Canadian fishers (Figure 6.2).[8]

Having been corked by the Americans, Canadians initiated a game of industrial leapfrog as they tried to intercept Fraser sockeye before their competitors. Canadian canners first countered the Point Roberts traps by erecting their own pound nets in Boundary Bay, just east and north of Point Roberts. When these traps failed to stem the American harvest, the Canadians moved to Vancouver Island, where they built a cannery at Victoria to service traps located farther west along the Sooke coast. They also toyed with the idea of retaliating against Americans by intercepting salmon bound for Southeast Alaska. Although nothing came of these plans, and little emerged from the Sooke traps, the Canadian strategy made sense within the existing context. If the Sooke fishery had succeeded in intercepting sockeye from the Fraser and Skagit Rivers before the salmon reached American traps, Canadians might have corked the Point Roberts fishery. Their greater failure, though, and that of the diplomats who soon followed, was not so much in their choice of trap sites but in not grasping the dynamic character of the fishery.[9]

Other fishers, primarily Americans this time, were already intercepting salmon before they reached any pound net. By 1900, Puget Sound fishers were equipping their boats with gas engines and perfecting the use of purse seines. These nets, which had been in use since the early 1880s, were an integral component of the sail-powered fishery around the San Juan Islands and Puget Sound. A purse seine's great advantage was its combination of mobility and scope. With nets as big as 250 fathoms long and 25 fathoms deep, fishers could surround entire schools, cinch the bottom tight, and brail salmon onboard with giant dip nets. The addition of internal combustion engines allowed fishers to build bigger boats, travel farther from shore, and deploy larger nets. Their migration offshore would have trumped the Canadians regardless of the efficacy of Sooke traps. By 1907 the purse seine fishery was an activity of "considerable consequence," according to later federal investigators. As vessels continued to grow in size, fishers ventured ever farther, to Juan de Fuca Strait, Cape Flattery, the Swiftsure Banks, the Columbia River, and Southeast Alaska. From the perspective of fishery managers, though, each strategic shift in location or technology further removed harvest from biological coherence. As fishers increased their distance from spawning grounds, they decreased the ability of managers to know the provenience of any given harvested fish.[10]

The free-for-all quality of this competition, conducted increasingly beyond the jurisdiction of state, provincial, or federal governments, soon inspired international efforts at accommodation. Claims and counterclaims from both sides of the border, in conjunction with uncertainties about the biology of fish, led Canadian and American administrators to jointly investigate Fraser sockeye issues as early as 1892. An initial committee, headed by Richard Rathbun of the Smithsonian Institution and William Wakeham of the Canadian Fishery Patrol, surveyed the fishery and made general recommendations. Their 1896 report did not indicate a need for greater restriction, but by 1900 the

Point Roberts trap fishery had drastically altered this assessment. In 1902, Canada launched a second investigation, and in 1905 and 1906, British Columbia and Washington state even tried to coordinate regulation at the state and provincial levels. Internal politics eventually stymied legislation, though, and broader problems in the fisheries led Britain and the United States to form the International Fisheries Commission to investigate a series of disputes ranging from the Atlantic through the Great Lakes to the Fraser River. The commission struggled constantly with nationalistic tensions but, under the direction of David Starr Jordan of Stanford University and E. E. Prince of the Biological Board of Canada, it did reach a series of accords recommending the creation of a regulatory commission, a bold research agenda, longer closed seasons, and stronger restrictions on traps. Officials in both countries objected to empowering an independent regulatory commission, but Canadians saw no alternative and complied with recommendations. Americans were less inclined to cooperate for a variety of reasons, and ratification stalled in the Senate as representatives from Ohio and Washington state effectively tabled the agreement.[11]

Though the 1896 and 1909 reports endorsed radically different solutions, in both cases negotiators suffered a similar absence of power and perspective. To begin with, negotiators struggled with a structural inconsistency between the nations regarding fishery issues. Constitutionally, only national representatives could conduct international negotiations. Although this caused no conflict in Canada because the Dominion regulated the fisheries, American diplomats could not enforce their agreements because the states retained jurisdiction over fishery management. Point Roberts trap owners and Puget Sound purse seiners could defy treaties with impunity as long as their representatives in Olympia and Congress thwarted restrictive legislation from key committee positions.

But the states were not wholly to blame for the resulting inertia. Rathbun, Wakeham, Jordan, and Prince also fell short of their mark because all had failed to comprehend the dynamic condition of the fisheries. Like a single frame of a movie, they saw only a static image of a process that was actually undergoing constant change. Even if governments had followed these early recommendations, they would have had little effect because the fishery was already morphing. Resistance to restrictions seemed absurd by 1900, and by 1909 a closed season on traps would have accomplished little because of high-seas purse seining. With fishers constantly developing new ways to corner the market in this "grown man's game," negotiators were usually a step behind the evolving technologies and spaces of the fishery. The conclusions of 1896 and 1909 thus failed in part because the conditions they addressed were already out of date.[12]

Conditions changed rapidly again following a disastrous series of rock slides in the Fraser River canyon at Hell's Gate. Sockeye runs collapsed, radically altering the terms of the international debate. The looming prospect of extinction encouraged fishers and governments to cooperate in researching and rebuilding runs, but allocation issues remained a key component of discussions. Like a tar pit, fishing rivalries entrapped anyone who dared tackle the problems surrounding Fraser River salmon.

By 1913 dams and slides blocked salmon from much of the Fraser system. Problems had begun in 1898, when miners dammed the Quesnel River, and in 1907 loggers built a similarly devastating dam on the upper Adams River. Much worse was the blockage at a narrows in the Fraser Canyon called Hell's Gate. The rapids had always tested salmon, but construction by the Canadian Pacific Railroad along one canyon wall in the 1880s, and by the Canadian Northern Railway along the other wall in 1911 and 1912, pushed huge amounts of debris into the river at its narrowest point. These slides, in conjunction with the river's natural fluctuation, created two alternating problems for sockeye. During periods of heavy runoff, the river accelerated at the debris-filled narrows, moving too fast for the salmon to ford. Conversely, when the river dropped later in the season, enormous boulders emerged to block fish passage. By 1913 few upper-river salmon could reach their spawning beds. The timing was even more unfortunate because 1913 was a big-run year in the four-year cycle. Although canneries on both sides of the border put up the largest pack ever, huge sockeye schools still escaped upstream. Unfortunately, most of the survivors died of injury or exhaustion in a vain struggle to pass Hell's Gate. The 1913 spawning was the poorest ever. Believing that predation and harvest were the real problems, Canadian managers removed only part of the debris field and assumed they had solved things, but not until the late 1930s did researchers grasp the full extent of the blockage. In the meantime runs plummeted. The 1917 harvest was only 23 percent of 1913; 1921 was only 6 percent; 1925 was no better.[13]

With its West Coast fishery crippled, and believing that Point Roberts and purse seines were the underlying reasons for the decline, Canada redoubled its efforts to limit American harvests. During the 1910s and 1920s Canada diligently pursued joint regulation of the sockeye fisheries, but intransigent resistance among U.S. fishers and politicians blocked increased regulation. In 1914, for example, Puget Sound fishers and state administrators were decidedly against the Jordan-Prince treaty because of its restrictive impact on their activities. U.S. Senator Miles Poindexter from Washington state did support ratification, but even if his constituents had been in agreement, which they most decidedly·were not, opposition from Midwesterners and Easterners over issues dealing with the Great Lakes and Atlantic fisheries killed the treaty. At that point Canada reluctantly withdrew its support of the treaty but continued to pursue negotiations. In 1918 diplomats completed a compact similar to the 1909 treaty, except that it also limited fishing licenses to citizens of Canada and the United States. This posed a considerable threat to the alien-dominated purse seine fishery, so purse seiners and the American canners who depended on their catch protested to Congress and succeeded in blocking ratification. Discouraged Canadians then tried to effect joint regulation with Washington state officials, but constitutional restrictions forced them back to federal negotiators. In any event Washingtonians were unwilling to cede control to federal managers, let alone an international commission, and negotiations foundered for much of the next decade.[14]

Although official diplomacy had stalled, various Canadian and American fishery agencies were achieving a remarkable degree of cooperation. British Columbia officials had suspected the significance of the Hell's Gate slides before the end of 1913, but they overestimated their success in excavating the offending debris over the next several years and preferred to indict fishers for any remaining problems. Thus continually diminishing runs deflected Canadian managers onto fruitless paths during the 1920s, but never completely. Lingering doubts about the cause of decline led to numerous investigations by provincial, Dominion, and U.S. researchers throughout the 1910s and 1920s. Individual investigators often disagreed about causes, extent, and solutions, but the ongoing contact among agencies had a salutary effect. Fishery managers and scientists began to recognize their common interest in resolving questions and sustaining runs. In 1923 fishers and managers persuaded the United States and Canada to create the International Fisheries Commission (IFC) to investigate and regulate troubled halibut fisheries in the northeastern Pacific. The IFC was an instant managerial and political success and became a standard for cooperation. Two years later the commissioner of the U.S. Bureau of Fisheries (USBF) and the director of the Biological Board of Canada persuaded fish commissioners in British Columbia, Washington state, Oregon, and California to help create the International Pacific Salmon Federation (IPSF) as a forum for addressing problems in the Pacific salmon fisheries.[15]

The IPSF was a quasi-governmental agency dedicated to addressing common issues plaguing fishery managers throughout the region. Although the federation had no enforcement powers, it quickly became a lens for focus-ing regional efforts in a timely and economical fashion. Administrators from the various agencies met annually, and their executive sessions became a forum for exchanging information and coordinating research. In 1926, for example, researchers from the USBF presented results from tagging studies that showed Columbia River chinook migrated as far north as Southeast Alaska. The direc-tor of the Biological Board and the USBF commissioner also used the meet-ing to coordinate sockeye research in Alaska and British Columbia. They agreed to conserve their meager resources by minimizing redundancy. The USBF would calculate the survival rates of juvenile and adult sockeye by meas-uring migration rates at Karluk, Chignik, and Alitak Rivers in Alaska; mean-while the Biological Board would evaluate the efficacy of artificial propagation at Cultus Lake, British Columbia. Later meetings reported on these and other projects and disseminated findings to a broad audience of scientists, managers, and administrators at state, provincial, and federal levels. Even as formal diplomacy foundered, the IPSF built a working community of international scientists and an admirable body of research. What they could not do, how-ever, was keep fishery politics completely at bay.[16]

The emergence of ocean trolling is a case in point. Salish Indians had long trolled for salmon in the open waters of the Strait of Georgia and Puget Sound, but immigrant fishers took this activity to a new level around the turn of the century. Using techniques first developed in northern Europe and the Medi-terranean, they sailed offshore to fish during the closed seasons for nets and to avoid conflicts with native whites over territorial claims within the fishery. The adaptation of internal combustion engines to boats in the 1900s allowed industrial fishers to venture even farther. From their home ports of Victoria, San Juan Island, Bellingham, Port Townsend, and Neah Bay, trollers began to work the Juan de Fuca Strait, Swiftsure Banks, and beyond. Keeping track of this fishery proved impossible. Much of the catch went unrecorded, as it was sold to fresh fish markets and salteries, and license records faltered because some fishers escaped regulation by only working the high seas or by selling fish under the table as they tramp-fished all the way from Monterey Bay to Sitka in pursuit of seasonal runs. Trolling was the final move in the spatial separation of harvest from spawning runs. The evolution of this fishery left no sense of the extent of harvest or provenience of individual fish.[17]

Members of the IPSF discussed trolling at length during their 1926 exec-utive meeting. Researchers complained about incomplete records for troller harvests, and some scientists and managers suspected trollers of withhold-ing information from government officials out of fear that it would be used against them. The irony behind these accusations was that trollers would have been correct to suspect the motives of officials. American members in particular expressed strong objections to trolling in any form. In addition to the problems of record keeping, managers also noted that trolling undermined the ability to regulate harvests of individual runs, ocean harvests sacrificed adult fish before they had reached their peak size, and incidental hooking killed many immature fish. Given their druthers, most American managers would have prohibited trolling altogether, but trollers refused to give them the necessary ammunition. Unfortunately, this circle of distrust also hamstrung researchers' ability to gauge the impact of various forms of gear on salmon. Managers and scientists saw their ability to understand and protect runs slipping through their fingers, and they were powerless to alter the contours of fishing or management.[18]

A related problem dogging the IPSF involved the political implications of the high-seas tagging experiments. From a scientific standpoint the research clearly refuted theories put forth by David Starr Jordan and other nineteenth-century naturalists that salmon never migrated far from the mouths of their natal streams. Recaptured tags from chinook originally marked in the ocean off Alaska and northern British Columbia revealed that many of these fish had originated in the Columbia River system. The research also implied that salmon raised in American waters were being caught in sizable numbers by Canadian trollers off the west coast of Vancouver Island. The marking studies raised concerns among American fishers and managers. Columbia River gillnetters objected to anyone harvesting what they considered *their* fish, while state and federal administrators regretted a further loss of control over where fish were caught because of the trollers' impact on scientific research.[19]

Such complaints rang hollow among Canadians, however. Fraser River gillnetters had been voicing similar concerns since the inception of the trap fisheries at Point Roberts and the San Juan Islands. Rather than a threat to rational management, Canadian managers viewed West Coast trollers as crucial leverage in their diplomatic negotiations. When a California fishery manager complained about high-seas trolling at the 1926 IPSF meeting, Major J. A. Motherwell, chief inspector of Fisheries for British Columbia, remarked that it did not "seem quite fair" to tell "a body of men who are living up on the west coast, say, of Vancouver Island, [that they] can't fish, but let . . . other men fish in the Fraser or the Skeena." Motherwell's point was ostensibly about fairness within the province, but the impact of his argument on treaty negotiations was patently obvious and not long in emerging.[20]

Charles Gilbert, a Stanford University ichthyologist who had performed extensive research on Fraser River sockeye for British Columbia, remarked: "It looks very much as though the old situation of Puget Sound and Fraser River, which has created so much hard feeling and controversy, was to be reversed when it comes to king [chinook] salmon in Canada, and I think it is a very genuine one, and no more could be asked in one case than in another." Motherwell leapt to concur: "That is very brilliant. I know on the west coast of British Columbia when they find, for instance, from these records we are getting from the tagging, [that] our spring salmon are going down [to] the Columbia River it will be pretty hard, I think, to stop them fishing."[21]

The IPSF was supposed to be an agency for coordinating research. It was supposed to be composed of nonpartisan scientists and managers whose foremost concern was the restoration of salmon runs, but just over a year into its existence IPSF members were already taking sides on a central political issue. Right before their eyes a quid pro quo had been laid on the table: if Puget Sound fishers wanted Fraser River runs, then American fishers had no grounds to oppose Canadians harvesting salmon from American streams. That they were the coveted chinook salmon from the Columbia River only elevated the stakes that much more.

In the ebb and flow of fishery rivalries, the tide had turned once more. Canadian diplomats used their newfound leverage to drive a hard bargain with U.S. representatives. Puget Sound fishers again opposed the treaty, but pressure from anglers eventually altered minds. The language of the treaty, however, reinforced the problem of regulating the harvest of individual runs.

By the time negotiators returned to the table in 1928, the terms of the debate had again shifted. Hell's Gate was still blocking salmon migrations, sockeye runs were still declining, and American traps and purse seines were still catching a majority of those runs; but Canadian negotiators were no longer powerless. Armed with the new information on ocean harvests, they crafted a new treaty essentially similar to the 1909 and 1918 documents but with one important change. In addition to agreeing to joint record keeping, restrictions, and recovery measures, U.S. representatives also agreed to share Fraser River sockeye equally with Canadian fishers. The terms of the 1929 agreement represented a clear shift in the political positions by both sides. The 50 percent clause was a significant concession by American negotiators because, at the time, canneries located south of the forty-ninth parallel were processing nearly two-thirds of the entire Fraser River pack. But clear-cut victories continued to elude either side. Although Canadian canners had gained a larger share of the catch, they resented the idea that American fishers were entitled to any fish originating from Canadian rivers. Agreeing to share Fraser salmon equally remained a significant concession on their part.[22]

Thus, although there was greater agreement in 1929, continued resistance by both sides eventually forced additional changes. One subject that the 1929 agreement did not cover was the high-seas fishery. By the late 1920s purse seiners were taking the largest share of the Fraser sockeye runs, yet much of this fishery occurred beyond the boundary delimited in the 1929 agreement. This suited purse seiners because they still opposed all restriction efforts, and for a time it looked as though they would once again stymie an agreement. With neither effective regulation of the whole fishery, nor explicit provisions granting Canada control of its own hatcheries, even Canada's Conservative-controlled parliament refused to ratify the 1929 agreement. This was the first time Canada had rejected a treaty outright. The U.S. Senate also rejected it after Washington representatives forwarded complaints about the fifty-fifty split and lack of language guaranteeing local participation on the international commission. Once again negotiators met, but this time they agreed to extend the treaty area to include high-seas fishing and to guarantee participation by Washington state citizens. Finally in 1930 both nations signed the revised treaty, since referred to as the Sockeye Convention, and Canada quickly ratified it.[23]

The 1930 convention revealed the extent to which management of any one salmon run had become hopelessly tangled with the fate of other runs. By 1930, American fishers were harvesting between two-thirds and three-quarters of all Fraser sockeye and, as purse seiners argued, the 50 percent concession made little sense within the narrow context of Puget Sound interests. But trap owners and purse seiners could never completely blinker the perspective of American negotiators, who had to consider a broader picture. As the tagging experiments and IPSF debates had demonstrated, salmon runs, canneries, and fishers ranging from Alaska to Monterey were affected as well. American negotiators most likely conceded to the equal share clause to create a precedent for protecting other, as yet unspecified, runs, and Columbia chinook were probably their primary concern. The evidence for this is indirect, but state fishery managers at the time were particularly worried about the impact of Canadian trollers on chinook stocks. In 1931, for example, Washington state manager Arthur Einarsen privately suggested that a second agreement "be drawn up on the same basis as the Sockeye Treaty giving the U.S.A. the same favorable consideration in regard to its chinook salmon."[24]

The Sockeye Convention again stalled in the U.S. Senate, but this time a tangential struggle between sport and net fishers broke the impasse. Purse seiners continued to protest what they saw as unfair restrictions, and Washington politicians still opposed any erosion of state powers. But these objections evaporated in 1934. That year Washington state voters passed Initiative 77, an angler-sponsored voter initiative designed to kill all fixed-gear fisheries in the Puget Sound and Columbia River. The measure outlawed the use of beach seines, fish wheels, and, most important for purse seiners, their chief rivals the pound nets. Initiative 77 was an attack on industrial and aboriginal fishers that had nothing to do with the Fraser River situation, but by radically reducing the number of participants in the industrial fishery, it had the effect of finally creating an incentive for purse seiners to support treaty ratification. The American harvest of Fraser sockeye plummeted with the elimination of traps. From 72 percent of the run in 1934, the U.S. share fell to 43 percent the next year, 18 percent in 1936, and 45 percent in 1937. Suddenly, 50 percent of the Fraser sockeye run looked good to purse seiners. Not only had they cornered the American harvest, but they had room to grow. With their endorsement the Senate ratified the convention in 1937, and the Canadian House of Commons rejected final objections by Liberal politicians in British Columbia. At last, Fraser River sockeye would be subjected to joint, coordinated, scientific management.[25]

On the surface the Salmon Convention would finally seem to have ushered in an era of rational conservation, but nothing has ever been a done deal in the fisheries: even agreements are best understood as tactical maneuvers in an endless contest to control resources. The 1937 ratification in fact did not immediately result in greater protection. Final approval in the Senate had been lubricated by an amendment postponing regulations for eight years while scientists continued to research the causes of the Fraser's depleted runs. To expedite this process, Canada and the United States had formed the International Pacific Salmon Fisheries Commission (IPSFC). The IPSFC effectively replaced the old IPSF, which fell dormant during the Depression because of budget constraints. There were, however, two critical differences between the agencies. While the IPSF had been strictly a forum for coordinating research, the IPSFC also became responsible for rehabilitating spawning habitat in the Fraser watershed *and* prescribing fishing regulations once the interim research period ended. Industrial fishers did their best to block this latter power. American purse seiners continued to oppose any regulation of fishing beyond the three-mile state boundary, and Canadian gillnetters tried to maintain their de facto allocation advantage for as long as possible. Nevertheless, in 1946 the IPSFC began to set seasons and regulate gear within waters covered by the treaty.[26]

The next few years should have been a period of waxing hope, but the IPSFC soon discovered serious flaws with the limited compass of the treaty. The 1930 agreement established an area of jurisdiction, called the "Convention waters," that extended from the Gulf of Georgia through Puget Sound and Juan de Fuca Strait out to sea between the forty-eighth and forty-ninth parallels. Although these boundaries covered the vast majority of relevant fishers in 1930, the purse seine and troll fisheries continued to expand geographically during the next quarter century. By the 1950s Canadian purse seiners had surpassed the American fleet, taking fully 35 percent of the regional catch. Now Canadian success began to cause political difficulties because treaty language was not flexible enough for the IPSFC to adjust fishing seasons for new imbalances. To further exacerbate matters, high-seas drift nets were beginning to take an untold, but probably significant, number of sockeye outside the boundaries of the convention waters; Canadian and American fishers were also competing for Fraser River pink salmon; and trollers from both nations patrolled the coast between California and Alaska. The IPSFC was powerless to regulate any of these new issues.[27]

Once again, a treaty had not anticipated the dynamic nature of fishing, and with new issues emerging and old ones festering, diplomats returned to the table. Realizing the original treaty needed amending, Canada and the United States reopened negotiations in the mid-1950s on an expanded front. In 1957 they agreed to extend the Sockeye Convention to cover pink salmon passing through convention waters, to allow the commission greater flexibility in setting seasons, and to prohibit the use of drift nets in the eastern Pacific. These new agreements quieted complaints for a time, but by the 1970s it was clear that further revisions were necessary to address an ever-growing trolling industry. The more researchers learned about salmon's movements, the more everyone conceded a need to regulate harvests throughout the northeastern Pacific. As Senator Daniel J. Evans of Washington state remarked, "The crux of the present fishery management problem has been that a single stock of salmon . . . may be harvested in many different fisheries in many different political jurisdictions, all of which may have goals and policies that are not only different, but incompatible." From this mutual recognition and distrust came a familiar chorus of concerns. Managers still wanted accurate information on harvests, Canadians still wanted to restrict American catches of Fraser and Skeena River runs, and Americans still wanted greater protection for "their" salmon passing along the west coast of Vancouver Island. What was remarkable about this was how little the basic problems and desires had changed. Even granting that discussions in the 1970s ranged over a much broader region, the problems themselves were age old. All sides were embroiled in a spatial struggle over a resource that defied socially constructed boundaries.[28]

The move toward the next agreement was slow, painful, and problematic. The crux of salmon diplomacy continued to be the structural inconsistency between the American and Canadian models of fishery management. The different locuses of jurisdiction—of Dominion control in Canada and of state control in the United States—had always produced divided agendas. Before 1940 the key region of conflict had been northern Puget Sound, but by the 1970s the hot spot had shifted to Alaskan waters. Researchers, managers, and fishers identified Alaska trollers as at the apex of a series of forces pressuring salmon runs, too many of which were in sharp decline, from their spawning beds to the Gulf of Alaska. Urgency dominated ensuing discussions, but negotiations dragged out to late 1984 as Alaska representatives blocked any proposal not to their liking. The eventual treaty did address problems with troubled stocks, but cooperation had hinged on an agreement that exempted Alaska fishers from court rulings on Indian treaties that restricted other non-Indian fishers. The new agreement also partitioned harvests so Canadian and American fishers gathered equivalent shares of salmon, but the comity provision had a contrary effect because whatever Alaska and Washington fishers caught of British Columbia–bound salmon had to be compensated by B.C. harvests on Washington- and Oregon-bound runs. Equal sharing thus had the effect of encouraging heavy catches on weakened Columbia River stocks to offset huge harvests on healthy Skeena River runs. Furthermore, enforcing these provisions required an expansion of the convention waters to include everything from Cape Suckling, Alaska, to Cape Flattery, Washington. The 1985 treaty also terminated the IPSFC and transferred its regulatory functions to the new Pacific Salmon Commission[29] (Figure 6.3).

These changes were supposed to eliminate problems that had plagued generations of fishery management, but conflict during the 1990s belied that hope. Canadians complained about Americans taking too many of *their* salmon; Oregon and Washington residents griped of Alaskans and Canadians catching *their* salmon; and Alaska fishers (many of whom reside in Oregon and Washington but migrate seasonally to fish) continued to perch like the Cheshire Cat atop a parabolic arc of salmon migrations. Rhythms of nature placed this ephemeral group of fishers proximate to where most salmon runs from northern California to the Skeena River migrated during the ocean phase of their lives, and for the past two decades these fishers have enjoyed a great boom that state representatives are loathe to throttle. As catches of Skeena

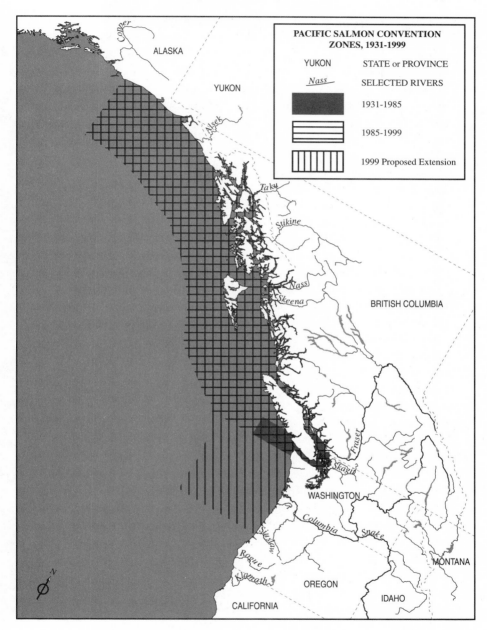

FIG. 6.3. Pacific salmon convention zones, 1931–1999.

and Fraser River stocks escalated off Alaska, however, Canadians took as many American salmon as possible to maintain equity. By the mid-1990s it seemed as if it was in no one's interest to restrain fishing. Similar to a classic tragedy of the commons—except one propelled by political negotiation rather than the marketplace—voluntary restraint had become irrational, only conceding an advantage to rivals farther south. Nobody gave quarter, and mutual assured destruction unfolded with fishing gear as the weapons of choice.[30]

While Americans and Canadians played chicken with extinction, diplomats returned to the table again and in June 1999 signed another agreement that signaled a remarkably conservative revision of salmon diplomacy. The latest proposed treaty would expand the present management structure to cover five salmon species (sockeye, pink, chinook, coho [*O. kisutch*], and chum [*O. keta*]) and all fishing from Cape Suckling, Alaska, to southern Oregon and inland to Idaho. This broad area would be governed by several regulatory panels as a series of discrete zones, but the goal of management remains the attainment of maximum sustained yield and parity through regional trade-offs. Americans hailed the agreement as a "new era in cooperation," a breakthrough deal that will "set the tone for fisheries management worldwide." Canada's ambassador crowed, "We have worked it out again," and an environmentalist called the agreement a "shining moment in the diplomacy of both countries . . . to put salmon first." British Columbia fishers remained less than sanguine about the continuation of trade-offs, however, and for all the document's attention to habitat restoration and scientific cooperation, this version of international salmon management remains astonishingly similar to that of the 1930s.[31]

The exercise of managing a shared natural resource both separates and joins Canadians and Americans. In 1846, British and American diplomats drew a line on a map to assert their independence from one another, but salmon have mocked that premise by regularly transgressing any and all socially constructed boundaries. By doing so, they have illustrated both the artificiality and power that lines possess. Salmon, the industry, and the state became enmeshed in complex layers of natural and social space. The local run, independent fisher, and sovereign state seemed increasingly fictive constructs, no more isolable in reality than any organism is from its environment, and they have remained so for a very long time. The survival of species, economies, and cultures has always depended on accommodation and cooperation, but the fate of Pacific salmon and salmon fishers now also hinges on convoluted pacts from the past.

Although the problems that plague two Pacific fisheries are hardly new, fisheries, managers, and diplomats only make matters worse by thinking and acting like their predecessors.[32] Contests to control Fraser River sockeye are but one example among many, but they may be the most salient because of the joint errors committed by the United States and Canada. Attempts to solve tensions only succeeded in ensnaring many other fisheries over time. Conceived in the spirit of diplomacy and justified on the laudable ideal of parity, the Fraser River Sockeye Convention and its descendant treaties have actually codified inequalities and perpetuated irrational management. What began as a local problem among Puget Sound and Fraser River fishers soon expanded as negotiators patched quarrels with additional trespasses. The resulting regional inequalities in allocations were masked by abstracting trade-offs under the rubric of national shares, but these measures did not solve underlying problems. Leapfrog competition continued unabated, and a local conflict metastasized into a cancerous blight that has enveloped most of the northeastern Pacific. Because the agreements sustain these poorly conceived trade-offs, they, in effect, legitimate them. This is irrational management, which is a polite way of saying crazy.

The solution to these problems is as obvious as it is unobtainable. The logical way to rationalize management is to kill the ocean fishery, return it to the rivers, reduce the number of fishers to an ecologically and economically sustainable number, and restore spawning grounds to a healthy state. Unfortunately, there does not seem to be any interest group or political representative willing to cooperate unless it gains immediate benefit. That may sound cynical, but there is nothing, *nothing,* in the entire history of the salmon fisheries to suggest a more charitable assessment. Technological solutions such as hatcheries have consistently failed to mitigate the environmental changes wrought by Euro-American resettlement, and no government has been willing to restrict damaging activities in a timely fashion. Change has only happened after the collapse. Unfortunately, the best—perhaps only—strategy is to understand where our predecessors have erred, wait for an opportunity, and try not to repeat past mistakes.[33]

NOTES

I wish to thank Ken Coates, Kurk Dorsey, Matthew Evenden, John M. Findlay, David Fluharty, Matt Klingle, Dianne Newell, Claire Strom, and the anonymous reviewers for their help in writing this chapter. The source for the epigraph is

Thomas C. Jensen, "The United States-Canada Pacific Salmon Interception Treaty: An Historical and Legal Overview," *Environmental Law* 16 (spring 1986): 369.

1. Daniel D. Huppert, "U.S./Canada Salmon Wars: Why the Pacific Salmon Treaty Has Not Brought Peace," in *New Directions in Marine Affairs,* A Report Series from School of Marine Affairs, University of Washington, vol. 1 (January 1996); "U.S. Talks with Canada on Salmon Hit Snag," (Portland) *Oregonian,* June 29, 1996, pp. A1, A13; "Canada Misplays Salmon Card," *Oregonian,* July 4, 1996, p. B8; "Canada Would Talk about Chinook if U.S. Would Bargain Fairly," *Oregonian,* July 26, 1996, p. C10; "NW Governors Seek New Canada Talks," *Oregonian,* August 28, 1996, p. D3; "Keeping Salmon Talks Alive," *Oregonian,* September 5, 1996, p. D4; "Fishing Groups Seek New Pacific Salmon Treaty," *Oregonian,* June 3, 1997, p. C8; "U.S., Canada Gear to Resume Salmon Talks," *Oregonian,* June 15, 1997, pp. B1, B6; "Canada Sets Salmon Quota after Talks Fail," *Oregonian,* June 28, 1997, p. C1; Timothy Egan, "Salmon War in Northwest Spurs Wish for Good Fences," *New York Times,* September 12, 1997, pp. A1, A14.

2. Cicely Lyons, *Salmon: Our Heritage* (Vancouver, B.C.: Mitchell Press, 1969), pp. 16–20; Patricia Ann Berringer, "Northwest Coast Traditional Salmon Fisheries: Systems of Resource Utilization," M.A. thesis, University of British Columbia, 1982; Wayne Suttles, "Central Coast Salish," in *Northwest Coast,* vol. 7, *Handbook of North American Indians* (Washington, D.C.: Smithsonian Institution Press, 1990), p. 457; Wayne Suttles, "Affinal Ties, Subsistence, and Prestige among the Coast Salish," *American Anthropologist* 62 (April 1960): 296–305; Wayne Suttles, "Coping with Abundance: Subsistence on the Northwest Coast," in Richard B. Lee and Irven DeVore, eds., *Man the Hunter* (Chicago: Aldine Publishing, 1968), pp. 56–68; Hilary Stewart, *Indian Artifacts of the Northwest Coast* (Seattle: University of Washington Press, 1973); Joseph E. Taylor III, *Making Salmon: An Environmental History of the Northwest Fishery Crisis* (Seattle: University of Washington Press, 1999), pp. 13–38.

3. John F. Roos, *Restoring Fraser River Salmon: A History of the International Pacific Salmon Fisheries Commission, 1937–1985* (Vancouver, B.C.: Pacific Salmon Commission, 1991), pp. 5–10; Robert T. Boyd, "Demographic History, 1774–1874," in Suttles, ed., *Northwest Coast,* pp. 135–48; Lyons, *Salmon,* p. 50.

4. Randall Schalk, "The Structure of an Anadromous Fish Resource," in Lewis R. Binford, ed., *For Theory Building in Archaeology: Essays on Faunal Remains, Aquatic Resources, Spatial Analysis, and Systemic Modeling* (New York: Academic Press, 1977), pp. 207–49; Dianne Newell, "Dispersal and Concentration: The Slowly Changing Spatial Pattern of the British Columbia Salmon Canning Industry," *Journal of Historical Geography* 14 (January 1988): 22–36; Taylor, *Making Salmon,* pp. 62–65.

5. Lyons, *Salmon,* pp. 137–219, 273; George A. Rounsefell and George B. Kelez, "The Salmon and Salmon Fisheries of Swiftsure Bank, Puget Sound, and the Fraser River,"

Bulletin of the Bureau of Fisheries 49 (1938): 817; Dianne Newell, ed., *The Development of the Pacific Salmon-Canning Industry: A Grown Man's Game* (Montreal: McGill-Queen's University Press, 1989), p. 12; John N. Cobb, "Pacific Salmon Fisheries," *Bureau of Fisheries Document 1092* (Washington, D.C.: Government Printing Office, 1930), pp. 579–80; Taylor, *Making Salmon*, pp. 105–12.

6. Newell, *The Development of the Pacific Salmon-Canning Industry*, p. 15; R. E. Foerster, *The Sockeye Salmon: An International Compendium of Scientific Research* (New Westminster, B.C.: International Pacific Fisheries Commission, 1968); Robert L. Burgner, *Pacific Salmon Life Histories*, ed. C. Groot and L. Margolis (Vancouver: University of British Columbia Press, 1991), pp. 3–117.

7. Kevin Hamilton, "A Study of the Variability of the Return Migration Route of Fraser River Sockeye Salmon (*Oncorhynchus nerka*)," *Canadian Journal of Zoology* 63 (August 1985): 1,930–43; Roos, *Restoring Fraser River Salmon*, p. 61.

8. Berringer, "Northwest Coast Traditional Salmon Fisheries," pp. 129–38, 169–70; Rounsefell and Kelez, "Salmon Fisheries of Swiftsure Bank," pp. 713–19; Jozo Tomasevich, *International Agreements on Conservation of Marine Resources, with Special Reference to the North Pacific* (Stanford, Calif.: Food Research Institute, 1943), p. 240.

9. Rounsefell and Kelez, "Salmon Fisheries of Swiftsure Bank," p. 719; Roos, *Restoring Fraser River Salmon*, p. 42. Dianne Newell aptly calls this period a "scramble for control"; see Newell, *The Development of the Pacific Salmon-Canning Industry*, pp. 65–73.

10. Rounsefell and Kelez, "Salmon Fisheries of Swiftsure Bank," pp. 725–30; Joseph A. Craig and Robert L. Hacker, "The History and Development of the Fisheries of the Columbia River," *Bulletin of the Bureau of Fisheries* 49 (1940): 181–82.

11. Kurk Dorsey, *The Dawn of Conservation Diplomacy: U.S.-Canadian Wildlife Protection Treaties in the Progressive Era* (Seattle: University of Washington Press, 1998), pp. 19–104; Tomasevich, *International Agreements on Conservation of Marine Resources*, pp. 250–53; Peter Neary, "Grey, Bryce, and the Settlement of Canadian-American Differences, 1905–1911," *Canadian Historical Review* 49 (December 1968): 357–80.

12. Dianne Newell, *Tangled Webs of History: Indians and the Law in Canada's Pacific Coast Fisheries* (Toronto: University of Toronto Press, 1993), pp. 10–11. For "grown man's game," see Newell, *The Development of the Pacific Salmon-Canning Industry*.

13. William F. Thompson, *Effect of the Obstruction at Hell's Gate on the Sockeye Salmon of the Fraser River,* International Pacific Salmon Fisheries Commission Bulletin 1 (New Westminster, B.C.: International Pacific Salmon Fisheries Commission, 1945); Roos, *Restoring Fraser River Salmon*, pp. 24–27; Richard C. Bocking, *Mighty River: A Portrait of the Fraser* (Vancouver, B.C.: Douglas & McIntyre, 1997), pp. 81–82, 145–46.

14. U.S. State Department, *Report of the American-Canadian Fisheries Conference,*

1918 (Washington, D.C.: Government Printing Office, 1920); Dorsey, *Dawn of Conservation Diplomacy*, pp. 97–99; Tomasevich, *International Agreements on Conservation of Marine Resources*, pp. 253–56; Roos, *Restoring Fraser River Salmon*, pp. 42–45.

15. Roos, *Restoring Fraser River Salmon*, pp. 24–33; Willis H. Rich to Henry O'Malley, March 1, 1930, folder 3 of 4, box 4, Records Concerning Societies, Councils, Conferences, and Other Groups, 1904–1937, Record Group 22, National Archives (hereafter cited as RG 22, NA). For the IFC, see Tomasevich, *International Agreements on Conservation of Marine Resources*, pp. 125–215.

16. "Meeting of International Pacific Salmon Investigation Federation, Executive Committee, Seattle, Washington, December 2, 1926," pp. 7–10, 72–56, 80–81, folder 1 of 4, box 4, Records Concerning Societies, Councils, Conferences, and Other Groups, 1904–1937, RG 22, NA; Willis H. Rich, "Growth and Degree of Maturity of Chinook Salmon in the Ocean," *Bulletin of the Bureau of Fisheries* 41 (1925): 15–90; Willis H. Rich, "Salmon-Tagging Experiments in Alaska, 1924 and 1925," *Bulletin of the Bureau of Fisheries* 42 (1926): 109–46; R. E. Foerster and W. E. Ricker, "A Synopsis of the Investigations at Cultus Lake, British Columbia, Conducted by the Biological Board of Canada into the Life History and Propagation of Sockeye Salmon, 1924–1937," Pacific Biological Station, Nanaimo, British Columbia, December 1937, copy in Fisheries Library, University of Washington. For later meetings see subsequent reports filed in Records Concerning Societies, Councils, Conferences, and Other Groups, 1904–1937, RG 22, NA.

17. John Earnest Damron, "The Emergence of Salmon Trolling on the American Northwest Coast: A Maritime Historical Geography," Ph.D. dissertation, University of Oregon, 1975; Irene Martin, *Legacy and Testament: The Story of Columbia River Gillnetters* (Pullman: Washington State University Press, 1994), p. 85; Rounsefell and Kelez, "Salmon Fisheries of Swiftsure Bank," pp. 749–50.

18. "Meeting of International Pacific Salmon Investigation Federation, Executive Committee, Seattle, Washington, December 2, 1926," pp. 38–40, folder 1 of 4, box 4, Records Concerning Societies, Councils, Conferences, and Other Groups, 1904–1937, RG 22, NA.

19. David Starr Jordan, "Salmon and Trout of the Pacific Coast," *Thirteenth Biennial Report of the State Board of Fish Commissioners of the State of California* (Sacramento: California State Printer, 1894). For gillnetter objections, see "Meeting of International Pacific Salmon Investigation Federation, Executive Committee, Seattle, Washington, December 2, 1926," appendix, folder 1 of 4, box 4, Records Concerning Societies, Councils, Conferences, and Other Groups, 1904–1937, RG 22, NA; Courtland L. Smith, *Salmon Fishers of the Columbia* (Corvallis: Oregon State University Press, 1979), pp. 87–90.

20. "Meeting of International Pacific Salmon Investigation Federation, Executive

Committee, Seattle, Washington, December 2, 1926," p. 40, folder 1 of 4, box 4, Records Concerning Societies, Councils, Conferences, and Other Groups, 1904–1937, RG 22, NA.

21. "Meeting of International Pacific Salmon Investigation Federation, Executive Committee, Seattle, Washington, December 2, 1926," p. 40, folder 1 of 4, box 4, Records Concerning Societies, Councils, Conferences, and Other Groups, 1904–1937, RG 22, NA. .

22. Roos, *Restoring Fraser River Salmon,* p. 44; Tomasevich, *International Agreements on Conservation of Marine Resources,* p. 240.

23. Canada, *Debates of the House of Commons,* 16th Parliament, 4th sess. (1930), pp. 2,798–2,814; Roos, *Restoring Fraser River Salmon,* pp. 44–45; Matthew Evenden, "Fish vs. Power: Remaking Salmon, Science, and Society on the Fraser River," Ph.D. dissertation, York University, 2000, chapter 4. Matthew Evenden has been extremely helpful in deciphering Canadian political battles within Parliament and between the Dominion and British Columbia during this period.

24. Roos, *Restoring Fraser River Salmon,* p. 47.

25. Lisa Mighetto, "Sport Fishing on the Columbia River," *Pacific Northwest Quarterly* 87 (winter 1995–96): 5–15; Daniel Boxberger, *To Fish in Common: The Ethnohistory of Lummi Indian Salmon Fishing* (Lincoln: University of Nebraska Press, 1989), p. 90; Tomasevich, *International Agreements on Conservation of Marine Resources,* pp. 239–41; Roos, *Restoring Fraser River Salmon,* pp. 46–51.

26. Roos, *Restoring Fraser River Salmon,* pp. 54–56, 110–13.

27. Ibid., pp. 132, 155; Damron, "Emergence of Salmon Trolling,"pp. 100–105; D. J. Milne and H. Godfrey, *The Chinook and Coho Salmon Fisheries of British Columbia,* Bulletin of the Fisheries Research Board of Canada 142 (Ottawa: Fisheries Research Board of Canada, 1964).

28. Daniel J. Evans, "Toward the Return of Pacific Salmon and Steelhead," *Environmental Law* 16 (spring 1986): 361; Jensen, "United States-Canada Pacific Salmon Interception Treaty," pp. 376–80; Roos, *Restoring Fraser River Salmon,* pp. 132–35, 156.

29. Jensen, "United States-Canada Pacific Salmon Interception Treaty," pp. 380–400; Roos, *Restoring Fraser River Salmon,* pp. 318–22.

30. William G. Pearcy, *Ocean Ecology of North Pacific Salmonids* (Seattle: University of Washington Press, 1992), pp. 20–21; C. Groot and L. Margolis, eds., *Pacific Salmon Life Histories* (Vancouver: University of British Columbia Press, 1991).

31. For "new era" and "shining," see *Oregonian,* June 4, 1999, pp. D1, D8. For "tone" and "worked," see www.state.gov/www/policy_remarks/1999/990630_pickering_salmon.html. For disappointment, see *Maclean's,* June 14, 1999, p. 33. For an Internet version of treaty, see Department of State, "Pacific Salmon Agreement," www.state.gov/www/global/oes/oceans/990630_salmon_index.html; for areal and species coverage, see Annex IV; for zones, see Attachment B; for habitat, see Attachments C and E; for cooperation, see Attachment D.

32. The concept of the fishery as a "public commons" is another example of a flawed idea handed down from the past. See M. Patricia Marchak, "What Happens When Common Property Becomes Uncommon?" *BC Studies* 80 (winter 1988–89): 3–23; Bonnie J. McCay, "The Culture of the Commoners: Historical Observations on Old and New World Fisheries," in *The Question of the Commons: The Culture and Ecology of Communal Resources,* ed. Bonnie J. McCay and James M. Acheson (Tucson: University of Arizona Press, 1987), pp. 201–15; Joseph E. Taylor III, "Politics Is at the Bottom of the Whole Thing: Spatial Relations of Power in Oregon Salmon Management," in Richard White and John Findlay, eds., *Power and Place in the North American West* (Seattle: University of Washington Press, 1999), pp. 233–63.

33. For a broader discussion of these issues, see Taylor, *Making Salmon.*

7 / Who Will Defend British Columbia?

Unity of Command on the West Coast, 1934–42

GALEN ROGER PERRAS

A utonomy in the face of centralizing forces emanating from the United
States has long been a vital theme in Canadian history, but one strand
in particular has attracted Canadian intellectuals and nationalists. Giving "critical emphasis to Canada's lack of domestic and socio-economic and external political independence from the United States and the world centred upon
it,"[1] the peripheral independence school is unique in that its adherents range
across the political spectrum—from Donald Creighton's and George Grant's
bemoaning of the decline of the British connection to the Marxist/neo-
colonialist musings of John Warnock and Gerard S. Vano.[2] Common to all
is the view that Canada has long been an American handmaiden, unable or
unwilling to resist Washington's biddings. Peripheral dependence, however,
has not gone unchallenged. Many prominent historians maintain that the
Canada–United States relationship, far from being that of master and slave,
is best described as an asymmetrical partnership dominated by ambivalence
and periods of convergence and divergence.

West Coast unity of command is an issue that demonstrates that these differing viewpoints need not be mutually exclusive. Concerned Canada was not
doing enough to protect its vulnerable West Coast, from 1934 until 1942 the
United States explored ways to integrate British Columbia into an American-
led system of unified command. But the much more powerful United States
did not prevail against the weaker Canada, a Canada that was unconvinced
of the threat to the eastern Pacific, united by a desire to preserve national
sovereignty in the face of perceived U.S. imperialism, and confronted by an

ambivalent ally that could not duplicate Canadian unanimity nor convince President Franklin Roosevelt to intervene personally. Ironically, Canada's victory may have proved, in fact, its military dependence.

The air power prophet William Mitchell was the first American to advocate integrating western Canada into the American strategic system. Testifying before a presidential aeronautical board in 1925, the former army air service officer wanted to transform Alaska into an aerodrome from which waves of bombers could sally forth against Japan in a future conflict. Pointing out that Canadian aid would be vital to make this dream reality, Mitchell was convinced such assistance would be forthcoming as Canada was "as much exposed to this danger [Japanese attack] as we are ourselves and Canada looks to this country for protection in an eventuality of this kind, rather than to Great Britain."[3]

Mitchell was a man before his time. Not only did much of the U.S. military reject his air power notions, but it was slow as well to view Canada as anything but a potential adversary at the side of a hostile Anglo-Japanese coalition; well into the 1930s U.S. officers continued to formulate "Red" plans to deal with a war with Britain, plans that emphasized invasions of Canada.[4] But by 1934, facing considerable public criticism for its disastrous attempt to deliver the mail, the army air corps was very eager to demonstrate that its new aircraft were capable of long-distance operations, and Canadian assistance was required. Therefore, in May 1934 the War Department asked Canada to allow twelve bombers to fly to Alaska across western Canada, arguing that the mission was designed "to further friendly diplomatic relations with Canada and to conduct a goodwill flight to Alaska."[5]

Precedent favored the United States. Canada had agreed in 1932 to an overflight agreement, but that pact applied only to the eastern half of North America because the Canadian military, citing concerns about security and sovereignty, had advised against allowing U.S. military aircraft to fly over western Canada.[6] But Chief of the General Staff A. G. L. McNaughton feared setting quite a different precedent. McNaughton had long been concerned that the previous one hundred years of history had demonstrated a pattern of consistent U.S. imperialism and hegemony in the western hemisphere. In 1931, McNaughton had formed a special joint services subcommittee to study the possibility of Canadian neutrality in a war between Japan and the United States. The subcommittee warned that if Canada could not prevent Japan from operating near British Columbia, the U.S. military might seize Canadian bases. Furthermore, expecting that American planes would overfly British Columbia to and from Alaska, the subcommittee concluded that "it would doubtless commend itself to the Canadian government to exercise great forbearance to the United States in this matter so long as it could convince Japan that it was not deliberately conniving at unneutral service." Intent on preventing the United States from gaining such rights, McNaughton opposed granting the American overflight request on the grounds it would constitute a "military reconnaissance" and that it might make it "very difficult to maintain our neutrality or to terminate the custom in a crisis."[7]

This thought was not new, however, as C. F. Hamilton, a militia officer and civil servant, had cautioned in 1921 that if Japan invaded Alaska, the United States could become "an uncommonly ugly neighbour and demand control of British Columbia."[8] As a soldier, McNaughton was obliged to present his civilian masters with such advice, but he was also a nationalist in a country where a great many nationalists, looking back on a long history of Anglo-American rivalry in North America, shared a former prime minister's opinion that Americans "have very many fine qualities but what they have, they keep and what they have not, they want."[9] Undersecretary of State for External Affairs O. D. Skelton was a nationalist too, but his brand was concerned more with combating imperial centralization than with American expansionism. Reminding McNaughton of the unique situation in that the United States "alone possesses territories on this continent between which a route through Canada is a natural one," Skelton doubted acceding to the American request would necessarily commit Canada to a permanent arrangement. If Canada denied the petition, Skelton thought "it preferable to refuse it on the grounds that the route is not available rather than bringing in any military defence issues."[10]

The overflight request was granted and then almost immediately regretted when a U.S. newspaper declared that the mission was designed to test the ability to reinforce Alaska quickly during wartime. Maintaining the piece would make it "impossible for us to permit any more passages of military planes from the United States to Alaska," a livid Skelton was not much comforted by the American minister's claim that the press report was sensationalist. The flight was permitted to go ahead, but as Minister Warren Robbins reported back to Washington, D.C., Canadian sensibilities had been offended and the hands of those in the Canadian military inclined "to view our military operations with some suspicion" strengthened. Robbins warned that "no doubt that part of the work of the National Defence Department consists of envisaging measures to be taken to render any incursions from the United States in time of war as difficult as possible."[11]

Robbins was right. Canadian officials already were worried that the United

States, which had surveyed the Aleutian Islands in May 1934 and was planning to hold major naval exercises in the North Pacific the following year,
would put military bases in the Aleutians once the Washington naval treaty's
ban on Pacific fortifications lapsed in 1936. Those worries were magnified by
the accidental spring 1935 release of hearing transcripts from the House of
Representatives' committee of military affairs. Not only was the U.S. Army
interested in placing air bases near the Canadian frontier, one of its officers
testified that if Canada could not prevent its territory from being used to attack
the United States, "we would have to do so, I imagine." Greatly displeased
by these revelations, McNaughton cautioned that failing to safeguard Canada's
neutrality could lead to an American occupation of British Columbia, a situation that would lead to a loss of independence and "the disintegration of
the structure set up by the Fathers of Confederation."[12]

McNaughton's apocalyptic warning, made just months before his resig-
nation, gained the military only two more maritime patrol squadrons and
four torpedo bombers for the West Coast. Had he remained, McNaughton
would have faced a new Liberal government led by William Lyon Mackenzie
King, who as prime minister in the 1920s had cut drastically the military budget.
But McNaughton's successor, Major General E. C. Ashton, had a new and
potentially powerful ally in his quest to bolster the nation's defenses. U.S.
President Franklin Roosevelt, concerned that the western democracies were
unprepared to confront Japan and Germany but bound by an isolationist
Congress, pursued a secret diplomacy. As early as 1934, he had suggested sharing the costs of Britain's bases at Singapore and Hong Kong, while two years
later he sought to exchange military data with the British. Unfortunately,
Roosevelt's refusal to make firm commitments prompted London to conclude
that he could not be relied on.[13]

Canada was quite another matter. By 1934, Roosevelt believed that the world
was moving toward continental power blocs, and he warned Britain that if
it appeased Japan, he might "be compelled in the interests of American security, to approach public sentiment in Canada" and the other Dominions to
make them "understand clearly that their future security is linked with us in
the United States."[14] Most important, the October 1935 defeat of the more
imperially minded R. B. Bennett by the Harvard-educated King offered new
opportunities. The new Canadian government was very interested in a trade
agreement with Washington, and both King and Skelton had told U.S.
officials that Canada sought closer relations with its powerful neighbor.[15] So
when Roosevelt and King finally met at Quebec City in July 1936, the president wasted little time in getting to the point. Noting that an Alaskan high-

way through western Canada would be an important means of transporting troops north, Roosevelt revealed that a group of senators favored intervening if Japan invaded British Columbia. In case King had missed the point, two weeks later Roosevelt announced publicly that "our closest neighbors are good neighbors. If there are remoter nations that wish us not good but ill, they know we are strong; they know that we can and will defend ourselves and defend our neighborhood."[16]

The ever-vigilant King had not missed Roosevelt's message, especially because it had come after an American officer had told a Canadian friend "that the major military schemes and problems discussed at the [U.S.] War College were all based on the general idea of a Far Eastern country making an attack on the United States by way of Canada."[17] King's frame of mind was not improved either by a military report that said U.S. and Japanese naval exercises, the rise of a "big navy" lobby in America, interest in an Alaskan highway, and requests to overfly Canada were "distinct portents of a trend to come." If the United States and Japan came to blows, Canada would face some unhappy choices: siding with the United States regardless of Britain's attitude; joining an Anglo-American coalition; or neutrality. Rejecting the first option, the Canadian services viewed the neutrality option as problematic, particularly if Japanese forces were to use Canadian waters and territory to attack American targets:

> Under the circumstances visualized, with American feeling running high and with a large army mobilized and impatient to intervene, it is to be expected that should Canada give the United States real reason to complain of Japanese infringement of Canadian neutrality owing to the lack of adequate armed supervision by Canada of its territorial waters, territory, or the air supervening, American public opinion will demand that the requisite protective measures along the Canadian seaboard be secured by what would amount to the military occupation of British Columbia by U.S. forces.[18]

As Canada's military considered itself incapable of ensuring anything approaching adequate supervision of its western coast, it prescribed a six-destroyer navy, a militia capable of speedily fielding a two-division mobile force, and a 23–squadron air force (400 planes) at a cost of $200 million over five years.[19]

Although the cost staggered the cabinet, there was a consensus that something had to be done to protect Canadian sovereignty from either Japanese but especially American incursions. Skelton agreed that Canada was fortunate in that it neighbored "a great and friendly state," but he believed that Canada could not "allow the United States to do for us what we can and should do for our own protection." King was less circumspect. Worried "that British protection means less & less, U.S. protection danger of losing our independence," the prime minister wanted to fortify the nation's coasts over ten years rather than five. Eventually a cheaper compromise was worked out, but as the reduced funds dictated, there would be enough money only for proper defenses on one coast, because the British fleet was strong in the Atlantic, "virtually without discussion, the government and military agreed" to strengthen the Pacific frontier.[20]

When King and Roosevelt next met in March 1937, King eagerly stated that Canada would not hide behind the Monroe Doctrine if attacked. Not much impressed, Roosevelt, spending much of his time discussing the Alaskan highway proposal, told King that he desired "Canada to have a few patrol boats on the Pacific Coast, and to see that her coast fortifications around Vancouver were of a character to be effective there." But by the following summer, Roosevelt's interest in Canadian West Coast defenses had grown. Told by Secretary of State Cordell Hull that Canada "had unfortunately shown little inclination even to discuss" an Alaskan highway, the president made British Columbia's capital a stop on his September 1937 West Coast tour. Warmly greeted in Victoria, Roosevelt found little keenness in Ottawa for the highway, despite assurances the U.S. Army was uninterested in the road's purported military value.[21] Finding the Canadian defenses to be "almost non-existent," Roosevelt told his minister in Ottawa, Norman Armour, that it might be time to formulate a coordinated defense plan for the territory, stretching from northern Washington state to the Alaskan Panhandle. But Roosevelt's proposal to covertly dispatch an officer to Ottawa to broach the matter with Canada attracted little support from his aides. If the president was serious, Armour proposed either sounding out King about a personal meeting with Roosevelt to avoid the chance of an embarrassing public disclosure, or pursuing informal military contacts including staff college exchanges. Assistant Undersecretary of State Sumner Welles agreed with Armour. Doubting there was much value in the military route, Welles thought that there was no hurry to proceed, as Hull had not yet been informed of the initiative.[22]

In a hurry after deciding on December 16 to initiate a secret exchange of intelligence with Britain about Japan, Roosevelt told Welles six days later that Canada should send an army and a navy officer to Washington, D.C., to talk "off the record" with their American counterparts.[23] Armour met with a wary

King on January 8, 1938. King was concerned with the international situation and was particularly worried that if Japan and Germany fought Britain and the United States, Canada would be "helpless" to counter an attempt to seize the country. But just days after Canadian newspapers had outlined how Canada's weak defenses constituted a menace to U.S. security, fearful that his traveling to Washington could threaten the success of ongoing trade talks, King accepted the proposal to dispatch two officers to Washington as soon as possible.[24]

General E. C. Ashton and Commodore Percy W. Nelles arrived in Washington, D.C., on January 18. Desiring assurances that the United States "would safeguard Canada's situation and not force her into a serious situation," Ashton was surprised to hear army Chief of Staff Malin Craig's offer for the United States to extend its operational zone to encompass British Columbia. Quite uneager to address the implications of that statement, Ashton explained that Canada had to prepare for three very different scenarios: participation with Britain in a war against Japan with the United States remaining neutral; Canadian neutrality in a United States-Japan conflict; and joining an Anglo-American alliance directed against Japan. While Craig asserted that only the latter contingency was worth considering, Admiral William Leahy, interested in confronting Japan in the western Pacific, described British Columbia's strategic situation as "minor." Leahy doubted Japanese forces would employ Canadian waters to assault U.S. targets, but if they did both Leahy and Craig confidently predicted those forces would be easily hunted down. Most important, despite his offer to extend the operational zone, Craig told his Canadian listeners that no formal commitments were possible.[25]

Pleased to hear that the threat in the eastern Pacific was insubstantial, Canadian officers viewed Craig's proposition with some alarm, alarm that found its way into the military's new neutrality defense plan. Believing that only Japanese cruisers and submarines (and not more dangerous battleships and aircraft carriers) would seek to hide in Canadian waters, the military worried that the United States nevertheless would seek overflight rights and might occupy Canadian territory unless Canada could prevent Japanese incursions. Canada's military was willing to exchange information with the U.S. services, but warning extensive contacts with the United States could be a problem if Britain remained neutral and maintaining war with Japan could not be seen in isolation from events elsewhere (i.e., Europe), it wanted the government to emphasize imperial ties and to "offer no military commitments in advance of an actual crisis developing."[26]

Roosevelt was not yet finished with Canada, however. Employing a bridge dedication on the Saint Lawrence River to send Germany a message, the president pronounced that "the people of the United States will not stand idly by if domination of Canadian soil is threatened by another empire." Although enthusiastically hailed throughout Canada, the Canadian military feared the promise of American aid would scuttle its own efforts to gain public support for rearmament and possible intervention in Europe. King's concerns were closer to home. Believing U.S. aid would mean that "Canada would become part of America," and complaining Roosevelt had only added to Canadian responsibilities in "that we would have to see that our coasts were so defended that no enemy forces could operate from Canadian territory against the United States," King played up the Dominion's obligation to defend itself in an August 20 speech.[27]

Canada's entry into World War II on September 10, 1939, and its subsequent dispatch of forces to Britain naturally drew attention away from the West Coast and home defense. Only once France collapsed the following June, leaving Canada as Britain's largest ally with no guarantee that Britain would survive an expected German onslaught, did home defense become a matter of some urgency. Not only had Germany become a major problem, but the government feared trouble in the Pacific if Japan took advantage of Allied weakness. Even before France's fall, King was considering approaching the United States for aid to defend a militarily denuded Canada, while a shaken Skelton, admitting Canada could not defend itself without U.S. aid, believed there was little choice but to "contribute our share to the common pool in a way that would appeal to United States opinion."[28]

But getting staff talks off the ground proved difficult initially. On June 14, King informed American minister Jay Pierrepont Moffat of Canada's desire for military discussions, but Washington responded that the timing was "not opportune." Although some senior U.S. officers favored meeting with their Canadian counterparts, army Chief of Staff General George C. Marshall doubted such talks would have any value until Roosevelt's administration had considered the consequences of a Royal Navy retreat to North America or supplying scarce equipment to Britain or Canada. But within days that decision was reversed and discussions between Ottawa and Washington, D.C., regarding access to bases, arms supplies, and the possible American reaction to an invasion of Canada were under way.[29]

Roosevelt again took the initiative. On August 14 he approved Rainbow Plan No. 4, a hemispheric defense scheme that recommended a defensive pact with Canada that would allow access to Canadian bases. Four days later Roosevelt and King met at Ogdensburg, New York, where the president pitched his idea of a ten-member permanent joint board on defense (PJBD) charged with studying "in the broad sense the defense of the north half of the Western Hemisphere." Very happy to agree, King assented and the PJBD was born. Despite complaints from imperially minded Canadians and Winston Churchill that the pact demonstrated little confidence in British staying power,[30] most Canadians were relieved to be under an American security umbrella in the dark summer of 1940. Within days the PJBD began formulating defensive plans including Joint Task Two, which bound Canada to secure its West Coast and to allocate forces to assist Alaska. In return, the United States promised to buttress British Columbia with a division and aircraft if needed. Control of forces operating together would be effected either by mutual cooperation or unity of command by consent of both governments or their designated commanders.[31]

But devising overarching defensive frameworks proved far more difficult than had been anticipated, the major stumbling block being Canadian concern about sovereignty especially on the West Coast. Leading the charge was the Canadian army. Praising the PJBD as a "major step forward," Chief of Staff General H. D. G. Crerar was more interested in promoting Britain as Canada's first line of defense and combating the Canadian tendency to think in terms of continental security. Intent on creating a five- to seven-division army that would contribute significantly to Germany's defeat but knowing King was reluctant to countenance such an effort, Crerar also wanted to make certain the United States would not be able to determine where or how Canadian forces might fight. Crerar thought that political considerations had led to Canada's agreement to aid Alaska. Dismissing a threat to Alaska as a remote possibility that should not be allowed to influence the PJBD, Crerar could see no reason why Canada should concentrate land forces in British Columbia for the support of Alaskan garrisons. This protest was successful. The final version of the joint Canadian-U.S. Defense Plan No. (ABC-22) contained no reference to Canadian army aid to Alaska.[32]

The unity of command problem proved far more stubborn. Canada was willing to accept American strategic control if Britain collapsed (basic Defense Plan No. 1), subject to the proviso that Canada's chiefs of staff be consulted before forces were employed. But Canada was unwilling to surrender control under ABC-22, the crucial difference being, as the PJBD's Canadian section head O. M. Biggar explained to King, that Plan 1 assumed the United States "would be Canada's sole as well as her overwhelmingly stronger ally," while ABC-22 dealt with a much less harsh reality. Concerned the vague definition of strategic control could allow the United States in either scenario to surrender Canadian territory or to determine if and when Canadian forces could be transferred domestically and overseas, Biggar wanted Ottawa to retain control of its forces in Canada while letting the United States assume command over certain specified areas at sea. The Cabinet War Committee agreed. Canada would accept American strategic control under Plan 1 if no other solution proved attainable but wanted the ABC-22 problem settled along the lines of Biggar's suggestion.[33]

Fiorello H. LaGuardia, Biggar's American counterpart, was greatly displeased. Arguing that acceptance of Biggar's proposals would place American units in Canada under Canadian control, LaGuardia lectured Biggar that in the grim struggle currently under way it was "far better to trust in the honor of the United States, than to the mercy of the enemy." Though LaGuardia appealed to Roosevelt to take up the matter directly with Prime Minister King, Roosevelt declined to do so, telling his PJBD appointee to make clear to Canada that "in view of the fact that in actual defense nine-tenths of the total effort will fall on the United States," America should wield strategic control.[34]

Told that the United States was reluctantly prepared to approach Britain or to plan for unilateral action, Crerar, asserting that it was foolish to "define the undefinable," wanted to establish broad and sound policies covering Canada's relations and responsibilities in "clearly definable *military situations*." Canada would retain control of its territory while letting the United States coordinate the interaction between the Canadian and American operational zones.[35] But when even that compromise proved too much for some Canadian officers to accept, Biggar sought political direction. Concerned the public's enthusiastic approval of U.S. aid to Britain and Canada might spur talk of a North American political union, the prime minister made clear it was better to have an understanding between two peoples and two governments "than to have anything like continental union." The Cabinet War Committee therefore ruled that it had no objections to giving the United States limited strategic authority subject to political approval but refused to countenance "unlimited authority over the disposition and employment of Canadian forces, in the circumstances contemplated."[36]

Admitting that progress was possible only if Canadian objections were acknowledged, the United States conceded in July 1941 that mutual cooperation would apply and strategic control would remain in national hands except when agreed to by either the chiefs of staff or by local commanders during an emergency. Even when unity of command was instituted, the local commander could create task forces, assign tasks, designate objectives, and exercise the coordinating control "necessary to ensure the success of the operations," but he was prohibited from interfering with the administration of the other nation's forces or from transferring them without chief of staff approval.[37]

Japan's attack on Pearl Harbor on December 7, 1941, not only brought the United States into the war as a full belligerent, it reopened the unity of command debate and suffused it with a real sense of urgency. A U.S. Army intelligence report, claiming that Japan seemed to have "complete information not only of our dispositions but of the habits, customs and traits of the American Army, Navy and people," said the enemy could strike in any direction including Alaska, Panama, and the North American West Coast.[38] What was to be done? Beyond marshaling forces, the Americans returned to unity of command, but this time the concept applied not just to the West Coast but to the entire Allied war effort up to the level of grand strategy. As a Council of Foreign Relations report made clear, unity of command was a necessary step "to produce the unity of purpose and effort, a wise allocation of resources in the common cause, and the elimination of friction" required to match the power of the Axis states.[39]

So while American and British officials sought to produce the unified grand war effort needed to achieve victory, the unity of command issue reemerged on the West Coast. Indeed, the matter had been raised just before the Pearl Harbor raid. Concerned Canada had not done enough to protect British Columbia—one American consul had rated the Canadian military personnel in the province as "exceptionally low"[40]—just two days before Pearl Harbor a war department officer had described the coast from the Arctic to Mexico as a single theater of operations that should be governed by one headquarters as "any step towards such unity of command will be an improvement over the present cumbersome and time-wasting organization." Assistant Chief of Staff Brigadier General L. T. Gerow agreed. Given the paucity of Canadian forces in British Columbia, the burden of defense was bound to fall on the United States, but only when the American services accepted unity of command as the governing principal for their own relations would the United States be in a good position to convince Canada to hand over control of its westernmost province. Still, believing the matter to be sufficiently urgent, Gerow asked the PJBD's American section on December 15 to take up the matter soon with its Canadian counterpart.[41]

Such a request had already been made. Moffat had approached King on December 9 about approving unity of command, but the Cabinet War Committee agreed only to meet the practical requirements of American request without acceding to a formal command system. King was more worried than that answer indicated. He anticipated an enemy landing in British Columbia, and hearing rumors that the prime minister might assign two divisions to the West Coast (the garrison numbered just six battalions), the Canadian military promised to place additional resources in the province as long as the cwc understood that the principal threat remained Germany and that the West Coast faced the prospect of raids only, not an invasion.[42]

Major General Maurice Pope, vice chief of the general staff, who had opposed Crerar's command compromise, doubted that a promise to pay more attention to British Columbia's defenses would satisfy Washington, but Pope opposed acceding to the American request. Despite Allied reverses, Pope believed Japan lacked the ships to land just one or two divisions on the West Coast and could not imagine what Japan could hope to accomplish by risking invaluable military assets in the eastern Pacific. Knowing that agreeing to the American proposal would be tantamount to admitting his service's threat assessment was in error, and concerned American dominance might engender unhappy consequences for Canadian sovereignty and the government's standing with voters, Pope firmly asserted "the need for a unified command over the land forces of the two countries is not indicated nor can it be admitted."[43]

Yet when the pjbd next convened on December 19–20, neither Gerow's hopes nor Pope's fears seemed justified. General S. D. Embick suggested only that local commanders be authorized to coordinate defensive activities, which the board was happy to pass as the twenty-second recommendation.[44] The expected confrontation had not occurred for two reasons. First, the American services, having wrestled for years about the control of joint operations before agreeing in 1935 to allow for a theater commander, found themselves unable to put this agreement into practice in December 1941. Despite the best efforts of George Marshall, charging that no army or naval commander was qualified to make all decisions for both services in an operational defensive situation, the navy refused joint command over Hawaii and Alaska in favor of mutual cooperation.[45] There also were bigger fish to fry. Having entered into wide-ranging and complex negotiations with the British regarding the direction of the total Allied war effort, the Americans were somewhat distracted.

LaGuardia, however, was very focused. Encouraged by Embick's small success, he again sought Roosevelt's aid in late December. Reluctant once more to personally lobby King about the need for West Coast unity of command, the president directed LaGuardia to employ other channels. LaGuardia proved to be that other channel. Describing British Columbia as a geographical enclave within the American western theater, LaGuardia insisted to Biggar that southern British Columbia and the Puget Sound area could not be effectively defended by a system of several commanders. Insisting "the problem presented is one of setting up, as a wise precautionary measure, in advance of an actual attack, that form of basic organization that will afford the greatest measure of protection against enemy operations," LaGuardia therefore proposed that Canada's westernmost province come under the sway of Lieutenant General John DeWitt's Western Defense Command.[46]

Believing that the Americans were trying to reverse their ABC-22 defeat and noting that the United States again had refrained from stating any forms and scales of enemy attack that would justify the change, Pope counseled rejection of LaGuardia's proposal. Biggar was more diplomatic. The Canadian chiefs of staff would consider the matter and then contact their American counterparts, but if that did not solve the problem, the PJBD could discuss the issue again when it met on January 20. The Canadian chiefs, however, made short work of the LaGuardia initiative on January 7. Having just returned from meetings in Washington, D.C., the Canadians insisted the American chiefs "had stated unequivocally that they did not subscribe to the necessity of Unified Command either in Newfoundland or on the West Coast." Moreover, they had no intention of taking any further action "unless or until this matter is brought to their attention by the United States Chiefs of Staff themselves."[47]

Informing Pope that the U.S. Navy might relinquish control of the North Pacific to the Japanese, and maintaining that unity of command over local air and ground elements was one of the most important means of improving defensive capabilities, Embick implored Pope to find a formula that would safeguard Canadian interests and provide for a more effective organization of the common defense. Quite unmoved, Pope in fact complained "the propriety of an officer of the War Department writing *in the name of his Government* to an officer of the Department of National Defence on a matter of this kind may be open to question." Arguing too that Embick had been too "vague in stating the premise on which his demand is based," and maintaining again that Japan could not conduct large-scale operations against North America, Pope firmly counseled denying Embick's request.[48]

Most important, the renewed American interest in unified command was met by a firm and negative response at the highest levels of the Canadian government. Although Ottawa was genuinely grateful for the support America had afforded to Canada, as the United States established much closer ties with Britain in early 1941, it had become very clear that Canada's role in continental defense and in Allied decision-making in general was fading. This discovery, as one Canadian historian has noted, "came as something of a shock to Canadian statesmen."[49] Shock soon gave way to other concerns. Even as Japan ran riot in December 1941, officials in the Canadian external affairs department were worrying more about American attitudes than the enemy threat. Norman Robertson, Skelton's successor as undersecretary (Skelton had died in January 1941) and a native British Columbian, saw the demand for unity of command as a strong indication that "the United States was turning everywhere to more direct and forceful methods of exerting its influence." And although Robertson thought the United States would continue to follow "a friendly, cooperative and unassuming policy toward Canada," he warned that Canadians "should not be too cavalier in our confidence that the United States will always regard Canadian interests as a close second to their own and appreciably ahead of those of any third country."[50] H. L. Keenleyside, Robertson's assistant and a fellow British Columbian, was more blunt. Citing unified command, Washington's reluctance to accept a Canadian military mission, and a recent *Fortune* magazine poll that 71 percent of all Americans displayed an "unblushedly imperialist attitude" in regard to their nation's foreign policy objectives, Keenleyside cautioned Canada's war effort could be hindered "if the authorities in Washington feel they can consider us almost as a colonial dependency."[51]

External affairs' political masters did not object. On January 14 the Cabinet War Committee formally approved the PJBD's twenty-second recommendation and sent Pope off to the next board meeting on January 20 with firm instructions that Canada could and would agree to unity of command only if mutual cooperation broke down. So when Embick again entreated the Canadians to alter their position, Pope told him that if the United States really desired unity of command, ABC-22's provisions demanded that Marshall should consult directly with the Canadian chief of the general staff. Giving up, the Americans insisted only that the PJBD's official journal note their opinion that the failure to establish unity of command was subjecting the West Coast "to an unnecessary hazard." The matter was not raised again.[52]

Canada had resisted what it perceived to be a significant threat to its sovereignty, but the victory proved short-lived. As America's effort grew exponentially in the Pacific, so did its presence in Northwest Canada. Under considerable pressure, Canada agreed in 1942 to allow the construction of an Alaskan highway, and other very large projects (including an oil pipeline and an airfield staging route) followed. By 1943 so many Americans were in western Canada that some locals were referring to the presence as an "army of occupation," while external affairs officials were warning the scale, intensity, and permanence of that effort seemed to indicate that the United States would seek postwar political and military concessions from Canada, perhaps including "a Maginot line of air defences in the Canadian North" that might lead to Canada "being involved in a future war either by a direct attack on our own territory or by an attack launched against one of our neighbours over our territory."[53]

Why did Canada succeed in resisting the pressure for unity of command? Nationalists likely would argue that Canada's determined resistance was the deciding factor, but that would greatly exaggerate the Dominion's power. In May 1942, after discovering the impending Japanese offensive against Midway and the Aleutian Islands, the United States forced a recalcitrant Canada to dispatch badly needed planes to Alaska despite protests the transfer would leave Canada's west coast dangerously exposed.[54] One must conclude Canada won the unity of command debate because American leadership at the very highest levels was largely uninterested in its outcome, especially in December 1941. Although Roosevelt had shown considerable interest in the subject before the war, and indeed had spearheaded the initiative in 1937 and 1938, by 1941 he demonstrated considerable ambivalence. Prime Minister King was in Washington, D.C., in late December 1941, as LaGuardia made his pitch to the president to personally intervene, but King's extensive diaries make no mention of Roosevelt raising the topic even in the most casual manner. The American historian Fred Pollock may have the answer to Roosevelt's puzzling inaction. Arguing that the president had proposed the PJBD's establishment to prepare the way for the acquisition of the Royal Navy should Britain succumb to a German invasion, Pollock believes Roosevelt lost interest in the board and continental defense generally once Britain's survival seemed likely.[55] And without Roosevelt's special influence with King, Canadian objections could not be overcome.

It is quite possible as well that by January 1942 the senior American military leadership realized that a formal unified command system, although desirable, was unnecessary. British Columbia's meager forces were willing to cooperate with DeWitt's command, possibly to an extent that made Ottawa uncomfortable.[56] Moreover, while Embick was trying to convince Pope that control of the North Pacific might fall into Japanese hands, the newly formed Anglo-American combined chiefs of staff had ruled on December 31, 1941, that even if Alaska and Hawaii were lost to the enemy, those defeats would not make a large-scale Japanese invasion of the continental United States any less improbable.[57] Whatever the reason, as one Canadian diplomat and

scholar so ably said in a brief survey of the history of Canadian-U.S. relations, the Americans possessed "a strong conscience that restrains them from
forcing their will on us."[58]

Although Canada's successful resistance to American demands for West
Coast unity of command from 1934 until 1942 would seem to offer evidence
that the peripheral dependence school's case for Canada's postcolonial status leaves much to be desired, one can argue in fact that this might not be so.
Canada could afford to battle on the command unity issue because, win or
lose, the Canadian West Coast would be protected by a U.S. military shield
because simple geography dictated that the North American coastline from
Alaska to Mexico was a single integral structure. Fundamentally dishonest at
its core, Canada's position was consistent at least with its historical practice
of low military expenditures and resistance to undertaking additional alliance
responsibilities. Before World War II, Canada's protector had been Britain,
but with the Ogdensburg agreement that mantle shifted across the forty-ninth
parallel. It is perhaps more than a little ironic that the vast majority of Canada's
military, the part serving overseas, had from the war's very start operated
within a command system that clearly subordinated Canada's needs to the
total Allied effort. Indeed, King made no real effort to gain a voice in the war's
direction at the grand strategic level, because to do so would mean a greater
military commitment and greater casualties, and possibly a repeat of the 1917
conscription crisis that had devastated his Liberal party and poisoned French-
English relations. It was very much safer then to insist on symbolic sovereignty at home when doing so limited military liability and certified the
government's nationalist credentials at no real strategic cost. But as Canadians
quickly discovered, the command unity victories of 1934 through 1942 proved
far more difficult to later duplicate as "the shift in power to the United States
was not something Canada willed. It was a fact to which Canada had to
adjust."[59]

NOTES

1. David B. Dewitt and John Kirton, *Canada as a Principal Power: A Study in Foreign
Policy and International Relations* (Toronto: Wiley, 1983), p. 29.

2. Donald Creighton, *The Forked Road: Canada 1939–1957* (Toronto: McClelland
and Stewart, 1976); George Grant, *Lament for a Nation: The Defeat of Canadian
Nationalism* (Toronto: McClelland and Stewart, 1965); John Warnock, *Partner
to Behemoth: The Military Policy of a Satellite Canada* (Toronto: New Press, 1970);

and Gerard S. Vano, *Canada: The Strategic and Military Pawn* (New York: Praeger, 1988).

3. Library of Congress Manuscript Division [LC], William Mitchell Papers, box 20, file Statements from Gen. Mitchell's Desk 1925, "Col. William Mitchell's Opening Statement before the President's Board of Aeronautic Inquiry on Conditions Governing Our National Defense and the Place of Air Power Beside Sea Power and Land Power," 1925.

4. The best account of war planning is Richard Preston's *The Defence of the Undefended Border: Planning for War in North America, 1867–1939* (Montreal: McGill-Queen's University Press, 1977).

5. National Archives and Records Administration [NARA], State Department Records, Decimal File 1930–1939, RG59, file 811.2342/422, Minister to Canada Warren Robbins to O. D. Skelton, May 21, 1934.

6. Directorate of History and Heritage, Department of National Defence [DHH], Skelton to U.S. Charge d'Affaires Pierre de L. Boal, September 16, 1932; and J.L. Granatstein and Norman Hillmer, *For Better or for Worse: Canada and the United States to the 1990s* (Toronto: Copp, Clark, Pitman, 1991), p. 121.

7. National Archives of Canada [NAC], A. G. L. McNaughton Papers, MG30 E133, vol. 109, file Otter Committee, McNaughton to Major General J. H. MacBrien, March 13, 1923; NAC, Department of National Defence Records [DND], RG24, vol. 2692, file HQS 5199–A vol. 1, subcommittee of the joint service committee report, "The Maintenance of Canadian Neutrality in the event of war between Japan and the U.S.A.," March 10, 1933; and NAC, Department of External Affairs Records [DEA], vol. 1763, file 53–BJ, DND Deputy Minister L. R. LaFleche to Skelton, June 9, 1934.

8. NAC, C. F. Hamilton Papers, MG30 D84, vol. 3, file 12, Hamilton memorandum, March 1921.

9. Wilfrid Laurier, quoted in Lawrence Martin, *The Presidents and Prime Ministers. Washington and Ottawa Face to Face: The Myth of Bilateral Bliss, 1867–1982* (Toronto: Doubleday, 1982), p. 54.

10. NAC, RG25, vol. 1684, file 53–AB, Skelton to LaFleche, June 12 and 13, 1934; and ibid., Skelton to Prime Minister R. B. Bennett, June 15, 1934.

11. NARA, RG59, Decimal File 1930–39, file 811.2342/431, Warren Robbins to Cordell Hull, "Projected Washington-Alaska Flight," June 22, 1934.

12. U.S. Congress, House, Hearings before the Committee on Military Affairs House of Representatives, 74th Congress, 1st sess. on H.R. 6621 and H.R. 4130, February 11–13, 1935, testimony by Lieutenant Colonel J. D. Reardon, February 12, 1935, p. 72; and DHH, file 74/256, vol. 2, McNaughton memorandum, "The Defence of Canada (A Review of the Present Situation)," May 28, 1935.

13. Richard A. Harrison, "Testing the Water: A Secret Probe towards Anglo-American Military Co-operation in 1936," *International History Review* 7 (May 1985):

215–17; and B. J. C. McKercher, "No Eternal Friends or Enemies: British Defence Policy and the Problem of the United States, 1919–1939," *Canadian Journal of History* 28 (August 1993): 279–80.

14. Franklin Delano Roosevelt Library [FDRL], Sumner Welles Papers, box 149, file Roosevelt 1934, Sumner Welles memorandum, June 14, 1934; and Robert Dallek, *Franklin D. Roosevelt and American Foreign Policy, 1932–1945* (New York: Oxford University Press, 1979), pp. 88–89.

15. FDRL, Franklin Roosevelt Papers, President's Secretary File [PSF], box 25, file Canada 1933–35, Norman Armour to William Phillips, October 22, 1935; and ibid., Armour memorandum, October 25, 1935.

16. NAC, William Lyon Mackenzie Papers, Diaries, MG26 J13, entry for July 31, 1936; and Stanley W. Dziuban, *Military Relations between the United States and Canada 1939–1945* (Washington, D.C.: Office of the Chief of Military History, Department of the Army, 1959), p. 3.

17. DHH, file 112.3 M1023 (D22), "Militia and Air Force Confidential Summary Volume XIV Serial No. 3/36," June 30, 1936.

18. DHH, file 74/256, vol. 1, Joint Services Committee memorandum, "An Appreciation of the Defence Problems Confronting Canada with Recommendations for the Development of the Armed Forces," September 5, 1936.

19. Ibid.

20. NAC, Loring Christie Papers, MG30 E44, vol. 27, file 9, Skelton memorandum, February 1937; NAC, MG26 J13, entries for September 9 and 10, 1936; and Roger Sarty, *The Maritime Defence of Canada* (Toronto: Canadian Institute of International Affairs, 1996), p. 99.

21. NAC, MG26 J13, entry for March 5, 1937; FDRL, Roosevelt Papers, PSF, box 73, file Hull, Cordell: 1933–37, Hull to Roosevelt, August 1937; and NARA, RG59, Records of the Office of European Affairs (Matthews-Hickerson File) 1934–1947, M1244, reel 1, John D. Hickerson memorandum, October 13, 1937.

22. FDRL, Welles Papers, box 161, file Canada, Norman Armour memorandum, November 9, 1937; ibid., Armour to Sumner Welles, November 17, 1937; ibid, Armour to Welles, December 10, 1937; and ibid., Welles to Armour, November 29, 1937.

23. Dallek, *Franklin D. Roosevelt and American Foreign Policy*, p. 154; and FDRL, Roosevelt Papers, PSF, box 70, file State 1937, Roosevelt to Welles, December 22, 1937.

24. NAC, MG26 J13, entry for January 19, 1938; and NARA, RG59, Decimal File 1930–39, file 842.20/68, Armour to Welles, January 8, 1938. The articles in question include "Canadian Defence Weakness 'Menace' to U.S. Security," *Ottawa Citizen*, January 6, 1938; and "Joint Coastal Defense Plan Envisaged," (Toronto) *Globe and Mail*, January 6, 1938.

25. DHH, file 112.3M2009 (D22), Ashton to Defense Minister Ian Mackenzie,

"Conversations held in Washington, D.C., on the 19th and 20th January, 1938," January 26, 1938; and NAC, William Lyon Mackenzie King Papers, Memoranda, MG26 J4, vol. 157, file F1411, Percy W. Nelles to Mackenzie, "Conversations held in Washington, D.C., on the 19th and 20th January, 1938," January 22, 1938.

26. DHH, file 322.016 (D12), "Defence Scheme No. 2 Plan for the Maintenance of Canadian Neutrality in the Event of a War between the United States and Japan," April 11, 1938; and ibid., Joint Services Committee to Mackenzie, April 14, 1938.

27. NAC, O. D. Skelton Papers, MG30 D33, vol. 5, file 5–6, Roosevelt speech, "Reciprocity in Defense," August 18, 1938; F. H. Soward, *Canada in World Affairs: The Pre-War Years* (Toronto: Oxford University Press, 1941), 107–11; NAC, MG26 J13, entries for August 20, 1938, and January 27, 1939; and NAC, MG30 D33, vol. 5, file 5–6, King speech, "Reciprocity in Defence," August 20, 1938.

28. NAC, MG26 J13, entry for May 23, 1940; and Skelton to King, July 1, 1940, in David R. Murray, ed., *Documents on Canadian External Relations,* vol. 8, *1939–1941.* Part 2 [DCER] (Ottawa: Queen's Printer, 1976), pp. 449–50.

29. Houghton Library, Harvard University [HL], Jay Pierrepont Moffat Papers, MS Am 1407, vol. 46, Moffat memorandum of conversation with the prime minister, June 27, 1940; Queen's University Archives [QUA], C. G. Power Papers, box 69, file D-2018, "Memorandum of conversation with the American Minister, Mr. Moffat, June 29th 1940," June 30, 1940; and HL, Moffat papers, vol. 46, "Memorandum of conversation with General Marshall, Chief of Staff," July 2, 1940. The talks are summarized in NAC, Minutes and Documents of the Cabinet War Committee [CWC], RG27C, vol. 2, CWC minutes, July 17 and August 7, 1940.

30. "Declaration by the Prime Minister of Canada and the President of the United States of America Regarding the Establishment of a Permanent Joint Board on Defence Made on 18 August 1940," in C. P. Stacey, ed., *Historical Documents of Canada,* vol. 5, *The Arts of War and Peace, 1914–1945* (Toronto: Macmillan, 1972), pp. 650–51. Roosevelt claimed later that the idea for such a board first occurred to him during his 1937 West Coast tour; NAC, RG25, vol. 2459, file C-10, Loring Christie to King, October 16, 1940. Churchill told King that if Britain was not beaten, "all these transactions will be judged in a mood different to that prevailing while the issue still stands in the balance"; Churchill to King, August 22, 1940, DCER, vol. 8, p. 142.

31. DHH, file 112.1 (D1A) vol. 1, "Joint Canadian-United States Basic Defense Plan—1940," October 10, 1940.

32. NAC, H. D. G. Crerar Papers, MG30 E157, vol. 1, file 958C.009 (D12), Crerar to McNaughton, September 9, 1940; DHH, file 82/196 vol. 1, Crerar to Stuart, September 14, 1940; NAC, Privy Council Records, RG2, vol. 4, file D-19–2 1940, Crerar to J. L. Ralston, October 14, 1940; and "Joint Canadian-United States Basic Defense Plan No. 2 (Short Title ABC-22)," July 28, 1941, in DCER, vol. 8, pp. 250–51.

33. DHH, file 112.11 (D1A) vol. 2, O. M. Biggar to King, April 22, 1941; and NAC, RG2 7c, Cabinet War Committee (CWC) minutes, April 23, 1941

34. NARA, RG59, box 8, file Correspondence of PJB on Defense, Fiorello H. La-Guardia to Biggar, May 2, 1941; FDRL, Roosevelt Papers, PSF, box 25, file Permanent Joint Board on Defense, LaGuardia to Roosevelt, early May 1941; and ibid., Roosevelt to LaGuardia, May 1941.

35. DHH, file 112.1 (D1A) vol. 2, Brigadier Kenneth Stuart to Crerar, May 14, 1941; and ibid., Crerar to Brigadier Maurice Pope, May 16, 1941.

36. NAC, MG26 J13, entry for April 23, 1941; and NAC, RG2 7c, CWC minutes, May 27, 1941.

37. "Joint Canadian-United States Basic Defense Plan No. 2 (Short Title ABC-22)," July 28, 1942, in DCER, vol. 8, pp. 250–51.

38. NARA, War Plans Division [WPD], RG165, file WPD 4544–28, Lieutenant Colonel P. M. Robinett to commanding general field forces, "Brief Estimate of the Situation in the Pacific," December 10, 1941.

39. General Frank R. McCoy, Hanson W. Baldwin, and Major George Fielding Eliot, War Planning, Council of Foreign Relations Report, December 15, 1941, in Yale University Archives, Henry L. Stimson Papers, reel 105.

40. NARA, RG59, Decimal Files 1940–1944, file 842.20 Defense/100, Robert Rossow, Jr., memorandum, "Observations on the General Defense Status of the Province of British Columbia," August 1, 1941.

41. NARA, RG165, WPD, file WPD 3512–146, Lieutenant Colonel Nelson M. Walker to the assistant chief of staff G-3, "Report of Observation—Alaska—General," December 5, 1941; and NARA, Office of the Director of Plans and Operations [OPD], RG165, Exec file 8, book 1, L. T. Gerow to George C. Marshall, "Defensive Preparations in Western Canada," December 15, 1941.

42. DHH, file 112.3 M2.009 (D133), H. L. Keenleyside to N. A. Robertson, "Developments in Canada-U.S. Defence Arrangements," December 10, 1941; NAC, MG26 J13, entry for December 11, 1941; and NAC, RG2 7c, chief of staff appreciation, CWC document no. 40, December 10, 1941.

43. DHH, file 72/145, Pope memorandum, "Note on Question of the United States-Canada Unity of Command," December 18, 1941.

44. DHH, file 82/196, PJBD minutes, December 20, 1941.

45. NARA, RG165, WPD, file WPD 2917–35, chief of naval operations to Marshall, "Unity of command over joint operations," December 1941.

46. NARA, RG59, box 8, file Correspondence of PJB on Defense no. 2, LaGuardia to Roosevelt, late December 1941; Dziuban, Military Relations between the United States and Canada, p. 120; and DHH, file 112.11 (D1 A) vol. 3, LaGuardia to Biggar, January 2, 1942.

47. DHH, file 112.11 (D1 A) vol. 3, Maurice Pope to Kenneth Stuart, January 3, 1942; ibid., Biggar to LaGuardia, January 3, 1942; and NAC, RG24, vol. 8081, file NSS 1272–2, vol. 6, chief of staff meeting minutes, January 7, 1942.

48. NARA, RG59, box 9, file Correspondence of PJBD 1942 Jan-March, Embick to Pope, January 14, 1942; DHH, file 112.11 (D1 A) vol. 3, Pope to Stuart, "Southern British Columbia—Puget Sound U.S. Request for Institution of Unity of Command," January 16, 1942.

49. J. L. Granatstein, "Getting on with the Americans: Changing Canadian Perceptions of the United States, 1939–1945," *Canadian Review of American Studies* 5 (spring 1974): 3.

50. NAC, RG25, vol. 810, file 614, Norman Robertson to King, December 22, 1941.

51. Ibid., vol. 5758, file 71 (s), H. L. Keenleyside memorandum, "Recent Trends in United States-Canada Relations," December 27, 1941.

52. NAC, RG2 7c, CWC minutes, January 14, 1942; NAC, RG24, vol. 13200, war diary of the vice chief of the general staff, entry for January 18, 1942; and NAC, MG26 J4, vol. 319, file F3369 (5), PJBD minutes, January 20, 1942.

53. NAC, William Lyon Mackenzie King Papers, Correspondence, MG26 J1, Keenleyside to King, "Canadian-American Relations in the Northwest," July 29, 1943; and NAC, Escott Reid Papers, MG31 E46, vol. 6, file 10, Reid memoranda, "Some Problems on the Relations between Canada and the United States," April 16, 1943, and "Canada's Position on the main air routes between North America and Northern and Central Europe and Northern Asia: Some general political and security considerations," August 2, 1943. The U.S. presence in Canada is ably discussed in K. S. Coates and W. R. Morrison, *The Alaska Highway in World War II: The U.S. Army of Occupation in Canada's Northwest* (Toronto: University of Toronto Press, 1992).

54. See Galen Roger Perras, "'The Defence of Alaska Must Remain a Primary Concern of the United States': Canada and the North Pacific, May-June 1942," *Northern Mariner* 7 (October 1997): 29–43.

55. Fred Pollock, "Roosevelt, the Ogdensburg Agreement, and the British Fleet: All Done with Mirrors," *Diplomatic History* 5 (summer 1981): 203–19.

56. Pacific command's head major general, R. O. Alexander, was removed from his post in June 1942, ostensibly because of poor performance. But an American naval liaison officer serving in Alexander's headquarters believed the firing had occurred "for the purpose of expressing displeasure in General Alexander's close cooperation with U.S. authorities," especially in the run up to Midway; Naval Historical Center, Strategic Plans Division Records, Series V, box 103, file EG-3 Alaska, Glenn Howell to commander [of the] northwest sea frontier, "Change in Commander-in-Chief, West Coast Defenses in Western Canadian Command," June 27, 1942.

57. NARA, RG165, OPD, file ABC 384 No. America (November 29, 1942), Section 1,

United States: ABC-4/ CS-1 British WW-1 (Final), "American-British Grand Strategy," December 31, 1941.

58. John W. Holmes, *Life with Uncle: The Canadian-American Relationship* (Toronto: University of Toronto Press, 1981), p. 105.

59. John W. Holmes, *The Shaping of Peace: Canada and the Search for World Order 1943–1957*, vol. 1 (Toronto: University of Toronto Press, 1979), p. 138.

8 / That Long Western Border

Canada, the United States, and a Century of Economic Change

CARL ABBOTT

At the start of the twenty-first century, according to the pundits of news-paper opinion pages, international borders were fast becoming relics. Germany and Italy had become members of the same European Union. Guest workers crossed and recrossed the borders of Europe, Asia, and the Americas. Transnational corporations sought workers and investments across dozens of national divides. Global financiers shifted wealth around the world with a few strokes on the computer keypad. The northwest quadrant of North America has heard the same message. NAFTA followed the Canada–United States Free Trade Agreement. Shoppers flow back and forth from one coun-try to the other depending on bargains and exchange rates, while tourist bureaus target cross-border recreationists. Competing for attention are new regional designations that span the long western border—the countercultural Ecotopia, the scholarly suggestions of a Great Raincoast, the recent idea of a sustainable Cascadia.[1]

This chapter offers a critical historical perspective on this vision of a unified Northwest. The stance is one of cautious skepticism. Despite the attractions of a Cascadian vision, I propose the counterintuitive suggestion that the national border actually divided the Northwest more thoroughly at the end of the twentieth century than it did at the beginning. Webs of regulations and layers of public bureaucracies now belie its physical openness. In the nine-teenth century life in the old Northwest reflected the international age of mobility. At the century's end, however, the new Northwest was deeply enmeshed in the global age of bureaucracy.

I begin this historical reflection on the economic and social implications of the border between the United States and Canada by casting some anchors into the firm ground of western literature. Wallace Stegner, one of the premier writers of the American West, remembered a childhood just north of the forty-ninth parallel in his memoir of the 1910s, *Wolf Willow*. It recounts Stegner's eloquent return to his early years and the sun-drenched plains of the continental dry-farming frontier. The family had already tried Seattle, Bellingham, and Iowa before arriving in Canada, and they would eventually move on again to Montana: "Our homestead lay south of here, right on the Saskatchewan-Montana border—a place so ambiguous in its affiliations that we felt as uncertain as the drainage about which way to flow. . . . Our lives slopped over the international boundary every summer day. Our plowshares bit into Montana sod every time we made the turn at the south end of the field. . . . We bought supplies in Harlem or Chinook. . . . In the fall we hauled our wheat, if we had made any, freely and I suppose illegally across to the Milk River towns and sold it where it was handiest to sell it."[2] In the summer the family sent its mail orders to Sears. In the winter it moved a few miles north to a small Saskatchewan town, where new school clothes came from the T. Eaton's catalog.

My second text comes from a novel set in the 1970s—a decade of crucial change for the United States and its global systems of economic and political interaction. The novel is *Yellowfish*, one of the fictional meditations on the tensions between western landscapes and the institutions of modernity that Washingtonian John Keeble wraps so effectively in the guise of a cross-border thriller.[3]

A red Datsun . . . whipped off [San Francisco's] Washington Street into the parking lot next to the Golden Phoenix restaurant. . . .

Wesley Erks . . . leaned around and rapped on the rear window. . . . Three Chinese youths stepped out. . . . [They] had about them a singular air of attention, receptivity, uncertain curiosity, the air of travelers, which is what they were, who have reached their destination, which they had, a place to which they have never before been, a strange place. . . .

The youths—he knew—were illegal aliens. That was why [he] had been hired. They entered Canada on tourist visas. He had driven them across the border at an unchecked point. . . .

Johnson's Immigration Act had attempted to regularize immigration. . . . It granted twenty thousand visas each year to each independent nation, but counted Hong Kong as part of Great Britain, and thereby reenacted, strangely, the "paper sons" and "uncles" entering surreptitiously from the north.

The contrast between Keeble's West and that of Stegner is a signpost for thinking about the ways in which the U.S.-Canadian border has affected the two overlapping economies of Northwest America in the twentieth century. By two economies I do not mean those of the United States and Canada. Rather, I mean the economies of the Old West and New West—fully understanding that both terms carry a variety of ideologically freighted implications that attract and repel different sets of North Americans. A review of long-term economic change is also a way to evaluate the idea of Cascadia as a binational region. Descriptions of Cascadia emphasize that similarities of climate and resource endowment from northern California to Alaska have shaped a common regional economy with similar political concerns and community values. They also suggest that the region's position on the Pacific Rim creates parallel economic opportunities on the two sides of the border and invites the construction of transnational institutions. Despite these commonalities, however, national connections (including the gravitational pull of California on the American Northwest) remain far more powerful than international ties.

In the Old West of the nineteenth century and early decades of the twentieth century, the tools of regional organization were water transportation, telegraph lines, and railroads. They created a northwestern version of the Old West that I sometimes think of as "Columbia." Literally, the dominant feature of Columbia was the Columbia River Basin, with its ranching, mining, farming, and logging enterprises tied to markets by the major railroads and shipping lines. Northwesterners ran sheep and cattle, grew fruit and grain, cut trees, and scooped fish from the cool waters. They dammed rivers for hydropower and dreamed of gardens in the drylands.[4] The majority of Columbians met the world with the help of Portland bankers, merchants, and transportation tycoons. In the nineteenth century, Portland was the point where riverboats shifted their cargoes to ocean-going steamers and lumber schooners. It was the channel and source for investment capital that ran rail and telegraph lines up the Willamette Valley and over the Siskiyous to California. It was the source of supply for miners and farmers in the interior of Oregon, Washington, Idaho, Montana, and British Columbia. To the north, Seattle, Tacoma, and Vancouver filled gaps in this early regional system. They vaulted into prominence in the Old West economy by grabbing railroad connections to the east. Their business leaders used enhanced accessibility to

organize Puget Sound and Georgia Basin resource regions and then to reach
northward to Alaska and the Yukon.

A century later the Old West economy remains central to our regional story
of the North Pacific Slope. The region's newspapers are filled with the ongoing history of resource controversies. Who gets to catch which species of
fish . . . and where . . . and when? Who gets to cut which sorts of trees . . . and
where . . . and how? Who gets to sell the most fruit to Japan and the most
wheat to China? Who gets to use how much of the Columbia Basin waters
for which beneficial use? Americans and Canadians argue among themselves,
First Peoples contend with latecomers, U.S. and Canadian regulations clash
and turn into headlines. Bookstores overflow with a new wave of powerful
and nuanced studies of timber communities, forest practices, the salmon crisis, and the mighty Columbia itself.[5]

However, the past fifty years have layered a new Northwest on the old.
Like the New Wests of the central Rockies and the Southwest, this new economy is a product of automobiles and airlines, not steam power. It reflects the
ongoing regional impacts of what we can call the "third urban revolution,"
involving the rise of new technologies of communication, the replacement
of manufacturing workers with service workers, and the increasing importance of information as a commodity in itself.[6] A defining feature of the new
Northwest is its intensively urbanized population. At the start of the 1990s,
the three metropolitan complexes of Greater Vancouver, Seattle-Tacoma, and
Portland-Salem housed 58 percent of the eleven million residents of British
Columbia, Washington, and Oregon.[7] The metropolitan Northwest is marked
by the high-volume movement of people and information. It is networked
internally along the Interstate-5 axis, interfaces with the global economy, and
pivots on Seattle. On both sides of the international border, new social patterns and clashes of community culture speak to the transforming impact of
the new economy. Indeed, much of the rhetoric of old and new economies—
or old and new Wests—assumes that borders count for little when wealth
comes in bytes rather than carloads. Information is so portable, say the enthusiasts of electronic communication, that national boundaries will erode
under a hail of faxes, e-mail messages, and hits on Web sites.[8] The vision is
a world reconstructed around direct connections of person to person, people
to people, and corporation to subcontractor.

I follow this scene-setting of the Old and New Wests by pursuing the suggestion that the forty-ninth parallel and its jagged extension through the Gulf
Islands and the Strait of Juan de Fuca have become *more* important rather
than less important during the course of the twentieth century. In the late

nineteenth and early twentieth centuries the northwestern quadrant of North America was in many ways a single arena for resource production. The United States–Canada border was permeable to migratory workers, settlers, and investors. Gold rush prospectors from California treated British Columbia as an American annex. Immigrant merchants and workers crossed and recrossed the border as members of binational family networks. Aboriginal Canadians provided a migratory labor force for Puget Sound mills. As Stegner reminded us, agricultural settlers on the western plains created a common borderland farming region and lifestyle that straddled the official border. For many years the competition between Great Northern and Canadian Pacific railroad builders pushed the border between trade zones substantially north of the diplomatic border.

All of these examples confirm the interpretive framework outlined more than half a century ago by the historian Marcus Lee Hansen in *The Mingling of the Canadian and American Peoples.* Hansen, of course, was the pioneer in the systematic historical study of the Atlantic migrations of the nineteenth century. His study of intra-American migration expanded this interest and emphasized the openness of the transcontinental border through most of its history.[9] In turn, Hansen's work is a key for placing the permeable forty-ninth parallel in the context of global history. The older Columbian economy of northwestern America developed within the framework of the great opening of the global economic system between 1815 and 1914.

The nineteenth century was an era of increasing mobility for Europeans, North Americans, and Asians. In this age of mobility serfs gained freedom in eastern Europe and slaves in the Americas. Industrializing economies drew farmers and peasants by the millions into Milan, London, Chicago, and Shanghai. They also required huge flows of workers across national borders—both permanent immigrants and temporary sojourners attracted by specific jobs. Nations in need of new workers eased international migration at both ends of the journey. Chinese moved to western America and Southeast Asia. Indians provided much of the labor force for British colonial Africa. The historian Walter T. K. Nugent estimates that roughly fifty million Europeans migrated across the Atlantic between 1815 and 1914; perhaps twice that many crossed national frontiers within Europe.[10] Immigrants flocked from Ireland to England, France to Algeria, Germany to Brazil, Italy to Argentina, Britain to Canada, Norway to the United States . . . and Quebec to New Hampshire, Minnesota to Manitoba, and Washington state to British Columbia.

That open economy changed with the onset of the Great War in Europe. Four years of devastating war, socialist revolutions, a Great Depression, a sec-

ond war, and a forty-year Cold War all helped to transform the growing
nationalisms of Europe and the Americas into rigid institutional barriers.
Nations erected protectionist barriers to trade that have taken half a century
to remove. The same governments created obstacles to international movement as they sought to hold their pool of workers and soldiers and to exclude
dangerous influences. In the United States pseudo-scientific racism coupled
with economic self-interest to limit Asian immigration, problematize Mexican
immigration, and curtail European immigration. Control of borders has
remained a central theme of U.S. policy, providing a story for Keeble's novel
and issues for the politicians. North of the international border, Canadian
nationalism also intensified after 1920, with results apparent in Canadian attitudes toward the Alaskan border and the Alaska Highway project, the
"Canadianization" of European immigrants, and even the effort to rename
Mount Eisenhower in the Canadian Rockies.

Thus if the nineteenth century for the Europeanized world was an age of
mobility, the twentieth century became an age of bureaucracy characterized
by fascist police and Soviet apparatchiks, by welfare bureaucrats in social democracies, and organization men in U.S. corporations. One of the central themes
of U.S. history since 1920 has been the rise of large-scale organizations—big
business, big labor, big science, "multiversities," and multinational corporations as shapers of what the economist Kenneth Boulding identified as an
organizational revolution.[11] Theories of social modernization describe the
replacement of local economic leaders with cosmopolitan representatives of
national corporations and conglomerates.[12] Even a relatively underdeveloped
nation-state such as the United States penetrates daily life in ways unheard
of in the nineteenth century, from income taxation to Medicare to automo-
bile safety regulation to neighborhood raids by the Immigration and
Naturalization Service.

Indeed, national borders are made to order for bureaucratization. Elaborate
border bureaucracies and institutions now regulate the surviving parts of the
old resource economy in northwestern America, forcing even loggers and
salmon fishers to be fluent with words and regulations. These regulatory systems are above all national (or nationally mandated) bureaucracies. Treaties
and agreements that regulate fisheries, boundary waters, and unfair exports
require constant adjudication. Even Indian peoples find that much of their
time and energy is devoted to negotiating the intricacies of a tightly regulated border. That they may be able to work out arrangements that protect
a vestige of their historical culture does not negate the fact that their lives are
embedded in the context of modernity, in the form of immigration and cus-

toms agencies, and that these differing regulations create diverging social and economic experiences.

It is this context of bureaucracy that makes me cautious about the popular idea of "Cascadia" as either a latent or an emergent region that transcends or ignores the international border. I worry that in both its ecological and economic versions, Cascadia is too good to be true. The ecological Cascadia has roots in the idea of a cultural "ecotopia" based on appropriate small-scale technologies and in the journalist Joel Garreau's definition of the Northwest Coast as one of the nine distinct "nations" of North America.[13] The most eloquent statement, however, has been Seattleite David McCloskey's map of a "great green land on the northeast Pacific Rim." McCloskey's Cascadia is an effort to forge a new awareness of human relationships with the regional landscape. But it also harkens back to the Old West economy and the age of mobility in which resources trumped political borders. McCloskey's evocative map (drawn in 1988) is a picture of water and its flows, embracing the Pacific drainages from Cape Mendocino to Yakutat Bay. Provinces, states, and nations disappear under the imperative of the hydrologic cycle that endlessly links the Pacific Slope and the Pacific Ocean, the same cycle that created and sustained forests and fish runs. Other depictions of an ecological Cascadia, such as the map of the "Coastal Temperate Rain Forest" issued by the Portland-based environmental organization Ecotrust, emphasize the north-south extensions of mountains and troughs that link the landscape (and carried early settlers and workers easily north and south).[14]

Ecological Cascadia also gains evocative power from the way in which water itself reverberates through Northwest regional literature. Rivers fill titles of our books—*The River Why, A River Runs Through It, Riverwalking, River Song*—and shimmer in the summer sun in Seattle native Richard Hugo's poem "West Marginal Way." Rainstorms pounding off the Pacific structure Ivan Doig's *Winter Brothers*, introduce H. L. Davis's *Honey in the Horn*, and drive the action in Ken Kesey's *Sometimes a Great Notion*.[15] The first paragraphs of Kesey's work are nearly a prose reproduction of McCloskey's map: "Along the western slopes of the Oregon Coastal Range . . . come look: the hysterical crashing of tributaries as they merge into the Wakonda Auga River. . . . The first little washes flashing like thick rushing winds through sheep sorrel and clover, ghost fern and nettle, sheering, cutting . . . forming branches. Then, through bearberry and salmonberry, blueberry and blackberry, the branches crashing into creeks, into streams. Finally, in the foothills, through tamarack and sugar pine, shittim bark and silver spruce—and the green and blue mosaic

of Douglas fir—the actual river falls five hundred feet . . . and look: opens
out upon the fields."

All this being said, we *still* find ourselves back at the bureaucratic realization that environments at the beginning of the twenty-first century are protected through laws, regulations, and plans. For an example close to my home,
the powerful Columbia River was confined by dams in the last gasp of the
Old West economy. Now it is managed by a Northwest Power Planning
Council, a Bonneville Power Administration, a Columbia River Gorge
National Scenic Area, a Columbia River Inter-Tribal Fish Commission, and
dozens of other complex organizations that try to balance the conflicting
demands of industries, nations, communities, and peoples.[16]

Economic Cascadia is a quite different take on a transnational region,
rooted in part in enthusiasm about the new economy. Proponents argue that
residents of the urbanized Vancouver-Eugene corridor share both values and
economic interests. The people of this Main Street Cascadia agree, says urban
scholar Alan Artibise, in their love of the outdoors, their respect for the natural environment, their sense of isolation from Ottawa or Washington, D.C.,
their orientation to Asian markets, their openness to Asian immigrants, and
their involvement in the rise of the information economy.[17] The idea of a Triple
Entente among Vancouver, Seattle, and Portland is thus an extrapolation of
the new Northwest economy. In the most expansive view this metropolitan
corridor carries along as many as five states (Oregon, Washington, Idaho,
Montana, and Alaska), two provinces (British Columbia and Alberta), and
the Yukon Territory.

However, this conception too invites cautious consideration because of the
paradoxical character of the new western economy itself. Even though the
economy of the new Northwest is heavily based on the highly fluid commodity
of ideas, it has still developed in the context of a controlled and regulated
border. To think about current effects, it is useful to differentiate between
the realms of consumption and production. The western border is permeable for personal consumption such as shopping and vacationing. The geographers Daniel Turbeville and Susan Bradbury demonstrate that loosened
trade restrictions have expanded the retail hinterlands of U.S. cities in the
interior Northwest. A study of Vancouver and Seattle news media by the political scientist Susan Holmberg suggests that each city thinks of the other primarily as a scene for consumption. The idea of a multinational Cascadian
region has been most visible in advertisements for a "two-nation vacation."[18]

Nevertheless, national pride and identity still override efforts to define common agendas for the organization of economic production. NAFTA has loos-

ened trade, but immigration and capital investment still take place within national borders. It makes a difference whether a Korean electronics firm decides to invest its $2 billion in Oregon or British Columbia. It makes a difference whether someone from Hong Kong decides to move to Vancouver or Seattle. The government of British Columbia blocked the implementation of a Cascadia Corridor Commission (authorized by both national governments) because of fears of subordination to Seattle—a sort of mirror of worries about the Alaska Highway fifty years earlier. Canadian concerns have been heightened by the effects of NAFTA on Canadian branch plant manufacturing. High-speed rail links south meet similarly mixed reviews because of their possible erosion of Canadian distinctiveness and Canadian businesses.

Cascadia to date is a set of committees and institutional arrangements— some formal, and some informal. Artibise does a masterful job in elucidating their overlapping origins and goals, their significant accomplishments, and next steps. Yet economic Cascadia remains organizationally embedded, a virtual region given life by bureaucracies, working groups, and "initiatives." Nor is it clear that Cascadia is really a natural economic unit. Artibise provides a compelling argument for the reality of an economic Cascadia that pools the economic capacity of Portland, Seattle, Vancouver, and their hinterlands into a globally competitive region. Depiction of such a Cascadia draws on the popular and plausible idea that "city-states" rather than nations are the real engines of contemporary economies. Originating with Jane Jacobs in the 1980s, the idea is now commonly accepted in both the United States and Europe (where it makes sense in the context of the emerging European Community).[19] As it has entered political debate in the United States, the idea that city-states are primary economic units is essentially an argument for metropolitan-scale planning and government. Journalist Neal R. Peirce, urban consultant David Rusk, former Housing and Urban Development Secretary Henry Cisneros, and many others use city-state arguments in efforts to persuade suburbanites that they have something to gain—a competitive edge relative to other cities—if they cooperate with central cities and that same edge to lose if they go it alone.[20]

A second version from the economic development field emphasizes the emergence of innovation centers or innovative milieus—urbanized regions in which a concentration of universities, scientific institutions, and high-tech companies drive the formation of new industrial complexes. In effect, an innovation center is a city or set of closely connected cities with a set of enterprises that flexibly complement and support each other's growth. What is important, say the case studies, are thick social networks among innovators, mobility of personnel among research and production enterprises, and instant access to suppliers and lenders. The resulting lists of global economic engines include the long-established superstars of the capitalist economy (greater Los Angeles, Tokyo, Paris), emergent high-tech cities (Munich), and closely knit sets of complementary cities as in the San Francisco Bay Area, where high-finance San Francisco, high-tech San Jose, thoughtful Berkeley, and brawny Oakland work as a metropolitan team.[21]

When we turn back to Main Street Cascadia, however, we find that the first version of the city-state idea doesn't help at all. Applied to the northern Pacific Coast, it is essentially an argument for Portland, Seattle, and Vancouver to compete more effectively against each other. It accentuates rather than erases both the Oregon-Washington border and the Washington-British Columbia border. The second version is also of little help. The three cities are too distant from each other for effective everyday interaction (ask any Portland basketball fan her opinion of having the Trail Blazers managed from Seattle). Most important, they may also be too similar to form a complementary whole on the analogy of the Bay Area. The cities originated, grew, and have continued to prosper as east-west gateways, not north-south connectors. Each is fundamentally a gateway to the Pacific and Asia for continental economies and a service center for interior hinterlands. British Columbia does *less* of its trade with the United States than does the rest of Canada.

Moreover, each metropolis is large enough to support a full range of consumer and producer services (NBA teams, research hospitals, advertising firms). Except for matters of taste, a Portlander need not go to Vancouver to seek out a sophisticated architectural firm, and a Vancouverite need not go to Seattle for transpacific container service or air connections. In other words it is not clear that the three cities working together are necessarily more than the sum of their parts. A realistic expectation for Main Street Cascadia may be less a merger of well-matched parts than a federation of otherwise similar city-states—a sort of Hanseatic League for the twenty-first century.[22] Anything more would require conscious decisions to generate economies of scale by systematically designating and developing agreed-on areas of economic specialization.[23]

Finally, western Americans can never forget California's looming presence, that vortex of economic power and engine of demographic and cultural change with the capacity to overwhelm a smaller Cascadia. Northward connections have been important for the northwestern United States, but southward even more so. In Oregon we *know* that we're a stubby little tail wagged by the very large California dog. California is the market, population pool, corporation headquarters, and consumption arena that pulls Oregon, Idaho, and Washington southward from Canada and Cascadia. Microsoft had to wait for California entrepreneurs to create the PC revolution. British Columbia's town of Campbell River may claim to be the salmon capital of the world, but California's Anaheim has Disneyland. Yakima has more in common with Bakersfield than with Kamloops. As the historian John Findlay points out, the northwestern United States has even forged its regional identity as a contrast to California.[24] The Golden State is the missing guest in discussions of Cascadia, waiting to take over the debate just as the statue of the Commandatore takes over the final act of *Don Giovanni*.

I'm left with a vision in which the three "Cascadian" cities go their separate ways rather than converging into a regional supermetropolis. Vancouver is likely to continue its development as a cosmopolitan gateway city—a Miami of the West, or Sydney of the North. Seattle is realizing a future as a globally competitive production city—an Osaka or Houston for the twenty-first century. Portland is following with one foot in both the old and new economies as a service center for regional resource communities and a bit player on the global stage—Kansas City with container ships or San Jose with steelhead swimming in its suburban streams. The bottom line is the continued importance of that long western border after a century of economic change.

I have framed this essay with a series of contrasts—the old western economy contrasting with the new western economy, an international age of mobility giving way to a global age of bureaucracy, an ecological Cascadia contending with an economic Cascadia. I have argued that the border has become more prominent rather than less in the second half of the twentieth century. The regulatory web that mediates U.S.-Canadian relations is firmly established and functional. Progress toward either an ecological or an economic Cascadia is likely to involve more coordinating committees and international agreements rather than fewer. The promised age of communication in the twenty-first century may make the regulations easier to navigate, but it is not likely to turn northwestern North America into a region where borders do not matter.

NOTES

1. Ernest Callenbach, *Ecotopia* (Berkeley, Calif.: Banyan Tree Press, 1975); Richard Maxwell Brown, "The Great Raincoast of North America," in David H. Stratton and George A. Frykman, eds., *The Changing Pacific Northwest: Interpreting Its Past* (Pullman: Washington State University Press, 1988), pp. 39–53; Gary Pivo, *Toward*

Sustainable Urbanization on Mainstreet Cascadia (Vancouver, B.C.: International Center for Sustainable Cities, 1995).

2. Wallace Stegner, *Wolf Willow: A History, a Story, and a Memory of the Last Plains Frontier* (New York: Viking Press, 1962), pp. 82–83.

3. John Keeble, *Yellowfish* (New York: Harper and Row, 1980), pp. 2–3, 7–8, 12–13.

4. For some of the vast literature on the rise of the Columbian economy, see D. W. Meinig, *The Great Columbia Plain* (Seattle: University of Washington Press, 1968); James B. Hedges, *Henry Villard and the Railways of the Northwest* (New Haven, Conn.: Yale University Press, 1930); Courtland Smith, *Salmon Fishers of the Columbia* (Corvallis: Oregon State University Press, 1979); Gordon Dodds, *The Salmon King of Oregon: R. D. Hume and the Pacific Fisheries* (Chapel Hill: University of North Carolina Press, 1963); Joseph Cone and Sandy Ridlington, eds., *The Northwest Salmon Crisis: A Documentary History* (Corvallis: Oregon State University Press, 1996); Robert Ficken, *This Forested Land: A History of Lumbering in Western Washington* (Seattle: University of Washington Press, 1987); Charles McKinley, *Uncle Sam in the Pacific Northwest: Federal Management of Natural Resources in the Columbia River Valley* (Berkeley: University of California Press, 1952); John Fahey, *Inland Empire: Unfolding Years, 1879–1929* (Seattle: University of Washington Press, 1986); Paul Pitzer, *Grand Coulee: Harnessing a Dream* (Pullman: Washington State University Press, 1994); Robert Ficken, *Rufus Woods, the Columbia River, and the Building of Modern Washington* (Pullman: Washington State University Press, 1995), p. 2.

5. On the forests, see Paul Hirt, *A Conspiracy of Optimism: Management of the National Forests since World War Two* (Lincoln: University of Nebraska Press, 1994); Nancy Langston, *Forest Dreams, Forest Nightmares: The Paradox of Old Growth in the Inland West* (Seattle: University of Washington Press, 1995); William Dietrich, *The Final Forest* (New York: Simon and Schuster, 1992); Kathie Durbin, *Tree Huggers: Victory, Defeat, and Renewal in the Northwest Ancient Forest Campaign* (Seattle, Wash.: Mountaineers, 1996); Robert Leo Heilman, *Overstory Zero: Real Life in Timber Country* (Seattle, Wash.: Sasquatch Books, 1995); Richard Rajala, *Clearcutting the Pacific Rain Forest: Production, Science, and Regulation* (Vancouver: University of British Columbia Press, 1998). On the Columbia system and its fish, see William Dietrich, *Northwest Passage: The Great Columbia River* (New York: Simon and Schuster, 1995); Richard White, *The Organic Machine: The Remaking of the Columbia River* (New York: Hill and Wang, 1995); Keith Petersen, *River of Life, Channel of Death: Fish and Dams on the Lower Snake* (Lewiston, Idaho: Confluence Press, 1995); Robert Clark, *River of the West: Stories from the Columbia* (San Francisco: HarperCollins West, 1995); Joseph Cone, *Common Fate: Endangered Salmon and the People of the Pacific Northwest* (Corvallis: Oregon State University Press, 1996); Blaine Hardin, *A River Lost: The Life and Death of the Columbia* (New York: W. W. Norton, 1996).

6. Some of these changes are discussed in Carl Abbott, *The Metropolitan Frontier: Cities in the Modern American West* (Tucson: University of Arizona Press, 1993), and "The American West and the Three Urban Revolutions," in Gene Gressley, ed., *Old West, New West: Quo Vadis* (Worland, Wyo.: High Plains Publishers, 1994). Also see William Riebsame, ed., *Atlas of the New West* (New York: W. W. Norton, 1998).

7. The 1991 population of Greater Vancouver was 1,602,000. The 1990 population of the Seattle-Tacoma-Bremerton Consolidated Metropolitan Statistical Area was 2,970,000. The 1990 population of the Portland-Salem Consolidated Metropolitan Statistical Area was 1,793,000.

8. George Gilder, *Microcosm: The Quantum Revolution in Economics and Technology* (New York: Simon and Schuster, 1989); Thomas Friedman, *The Lexus and the Olive Tree* (New York: Farrar, Straus and Giroux, 1999).

9. Marcus Lee Hansen, *The Mingling of the Canadian and American Peoples*, vol. 1, *Historical*. Completed by John Bartlett Brebner (New Haven, Conn.: Yale University Press, 1940); Marcus Lee Hansen, *The Atlantic Migration, 1607–1860* (Cambridge: Harvard University Press, 1941).

10. Walter T. K. Nugent, *Crossings: The Great Transatlantic Migrations, 1870–1914* (Bloomington: Indiana University Press, 1992); Geoffrey Barraclough, *The Times Atlas of World History* (London: Times Books Limited, 1978), pp. 208–209.

11. Kenneth Boulding, *The Organizational Revolution* (New York: Harper, 1953); Louis Galambos, "The Emerging Organizational Synthesis in American History," *Business History Review* 44 (1970): 279–90; John Kenneth Galbraith, *American Capitalism: The Concept of Countervailing Power* (Boston: Houghton Mifflin, 1952); Robert Wiebe, *The Segmented Society: An Introduction to the Meaning of America* (New York: Oxford University Press, 1975).

12. A model case study of the erosion of local economic control for the industrial East is John Cumbler, *A Social History of Economic Decline: Business, Politics, and Work in Trenton* (New Brunswick, N.J.: Rutgers University Press, 1989); comparable for the resource-producing West is William Robbins, *Hard Times in Paradise: Coos Bay, Oregon, 1850–1986* (Seattle: University of Washington Press, 1988).

13. Callenbach, *Ecotopia;* Joel Garreau, *The Nine Nations of North America* (Boston: Houghton Mifflin, 1981).

14. David McCloskey, "Cascadia," in Doug Aberley, ed., *Futures by Design: The Practice of Ecological Planning* (Philadelphia: New Society Publishers, 1994), pp. 98–105; Peter K. Schoonmaker, Bettina von Hagen, and Edward C. Wolf, eds., *The Rain Forests of Home: Profile of a North American Bioregion* (Washington, D.C.: Island Press, 1997); Rain Collective, *Knowing Home: Studies for a Possible Portland* (Portland, Oreg.: Rain magazine, 1981).

15. David James Duncan, *The River Why* (San Francisco: Sierra Club Books, 1983);

Norman MacLean, *A River Runs Through It, and Other Stories* (Chicago: University of Chicago Press, 1976); Craig Lesley, *River Song* (Boston: Houghton Mifflin, 1989); Kathleen Dean Moore, *Riverwalking: Reflections on Moving Water* (New York: Lyons and Burford, 1995); Ivan Doig, *Winter Brothers: A Season at the Edge of America* (New York: Harcourt Brace, 1980); H. L. Davis, *Honey in the Horn* (New York: Morrow, 1935); Ken Kesey, *Sometimes a Great Notion* (New York: Viking Press, 1964), p. 1.

16. For one example, see Carl Abbott, Sy Adler, and Margery Post Abbott, *Planning a New West: The Columbia River Gorge National Scenic Area* (Corvallis: Oregon State University Press, 1997).

17. Alan Artibise, "Cascadian Adventures: Shared Visions, Strategic Alliances, and Ingrained Barriers in a Transborder Region," paper delivered at the conference "On Brotherly Terms: Canadian-American Relations West of the Rockies," Seattle, September 13, 1996.

18. Daniel E. Turbeville and Susan Bradbury, "From Fur Trade to Free Trade: Rethinking the Inland Empire," paper delivered at the conference "On Brotherly Terms: Canadian-American Relations West of the Rockies," Seattle, September 13, 1996.

19. Jane Jacobs, *Cities and the Wealth of Nations* (New York: Random House, 1984); Artibise, "Cascadian Adventures."

20. Neal R. Peirce, Curtis W. Johnson, and John Stuart Hall, *Citistates: How Urban America Can Prosper in a Competitive World* (Washington, D.C.: Seven Locks Press, 1993); David Rusk, *Cities without Suburbs* (Baltimore, Md.: Johns Hopkins University Press, 1993); Henry Cisneros, *Regionalism: The New Geography of Opportunity* (Washington, D.C.: U.S. Department of Housing and Urban Development, 1995).

21. Manuel Castells and Peter Hall, *Technopoles of the World: The Making of Twenty-First-Century Industrial Complexes* (New York: Routledge, 1994); Annalee Saxenian, *Regional Networks: Industrial Adaptation in Silicon Valley and Route 128* (Cambridge: Harvard University Press, 1993); Ann Markusen, Peter Hall, and Amy Glasmeier, *High Tech America: The What, Where, Why, and How of the Sunrise Industries* (Boston: George Allen and Unwin, 1986); Saskia Sassen, *The Global City: New York, London, Tokyo* (Princeton, N.J.: Princeton University Press, 1991); Allen J. Scott, *Technopolis: High-Technology Industry and Regional Development in Southern California* (Berkeley: University of California Press, 1993).

22. There is now a substantial literature on the international or Cascadian dimensions of economic development and public policy in Portland, Seattle, and Vancouver. Some of the studies argue the importance of similarities and cooperative potential. Others directly or indirectly stress continued competition among the metropolitan economies. Representative of the first cluster are Alan F. J. Artibise, "Achieving Sustainability in Cascadia: An Emerging Model of Urban Growth Management in the Vancouver-Seattle-Portland Corridor," in Peter Karl Kresl and Gary Gappert, eds.,

North American Cities and the Global Economy (Thousand Oaks, Calif.: Sage Publications, 1995), pp. 221–50; and Artibise, Anne Vernez Moudon, and Ethan Seltzer, "Cascadia: An Emerging Regional Model," in Robert Geddes, ed., *Cities in Our Future* (Washington, D.C.: Island Press, 1997), pp. 149–74. In the second cluster Theodore H. Cohn and Patrick J. Smith, "Developing Global Cities in the Pacific Northwest: The Cases of Vancouver and Seattle," in Peter Karl Kresl and Gary Gappert, eds., *North American Cities and the Global Economy* (Thousand Oaks, Calif.: Sage Publications, 1995), pp. 251–85; John Hamer and Bruce Chapman, *International Seattle: Creating a Globally Competitive Community* (Seattle, Wash.: Discovery Institute, 1992).

23. Differences of political cultures and styles might also make such agreement difficult. Oregon and Washington have very different styles of doing the public business. British Columbia politics look eccentric from south of the border. And Alaskans definitely march to their own drummers. For balance, it should be noted that Richard Maxwell Brown argues for similarities in political culture in "The Other Northwest: The Regional Identity of a Canadian Province," in David Wrobel and Michael Steiner, eds., *Many Wests: Place, Culture, and Regional Identity* (Lawrence: University Press of Kansas, 1997), pp. 285–90.

24. John Findlay, "A Fishy Proposition: Regional Identity in the Pacific Northwest," in Wrobel and Steiner, eds., *Many Wests*, pp. 37–70.

PART THREE

NATIONAL DISTINCTIONS

9 / Borders of the Past

The Oregon Boundary Dispute
and the Beginnings of Northwest Historiography

CHAD REIMER

Traveling south from British Columbia to Washington State, one passes
the whitewashed Peace Arch that straddles the border between Canada
and the United States. Marking a boundary that has stood 150 years, the arch
proclaims these two nations "Children of a Common Mother." Of course,
time has a way of calming nerves and tensions and of making boundaries
such as this appear natural. But as Ken S. Coates notes in his introduction to
this collection, there is little that is natural about these "artificial lines." Like
all such boundaries, the border separating British Columbia and Washington
is the product of history—of a dispute that threatened war and a final resolution in the Oregon Treaty. Boundaries need to be drawn, not just on maps,
but also in the minds of those living on either side of them. This border has
been a peaceful one; over the decades citizens and historians on both sides
largely have accepted it as a reasonable compromise in an ancient dispute
that threatened relations between Britain and the United States. Not all scholars have been so sanguine, however. In a fit of pique, the Canadian historical ethnographer James Gibson has written recently that "present day
Canadians have valid reasons for regretting and even resenting the Oregon
settlement. . . . [they] should not forget that they were dispossessed of part
of their rightful Columbia heritage. . . . Canada has an irredentist legacy, to
which the Oregon 'compromise' was the chief contributor."[1] But over the past
century there has been little talk north of the border of sending forces south
across the "undefended" border to grab the Puget Sound, Canada's irredenta.
The forty-ninth parallel has stood firm since the Oregon Treaty of 1846.

The history of the Oregon boundary dispute has been covered well in the existing literature, at least from the American side, and therefore only a bare outline of events is visited in this chapter.[2] Until the later part of the eighteenth century, while a vital and culturally diverse population of Native peoples flourished, the Northwest Coast of North America remained unknown to the European world. For a brief moment after its delayed "discovery," the region attracted the interest of a "swirl of nations" competing for commercial and strategic advantage. By the 1820s, however, only Great Britain and the United States maintained an active interest in and claim to the region west of the Rocky Mountains that came to be known as Oregon. Spain had agreed in the 1819 Treaty of Florida to remain south of the forty-second parallel; a few years later Russia negotiated agreements with both Britain and the United States, setting the northern limits of "Oregon country" at 54°40' north latitude.

Meanwhile, beginning in 1818, Great Britain and its former colony began a series of negotiations aimed at dividing the remaining territory between them. The two governments soon established their bottom-line positions on the Oregon boundary. Determined to protect the strategic position and interests of British fur companies (which represented the only non-Native presence in the majority of the Oregon country), British negotiators held out for a boundary running west along the forty-ninth parallel until the Columbia River, and then down the river to the Pacific. American diplomats, meanwhile, would settle for no border further south than the forty-ninth parallel all the way to the Pacific. For there resided the region's only adequate harbor, the Puget Sound, and the land most suited for any future occupation by American settlers. Thus only the tract north and west of the Columbia River remained seriously at issue. These negotiations ended in stalemate and, with more pressing matters elsewhere, the two parties agreed at this time to leave Oregon open to joint use and occupation.

The issue was left to drift unresolved into the 1840s, when domestic politics turned Oregon into a source of increasing Anglo-American tension and the two nations flirted with war. The most significant force fueling this rising tension was the expansionist fever that swept the United States in that decade. Through war with Mexico, and negotiation with Britain, the United States would add more than 1.2 million square miles of territory between 1845 and 1848, including Texas, California, and Oregon.[3] James Polk tapped into this expansionist sentiment during his successful campaign for the White House. In 1844 he was elected president on a Democratic platform that eschewed the traditional U.S. diplomatic position, calling instead for the "reoccupation" of the Oregon country; and in his 1845 inaugural address Polk explicitly demanded all of Oregon, up to 54°40'. The bellicose language of Polk and other American "ultras" challenged the imperial honor of Britain, which responded with saber rattling of its own. A looming war was averted when more moderate voices gained authority on each side; in the end neither government valued Oregon enough to justify all-out hostilities, and the Oregon Treaty was signed in 1846. The treaty largely followed the traditional U.S. position, setting the boundary at the forty-ninth parallel from the Rocky Mountains to the Strait of Georgia, but jogging south here to include Vancouver Island in the British sphere. Within the broader context of Anglo-American relations, the Oregon Treaty contributed greatly to an Anglo-American rapprochement that emerged through the nineteenth century.[4] More directly, the treaty drew the line between British and American possessions in the Northwest and set the contours for future developments there.

The Oregon boundary question also produced the first historical literature on the region, which is examined in this chapter. The earliest of that literature, sponsored by the U.S. Senate, appeared in 1840; the next work was not published for four years, but as tensions rose in the crucial period of 1844 through 1846, a spate of histories by British and American writers was produced. Written in support of competing national and imperial claims, these inaugural histories of Oregon sought to provide the respective nations with legitimate historical lineages in the region. As the Oregon Treaty defined the region's boundaries on maps, so this literature constructed borders out of the past. This chapter shows that these histories, products of controversy, were molded by the contours of the Oregon dispute and in turn played an active role in the Oregon debate itself. Here, British and American authors shaped the past to support the region's current identity and future destiny. In so doing, they drew borders in the past, constructing competing narratives to uphold their nation's claim to the region based on historical events and evidence. The early histories of Oregon, then, laid the foundations of diverging historiographical traditions for the Pacific Northwest.

This examination of the beginnings of Oregon historiography has profited from recent studies by scholars who have turned their attention to the process of writing history, thereby contributing to our understanding of the ways in which historians rework the past in writing historical narratives. Such scholars as Dominick LaCapra and Hayden White have rejected any lingering suggestions of the historian as a passive mirror reflecting a pre-made "history."[5] Rather, they argue for the historian's active role in making history, not only through the selection and ranking of material considered relevant but also through the narrative form or strategy chosen to give meaning to the raw material of the past. Other scholars have shown how written history is profoundly affected by the social, intellectual, and institutional context within which history is produced. Most of these studies examine the role of historians in empire- and nation-building from the nineteenth century on.[6] With the rise of nationalism and the nation-state, historians worked to provide unifying and founding myths for their countries, building a common identity on a common past, while justifying the nation's current or expanding borders—distinguishing "us" from "them"—or establishing a sense of grievance and irredentism over allegedly unjust boundaries.

American writers made the earliest and most substantial contribution to the historical debate surrounding the Oregon boundary dispute. This was due in part to the fact that public opinion (through the press, party politics, and Congress) was beginning to play a more active role in the formation of foreign policy through the first half of the nineteenth century. In both public and official circles, Oregon had been a topic of interest since the 1820s, when the U.S. Congress first took up the possibility of occupying the region. Events of the late 1830s and 1840s, the high point of Manifest Destiny, heightened American interest in the Far West. In this atmosphere U.S. political leaders supported the first efforts at writing Oregon's history in an attempt to put their case before the American public and the world.

In 1840 the U.S. Senate ordered the publication of twenty-five hundred copies of Robert Greenhow's *Memoir, Historical and Political, on the Northwest Coast of North America*.[7] And four years later, when Greenhow released *The History of Oregon, California, and the Other Territories on the North-West Coast of North America*, the Senate ordered fifteen hundred copies of this expanded version of the earlier work.[8] Greenhow was a State Department translator and librarian who through the late 1830s, on instructions from Secretary of State John Forsyth, had collected and arranged historical information on Oregon.[9] Accordingly, Forsyth looked to him upon receiving a request from Senator Lewis Linn of Missouri in January 1840. Linn, chair of the Select Committee on the Territory of Oregon and leader of the Oregon cause in Congress, was seeking any information that might help bolster the American claim to the region. Greenhow's material was dispatched, and Linn immediately ordered that it be published.[10] Subsequently, Greenhow's works played a direct part in congressional debates on Oregon throughout that decade. The Committee on Military Affairs used his *Memoir, Historical and Political* in drafting its 1843 report on Oregon and reprinted the piece as an appendix.[11] During the decisive spring 1846 debate, one expansionist senator used Greenhow's

History of Oregon, California, and the Other Territories to buttress his argument that, contrary to the opinion of many, earlier international agreements had not set the precedent for a boundary running along the forty-ninth parallel to the Pacific.[12]

Interestingly, Greenhow himself would argue that there was a certain naturalness to a boundary along the forty-ninth parallel, if not in international diplomacy, then in the region's geography. As was common in nineteenth-century histories, both *Memoir, Historical and Political* and *History of Oregon, California, and the Other Territories* opened with lengthy descriptions of Oregon's geographic features.[13] Here Greenhow delineated the crucial boundary—that between American and British possessions—as running along the Juan de Fuca Strait and inland between the Columbia and Fraser watersheds. Echoing a prevalent skepticism in Britain and the United States about the fertility of the land in the Far Northwest, Greenhow argued that the only desirable land lay south of this line, in Oregon proper. The rest (what would become the province of British Columbia) could be left to the British, for it was "a sterile land of snowclad mountains, tortuous rivers, and lakes frozen over more than two thirds of the year; presenting scarcely a single spot in which any vegetables used as food by civilized people can be produced."[14] Thus, in suggesting a natural division of Oregon, Greenhow provided no geographic basis for "ultra" American claims up to 54°40'. At the same time his inclusion of Puget Sound in an American Oregon was consistent with the State Department's goal of acquiring an adequate port in the Northwest, and its recognition that the Columbia River, although a defining and dominating feature of the region, could not serve as such.[15]

After dispensing with the geographic boundaries of his subject, Greenhow proceeded to construct an American history for the region. Once again, the diplomatic context molded the contours of the narrative. In the decades of negotiations over Oregon, both Britain and the United States asserted priority of discovery, exploration, and settlement, from which each claimed sovereignty over the region. Of course, the United States did not even exist at the time that British ships first appeared on the Northwest Coast.[16] Yet American diplomats and historians could assert that their country's claim reached far back in history by making a crucial link: the United States was heir to Spanish historical presence and rights north of the forty-second parallel as a result of the 1819 Florida Treaty. Thus the opening chapters of both *Memoir, Historical and Political* and *History of Oregon, California, and the Other Territories* presented a Spanish story—from Spain's entry into the New World in the early 1500s, through to Spanish explorations and presence along the Pacific Coast in the two following centuries.[17] Thanks to this inheritance from Spain, Greenhow and other American writers could provide their country with a history in Oregon dating back to the sixteenth century, a historical lineage anchored in more than two hundred years.

A second element of the U.S. claim to Oregon rested on the presence of American citizens in the region from the 1780s on. Despite their relatively late appearance, Greenhow was determined to place his compatriots' activities in the foreground. From Robert Gray's entrance into the mouth of the Columbia River—"the most important discovery on the coast to date"[18]—to the expedition of Meriwether Lewis and William Clark and the American settlement of the Willamette Valley, Greenhow argued that American citizens took over from the Spanish in opening up the Northwest.[19] The discovery of the Columbia River, for instance, was depicted as a Spanish-American discovery, as Gray entered the river first sighted by Heceta in 1775. American exploration and settlement picked up where Spaniards left off, with almost no time gap between them.

While shaping his historical narratives to uphold the American claim to Oregon, Greenhow also sought to undermine the British case. To his credit, Greenhow did provide a scholarly presentation of British explorations and settlement, recognizing in particular the achievements of James Cook and George Vancouver.[20] However, at each crucial point in Greenhow's histories, British explorers were bested by either Spaniards or Americans: Juan Perez, not Cook, discovered the coast past the forty-second parallel; Gray, not Vancouver, discovered the Columbia; and so forth. Thus "neither Cook nor any other British navigator discovered any part of those coasts south of the 49th."[21] Greenhow conceded that Britain had a legitimate historical presence north of this line, based partially on exploration and more solidly on the presence of the Hudson's Bay Company. Consistent with the traditional, more moderate position of American diplomats, he implicitly rejected the arguments of the "ultras" that the British were alien intruders with no rights in the Northwest and that the American claim accordingly ran up to 54°40'.[22] But Greenhow dismissed the worth of the northern section of the Northwest Coast, even defining it as outside Oregon proper. The history of "Oregon" was an American, not a British, tale.

Greenhow's *History of Oregon, California, and the Other Territories* was the most substantial and scholarly history to emerge from the Oregon boundary question, and it structured the historical debate sparked by the international dispute. In many ways this work remained the most significant on the Pacific Slope until H. H. Bancroft's publications in the 1880s. Although both

Memoir and *History* bore the marks of the partisan context that produced them, Greenhow's two seminal histories were firmly based on primary material (most notably exploration accounts and government records, to which Greenhow had easy access) and reprinted important documents in appendixes. But the State Department official's writings were not the only contribution to the beginnings of the American historiography of the Northwest, for in the two years prior to the Oregon dispute's resolution a handful of Greenhow's compatriots added narratives of their own.[23] These histories were largely derivative of Greenhow's, with sections of some simply paraphrasing the latter's work and research. Not surprisingly, they followed the contours of the American narrative he had constructed—most important, in asserting the link between early Spanish and American activities on the Pacific Slope.[24] These histories also addressed the main points of contention in the Oregon dispute, marshaling historical evidence and legal arguments in partisan assertions of the American position. While Greenhow's works remained solid pieces of scholarship, even with their focus on the American side of the question, the writings of Thomas Farnham, Ephraim Tucker, and George Wilkes were more directly polemical and partisan. Taking up the "ultra" position, each discarded the traditional third-person voice of the historian for the first-person "we" and "us" in discussing the history and claims of the United States.

This tone was backed by substance. The "ultra" historians assumed a strong anti-British stance, which contributed new elements to the American historiography of Oregon, while echoing time-honored themes in American thought. A potent, negative image of Britain dated back to pre-Revolutionary days—the image of a grasping, tyrannical monarchy, determined to thwart the existence and growth of a democratic American Republic, using tactics such as inciting Natives to do so. And a "residue of suspicion and reflex of Anglophobia" dogged American attitudes through the first half of the nineteenth century.[25] Although such Anglophobia had waned somewhat, and certainly did not dominate all leading American opinion of the time, the Oregon dispute gave new life to Britain's negative image. Wilkes explicitly attacked "calculating monarchists" and British "tyranny," arguing that as a republic, the United States need not adhere to the international law of old monarchies in claiming Oregon.[26] Farnham wrote of the "insolent selfishness of Great Britain, her grasping injustice, her destitution of political honesty," while Tucker darkly warned of Britain's designs to control the world's commerce and suggested that it had plans to incite Natives to attack along the western frontier of the United States.[27] These American historians echoed the contemporary argument of "ultra" expansionists that Britain was an intruder in the region, an aggressively threatening presence that violated the noncolonization principle of the Monroe Doctrine. Moreover, they rejected compromise with Britain, called for "ALL OREGON" up to 54°40', and demanded that the United States immediately occupy it.[28]

Meanwhile, the sins of the British government were projected onto its supposed imperial agent in Oregon, the Hudson's Bay Company. The official American demonization of the company began in 1837, when navy purser William Slacum toured the region and submitted reports to the State Department and Congress. Slacum aired accusations that would be repeated in congressional debates on Oregon: the company exercised an active hostility to American competition and settlers, using its control over Natives to accomplish this, even to the point of inciting them to violence.[29] The American historians of the 1840s replayed these charges. They portrayed the company as an "irresponsible" and "foreign corporation," an agent of imperial Britain that unjustly exercised power over U.S. citizens, and put up "continual opposition" to American traders and settlers.[30] Tucker was particularly harsh: aside from sundry injustices to American settlers, he charged the Hudson's Bay Company with virtual genocide; through alcohol, murder, and enslavement, he wrote, it had been responsible for the dwindling numbers of Native people in Oregon.[31] Tucker, himself trained as a minister, also contrasted the strong moral influence of American Protestant missionaries to the company's spiritual negligence, thereby anticipating the myth of the founding missionary that would be so strong in subsequent Oregon historiography.

The American histories of Oregon, then, incorporated the Northwest Coast within the narrative of an expanding American nation. Each writer called on the U.S. government to occupy and annex all of Oregon, and each foresaw the expansion of American settlers and institutions there. "Oregon is ours," cried Tucker, while Wilkes intoned that "the course of empire has Westward found its way."[32] These early U.S. histories were part of and contributed to the larger context of nationalist and expansionist thought in the mid-nineteenth century. During this time older Jeffersonian concerns about the threats expansion posed to republican democracy were alleviated, and territorial expansion became part of the nationalist discourse.[33] The vision emerged of an American nation that reached to the Pacific, spreading its people and institutions across the continent in the realization of its "manifest destiny." John O'Sullivan himself stated in 1845 that Oregon belonged to the United States because of the nation's "manifest destiny to overspread and to possess the whole of the continent which Providence has given us for the development of the great experiment of Liberty and federated self-government entrusted to us."[34] The appeal of American expansionists to a higher law was echoed in the Oregon histories. Rejecting international law as a product of the old monarchical regime, Wilkes argued that "justice and natural rights" further strengthened an American claim already established by historical events.[35]

Not all American writers on the Oregon dispute were as expansionist and nationalistic as the "ultra" historians. During the crucial years of 1845 and 1846, William Sturgis (a naval captain active in the Northwest maritime fur trade and a partner in a major Boston trading company) and Albert Gallatin (an American diplomat at various negotiations with Britain concerning Oregon) put forward strong cases for compromise.[36] These two argued that history and international law provided neither the United States nor Britain with an exclusive claim to Oregon. While eschewing the demonization of Britain and the Hudson's Bay Company, the pair also rejected the "covetous" calls of their compatriots for all of Oregon, arguing that only an "amicable division of territory"—the border subsequently drawn by the Oregon Treaty—could prevent war between "kindred nations."[37]

The suggestion of an Anglo-American rapprochement here was significant; as with the other American historians, the compromisers believed that it was the destiny of the Anglo-Saxon people to populate the Northwest. But rather than using such rhetoric to justify U.S. possession, Sturgis and Gallatin expressed their preference that the region not be divided at all, and foresaw the emergence of Oregon as a "kindred and friendly Power," independent from both the United States and Britain.[38] As Frederick Merk notes, the idea of an independent maritime republic had been popular in Jeffersonian circles since 1812, when the former president himself wrote of the Pacific Slope's future as populated by "free and independent Americans, unconnected with us but by ties of blood and interest, and employing like us the rights of self-government."[39] The vision of the Northwest as independent, rather than an integral part of the United States, emerged from the Jeffersonian fear of over-expansion, that too large a territory would threaten republican democracy in America. Moreover, the prospect of absorbing Oregon as a colony was anathema to the self-image held by most Americans, whose nation was itself a former colony that had revolted against its European imperial master.[40]

What all American writers on Oregon shared, compromisers and "ultras" alike, was a profound belief in the superiority of Anglo-Saxon peoples. The diplomat Gallatin, whose view of this superiority was more cultural than racial, wrote that Oregon, free of Russian and Spanish/Mexican presence, was the only territory on the West Coast that could be "occupied and inhabited by an active and enlightened nation, which may exercise a moral influence over her less favored neighbors, and extend to them the benefits of a more advanced civilization."[41] Greenhow and the "ultra" historians, meanwhile, were more profoundly racist and nationalistic. He wrote that Oregon was to be settled by "enterprising and industrious" Anglo-Saxons, not by "savage" Indians, "listless" Spanish, or "feudal" Russians.[42]

At the same time these latter writers also disqualified Anglo-Saxon Britain as legitimate heir to Oregon. To distinguish between American and British claims to the region, Greenhow added the dimensions of race and national character to the anti-British arguments of "ultra" historians. For him, Britain's primary agent in the region, the Hudson's Bay Company, had left a tainted racial legacy. The combination of the barrenness of company land north of the forty-ninth parallel and interracial mingling under its aegis meant that there was "little prospect of the diffusion of the pure Anglo-Saxon race through countries possessed by the Hudson's Bay Company."[43] Moreover, he believed that the character of the American people rendered them more fit as founders of a new society on the Northwest Coast. In a Turnerian passage, Greenhow concluded *History of Oregon, California, and the Other Territories* by contrasting the prospects of British and American occupation of Oregon: "The contrast becomes still stronger, when we compare the character and traits of Americans, trained from their childhood to struggle and provide against the hardships and privations incident to the settlement of a new country, with those of Europeans, accustomed only to a routine of labor the most simple, and the least calculated to nourish energies or to stimulate invention."[44]

In the end these writers were convinced that the United States not Britain now represented the highest stage and leading edge of civilization. It had a providentially sanctioned mandate to carry the Anglo-Saxon race, Protestant religion, and republican democracy westward and southward across North America.[45] Russia, Mexico, and even Britain thus were disqualified as legitimate heirs to Oregon. Yet even more profound was the exclusion of those who had inhabited the region for thousands of years. In the American history of Oregon, Native peoples were either contemptuously dismissed as without history, or vilified as a threatening backdrop to the activities of non-Natives. To Greenhow, the Pacific Slope's Native Indians were "all savages incapable of civilization," who played no part in the history of Oregon.[46] The few times Natives did appear in his *Memoir* or *History*, it was as violent and treacherous threats willing to rob and murder visiting Americans.[47] Other American historians also alternated between dismissal and vilification of Oregon's Native peoples. Expressing a conviction that would only become more pervasive as the nineteenth century went on, Wilkes argued that Native peoples were "rapidly passing away before . . . [a] superior race."[48] Meanwhile, Tucker suggested the danger of the British inciting an Indian uprising on the western boundaries of the United States, a timeworn specter that denied Native peoples were capable of acting on their own and could easily be manipulated or used by foreign powers.[49]

The views expressed in the American histories of Oregon were consistent with North American historical writing on Native peoples through the nineteenth century. As Bruce Trigger writes: "Native people were treated as part of a vanishing past . . . seen as more akin to the forest in which they lived and the animals they hunted than as competitors for control of North America."[50] The early American historians of Oregon reinforced the "civilization versus savagery" opposition, which was the foundation for nineteenth-century views of Native peoples, with a national expansionist creed. They incorporated the region within the narrative of an expanding United States: American settlers, commerce, and political institutions left no room for Oregon's prior inhabitants. Indeed, the latter could be moved aside, violently if need be; and although their physical extinction was not explicitly called for, it was not seriously mourned either.[51]

The Oregon country aroused far less active and animated interest in Great Britain than it did in the United States. To the British public, and indeed to many leaders, Oregon remained a distant land of pine swamps, mist, and ice, a fur trade preserve ruled over by the monopolistic Hudson's Bay Company. As the British Columbia historian Frederic Howay later noted, "The British people knew nothing and cared less about Oregon—they had not been so continuously educated in the matter as the Americans."[52] However, through 1844 and 1846, and particularly after James Polk's expansionist State of the Union address in 1845, the British public was aroused by what they perceived to be an American threat to their national and imperial honor. Even Britain's chronically pacific foreign secretary, Lord Aberdeen, warned that "our honour is a substantial property" that could not be trifled with.[53] It was in this atmosphere, apparently with some official support, that British authors produced their first histories of the Oregon country.[54] Determined to counter what they saw as the "very ridiculous trash" of the American histories, English authors constructed their own historical narratives for Oregon, designed to replace the nationalist American histories with a more properly British, imperial story.[55]

First, these historians rejected the crucial link made in the U.S. literature between Spanish and American rights to the region. To British writers, the United States could not inherit historical rights from Spain because the latter had none to give. "If Spain had any rights," they argued, "Great Britain had acquired them"—either through treaties or by priority of exploration and occupation.[56] In support of this second point, English writers constructed a historical narrative that privileged the British presence in the Northwest over Spanish and American activities. Great pains were taken to argue that, as early as 1578, Sir Francis Drake had indeed sailed as far north as the forty-eighth parallel, contrary to the assertions of American writers.[57] Moreover, Cook and Vancouver were credited with inaugurating Britain's "continuous occupation" of the Northwest Coast two centuries later.[58] Thus the British view of Oregon's early history differed fundamentally from that of American historians: the early Spanish presence receded into the background, as British explorers took center stage. Indeed, some English writers felt free to ignore completely Spain's early efforts on the Pacific Coast.[59]

Likewise, the efforts of U.S. citizens were slighted. Convinced of their own nation's superior historical lineage, British historians pointedly noted that the United States had not come into existence until 1783. And it was another five years before "Americans appear for the first time on the shores of North West America," when Gray and John Kendrick came to trade furs, and still another four years before Gray and his men sailed into the Columbia River.[60] Even here, British writers rejected any American claim based on Gray's voyage, labeling it as "trivial" and a "pretended discovery," and asserting instead that Vancouver's efforts provided their country with the better claim.[61] Thus on all the contentious questions brought up by American diplomats and historians—from Drake's voyage to the discovery of the Columbia River—the British history of Oregon turned Greenhow's American trajectory on its head. Here, history unfolded as a British, not American, story.

As with the American histories, British works on Oregon were molded by the diplomatic controversy that produced them. British diplomats stressed the importance of actual occupation in assessing competing claims; their countrymen's histories followed suit by placing greater emphasis on land explorations and trade.[62] For both British officials and historians recognized that the long history of the region's two great fur companies (the Canadian North West Company, followed by the British Hudson's Bay Company) gave their cause a decided advantage, at least north of the Columbia. Overall, the British history of Oregon corroborated the Foreign Office's bedrock position, held through decades of negotiations, that it should possess the region north of the Columbia River.[63] Accordingly, the forty-ninth parallel does not emerge from these histories as a natural or satisfactory border.[64]

Both American and English writers recognized that the Hudson's Bay Company represented the strongest British presence in Oregon. Upon its move west of the Rockies in 1821, the company had emerged as the Foreign Office's primary source of information on the region; and it continued to affect Britain's perception of and policy toward the Northwest Coast well into the 1840s.[65] The Hudson's Bay Company, then, loomed large in the British history of Oregon, and British historians were determined to counter the company's demonization by American writers. In doing so, they laid the foundations for a powerful mythology that would persist in British Columbia historical writing. This mythology portrayed the Hudson's Bay Company as an agent of empire and civilization that saved the North Pacific Slope for Britain (and, in turn, Canada). John Dunn, a company employee in Oregon through the 1830s, used all 359 pages of his *History of the Oregon Territory* (1844) to praise the company. He described his former employer as "the greatest commercial association that ever appeared in England, next to the East India Company . . . diffusing wealth at home and spreading civilization abroad—ransacking the wildest, the dreariest, and most ungenial regions of the earth to provide comfort and luxury and wealth for the people of England; and pointing out to the benighted savage the means of improvement, comfort and happiness."[66] A second abiding tenet of this mythology was the sharp contrast drawn between the "benevolent" and "humane" treatment the company afforded Native peoples and the violent actions and policies of Americans.[67] Some even argued that Britain had a moral responsibility to hold on to Oregon, to maintain the company's benevolent regime and save the Native inhabitants from a possible American "war of extermination."[68]

Yet from the start, the Hudson's Bay Company's shortcomings as a founding figure of a British Northwest were recognized. For instance, the Anglican missionary Charles Nicolay acknowledged that the company focused on its own economic self-interest as much, if not more, as on the empire's imperatives. In past years it had used alcohol as a trading item, with devastating effects for Natives, and more recently it had been less than enthusiastic in bringing Christian civilization to the Native people.[69] This ambivalence concerning the company also would persist in British Columbia historical writing, causing difficulties for those in search of dependable founding myths.

Native peoples, then, played an important role in British historians' portrayal of the Hudson's Bay Company. This greater attention paid to Natives, along with a less harsh portrayal of them, marked the British histories apart from the dismissive tack of American writers.[70] In the British histories Native peoples did not assume the role of violent and treacherous threat, but instead they appeared as a population of wards destined to be led by either company officials or Christian missionaries. Without doubt, British historians shared with the Americans the same racial and cultural beliefs that formed the basis for nineteenth-century historians' treatment of Native peoples. The former were convinced as well that the Native way of life was fated for extinction, that the victory of "civilization over savagery" was both desirable and inevitable. Nicolay considered it a "sad reflection," though necessary for "universal advantage and progress," that "before the advance of civilization, savage life melts away like snow before the beams of spring."[71]

Before they passed off the scene, though—and the logic of the British histories seemed to suggest that this would be a cultural rather than physical passing—Natives had a role to play. Most notably, through the reputed contrast between their treatment by the Americans and the British, the presence of Native peoples served to discredit the Americans while salvaging the reputation of the British. In this, British historians of Oregon anticipated a tradition among Canadian historians who, as Bruce Trigger writes, "also relished comparing the brutal treatment of native people by the Americans with the 'generous' treatment they received from Euro-Canadians"—an interpretation requiring "great self-deception, or hypocrisy" in the face of British and Canadian government policy.[72] With respect to Oregon in the 1840s, there was less room for Native peoples in the nationalist narrative of American historians than in the British vision. The former assumed the inexorable march of American settlers, commerce, and government. The latter portrayed Britain as a benevolent landlord, most notably through its agent, the Hudson's Bay Company, which had built a reciprocal relationship with the Natives during the fur trade and which, through a firm yet "humane" policy, had prepared them to be what later British Columbian historians would label "docile and useful" citizens in a new non-Native society.[73]

Ironically, the British historians made room for Natives because they were more willing than American writers to see Oregon within a colonial framework, of Britain extending its "benevolent" imperial power over the region. It was suggested above that most Americans could not view their country as an expansive, imperial power. As Frederick Merk notes, the expansionist creed embodied by the phrase "manifest destiny" was not imperialistic at its ideological core. Rather, it was premised on the notion of consensual, contract government—Americans moving westward and southward would set up their own governments and apply to join a federated United States in due course. Native peoples and Mexicans could not easily be incorporated within this vision because they were "unenlightened" peoples not yet capable of self-government.[74] Yet to American historians, the settlers moving into Oregon sealed its fate.

Throughout, British leaders and writers accepted the global colonial regime and used its rules to assert their nation's claim. Britain had a right to the Northwest, they argued, based on the same "law of nations" that upheld the legitimacy of all colonial possessions held by European powers (these were the very rules rejected by American expansionists and historians).[75] British historians thus could envision Oregon as a colony within the British empire. They predicted that the region would be settled by British not American immigrants, for they considered overland emigration too difficult.[76] Of course, as with American apologists, British writers viewed their resolution of the Oregon question as good for both themselves and Oregon. Their arguments followed a typically colonial rationale for acquiring new possessions: the Northwest would open new opportunities for immigrants, while solving the problem of the home country's surplus population; it would provide new markets and avenues for commerce; and extending British colonial rule there would result in the "spread of our free institutions, equal laws and holy religion."[77]

From the British perspective Oregon also found its place within a global imperial framework. Strategically, a British Northwest would provide valuable ports on the East Pacific; and it would restrain American expansion on both land and sea, which was a serious concern for Britain.[78] Visions of a British Oregon also were predicated upon national and imperial pride, not least because the region offered the prospect of Britain spreading its dominion over such a distant land. Moreover, American bluster on Oregon threatened British honor and sparked a "burst of British patriotism."[79] "The thing attacked is *our own*," cried the London *Times* in April 1845, an opinion shared by British historians of the region.[80] Indeed, by dwelling on the Nootka Sound controversy, these writers reminded readers that the Northwest Coast had been a scene of imperial triumph, when in the face of war Britain stared down an over-reaching Spain. In the end the early British historians provided an imperial narrative for Oregon to compete with the American writers' nationalist histories. British protagonists—from daring naval captains such as Drake and Cook, to the stolid presence of the Hudson's Bay Company—acted out a

British plot line, concluding with Oregon taking its place within a worldwide empire, populated by colonists living under Britain's "free institutions."

Despite the heated emotions and rhetoric surrounding the Oregon question, compromise-seeking leaders in Britain and the United States were able to steer their countries toward a peaceful resolution of the simmering dispute. The Oregon Treaty of 1846 fixed the boundary between the two nations' holdings on the Northwest Coast. Although confusion over the exact location of the line through the Juan de Fuca Strait would spark local war talk and preparations a decade later, the Oregon Treaty contributed to the drift toward a larger Anglo-American rapprochement through the nineteenth century. At the same time the Oregon dispute convinced both nations that they had to strengthen their grip on the respective holdings of the Pacific Slope; in 1848 and 1849 both did so: the United States by organizing the Oregon Territory, Britain by creating the colony of Vancouver Island.

As with the diplomatic repercussions of the Oregon question, the latter dispute also left a mixed legacy for the region's historiography. The region's first histories were written before Oregon had been divided between the competing nations. Thus the earliest historiography of Oregon was a common one, with a common set of events occurring over a shared landscape. The fact that the Oregon dispute revolved around the issue of priority of exploration and occupation meant that these were dominating themes in early historical writing on both sides of the border, as was the determination to assert the British or American nature of each portion of the Northwest. Both American and British writers faced the more profound common task of writing the history of such a new region, a land that to them remained "almost entirely in a state of nature."[81] Most directly, there was a need to legitimate the presence of newcomers (American and British alike), while excluding the region's Native peoples from any claim by denying that they had a history. Operating on the intellectual premises of western historical thought, Oregon's first historians viewed Native peoples as being outside the march of history— that is, outside the progress of civilization, which to them was being pushed forward by Anglo-Saxon peoples. Indeed, Natives were viewed as without history because they lacked a written record of their past; they were "prehistorical" societies bereft of written languages. A written record of the past, then, was considered a constituent element of a "civilized" society; by constructing historical narratives for the Northwest Coast, these writers were actually incorporating the region within the realm of their "civilization."

The immediate purpose of these early histories, however, was to differentiate between British and American claims to Oregon, to draw borders out of the past in support of diplomatic efforts to delineate borders on maps. Born in controversy, the histories were molded by the currents of the Oregon dispute; and in turn, they contributed to the debate swirling around this boundary in the far distant Northwest. In upholding competing national claims on the basis of historical evidence, these writings provided the basis for diverging historiographical traditions south and north of the forty-ninth parallel.

For the American Pacific Northwest the most significant contribution was the incorporation of Oregon within the narrative of an expanding United States.[82] These nationalistic inaugural histories defined Oregon in terms of the United States's historical march across the continent—as such they contributed to the rise of a nationalist historiography that would come to dominate historical writing in the United States through the nineteenth century. Oregon's destiny was to be populated by American settlers, setting up a way of life founded on republican democracy, commerce, and agriculture. Although early American writers anticipated the theme of overland settlement—which would be expressed in the near mythical status attached to the Oregon Trail— they only hinted at the "founding missionary" motif to be found in so many later histories.[83] Definitely explicit, though, was a strong anti-British, anti-Hudson's Bay Company theme that, if anything, only grew stronger in Oregon historical writing through the nineteenth century.[84] Interestingly, in their focus on the Spanish presence or inheritance in Oregon history, the early American historians suggested a theme that would only be taken up sporadically, and much later, in American writing on the Pacific Slope.[85] The early histories also contributed less nationalistic, more critical traditions. William Sturgis's harsh criticism of the hypocritical treatment of Native peoples by Christian nations would be repeated later in the century by H. H. Bancroft.[86] And the Jeffersonian vision of a "free and independent" Oregon expressed by Sturgis and Gallatin would find a faint echo in the modern concept of Cascadia.

Meanwhile, British Columbian historians would struggle with the historiographical legacy of the first histories on Oregon.[87] The province's historians would have to deal with both the influence of American historians in the writing of their history, and the influence of the United States in the development of that history. Accordingly, they were determined to distinguish their province from its southern neighbors, and here the early British historians provided useful themes. Most prominent was the contrast between the vio-

lence of the American frontier—notably with reference toward treatment of
Native peoples—and the peaceful, benevolent regime of the Hudson's Bay
Company and British authorities. Early protagonists such as James Cook and
Alexander Mackenzie, along with the extended presence of the Hudson's Bay
Company, provided the elements for a *British* Columbia narrative of the
Northwest. Moreover, the imperial theme of the British Oregon histories
would be taken up; British Columbia historians would maintain the view of
the North Pacific Coast as a loyal part of the British empire. Well into the
twentieth century imperial motifs remained strong in their writings, while
the theme of nation-building would be much weaker than elsewhere in
Canada.

Nevertheless, British Columbia historians were left with a more difficult
historical and historiographical legacy than their American counterparts. For
one, the early Oregon histories gave them a less auspicious start. The American
Robert Greenhow produced the best inaugural history of the Oregon country, and the American H. H. Bancroft produced the first substantial narrative history of British Columbia proper. This historiographical legacy only
added to British Columbia historians' determination to distinguish the
province from the United States, a determination further fueled by the anxious realization that the Oregon boundary could have been drawn farther
north. However, unlike American historians, who could construct a nationalist narrative for the Northwest from the very start, British Columbia became
Canadian a quarter century after the Oregon Treaty. Even with Confederation,
British Columbia historians recognized that their province remained isolated
from its own national center and from the nation-building themes of central Canadian writers. Ambivalence about the Hudson's Bay Company presented additional difficulties. Although some writers looked to the company
as a successful agent of empire and a pacifier of Natives, others would question its role as founding figure by pointing to its self-serving monopoly and
failure to bring in British settlers. Finally, there was a lingering feeling that
Britain had let British Columbia down, that despite British Columbians' heart-
felt support for empire, the British government had sacrificed a good portion of what would have become British Columbia for the sake of peace with
the United States. This simmering dissatisfaction has rarely found expression
in irredentist outbursts; the words of the Canadian historical geographer James
Gibson quoted at the outset of this chapter represent an exception to the rule.
However, one might have coaxed Gibson's sentiments out of some British
Columbia historians with a few pints of ale—the stronger Canadian brew,
of course.

NOTES

1. James Gibson, *Farming the Frontier: The Agricultural Opening of the Oregon Country, 1786–1846* (Vancouver: University of British Columbia Press, 1985), p. 205.

2. The longtime standard in the field has been Frederick Merk, *The Oregon Question: Essays in Anglo-American Diplomacy and Politics* (Cambridge: Harvard University Press, 1967). Renewed interest in the topic is evidenced by Donald Rakestraw's *For Honor or Destiny: The Anglo-American Crisis over the Oregon Territory* (New York: Peter Lang, 1995). Works that deal with Oregon within the context of U.S. expansionism during the 1840s include Norman Graebner, *Empire on the Pacific: A Study in American Continental Expansion* (1955; reprint, Claremont, Calif.: Regina Books, 1983); and David Pletcher, *The Diplomacy of Annexation: Texas, Oregon, and the Mexican War* (Columbia: University of Missouri Press, 1973). Despite a chronic Canadian concern for those things that separate the two nations, the Oregon boundary has received surprisingly little attention from historians north of the border. However, Oregon is discussed within a larger, continental perspective in Reginald Stuart, *United States Expansionism and British North America, 1775–1871* (Chapel Hill: University of North Carolina Press, 1988).

3. Pletcher, *Diplomacy of Annexation*, p. 577. This nascent rapprochement would be sorely tested in the 1860s, during the U.S. Civil War.

4. Rakestraw, *For Honor or Destiny*, p. 3.

5. Dominick LaCapra, *History and Criticism* (Ithaca, N.Y.: Cornell University Press, 1985); Hayden White, *The Content of the Form: Narrative Discourse and Historical Representation* (Baltimore, Md.: Johns Hopkins University Press, 1987).

6. Most notably, see Peter Novick, *That Noble Dream: The "Objectivity Question" and the American Historical Profession* (Cambridge: Cambridge University Press, 1988); Carl Berger, *The Writing of Canadian History: Aspects of English-Canadian Historical Writing since 1900*, 2d ed. (Toronto: University of Toronto Press, 1986); and William Keylor, *Academy and Community: The Foundation of the French Historical Profession* (Cambridge, Mass.: Harvard University Press, 1975).

7. Robert Greenhow, *Memoir, Historical and Political, on the Northwest Coast of North America* (Washington, D.C.: Blair & Rives, 1840).

8. Greenhow, *The History of Oregon, California, and the Other Territories on the North-West Coast of North America* (London: John Murray, 1844). See "Preface to the Second Edition," reprinted in the third edition of *History of Oregon, California, and the Other Territories* (New York: Appleton, 1845).

9. Biographical information is from Reuben G. Thwaites, introduction to Thomas Farnham, *Travels in the Far Northwest, 1839–46*, vol. 1 (Cleveland, Ohio: A. H. Clark Co., 1906). Greenhow's star at the State Department faded during the Polk years.

Secretary of State James Buchanan did not trust Greenhow enough to translate Spanish documents. David Pletcher charges that Greenhow's wife was actually a paid British spy, passing on confidential documents; Pletcher, *Diplomacy of Annexation*, pp. 234–35.

10. See Greenhow, *Memoir, Historical and Political*, pp. iii–iv.

11. The Committee's report was reprinted in Thomas Farnham, *History of Oregon Territory, It Being a Demonstration of the Title to These United States of North America to the Same* (New York: New World Press, 1844), pp. 63–80.

12. Merk, *Oregon Question*, pp. 385–86, 397. The senator in question used Greenhow's rebuttal of the widely held notion that the Treaty of Utrecht of 1713 had set the forty-ninth parallel as the boundary between French and British possessions to the Pacific Ocean; Greenhow, *History of Oregon, California, and the Other Territories*, pp. 281–83.

13. Greenhow, *Memoir, Historical and Political*, pp. 1–19; *History of Oregon, California, and the Other Territories*, pp. 1–42.

14. Greenhow, *History of Oregon, California, and the Other Territories*, pp. 28–29.

15. In his *Empire on the Pacific*, Graebner argues that the desire for ports was the primary factor determining U.S. policy in the Oregon question.

16. Citizens of the United States did not enter the picture until p. 89 in Greenhow, *Memoir, Historical and Political*, and p. 178 of Greenhow, *History of Oregon, California, and the Other Territories*.

17. See Greenhow, *Memoir, Historical and Political*, pp. 69–85, and *History of Oregon, California, and the Other Territories*, pp. 114–26. Notably, the map reprinted in *Memoir* charted the "Northernmost point reached by Spain" in various years, from 1543 to 1775; no other nation's explorations were noted.

18. Greenhow, *Memoir, Historical and Political*, pp. 125–29; *History of Oregon, California, and the Other Territories*, pp. 232–59.

19. Greenhow, *Memoir, Historical and Political*, pp. 149–62, 199; *History of Oregon, California, and the Other Territories*, chapters 13–15, pp. 375–77.

20. Greenhow, *Memoir, Historical and Political*, pp. 79–83, 118–39; *History of Oregon, California, and the Other Territories*, pp. 147–59, 232–59. However, Greenhow was harshly critical of Vancouver for harboring "the most bitter animosity" toward all Americans, and of denying Gray of his just credit; *History of Oregon, California, and the Other Territories*, p. 256.

21. Greenhow, *Memoir, Historical and Political*, p. 170.

22. In *Oregon Question*, pp. 410–11, Merk lays out the principal tenets of the "ultra" stand.

23. Farnham, *History of Oregon Territory*; Ephraim Tucker, *History of Oregon* (1844; reprint, Fairfield, Wash.: Ye Galleon Press, 1970); George Wilkes, *The History of Oregon, Geographical and Political* (New York: Colyer, 1845). Unlike Greenhow, who wrote

from Washington and only ventured out to the West Coast in 1850, some authors of these histories had personal experience in Oregon. Farnham led a group of settlers to the region in 1839; apparently, Wilkes did likewise four years later. George Wilkes should not be confused with Lieutenant Charles Wilkes, who as commander of the 1839–42 American naval expedition to the Pacific Coast also visited and wrote about Oregon.

24. Farnham was the most explicit in making this link; *History of Oregon Territory*, pp. 58–59.

25. Stuart, *United States Expansionism,* p. 79, also see pp. 36–37, 55, 58, 73; Graebner, *Empire on the Pacific,* pp. 87–89.

26. Wilkes, *History of Oregon,* pp. 3–6, 28.

27. Farnham, *History of Oregon Territory,* p. 5; Tucker, *History of Oregon,* pp. 82–83.

28. Wilkes, *History of Oregon,* pp. 5, 33; Farnham, *History of Oregon Territory,* p. 62; Tucker, *History of Oregon,* pp. 81–84.

29. Rakestraw, *For Honor or Destiny,* pp. 32–34, 59–62.

30. Wilkes, *History of Oregon,* pp. 32–33; Tucker, *History of Oregon,* pp. 53, 81.

31. Tucker, *History of Oregon,* pp. 71–76. Greenhow, in the more partisan *Memoir, Historical and Political,* had aired some of these charges against the Hudson's Bay Company: an autocratic institution hostile to the existence of a "free population," it manipulated Native peoples as "willing slaves" to strike against its adversaries (pp. 191–94). These charges were not repeated in Greenhow's *History of Oregon, California, and the Other Territories,* which described the company in more favorable terms, recognizing that it was acting in its own economic self-interest (pp. 394–99).

32. Tucker, *History of Oregon,* p. 81; Wilkes, *History of Oregon,* p. 35.

33. On the evolution of expansionist thought, and competing anxiety over expansion, see Stuart, *United States Expansionism,* notably "Part 2: The Era of Manifest Destiny, 1815–1860"; and Frederick Merk, *Manifest Destiny and Mission in American History: A Reinterpretation* (New York: Alfred A. Knopf, 1963), pp. 8–14, chapter 2. Elsewhere, Merk argues that by the 1840s, changes in technology—most notably the advent of the steam locomotive—convinced most Americans that the extension of their political institutions over great distances was feasible; Merk, *Oregon Question,* p. 404.

34. John O'Sullivan, quoted in Merk, *Manifest Destiny,* pp. 31–32.

35. Wilkes, *History of Oregon,* pp. 5–6. On the higher law arguments invoked by American expansionists, see Graebner, *Empire on the Pacific,* pp. 123–25.

36. In January 1845, William Sturgis gave an influential lecture to the Mercantile Library Association of Boston, later published as Sturgis, *The Oregon Question* (Boston: Swift & Wiley, 1845). A year later, Albert Gallatin published a series of calming letters in the Washington, D.C., journal *National Intelligencer;* these were reprinted in Gallatin, *The Oregon Question* (New York: Bartlett & Welford, 1846).

37. Sturgis, *The Oregon Question*, pp. 23–24; Gallatin, *The Oregon Question*, pp. 25, 50. As early as 1818, Gallatin had proposed such a boundary, running along the forty-ninth parallel to Georgia Strait then veering south of Vancouver Island on the way to the Pacific; Rakestraw, *For Honor or Destiny*, p. 14.

38. Gallatin, *The Oregon Question*, p. 50.

39. Merk, *Oregon Question*, p. 42; Jefferson quote on p. 117.

40. Ibid., pp. 14, 116–18. As noted earlier, for many Americans technology had alleviated these concerns. And Graebner, *Empire on the Pacific*, p. 220, argues that by the 1840s, U.S. leaders and expansionists had flatly rejected the notion of an independent Oregon.

41. Gallatin, *The Oregon Question*, p. 50.

42. Greenhow, *History of Oregon, California, and the Other Territories*, p. 153.

43. Greenhow, *Memoir, Historical and Political*, p. 199.

44. Greenhow, *History of Oregon, California, and the Other Territories*, p. 401.

45. Merk, *Manifest Destiny*, p. 265; Stuart, *United States Expansionism*, pp. 258–59.

46. Greenhow, *Memoir, Historical and Political*, p. 20; Greenhow, *History of Oregon, California, and the Other Territories*, p. 31.

47. Greenhow, *Memoir, Historical and Political*, pp. 90, 143–44; Greenhow, *History of Oregon, California, and the Other Territories*, pp. 266–68.

48. Wilkes, *History of Oregon*, p. 44.

49. Tucker, *History of Oregon*, p. 82; Stuart, *United States Expansionism*, pp. 36–37.

50. Bruce Trigger, *Natives and Newcomers: Canada's "Heroic Age" Reconsidered* (Kingston and Montreal: McGill-Queen's University Press, 1985), p. 3. On the treatment of Native peoples in North American historical writing, see also Janet Cauthers, "The North American Indian as Portrayed by American and Canadian Historians, 1830–1930," Ph.D. dissertation, University of Washington, 1974.

51. There was one dissenting voice in the chorus of American writers—the exception that underlined the rule. While arguing that Oregon's fate was to be settled by Anglo-Saxon people, Sturgis caustically attacked the negligence and mistreatment of the Native inhabitants. He noted that the Natives' claim to the region was based on "actual . . . undisputed possession" reaching well back in history. And he concluded with an apocalyptic passage, foretelling the final day of judgment when "equal justice will be meted out to Christian destroyer and his heathen victim—and that will be a woful [*sic*] day for the white man"; Sturgis, *The Oregon Question*, p. 32.

52. Frederic Howay, *British Columbia and the United States: The North Pacific Coast from Fur Trade to Aviation* (New York: Russell & Russell, 1942), p. 129.

53. Lord Aberdeen quoted in Kenneth Bourne, *The Foreign Policy of Victorian England, 1830–1902* (Oxford: Clarendon Press, 1970), p. 263. Rakestraw uses the "hon-

our" argument to explain British policy toward Oregon and the ensuing crisis of 1845 and 1846.

54. The pamphlet *Comparative Chronological Statement of the Events Connected with the Rights of Great Britain and the Claims of the United States to the Oregon Country* (London, 1845) appeared to be an official government publication. Books that quite possibly enjoyed official or semi-official approval were: *The Oregon Question* (London: Samuel Clarke, 1845), by the barrister and Royal Geographic Society member Thomas Falconer; and *The Oregon Territory, Its History and Discovery* (New York: Appleton, 1846), by Travers Twiss, a barrister and professor of political economy at Oxford. Other works, most likely undertaken without government support, included: n.a., *Oregon Historical and Descriptive*, 3d ed. (Bradford, England: J. Ibbetson, 1846); John Dunn, *History of the Oregon Territory and British North American Fur Trade* (London: Edwards & Hughs, 1844); and Charles Nicolay, *The Oregon Territory* (1846; reprint, Fairfield, Wash.: Ye Galleon Press, 1967).

55. Falconer, *Oregon Question*, p. 43. Twiss viewed his book, *Oregon Territory,* as a corrective to Greenhow's *Memoir, Historical and Political* and *History of Oregon, California, and the Other Territories*; p. v. Meanwhile, the publication of Greenhow's *History of Oregon, California, and the Other Territories* sparked a back-and-forth pamphlet war between Falconer and the American, each faulting the other for various errors and misrepresentations. See Thomas Falconer, *On the Discovery of the Mississippi, and On the South-Western, Oregon, and North-Western Boundary* (London: Samuel Clarke, 1844); Greenhow, "Answer to the Strictures of Mr. Thomas Falconer," in the third edition of Greenhow, *History of Oregon, California, and the Other Territories*; and "Mr. Falconer's Reply to Mr. Greenhow's Answer: With Mr. Greenhow's Rejoinder," published as a pamphlet in 1845 and reprinted as a postscript in the second edition of Falconer's *Oregon Question*.

56. *Comparative Chronological Statement*, p. 14; Twiss, *Oregon Territory,* pp. 86–91; Falconer, *Oregon Question*, p. 24; *Oregon Historical and Descriptive*, p. 8.

57. Twiss, *Oregon Territory,* pp. 27–49; also see Falconer, *Oregon Question*, pp. 12–19; *Comparative Chronological Statement*, p. 1; and *Oregon Historical and Descriptive*, p. 5.

58. *Oregon Historical and Descriptive*, p. 8; Twiss, *Oregon Territory,* p. 61; Falconer, *Oregon Question*, pp. 19–24.

59. See, for example, *Comparative Chronological Statement*, pp. 1–3.

60. *Comparative Chronological Statement*, pp. 2–3.

61. *Oregon Historical and Descriptive*, p. 2; Twiss, *Oregon Territory,* pp. 102–108; Falconer, *Oregon Question*, pp. 27–29; *Comparative Chronological Statement*, p. 3.

62. Graebner, *Empire on the Pacific,* pp. 23–24. See, for instance, Nicolay, *Oregon Territory,* chapters 3, 4, 8.

63. As Merk shows, the Hudson's Bay Company dominated the region north of the Columbia up to the signing of the Oregon Treaty in 1846; at that time there were only eight American settlers between the river and the forty-ninth parallel; Merk, *Oregon Question*, pp. 236–38.

64. See, for instance, Nicolay, *Oregon Territory*, pp. 215–26.

65. Merk, *Oregon Question*, pp. 139, 244 n. 31; Pletcher, *Diplomacy of Annexation*, pp. 225, 243–44.

66. Dunn, *History of the Oregon Territory*, p. 12.

67. Nicolay, *Oregon Territory*, pp. 14, 76; in Dunn, *History of the Oregon Territory*, see particularly chapter 5.

68. Nicolay, *Oregon Territory*, p. 220.

69. Ibid., pp. 162–71.

70. See, for instance, Nicolay's ethnological treatment in ibid., chapter 7, "Native Tribes."

71. Ibid., pp. 139, 141.

72. Bruce Trigger, "The Historians' Indian: Native Americans in Canadian Historical Writing from Charlevoix to the Present," *Canadian Historical Review* 67 (September 1986): 321.

73. R. E . Gosnell and R. Coats, *Sir James Douglas* (Toronto: Morang, 1908), p. 266.

74. Merk, *Manifest Destiny*, pp. 4–10, chapter 2 passim.

75. *Comparative Chronological Statement*, p. 15; Twiss, *Oregon Territory*, p. 264.

76. Twiss, *Oregon Territory*, p. 264; Nicolay, *Oregon Territory*, p. 224.

77. Nicolay, *Oregon Territory*, pp. 224–25.

78. On the currents of British imperial thought regarding Oregon, see Merk, *Oregon Question*, pp. 140–42, 148–94.

79. Pletcher, *Diplomacy of Annexation*, p. 339.

80. Quoted in Pletcher, *Diplomacy of Annexation*, p. 594.

81. Greenhow, *Memoir, Historical and Political*, p. iv.

82. On the historiography of Oregon and the Pacific Northwest, see Kent Richards, "In Search of the Pacific Northwest: The Historiography of Oregon and Washington," *Pacific Historical Review* 50 (November 1981): 415–43.

83. See Tucker, *History of Oregon*, p. 75.

84. The most determined expression of this was W. H. Gray's *A History of Oregon, 1792–1849* (Portland, Oreg.: Harris & Holman, 1870), which expressed, and embellished on, all the elements of the demonization of the Hudson's Bay Company.

85. Gerald Nash, *Creating the West: Historical Interpretations, 1890–1990* (Albuquerque: University of New Mexico Press, 1991), p. 213.

86. H.[ubert] H.[owe] Bancroft, *History of the Northwest Coast* (San Francisco: History Co., 1890), vol. 2, pp. 317, 569–70, 697.

87. On the evolution of B.C. historiography, see Chad Reimer, "The Making of British Columbia History: Historical Writing and Institutions, 1784–1958," Ph.D. dissertation, York University, 1995; and Allen Smith, "The Writing of British Columbia History," *BC Studies* 45 (spring 1980): 73–102.

10 / Wild, Tame, and Free

Comparing Canadian and U.S. Views of Nature

DONALD WORSTER

"I wish to speak a word for Nature, for absolute freedom and wildness, as contrasted with a freedom and culture merely civil,—to regard man as an inhabitant, or a part and parcel of Nature, rather than a member of society." Those oft-quoted words from Henry David Thoreau, published in 1862, ring through the subsequent years of American history. Although they were made deliberately extreme and one-sided and although they came from a man who often felt marginal to his society, they express some central ideas in American national culture, ideas that are among our most distinctive contributions to the human story.

Over the past century and a third, following Thoreau's manifesto, the United States has arguably been the world leader in cherishing and preserving wildness—in terms of path-setting legislation, size of acreage, and the passion and intellectual rigor of debate. Beginning with the creation of Yellowstone in 1872, the country has extended protection to more than eighty million acres in its national park system and a comparable expanse in its wildlife refuges. Both programs, it should be said, have been widely copied by other nations, and the idea of nature preservation has become a global movement. Although it is now fashionable on both the right and left to attack the entire movement as elitist or racist and even to criticize it for alienating humans from nature—a strange, contorted piece of reasoning that holds that we are spiritually estranged from places we cannot farm, mine, or drive our cars through—the common sense of humankind has come around to the view that nature preservation is, at least theoretically, a moral obligation. The 1992

Earth Summit in Rio recommended that every nation set aside at least 12 percent of its land base from economic use—a goal that even the United States does not quite meet and most nations fall short of meeting. Canada, for example, protects less than 3 percent of its gigantic territory from logging, mining, or other exploitation.

But the most stringent way to protect nature is not merely to designate "parks" or "bioreserves" but to designate land as "wilderness," and so far only the United States has set up a comprehensive system for doing that. Passed by overwhelming majorities in both houses of Congress and signed into law on September 3, 1964, the Wilderness Act established a system of preserving wild lands within the national parks, forests, wildlife refuges, or public domain. With few exceptions, those lands will never have to provide any crops, minerals, reservoir sites, timber, gravel, meat, suburbs, or golf courses—they will never have to earn any dollars for the greater good of the United States. Remarkably, in a nation that often seems driven solely by economic calculation, these lands have been put beyond the demands of commodity production.

To date the nation has set aside about one hundred million acres of wilderness, an area larger than California.[1] Most of that land has come from the national forests and fish and wildlife refuges, although the national parks have contributed a large share too. More than half of the one hundred million acres is in Alaska, including 8.7 million acres in the Wrangell–St. Elias National Park; but also in the lower forty-eight states there are immense stretches of protected wild country, some of the largest in the Pacific Northwest. There are small remnant pieces of wilderness scattered from Florida's Keys to Vermont's Green Mountains and westward to Missouri's hardwood forests, indeed scattered through all but a handful of states. Conservationists have identified another eighty to one hundred million acres they feel deserve protection, while they have begun to talk boldly of still more acres that can be *restored* to wilderness—lands that may have been heavily used but can be put back into a more natural condition through a program of "wilderness recovery."[2]

Inspiration for the 1964 law, I have suggested, lies far back in the nation's past. Particularly, as scholars have argued, it owes much to Europe's Romantic movement of the late eighteenth and early nineteenth centuries and to the search for a new secular religion in the sublimity of nature. After Thoreau, passionate defenders of the wild included John Muir, Robert Marshall, and Aldo Leopold, who together made wilderness into a national political cause, although it was the indefatigable Howard Zahniser (1906–64), a less well-known figure but a highly effective advocate in congressional hearing rooms, who achieved the final victory, dying just before wilderness preservation became law.[3] Because of such persistent efforts, the principle of wilderness preservation has become firmly entrenched in the nation's political culture, and today the main issue we face is the size of the protection we are willing to grant.

Definitions are the stuff of intellectual history, and a long treatise on the many complex, shifting meanings of this word could be written.[4] The Wilderness Act, to choose one definition among many, defined wilderness as "an area where the earth and its community of life are untrammeled by man, where man himself is a visitor who does not remain."[5] The word "untrammeled" is a striking choice—not "virgin" or "untouched" or "pristine" but "untrammeled," meaning free, unconfined, a natural world that has not yet been put into bondage or shackled by human demands. How truly free or wild those one hundred million acres ever were, however, is a question getting attention these days from many American Indians and their supporters. They argue that much, if not all, of the protected land was not true wilderness but a long-occupied, domesticated homeland; throughout its past the land had felt the manipulative hand of native hunters, gatherers, or farmers.[6] Some of those acres may even have experienced dense settlement long before the coming of the white man.

The Native peoples of North America left their footprints all over the continent; they burned, planted, hunted, and dug in the wild for at least ten thousand years, and their labor, their history of occupancy, should not be effaced by "virgin land" mythmakers. To a point this argument seems indisputably true. On the other hand, we have not done much careful investigating of those one hundred million protected acres to determine precisely whether or to what extent they ever served as human habitat. Was the River of No Return Wilderness in Idaho ever regularly lived in by Native Americans, and if so, what lasting impact on soils, wildlife, vegetation, or stream flow did they leave? We do not really know. Because white Europeans tended to settle where Indians had prepared the way, it seems reasonable that most currently designated wilderness areas were less affected by Native peoples than, say, the coast of California or floodplains along the Mississippi. In any case the standard set by the law is not whether the wilderness we have protected was always free of *any* degree of human impact, from a campfire to a tissue, at any point in time, but whether it had become "trammeled" or not at the time of its protection. Trammeling is not an easy act to describe, nor to witness. One man's act of bondage may be another's act of bonding. For that reason how wild North America ever really was is a question that cannot be answered simply by compiling a record of aboriginal land use or changing vegetation. It is not really a scientific concept.

For Thoreau and others a condition of wildness meant being free of agriculture, free of urban development, free of permanent settlement, and free of roads.[7] It was a place that had not yet been shackled in the bonds of modern economy and technology. Such thinking was undoubtedly ethnocentric in that it emphasized the specific impact of Europeans, but it was not necessarily racist.[8] Although some early wilderness advocates did not acknowledge any Indian impact on the lands they wanted to protect, there were those who did—the literature of wilderness is actually full of Indians. Yet those seekers after the wild did not regard Indian impact as a shackling in the bonds of economy. Indians, that is, did not trammel. If they burned and planted, they did not leave the land in a state of permanent bondage. Gary Snyder, one of the most enthusiastic students of Indian cultures while also being a wilderness philosopher, talks of a native "culture of wilderness," a culture unlike our own in coexisting harmoniously with wild species. He does not sentimentalize or trivialize those cultures when he suggests that they may once have lived in a respectful, nondegrading relation with the wild things of the earth.[9]

In the eyes of nonpurist preservationists, wilderness might include not only former Indian economic zones but also lands that had once been occupied by whites: a log cabin now crumbling back to dust, a cutover forest now regenerating, an old horseman's trail now used for backpacking into the high country. Even a long record of white habitation might not disqualify a piece of land from being considered wild if all economic use has ceased and the natural community has been liberated from human demands. Wilderness is undeniably a cultural ideal and, like other ideals, it has its more and its less thoughtful expressions, more or less rigid standards of evaluation, more or less dedicated advocates. It is an ideal constantly up for dispute and revision. At the same time wilderness can be an actual physical place that we point to on a map, define with reasonable clarity, and even visit. This tension between ideal and real is always present in the history of wilderness preservation. Hubris enters when the act of discussing, idealizing, or even protecting is itself taken to be an act of "creating," as if whatever we decide to defend or protect can in no sense enjoy an independent existence.

My emphasis in this chapter is on wilderness as a cultural ideal, not because I regard the wild as merely a cultural construct but because I want to understand the American motive behind defending and protecting wilderness. I want to do so by comparing that thinking to Canadian attitudes. Above all, I want to focus on one critical element: the wilderness as a vital part of the American dream of freedom—freedom pure and absolute, as Thoreau put it, but also freedom relative to modern conditions. That freedom has, from early on, included not only a search to recover the natural self lurking beneath civilization, to restore our deep ties with the earth that go back before civilization, but also—and very significantly—a call for freedom for all species, for life in all its manifestations. As Thoreau put it, "We need to witness our own limits transgressed, and some life pasturing freely where we never wander."[10] Defined thus, wilderness becomes a freedom that can be recovered if lost, but it cannot coexist in the presence of a more or less permanent agriculture or other intervention—plows, fences, dams, automobiles, snowmobiles, villages, or cities, all of which are necessarily infringements on the freedom of the wild.

Ironically, this ideal of wilderness as multifaceted, multi-being freedom can be undermined by the very strategies we adopt to realize it. Putting wild areas into a legal system of preservation, fencing it against our depredations, the philosopher Thomas H. Birch has warned, can become a form of incarceration.[11] We can, that is, trammel wild nature by governmental decree as well as by invading technology. Wilderness areas can become carefully patrolled places like zoos in which the wild survives as an object of amusement, safely imprisoned within its cage by the rules and regulations of a protective bureaucracy. By designating a particular landscape as wild and putting fences around it, we may, if we are not careful, practice a more subtle form of domination, just as setting aside Indian reservations has often created places not of cultural autonomy but of cultural containment. Nonetheless, as Birch himself argues, the wilderness, even when carefully fenced in by law, can remain a subversive presence in our midst. Like a beast shut up in a pen, the wild may still stare defiantly at civilization, reminding us that there are powerful natural forces on this planet that we can never wholly understand nor domesticate.

Before taking up the wilderness ideal, I recognize that, defined as an actual place on the map, one we can designate by fairly objective, transcultural criteria, there is still plenty of wilderness around. Americans are likely to assume, because of our constant talk of wilderness, that we have a near monopoly among the world's nations, but in truth most of the great wild areas of the earth lie outside U.S. borders. A recent global inventory looked for areas of more than four hundred thousand hectares (one million acres) that lacked any "permanent human settlements or roads," lands that were "not regularly cultivated nor heavily and continuously grazed" but that might have been "lightly used and occupied by indigenous peoples at various times who practiced traditional subsistence styles of life."[12] Researchers found forty-eight million square kilometers qualifying as wilderness, or about a third of the earth's land surface. (Forty-eight million square kilometers is equivalent to twelve billion acres, an expanse larger than the continents of the Western Hemisphere.) Fifteen million of those square kilometers are in Antarctica and Greenland—a wilderness of ice.

The other leading wilderness-rich countries include Algeria, Australia, Brazil, Canada, Russia, and the Sudan, all well ahead of the United States in having large unoccupied spaces. But even heavily populated countries like China, India, Laos, Mexico, and Iraq have their empty quarters too. China, for instance, despite its billion-plus human population, still has 22 percent of its territory in a wild state, a higher percentage than in the United States. Much of the earth's surface in the higher latitudes is wild, as are much of the world's deserts and tropical rainforests. This broad-gauged inventory does not, of course, exhaust the possibilities of wilderness, for there are many places under four hundred thousand hectares that might qualify under the same criteria, and then there are all the tiny patches of wildness lurking even in our backyards.[13]

Some of those global wild places lie within national parks, but many do not. Most are de facto wilderness because no other country has established a program of preservation comparable to that of America. As the world's population mounts to ten or fifteen billion people, all seeking a more affluent life, much of this marginal land may be invaded and transformed. In some countries citizens may reject any call for preserving their last wilderness, especially if the call comes from an overly self-righteous America; already in poorer nations critics are charging that the wilderness movement is anti–poor people, or anti–indigenous people, or simply anti-people in general, that it is a romantic fetish of well-fed American environmentalists.[14] So what is to be the fate of those lands? Will the international community heed the call from Rio to protect them? Or on the contrary, will the U.S. wilderness movement go on expanding within our own borders, though always against strident opposition, but elsewhere get little popular support? Is the United States in this regard to remain an anomaly on the globe and, if so, why? What explains the peculiar call of the wild in American ears?

To answer these questions, I have been reading about the environmental history of our friendly neighbor to the north. For a long time Canada was not very familiar terrain to me, nor I suspect to most Americans; we tend to ignore its huge, looming presence, although now and then we notice that they do things a little differently up there, like adopting a national health care system or stringent gun-control laws. It is time we Americans began to admit that we have a lot to learn from the Canadians about how to live on the continent we share, and a lot to learn about ourselves—our virtues as well as our vices—by studying their history. We share a common landscape with many common ecosystems, waterways, and climates. We are alike in being nations of populations gathered together from many parts of the world, now grown well advanced in wealth, education, and technology. Most of us speak the same language, and we share many traditions of government, economics, and religion derived mainly from the same European roots.

And both Canada and the United States have an abundance of wilderness in our past and present. According to the inventory I mentioned, 65 percent of Canada is still covered by large stretches of wilderness, more than 6.5 million square kilometers (1.6 billion acres) in all.[15] Yet despite sharing many cultural traits and a common North American environment, the Canadians still do not seem inclined to follow our wilderness preservation lead quickly, enthusiastically, or faithfully. There is distinctly less wilderness under legal protection in Canada today than there is in the United States; indeed, there is no nationwide system of wilderness preservation north of the border. We need to understand why that is so—not to criticize Canadians, who may have their own environmental priorities to follow, nor to hold up one nation as more or less "destructive" than the other (a nearly impossible judgment to make), but to know ourselves better.

The simple fact is that, generally speaking, Canadians—whether Anglophone or Francophone, old or new immigrant—have not felt about wilderness quite the same way Americans have. The two nations have followed distinctive lines of thinking about nature from the beginning of European settlement down to the present and have expressed that thinking differently in legislation, art, and literature. In the early period of white pioneering in what is now Canada, nature was regarded as a less hostile antagonist than it was in what is now the United States. While the Puritans were taking over New England and preaching against the howling wilderness and the bloody savages, the French voyageurs were ranging far into the continental interior for beaver pelts, adopting Indians' mode of dress and travel. One might suppose that such an original contrast would endure: that the legacy of Puritanism would make the United States forever hostile to the back country, while Canadians would still be wearing deerskin leggings. Instead, a shift in attitudes on both sides of the border seems to have occurred. The children of the Puritans eventually went wild, while later Canadians (particularly the English settlers of Ontario) came to view their wilderness more warily.

That old divergence from American thinking helps explain why there is no national wilderness system to the north.[16] The province of Ontario established Algonquin Provincial Park as a wilderness in 1893 (not long after New York state set aside the Adirondacks to be kept "forever wild"), but then permitted logging companies to enter. The Federation of Ontario Naturalists, founded in 1931, lobbied to stop the logging and establish nature preserves throughout the province, but not until the 1970s and 1980s did wildness become a more popular cause. The founding of the Algonquin Wildlands League marks a more recent trend away from traditions of resource exploitation and outdoor recreation as the only sanctioned approaches to nature. In its 1972 statement of principles and policies, the league called on Ontarians to honor their cultural heritage of going into the wild: "We are the spiritual descendants of Etienne Brule and David Thompson, La Verendrye and Simon Fraser, as well as thousands of unsung wilderness voyageurs and frontier farmers." The provincial government responded to such memories by passing a Wilderness Areas Act, which authorized the protection of wild areas not to exceed 640 acres each—about the size of a Midwestern farm.[17]

Only very recently has there been much wilderness set aside in the vast stretches of the Yukon or the Northwest Territory, except for Kluane National Park, which was protected in 1942 at U.S. instigation. Even now, the contrast with next-door Alaska is striking: the Northern Yukon National Park, established in 1984 along the Beaufort Sea, is one-seventh the size of the Arctic National Wildlife Refuge, which adjoins it across the border. The "Endangered Spaces" campaign, launched in 1989 by the World Wildlife Fund and the Canadian Parks and Wilderness Society, promised to try to improve on that record, and in fact new national parks have been added on Banks and Baffin Islands above the Arctic Circle. Most of the great northern wild lands, nonetheless, remain unprotected from exploitation, and the chief interest of the Ottawa government seems to be finding an accommodation between urban corporate interests and Native land rights—not an unworthy goal but different from the preservation of nature.

In British Columbia it is true that one can find a fairly strong grassroots wilderness movement, but then British Columbia is perhaps more American-like than the eastern provinces and has been highly influenced by "ecotopian" regional images creeping up from Seattle, Eugene, and San Francisco. Even so, B.C. wilderness advocates have had a hard fight against the well-entrenched alliance of the Ministry of Forestry with large private timber companies. As late as 1987 the province could boast of many national parks and wildlife areas, along with many provincial parks—but only one wilderness area. Using less rigorous standards, the total extent of reserves permitting no logging, mining, or sport hunting amounted to twenty-three thousand square kilometers (5.6 million acres), but that is only 2.4 percent of the land base in that province.[18] The adjoining state of Washington, in contrast, although much smaller in area and more densely populated, counted in that same year more than four million acres within the national wilderness system or pending such protection—fully 10 percent of its land base—as well as millions of more acres reserved from economic use within parks and refuges.[19]

I do not want to overstate the difference here. Canada has had powerful voices for appreciating wild nature and wild places, including the British immigrant Archie Belaney (who adopted Indian ways, taking the name Grey Owl), Ernest Thompson Seton and Charles G. D. Roberts (who told popular wild animal stories), Frederick P. Grove (a passionate lover of the undeveloped Manitoba landscape, as seen from his buggy seat on weekend travels), and Farley Mowatt (another great teller of wildlife tales and defender of the arctic lands and peoples).[20] Several of the country's historians have likewise been drawn to wilderness themes in narrating the past—such scholars as Arthur Lower, W. L. Morton, and more recently Ramsey Cook. Morton, in his book *The Canadian Identity*, has summed up these themes with typical eloquence:

> In Canadian history the St. Lawrence valley, the Ontario peninsula, and the western prairies have been the regions of settlement which have furnished and fed the men, the fur traders, the lumberjacks, the prospectors, and the miners who have traversed the [Canadian] Shield and wrested from it the staples by which Canada has lived. And this alternate penetration of the wilderness and return to civilisation is the basic rhythm of Canadian life, and forms the basic elements of Canadian character whether French or English: the violence necessary to contend with the wilderness, the restraint necessary to preserve civilisation from the wilderness violence, and the puritanism which is the offspring of the wedding of violence to restraint. Even in an industrial and urban society, the old rhythm continues, for the typical Canadian holiday is a wilderness holiday, whether among the lakes of the Shield or the peaks of the Rockies.[21]

Violence and puritanism may not seem like good bases for developing a protective ethos toward the wild, but Morton is undoubtedly right in pointing to the powerful impact that the untamed landscape has had on his country's imagination.

Perhaps most eloquent of all in expressing that impact were the extraordinary wilderness painters who became known as the Group of Seven—Lawren Harris, Frederick Varley, and the others. When the group's inspirational figure Tom Thomson made his first trip north from Toronto to Algonquin National Park in 1912, Canadian painting began to discover for the first time the northern landscape of woods and lakes. Wildness was what Thomson came to see: jack pines and tamaracks silhouetted against low mountains, sunsets reflecting off the water, thundering cascades deep in the interior, far from the artificial ways of the city. Thomson died on a lonely canoe trip, and his epitaph described him as one who "lived humbly but passionately with the wild; it made him brother of all untamed things of nature." Canadians have honored him as a tragic hero, and the Group of Seven remains the country's best-known, best-loved group of artists, along with Emily Carr, who began painting the Pacific Coast rainforests with revolutionary vision in the 1920s (although she was treated by the male artists as an outsider). Yet these popular outdoor painters seem hard to read in terms of cultural significance. They came along well after the nineteenth-century vogue of Romantic landscape art had passed and just at the point when most artists internationally were turning to more urban, indoor, or abstract themes. They told Canadians that their identity lay in the land, particularly the north woods—"the true north strong and free"—but the message did not resonate equally over the entire country nor leave much of a model for later artists. Above all, those painters, like the nature writers and the historians mentioned, failed in their day to stimulate a powerful nationwide preservation movement.[22]

On the philosophical as well as political front, Canadians have been slower to speak up for the defense of nature or natural resources, and that is so even along utilitarian lines. No one among them quite matches the Americans Thoreau, Muir, Leopold, Snyder, or Rachel Carson as widely influential philosophers of the wild, nor do they quite match John Wesley Powell or Gifford Pinchot as leaders in resource conservationism, although Sir Clifford Sifton certainly learned much from Pinchot and tried to put into practice Pinchot's prudent managerial program.[23] Again, my purpose here is not criticism; and I readily add that in other areas of public policy, or the history of ideas, or social reform, Canada has been the innovator, and the United States the follower.

The most thorough study to date of distinctive national traditions in policy and attitudes toward nature comes from Marilyn Dubasak, who argues that "support for wilderness preservation as a general, long term goal [has] had much less appeal in Canada than in the United States. Canadian historical tradition does not contain the same degree of romantic veneration of land as a component of national character. In Canada, the vast northern wilderness and the perception of being a small population group dwarfed by a huge land mass makes it more difficult to credit the need to preserve wilderness."[24]

Other observers have also noted a transition in attitudes toward nature when one crosses the border. Twenty years ago Robert D. Turner and William E. Rees argued that "membership in conservation organizations in Canada is proportionately much lower than in the United States."[25] The closest equivalent to the Sierra Club at the time they wrote was the National and Provincial Parks Association of Canada (which later changed its name to the Canadian Parks and Wilderness Society), founded in 1963, more than seventy years after the founding of the Sierra Club and attracting a membership nowhere proportionate to the American organization. The radical group Greenpeace, established in Vancouver, British Columbia, in 1979, may seem an exception to that pattern, but note that it was founded by an American-born conscientious objector, Paul Watson, and its confrontational tactics seem distinctly imported to the country. Moreover, from its beginning Greenpeace has emphasized the protection of charismatic ocean species like whales and seals more than the protection and restoration of the north country's wilderness. The gap may be narrowing, however. The Western Canada Wilderness Committee now has more than twenty-five thousand members, and according to a recent poll, 9 percent of the Canadian population (or two million people) claim to be members of some sort of environmental organization.[26] But even if a new politics of the environment may be emerging across Canada, some divergence from the United States is more than likely to continue.

A contrast in the philosophy and management of national, provincial, and state parks has long persisted in the two countries, although here too it is a contrast more of *degree* than of category. Canada, as noted earlier, has been closely behind the United States in setting aside parks, but those parks have commonly been less wild and more civilized than most American conservationists would like, allowing golf courses, hotels, even logging trucks, towns, mines, and railroads. "Parks," writes Dubasak, "were imagined as landscaped gardens, as they were in England and Europe."[27] Canada's first parks, Banff, Yoho, and Glacier (all established in the mid-1880s), were openly commercial ventures, set aside for no other reason than to attract tourist trade westward, and so they have remained to this day; at no point were the major Canadian parks ever conceived as wilderness. American parks, to be sure, have had similar touristic purposes and have permitted several hotels of their own, but there has always been a powerful, articulate group protesting any over-civilizing of our parks, beginning with the bitter, prolonged battle over damming Hetch Hetchy Valley Reservoir in Yosemite National Park in the first two decades of the twentieth century.[28]

The differences may go deeper than styles of park administration or levels of conservation group membership or the content of environmentalist politics. Several Canadians have argued that their countrymen tend to take a less positive view of nature than most Americans do—that there has long been a strain of fear and hostility that has kept Canadians from embracing the wild. The eminent literary critic Northrop Frye once wrote, "I have long been impressed in Canadian poetry by a tone of deep terror in regard to nature." Vast, unconscious nature has seemed a threat to civilized, humane values and must be resisted, the poets have felt, if Canadians want to preserve their moral integrity, their link with established culture, their very sanity.[29]

This hostility is noted also in Margaret Atwood's less scholarly but perceptive book *Survival: A Thematic Guide to Canadian Literature*, where she includes a chapter on "Nature the Monster." "Canadian writers," she senses, "as a whole do not trust Nature, they are always suspecting some dirty trick. . . . Nature seen as dead, or alive but indifferent, or alive but actively hostile toward man is a common image in Canadian literature."[30] I have no reason to question such well-informed cultural observers, but it would be unthinkable to describe American writing so, although we have had our writers, from Herman Melville to James Dickey, who have been aware of the dark side of nature. Why should there be any national difference in thinking about wild nature? Why should the untrammeled wild get less enthusiasm or protection in Canada than in the United States?

There are relatively superficial answers to those questions, too easy to be fully convincing, and then there are more complicated, less obvious ones. First, on the superficial side, I should note that the Canadian economy is still heavily dependent on natural resource extraction, as it has been since the days of beaver hats, while the U.S. economy, because of a greater diversification into agriculture, manufacturing, and services, may allow us the privilege now and then to value the wilderness as something more than raw material to be harvested. Also, it is worth noting that many of those surviving wild lands in Canada still belong to the provinces, not to the federal government, which means that new parks, wildlife refuges, or wilderness reserves must often wait on provincial initiatives and compete against powerful extractive industries active in the provinces.[31]

In the United States, however, almost all protected wilderness is located on federally owned land, except for New York's Adirondacks or Maine's Baxter State Park. We Americans might have saved less of the wild if it had been left up to our state governments to act, or if farsighted Americans had not saved western lands from privatization in the nineteenth century. But such answers to my questions, although convincing to a point, do not take us far enough. As I have indicated, even where it still has a huge federal domain in the far north, Canada has not matched the example of the Americans. Hostility, indifference, or wariness toward the wild seem to be found at all levels of Canadian government.

Perhaps, some have suggested, the fact that Canada enjoys an abundance of wilderness in relation to its population size accounts for the national contrast. Roderick Nash, our leading historian of the wilderness movement in the United States, argues that wilderness is like any economic commodity: the scarcer it gets, the more value people put on it.[32] Americans did not set up a wilderness system until the U.S. population had reached nearly two hundred million. But if scarcity or a sense of endangerment is all that is required to save wilderness, then the most active wilderness movements in the world would be found in far more crowded countries than the United States. India or Japan, for example, ought to be world leaders in nature preservation, and they are not. A little comparative analysis quickly suggests that preservation of the wild cannot be reduced simply to demographics or population density, or for that matter, simply to levels of economic development or pressure on space.

Nor for that matter, simply to such environmental factors as climate. Margaret Atwood has suggested that Canadians have learned their hostility toward nature from having to endure their legendary cold weather. "The true and only season here," she writes, "is winter."[33] Who could love nature when it is thirty degrees below zero outside, a timber wolf is sniffing around the cabin door, the wood supply is running low? Americans have it easier, she implies; living as we do in the Garden of Eden, we can afford to take a happier view of nature. I am sure that Atwood is right when she says that life in Virginia or California can encourage a different outlook on nature than life on the Saskatchewan prairies, but I fear her argument is too glib and superficial, overlooking the fact that many, if not most, wilderness enthusiasts in America have come from our harsher northern latitudes, not the sunny South, and they have deliberately sought out even more dangerous, inhospitable places: Thoreau going to the Maine woods, John Muir to the Alaskan glaciers, Sigurd Olson to the mosquito coasts of Quetico-Superior. For many Americans the call of the wild comes keening on a sharp wind and we thrill

to the sound in our ears, longing to be up there on Great Slave Lake or in the
Brooks Range with a canvas tent and a tin coffee cup.

Something in American national culture loves wildness, and that something is weaker in Canada. A fuller explanation for the difference, I now suggest, requires us to dig deeper into our distinctive cultures and histories, our
distinctive national myths and ideologies. From reading Canadian historians and writers, one gets the feeling that as America has grown big and aggressive, Canada has purposely diverged from us, trying somewhat desperately
to become an "other," a counterculture to the United States. What Europe
has been to the United States, a model to avoid, the United States has been
to Canada. This distancing goes back more than two centuries. When the
American Revolutionary War broke out, thousands of men and women loyal
to the English king fled across the St. Lawrence River to establish Upper
Canada, now Ontario. That event, many have argued, was the moment of
divergence. Canadians henceforth saw themselves as the people who chose
not to rebel against authority, the state, or the crown, and they rejected much
of the libertarian rhetoric of America's Declaration of Independence—"life,
liberty, and the pursuit of happiness."[34] Whether French or English, they were
skeptical of the American insistence on freedom from government inter-
ference. "Freedom," they believed, "wears a crown." The monarchy was not
seen as an evil foreign oppressor but rather as the only force that could protect them from the feverish mobs to the south and ensure a more genuine
freedom, a real diversity of thought, a right to be different.

The most thorough, if controversial, study of these diverging national cultures is Seymour Martin Lipset's *Continental Divide: The Values and Institutions of the United States and Canada*, which emphasizes the Revolutionary
War's role in making Americans what we are today, and Canadians too. We
still are Whigs, he says, they still are Tories. Lipset takes such broad charac-
terizations seriously, backing them up with an impressive array of public opinion surveys that show significant cultural variation. Those differences linger
on and on, even in the face of spreading Americanization. Sometimes the
differences are only on the order of a 5 percent to 10 percent variation in survey sampling, but they are differences all the same, with telling consequences
for such issues as taxation, social services, immigration, trade unions, free
speech, foreign affairs, and even—although Lipset does not make the point—
the conservation of nature.[35]

Whether they can be traced unbrokenly back to the eighteenth century or
not, those cultural differences had clearly emerged and solidified in the later
nineteenth century, as Americans developed a single, encompassing, grandiose

national mythology about ourselves, while Canadians did not. The American national myth is, of course, about the frontier. A poor, ordinary people, it tells us, went out from civilization into a vast wilderness where they found an unfamiliar but delicious freedom. They used that freedom to make something of themselves. As they advanced into the interior, a continental nation grew up—richer than any nation had ever been before, larger than almost any other had been, but above all, a nation more open, more democratic, more free in spirit and institutions.

That much celebrated story of the frontier may not actually describe American history very well, but it does express well some core ideals, and it powerfully organizes them into a compelling tale of heroic action. Among those ideals is wilderness. In his well-known 1893 essay, "The Significance of the Frontier in American History," Frederick Jackson Turner uses the word "wilderness" no less than ten times. The wilderness is said to break complex European life into "the simplicity of primitive conditions," and one senses that for Turner such breakage makes people more virtuous. Thus, at its heart the American myth of the frontier, which Turner did not create but only came upon and made over into historical narrative, depends on an idealization of wild nature. Nature becomes the elemental source of all blessings and goodness, even if that nature must be conquered and destroyed in the movement west. "Freedom" is another of Turner's favorite words, as it long has been of Americans generally; indeed it may be the most powerful word in our vocabulary. The action taking place in the American myth has millions of individuals making a private escape from their bondage to oppressive, confining social forces. Turner writes that the act of escape "produces antipathy to control, and particularly to any direct control." His first example of such antipathy is toward the tax collector, a hated agent of the state, but other forms of centralized power are despised too, including hierarchies of wealth and credit, of church and class, which in Europe had long managed to keep the lower orders under their fist.

The two ideals of wilderness and personal freedom became fused into one by the frontier myth, so that the wilderness became a landscape of freedom and freedom became a promise of the wild. Thus it happened in the United States—but not in Canada. Farther north, there was nothing quite like the frontier myth, indeed there was little national myth-making of any kind that told all Canadians, on both sides of the Ottawa River, who they were and where they were driving.[36] To this day they have continued to search anxiously for a shared or common identity, something that binds them together "from sea to shining sea," and they have found little except a tolerance toward each other's idiosyncrasies and a wariness toward the United States and its expansionist designs. For a while, it is true, a handful of Canadian historians, led by Arthur Lower, Walter Sage, and A. L. Burt, tried to maintain that Canada was a frontier society like the United States, but the argument did not quite take, either among historians or the public.[37] No unifying national cults developed around freedom-seeking wagon trains, gunslingers, cowboys, or even the voyageurs. Canadians have fantasized less than Americans about leaving the settlements behind and striking off alone toward the setting sun, nor have they so fervently believed in a great single saga of inexorable westward movement or manifest destiny.

Again, Northrop Frye, writing about his nation's literary imagination, best explains this contrast. The Canadian writer, he writes, has typically focused not on a broad, confident march into the wilderness but on "small and isolated communities surrounded with a physical or psychological 'frontier,' separated from one another and from their American and British cultural sources: communities that provide all that their members have in the way of distinctly human values, and that are compelled to feel a great respect for the law and order that hold them together, yet confronted with a huge, unthinking, menacing, and formidable physical setting. [S]uch communities are bound to develop what we may provisionally call a garrison mentality." A garrison mentality, he continues, is the outgrowth of "a closely knit and beleaguered society" in which moral and social values are "unquestionable."[38] Others have noted the same closed or fortress-like mentality widespread in Canada. Margaret Atwood, for one, suggests that although the symbol for the United States is "the Frontier," implying "a place that is *new*, where the old order can be discarded," the central image for Canada is "Survival, *la survivance*, hanging on, staying alive."[39]

I have cited some of Canada's most intelligent, distinguished, and probing self-observers to help us understand why their country has never embraced wilderness in the way Americans have. If there were space here, it would be instructive to trace in turn the long tradition in which Americans have associated wilderness with freedom—freedom for oneself, freedom for one's group, freedom for humans and nonhumans alike, a tradition that runs from Thoreau down to recent writers like the anarchistic desert rat Edward Abbey.[40] I offer only a single example of the familiar association—a man who, although born in the United States, spent a large part of his childhood growing up on the Saskatchewan prairie, the late Wallace Stegner. Though always sympathetic toward the more communitarian Canadian ethos, when he talked about nature, Stegner found himself defending America's liberty-loving tradition. Nearly four years before the Wilderness Act became law, Stegner set down his views about the value of wilderness in a famous public letter. For him wilderness was not merely a place for outdoor recreation but a powerful symbol of who Americans are—even the best part of who we are. The encounter with wilderness, he wrote, has given Americans a recurring chance to see ourselves "single, separate, vertical and individual in the world, part of the environment of trees and rocks and soil, brother to other animals, part of the natural world and competent to belong to it." Note the seeming paradoxical pairing of personal freedom and ecological community. The wilderness has nurtured a dream of liberty and dignity for all, Stegner suggested, and it has given us reason to be optimistic and confident. The wilderness, he continued, is part of "the geography of hope." Our most cherished values and experiences, he feared, would not survive without carefully preserving the physical presence of the wilderness, or without allowing for the presence of the other than human creatures that live in the wilderness and constitute our larger brotherhood.[41]

By the time of Stegner's writing, a serious threat to personal freedom had appeared within the national borders—an immense, complicated, ubiquitous industrial civilization that often seemed as oppressive, undemocratic, and unfree as England's imperial regime had once been. Stegner called that industrial order our "termite life," our "Brave New World of a completely man-controlled environment." Foreign governments still remained part of the threat to freedom (at least for some), although it was now a government in Moscow or Beijing, not London. But increasingly, if we listen to writers like Stegner and Abbey, the greatest threats now come from *within* the republic: from the business world, the research lab, the engulfing urban-industrial complex. All those institutions are hotly in pursuit of the conquest of nature, and the conquest of nature leads to the unfreedom of humankind. We have become victims, these critics warn, of our own driving urge to dominate the continent. Wilderness offers a place to go to escape that technological oppression, a zone of resistance to that urge to manipulate and manage. It is our last chance to experience a world outside humankind's collective control, our last chance for escape.

Saving the wilderness from those trammeling powers of economy and technology has been a defining theme in the American environmental movement throughout the twentieth century, perhaps its deepest and most important theme. I do not think we can explain that movement by any rigid class analysis, as critics of the wilderness ideal often try to do, arguing that the wilderness is desired simply as a rich white man's playground. Stegner was no spokesman for upper-class or racial elitism, wanting to save the wilderness only for himself and his friends; he grew up poor and insecure, spending some of his youth in rural shacks, even temporarily in an orphanage. Similarly humble backgrounds link Muir, Carson, Abbey, Snyder, Olaus and Margaret Murie, David Brower, and Dave Foreman. Theodore Roosevelt may closely fit the debunkers' stereotype, but then he was never one of the key leaders of the wilderness movement; he was more of a big-game hunter and rancher. Robert Marshall alone of the major movement leaders fits the rich white boy model, but then he was an ardent socialist and feminist. Historians who have tried to explain, and often explain away, the wilderness movement as a function of class status have missed a crucial element. They have failed to see how embedded this movement has been in traditional American frontier mythology, which itself is embedded in a political ideology that celebrates the struggle of people to revolt and achieve their independence from dictatorial power. They have also failed to see how deeply that myth has influenced Americans (though mainly white Americans) at all social levels.

Canadians, so near to the United States geographically and so similar economically, have not shared that ideology, not at least to the extent that it has gripped so many American minds. Indirectly by this line of argument, I suggest that Canadians may tend to look on modern technological civilization somewhat differently than many Americans. They may be a little less worried about its dangers, a little more hopeful that technology can become a positive civilizing force—well-governed, decently organized, and supportive of human freedom. What Stegner feared might become a termite life might not appear so to the average Canadian. Technological civilization might appear as a better-stocked garrison, offering a more secure life against the savage elements, the dangerous winter cold. Make no mistake, Americans have shown considerable enthusiasm for material comforts too; the differences here are not clear cut. But everything we have heard about Canadian values suggests that they have fewer doubts than Americans about the benevolence of their government, corporations, or other institutions, about the moral legitimacy of their laws and regulations, about the human-made infrastructure that supports their lives. Canadians seem inclined to want to make technological civilization work more efficiently, while many Americans would like to walk away from it.

That tendency of our northern neighbors to work within the established order to achieve the common good has much to commend it, in environmental as well as social terms. Canadians may find it a little easier to pass tough air-pollution laws and get them enforced than we do in United States.

A people who expect much of government, who honor thrift, who tend to feel highly responsible toward the next generation can offer exemplary leadership to a world that desperately needs all those virtues. In recent years Canada has in fact offered such leadership on many important international issues. In 1990, for example, it became the first nation anywhere to draw up a comprehensive "Green Plan" to reshape its economy toward a more "sustainable" future. Projected to cost $3 billion, the plan was described as "the most complete, big-picture strategy ever proposed by any nation."[42] It aimed to eliminate almost all toxic discharges into the environment, stabilize carbon dioxide and other greenhouse gases, reduce solid waste by 50 percent within a decade, add new national parks and other recreational areas, and put the country on the path to a leaner, cleaner lifestyle. Whether Canada will actually achieve all those objectives is uncertain; soon after it was proposed, in fact, the plan had to be tabled indefinitely.[43] But the very idea of drawing up such a blueprint has placed Canada in the forefront of environmental stewardship, and at the 1992 Rio conference Canada stood forth as one of two or three pacesetters in reconciling economic development with ecological protection. Meanwhile, the United States, in the opinion of many observers, failed to exert comparable leadership by significantly reducing air and water pollution, by redesigning its wasteful transportation system, or by sharing resources with less fortunate nations.

American environmentalism may have to share some responsibility for the country's failing to address adequately the global human predicament. To the extent that a passion for wilderness, a search for freedom from the modern political-economic juggernaut, works against the kind of collective national planning that the Rio summit stressed, the American environmental community may bear some responsibility and need to reassess its priorities. The Achilles heel of U.S. environmentalism is the fact that, despite all their calls for government activism and regulatory power, environmentalists in their heart of hearts share much the same ideology of liberty and self-determination that has created a degraded environment. The distance between the "wilderness freedom" of an Abbey or a Muir and the "economic freedom" of laissez-faire capitalism may at times seem not very great. This confusing overlap of a liberty-seeking ideology among avowed enemies may pose the greatest intellectual difficulty the wilderness movement has, one that even its most thoughtful philosophers have never fully addressed or clarified.[44]

But achieving Canada's "green" goal of a more socially responsible use of resources, although not a foreign idea to American environmentalists, has not been radical enough for many. They have called for something more subversive, more wild, more liberating. Thoreau would have scorned the making of Green Plans as a shallow achievement: "In saving more wildness, not in making more provident use of resources," he would have retorted, "lies the preservation of the world." I expect that Thoreau would have pointed out, with some impatience, that Canada's Green Plan is not a plan aimed at saving wilderness in the taiga. And Wallace Stegner, who, though no backwoods renegade from law and order nor enemy of government planning, probably would have shared some of Thoreau's reservations and wondered whether cleanliness, efficiency, sustainability, or even distributive justice are all that one should fight for in the environmental movement. "We need to demonstrate our acceptance of the natural world, including ourselves," he would have said to Canada's planners just as he did to American officials in 1960; "we need the spiritual refreshment that being natural can produce."[45]

At least one Canadian (and undoubtedly there are others) would agree wholeheartedly with Thoreau's or Stegner's critique of green planning. The novelist Wayland Drew, author of *The Wabeno Feast* (1973), has written that wilderness advocates like himself are always apt to be a little out of step with the planners, environmental or otherwise, for such an advocate "has bypassed the mass of alternatives posed by the assumptions of the technological society and glimpsed a possibility which his society will tell him is reactionary, archaic, and impossible, but which his body and his spirit tell him is absolutely correct. He has positioned himself to breach the Reason of his society; to jump the Green Wall [which we erect between ourselves and nature] and confirm that there is something better than being a drugged and gratified utopian." Everywhere, Drew complains, even in the politics of conservation, "we are acceding to the technocratic dictum that what is not known by experts cannot be known." Like Stegner, Drew looks to the wilderness as a refuge from technocracy, from a reduction of nature to instrumental values, from a denatured civilization.[46]

Drew reminds us that Canada has its impassioned, dissident voices for the wild, as do other countries, and that no nation is homogenous in its ideology. Comparative history always runs the danger of ignoring complex internal differences, the full spectrum of possibilities that lie within any society, in its tendency to locate what is different between nations. I do not want to fall into that trap here. Nonetheless, national cultures do exist—cultures that are bounded and shaped by the nation-state—and they do differ in their emphases, their structure of values, their myths and fantasies. Canada is not the United States in every particular, nor does it want to be, nor should it want to be. It is not on a path of cultural evolution that one day will make it exactly like the United States, either in terms of wilderness preservation or any other ideal.

If I were now to leave North America and go on to examine China, Brazil, or the Sudan, scrutinizing their national myths of creation, their attitudes toward wild nature, their political and economic ideologies, I would surely find even more striking differences than those that separate Canadians from Americans. Such differences have profound consequences for the natural world, for they determine how nations set about defining their environmental problems, deciding what needs to be protected and what will be done. In nearly two hundred national capitals, and in thousands of small communities, the earth's future is currently being debated and decided. Policies that American environmentalists find compelling may not be so across the borders and the oceans that divide us as a species. In some ultimate sense the earth may be a single living whole, but we humans do not normally see it as such nor agree on a single united response.

Forty-eight million square kilometers exist around the earth in a state of wildness—often unprotected and unacknowledged. Six and a half million square kilometers are in Canada alone. Smaller, fragmented pieces of the wild are scattered across the United States and other countries. What will the world do with these wild lands? A strong American tradition says let those places alone. We already have enough resources to go around, to feed and clothe all of our kind, without forcing the last wild areas into the role of raising the GDP. We need, and will always need, such places as a refuge for ourselves and other forms of life. Those are arguments that come out of the American experience. Such arguments, however, may not easily persuade nations where there is a different history and national ethos, a different cultural tradition. Decades after the passage of the Wilderness Act, the American wilderness still survives, although it is only a fragment of what people once saw, or imagined they saw. But of the Canadian wilderness, the world wilderness, what is to be its fate? If that greater wild earth is to be preserved, or any significant part of it, the world may need other reasons than we in the United States have given. It may need words other than freedom.

NOTES

1. U.S. Department of Agriculture, *Twenty-Fourth Annual Wilderness Report to Congress* (Washington, D.C.: Government Printing Office, 1987), is the latest official summary I have found; it gives a total of 88,993,429 acres in the wilderness system

(36.7 million acres in the national parks, 32.5 million in the national forests, 19.3 million in the wildlife reserves, and a tiny remnant in the public lands administered by the Bureau of Land Management). Congress has added several million more acres since that summary, particularly in the California deserts.

2. See "The Wildlands Project: Plotting a North American Wilderness Recovery Strategy," special issue of *Wild Earth* (1992), which proposes "to protect and restore the ecological richness and native biodiversity of North America through the establishment of a connected system of reserves."

3. The best account of the legislative history of the Wilderness Act is Craig W. Allin's *The Politics of Wilderness Preservation* (Westport, Conn.: Greenwood Press, 1982), pp. 102–42. Zahniser is discussed in Stephen Fox, *John Muir and His Legacy: The American Conservation Movement* (Boston: Little, Brown, 1981), pp. 266–72

4. Roderick Nash has written an important history, *Wilderness and the American Mind*, 3d ed. (New Haven, Conn.: Yale University Press, 1982). See also Max Oelschlager, *The Idea of Wilderness: From Prehistory to the Age of Ecology* (New Haven, Conn.: Yale University Press, 1991), which is especially valuable for its effort to define a contemporary wilderness philosophy. William Cronon's critique of radical preservationists, "The Trouble with Wilderness or, Getting Back to the Wrong Nature," *Environmental History* 1 (January 1996): 7–28, 47–55, appeared after my essay was largely conceived and written.

5. The act is also known as Public Law 88–577, and the quotations are from Sec. 2 (c).

6. See, for example, Mark David Spence, "Crown of the Continent, Backbone of the World: The American Wilderness Ideal and Blackfeet Exclusion from Glacier National Park," *Environmental History* 1 (July 1996): 29–49.

7. Morgan Sherwood warns that new forms of technology—including all-terrain vehicles, nuclear radiation, and wildlife managers' radio-tracking collars and tranquilizer guns, all unheard of in Thoreau's day—have already begun to invade the wilderness, without much public awareness or resistance. See his "The End of American Wilderness," *Environmental Review* 9 (fall 1985): 197–209.

8. The view that wilderness is a racist ideal is expressed in J. Baird Callicott, "The Wilderness Idea Revisited: The Sustainable Development Alternative," *The Environmental Professional* 13 (1991): 236–45.

9. Gary Snyder, "The Etiquette of Freedom," in *The Practice of the Wild* (San Francisco: North Point Press, 1990), p. 7.

10. Henry David Thoreau, *Walden* (1854; reprint, Princeton, N.J.: Princeton University Press, 1971), p. 318.

11. Thomas H. Birch, "The Incarceration of Wildness: Wilderness Areas as Prisons," *Environmental Ethics* 12 (spring 1990): 3–26.

12. J. Michael McCloskey and Heather Spalding, "A Reconnaissance-Level Inventory of the Amount of Wilderness Remaining in the World," *Ambio* 18, no. 4 (1989): 221–27.

13. Ibid. The United States ranks sixteenth on the world list in large wilderness areas, with 440,580 square kilometers (109 million acres), or 4.7 percent of its total area.

14. This charge has been made by Ramachandra Guha, "Radical American Environmentalism and Wilderness Preservation: A Third World Critique," *Environmental Ethics* 11 (spring 1989): 71–83. I know of no leading wilderness advocates, however, past or present, from Henry Thoreau to Dave Foreman, who exclude all questions of human welfare or justice from consideration; they may, of course, place a higher value on saving wilderness than on abolishing poverty or increasing wealth.

15. McCloskey and Spalding, "A Reconnaissance-Level Inventory," p. 222.

16. Canada also has no national endangered species act, although the United States passed one in 1973.

17. Algonquin Wildlands League, *Wilderness Now: A Statement of Principles and Policies* (Toronto: Algonquin Wildlands League, 1972), p. 6. According to a recent history of the league and its predecessors, the Ontario wilderness movement failed to attract much public support until the late 1980s. See George M. Warecki, "Protecting Ontario's Wilderness: A History of Wilderness Conservation in Ontario, 1927–1973," Ph.D. dissertation, MacMaster University, 1989. Seventy-five percent of Algonquin Provincial Park is still subject to controlled logging.

18. I take these figures from the 1987 publication *Heritage Conservation—The Natural Environment;* they are conveniently reprinted as an appendix to Monte Hummel, ed., *Endangered Spaces: The Future for Canada's Wilderness* (Toronto: Key Porter Books, 1989).

19. Since that tally, British Columbia has added (after much controversy) South Moresby in the Queen Charlotte Islands and the Tatshenshini River corridor, flowing into the Pacific Ocean above Glacier National Park, to its protected areas.

20. See John Henry Wadlund, *Ernest Thompson Seton: Man and Nature and the Progressive Era, 1880–1915* (New York: Arno Press, 1978); Thomas R. Dunlap, "'The Old Kinship of Earth': Science, Man, and Nature in the Animal Stories of Charles G. D. Roberts," *Journal of Canadian Studies* 22 (spring 1987): 104–28; T. D. MacLulich, "Reading the Land: The Wilderness Tradition in Canadian Letters," *Journal of Canadian Studies* 20 (summer 1985): 29–44; George Altmeyer, "Three Ideas of Nature in Canada, 1893–1914," *Journal of Canadian Studies* 11 (August 1976): 21–35; and Elaine Theberge, "The Untrodden Earth: Early Nature Writing in Canada," *Nature Canada* 3 (April-June 1974): 3–36.

21. W. L. Morton, *The Canadian Identity* (Toronto: University of Toronto Press,

1972), p. 5. Arthur R. M. Lower was a pioneer in Canadian forest history and a lover of the forested wilds; see, for example, his book *Canadians in the Making* (Toronto: Longmans, Green, 1958), especially p. 443. Among Ramsey Cook's many writings, I particularly recommend his Robarts Lecture at York University, *1492 and All That: Making a Garden out of a Wilderness* (York, Ont.: Robarts Centre for Canadian Studies, 1992). I have also profited greatly from Bruce Litteljohn's "Wilderness and the Canadian Psyche," in Hummel, *Endangered Spaces,* pp. 13–19.

22. The Group of Seven was "organized" at its first exhibition in 1920, three years after Thomson died, though some members regarded him spiritually as one of the group. On the Canadian artist and nature, see Peter Mellen, *The Group of Seven* (Toronto: McClelland and Stewart, 1970); Joan Murray, *The Best of the Group of Seven* (Toronto: McClelland and Stewart, 1984); Ramsey Cook, "Landscape Painting and National Sentiment in Canada," *Ariel* 1 (1974): 263–83; Margaret Tippett and Douglas Cole, *From Desolation to Splendor: Changing Perceptions of the British Columbia Landscape* (Toronto: Clarke, Irwin, 1977); and Jonathan Bordo, "Jack Pine—Wilderness Sublime or the Erasure of the Aboriginal Presence from the Landscape," *Journal of Canadian Studies* 27 (winter 1992–93): 98–128. Thompson's epitaph can be found in Mellen, *Group of Seven,* p. 82.

23. Clifford Sifton was a Liberal businessman from Manitoba who served as minister of the interior under Wilfred Laurier, in charge of western settlement. He was a key figure in the founding of the Conservation Commission (1909–21), which brought Pinchot-style thinking into national planning. See Alan F. J. Artibise and Gilbert A. Stelter, "Conservation Planning and Urban Planning: The Canadian Commission of Conservation in Historical Perspective," in Chad Gaffield and Pam Gaffield, eds., *Consuming Canada: Readings in Environmental History* (Toronto: Copp Clark, 1995), pp. 152–69.

24. Marilyn Dubasak, *Wilderness Preservation: A Cross-Cultural Comparison of Canada and the United States* (New York: Garland, 1990), pp. 204, 206.

25. Robert D. Turner and William E. Rees, "A Comparative Study of Parks Policy in Canada and the United States," *Nature Canada* 2 (January-March 1973): 35.

26. Jeremy Wilson, "Green Lobbies: Pressure Groups and Environmental Policy," in Robert Boardman, ed., *Canadian Environmental Policy: Ecosystems, Politics, and Process* (Toronto: Oxford University Press, 1992), pp. 110–11. See also Wilson's "Wilderness Politics in B.C.: The Business Dominated State and the Containment of Environmentalism," in William D. Coleman and Grace Skogstad, eds., *Policy Communities and Public Policy in Canada: A Structural Approach* (Mississauga, Ont.: Copp Clark Pitman, 1990), pp. 141–69. A valuable study by G. Bruce Doern and Thomas Conway, *The Greening of Canada: Federal Institutions and Decisions* (Toronto: University of Toronto Press, 1994), examines the federal Department of Environment,

founded in 1970 by the Trudeau Liberal government, as a reflection of changing national attitudes. "Green" does not mean wilderness, apparently; the book scarcely mentions the subject. What it does mean is the concept of "sustainable development," a more conservative ideal that continues Canada's traditional preference for a more utilitarian or "wise use" set of attitudes.

27. Dubasak, *Wilderness Preservation*, p. 23.

28. The best history of a single park is Bill Waiser, *Saskatchewan's Playground: A History of Prince Albert National Park* (Saskatoon, Sask.: Fifth House Publishers, 1989). See also Robert Craig Brown, "The Doctrine of Usefulness: Natural Resource and National Park Policy in Canada, 1887–1914," in J. G. Nelson, ed., *Canadian Parks in Perspective* (Montreal: Harvest House, 1969), pp. 46–62; J. I. Nicol, "The National Parks Movement in Canada," in Nelson, ed., *Canadian Parks*, pp. 19–34; and W. F. Lothian, *A Brief History of Canada's National Parks* (Ottawa: Minister of Supply and Services Canada, 1987). The most comprehensive history of parks and wildlife policy is Janet Foster, *Working for Wildlife: The Beginning of Preservation in Canada* (Toronto: University of Toronto Press, 1978). A key figure in that history was James Harkin, who was appointed commissioner of Dominion parks in 1912. His attitudes toward wilderness, Foster writes, "were well grounded on the philosophy and writings of the American wilderness preservationist, John Muir. Indeed, the Parks Commissioner lost few occasions to quote the American author at length in his departmental reports to the Minister of the Interior on the need for wilderness areas and the importance of dominion parks" (p. 14). For an account of more recent developments in parklands, see Karen Twichell, "The Great Canadian Parks Debate," *Canadian Geographer* 112 (July-August 1992): 6, 8; and Philip Dearden, "Parks and Protected Areas," in Bruce Mitchell, ed., *Resource and Environmental Management in Canada: Addressing Conflict and Uncertainty*, 2d ed. (Toronto: Oxford University Press, 1995), pp. 236–58.

29. Northrop Frye, *The Bush Garden: Essays on the Canadian Imagination* (Toronto: Anansi, 1971), p. 225. Perhaps Frye's views are colored by the fact that he grew up in the eastern provinces of Quebec and Ontario, rather than in the West, and they may not be altogether representative of national opinion. But there are corroborative national analyses in other works, including Marcia B. Kline, *Beyond the Land Itself: Views of Nature in Canada and the United States* (Cambridge, Mass.: Harvard University Press, 1970); Gaile McGregor, *The Wacousta Legend: Explorations in the Canadian Landscape* (Toronto: University of Toronto Press, 1985); and D. G. Jones, *Butterfly on Rock: A Study of Themes and Images in Canadian Literature* (Toronto: University of Toronto Press, 1970), pp. 6–8.

30. Margaret Atwood, *Survival: A Thematic Guide to Canadian Literature* (Toronto: Anansi, 1972), pp. 49, 54.

31. All but a tiny fraction of the one billion acres owned by the Canadian federal

government lie north of the sixtieth parallel, and their major use is for Native subsistence and for mineral exploration and production. Within the provincial boundaries, the federal government owns only 7.8 million acres. The provinces together control more than 1.2 billion acres, while Quebec, Ontario, and British Columbia each control more land than there is in the entire U.S. national forest system. See Christopher K. Leman, "The Concepts of Public and Private and Their Applicability to North American Lands," in Elliot J. Feldman and Michael A. Goldberg, eds., *Land Rites and Wrongs: The Management, Regulation and Use of Land in Canada and the United States* (Cambridge, Mass.: Lincoln Institute of Land Policy, 1987), p. 29.

32. Nash, *Wilderness and the American Mind*, p. 343. See also his essay, "Wilderness and Man in North America," in J. G. Nelson and R. C. Scace, eds., *The Canadian National Parks: Today and Tomorrow* (Calgary: University of Calgary, 1968), vol. 2, pp. 66–93. Nash argues that "the Canadian public's sensitivity to and enthusiasm for wilderness values lags at least two generations behind opinion in the United States" (p. 75). The word "lags" is probably not one that Canadians would find pleasing.

33. Atwood, *Survival,* pp. 49, 65–66.

34. According to W. L. Morton, "not life, liberty and the pursuit of happiness, but peace, order, and good government are what the national government of Canada guarantees." From Morton, "The Relevance of Canadian History," in Eli Mandel, ed., *Contexts of Canadian Criticism* (Toronto: University of Toronto, 1971), p. 68.

35. Seymour Martin Lipset, *Continental Divide: The Values and Institutions of the United States and Canada* (New York: Routledge, 1990). Lipset's book has been criticized by some Canadians for drawing too sharp a contrast between the two nations and for characterizing Canada as consistently more "socialistic" than the United States from its founding on down to modern day. But for a supportive line of argument, see John Conway, "An Adapted Organic Tradition," *Daedalus* 117 (fall 1988): 381–96. Conway argues that "Americans cherish individualism and individuality above community. Canadians have exactly the reverse of political priorities" (p. 382).

36. "Alternatives to the Frontier Thesis: Paul Fox Interviews Donald Creighton," in Michael Cross, ed., *The Frontier Thesis and the Canadas: The Debate on the Impact of the Canadian Environment* (Toronto: Copp Clark, 1970), pp. 39–42. Creighton's alternative was the idea of "metropolitanism," which puts the city at the core of national development.

37. A. R. M. Lower, "Some Neglected Aspects of Canadian History," in Cross, *Frontier Thesis,* pp. 34–35. See also Cook, "Landscape Painting," p. 265; and Robin W. Winks, *The Relevance of Canadian History: U.S. and Imperial Perspectives* (Toronto: Macmillan, 1979), pp. 10–22. See also George F. G. Stanley, "Western Canada and the Frontier Thesis," in *Canadian Historical Association Report* (Toronto: University of Toronto Press, 1940), pp. 105–14; Paul F. Sharp, "Three Frontiers: Some Comparative

Studies of Canadian, American, and Australian Settlement," *Pacific Historical Review* 24 (November 1955): 369–77; Robin Fisher, "Duff and George Go West: A Tale of Two Frontiers," *Canadian Historical Review* 68 (December 1987): 501–28. The idea that the north country will provide a common unifying environment for Canadians has been a recurring dream. See Carl Berger, "The True North Strong and Free," in Peter Russell, ed., *Nationalism in Canada* (Toronto: McGraw-Hill, 1966), pp. 3–26; Cole Harris, "The Myth of the Land in Canadian Nationalism," in Russell, *Nationalism in Canada*, pp. 27–43; Allison Mitcham, *The Northern Imagination: A Study of Northern Canadian Literature* (Moonbeam, Ont.: Penumbra Press, 1983); and Morris Zaslow, *The Opening of the Canadian North, 1870–1914* (Toronto: McClelland and Stewart, 1971), and *The Northward Expansion of Canada, 1914–1967* (Toronto: McClelland and Stewart, 1988).

38. Frye, *Bush Garden*, pp. 225–26.

39. Atwood, *Survival*, p. 33. See also Lipset, *Continental Divide*, pp. 51–52, 67.

40. Such an account would have to examine Edward Abbey's "Freedom and Wilderness, Wilderness and Freedom," in *The Journey Home: Some Words in Defense of the American West* (New York: E. P. Dutton, 1977), pp. 227–38. Wilderness, he argues, is our only real defense against "the thoroughly organized society, where all individual freedom is submerged to the needs of the social organism" (p. 233).

41. Wallace Stegner, "Coda: Wilderness Letter," in *The Sound of Mountain Water* (Lincoln: University of Nebraska Press, 1980), pp. 145–53.

42. Huey D. Johnson, "Canada Heralds Green Plan," *Whole Earth Review* 72 (fall 1991): 52. See also Robert Cahn "Where Green Is the Color," *The Amicus Journal* 14 (fall 1992): 10–11.

43. Introduced by Conservative Brian Mulroney's government, the plan ran afoul of business interests that felt overburdened by federal regulation, and it was opposed by fossil fuel–rich Alberta, which did not want to see national energy consumption go down. Moreover, a shaky economy made the plan seem too expensive. See Doern and Conway, *Greening of Canada*, pp. 56–58, 78–81, 98–99, 121–22, 239–40.

44. The only comparative study of this subject I have found is George Hoberg, "Comparing Canadian Performance in Environmental Policy," in Robert Boardman, ed., *Canadian Environmental Policy: Ecosystems, Politics, and Process* (Toronto: Oxford University Press, 1992), pp. 246–62. He argues that Canadians have an unjustified sense of superiority on environmental matters, derived from the fact that American coal-burning power plants cause acid precipitation in their country. In controlling water pollution, however, the United States is performing better than its neighbor. Overall, in 1986 the United States spent .65 percent of all its governmental budgets on environmental protection compared with .49 percent by Canada. If parks are included in

the sum of expenditures, the United States spent .68 percent, compared with .64 percent by Canada (p. 249).

45. Stegner, "Coda: Wilderness Letter," p. 149.

46. Wayland Drew, *The Wabeno Feast* (Toronto: Anansi, 1973); and Drew, "Killing Wilderness," *Ontario Naturalist* (September 1972): 22. See also his essay "Wilderness and Culture," *Alternatives* 3 (summer 1974): 8–11; along with John Wadlund, "Wilderness and Culture," in Bruce W. Hodgins and Margaret Hobbs, eds., *Nastawgan: The Canadian North by Canoe and Snowshoe* (Toronto: Betelgeuse Books, 1985), pp. 223–36; and Neil Evernden, *The Natural Alien: Humankind and the Environment,* 2d ed. (Toronto: University of Toronto Press, 1993).

11 / Sleeping with the Elephant

Reflections of an American-Canadian on Americanization
and Anti-Americanism in Canada

MICHAEL FELLMAN

Arriving in Canada in 1969, direct from the doctoral program at North-western University, wet behind the ears, and as ignorant of my new homeland as are almost all Americans, I had no idea of what subtle and not so subtle differences I might encounter. As do most Americans in Canada, I have stayed on and contributed and more or less disappeared into the Anglo-Canadian mainstream. Indeed, almost uniquely among immigrant groups to Canada, we Americans have little visibility as a group. Despite a proud (if not always observed) post–World War II advertisement of cultural plural-ism, where very large numbers of Italian-Canadians, Indo-Canadians, and Chinese-Canadians in particular have been generally welcomed into the social "mosaic," no one has ever heard of an American-Canadian, although in Canada we number in the millions, if one looks back historically. This chap-ter marks the first time I have seen anyone declare that she or he is an American-Canadian. This reflects both our accommodation to the high level of anti-Americanism in Canada and the degree to which, subtle language cues excepted, Americans (white Americans at least) are so close to white Canadians, Quebecois excepted, as to assimilate without an apparent trace, bred as we all have been in that shared North American pool of cultural values and social practices called liberal capitalism.

Anglo-Canadians, or at least the ideological trendsetters in Canadian soci-ety, vastly exaggerate both their small differences from Americans and their minor resemblances to the British. They often refuse to acknowledge the depth to which their society is bound to their very powerful American neighbors by voluntary and organic relationships rather than coercion. Demographically, economically, politically, culturally, and historically, the American impact on Canada has been enormous, in progressive as well as regressive ways. Concomitantly, anti-Americanism has been the chief ideological manner, as often reactionary as positive, in which Canadians have attempted to hold at some remove the colossus to the south. Yet the focus on anti-Americanism is often inaccurate and distorting: it tends to lead Canadians to refuse to acknowledge the depths of Americanization that they have absorbed, to see the Americans in their midst, to recognize the degree to which Canadians have always migrated to the United States in large and eager numbers, and to admit how well they have done in their *pas de deux* with their U.S. partner.

The sheer numbers are impressive even before one interprets them. In 1900 there were 5.37 million Canadians in Canada and 1.2 million Canadians who had migrated to the United States, where they comprised 11.4 percent of foreigners living there. From 1820 until 1950, 4.3 million Canadians emigrated to the United States, which matched the size of the more readily recognizable and hence more prominent Italian immigration. During the height of the Industrial Revolution, between 1840 and 1900, subtracting the sizable American movement to Canada, a net of 427,000 Maritimers and 582,000 Quebecers settled in the United States, mainly as workers in the mill and factory towns of New England, while a net of 521,000 left Ontario, mainly for points further west in the United States. As the U.S. border was open to them, Canadians could join freely in the mass European and internal American migration from countryside to industrial cities: they sought better jobs, more promising futures for their children, and the bright lights of the metropolis. Although Canada was changing then in similar fashions, in part because of the restrictive National Policy that traded rapidity of growth for social and economic control, Canadian industrial and urban development was too slow to contain the hundreds of thousands of ambitious Canadians who thus became parts of an American as well as a Canadian transformation.

Although the number of Canadians migrating has outnumbered Americans coming north, with the exception of the Vietnam War period, American migration has always been considerable. In 1921, for instance, 375,000 or 20 percent of those of foreign birth living in Canada were Americans (which can be compared to the 52 percent then from Great Britain and Ireland), and in the following decade, 933,000 more Americans arrived, while 1,658,000 more Canadians migrated south.[1]

Significant cross-border immigration was not a new phenomenon after 1840. Indeed, after the British conquest of the French at the gates of Quebec

in 1759, the first wave of English-speaking settlement was American, beginning with the New Englanders who settled in Nova Scotia after the Acadians
were expelled in 1755. Americans also flooded into what would become New
Brunswick, Upper Canada, and the eastern townships of Lower Canada after
the American Revolution. Although most Canadians believe that these
migrants were all committed United Empire Loyalists, in fact perhaps 80 percent of this wave of American settlers were more or less apolitical scramblers
for cheap land. The War of 1812 halted American immigration, which returned
after the war, but at a slower pace, in part because Americans expanded along
the new Erie Canal and the Great Lakes into the upper Midwest. The end of
the Napoleonic wars in 1815 also triggered a flood of British immigration, but
until that point Americans composed the majority of English-speaking settlers in Canada.[2]

Many of these Americans supposed that their expansion northward would
lead to the annexation of Canada, an idea popular enough to the south to
lead to the two invasions of the Revolutionary War and the War of 1812, which
with Canadian help the British army was strong enough to repel. Nevertheless,
Americans continued to cross the Canadian border as part of their westward
expansion, which along with climate, transportation routes, and the presence
of hungry American markets, explains why 90 percent of Canadians live within
fifty miles of the United States even today. Indeed, in a recent study the historian Reginald C. Stuart focuses on what he calls a "borderland culture" of
local self-interest shared by generations of settlers spanning the border, who
basically ignored the forty-ninth parallel and both national governments.
"Family and friendship ties reinforced economic linkages to produce the borderland mentality," he has written, "a product of American frontier expansion where the people from one society intermingled with the people of
another. . . . For American borderlanders [Canada contained] neighbors, markets, relatives and friends."[3]

Perhaps the relative ease, even the obviousness of this permanent demographic intermingling contributes to a lack of Canadian awareness of
Americans in their midst. It is notable, however, that although the extensive
Canadian Historical Association series—Canada's Ethnic Groups—has com-
missioned pamphlets on the Belgians and the Welsh in Canada, they have
ignored the vastly more sizable and influential Americans. And the authors
of the semiofficial history of Canadian immigration, 'Coming Canadians', published in association with the multiculturalism program of the Secretary of
State of Canada, which breaks down figures for the settlement of thirty-six
ethnic groups of foreign-born Canadians as of 1981, including 10,055 West

Asians and 10,545 North African Arabs, fails to mention Americans. They are, however, subsumed under the heading "British and other," defined as "immigrants of British origin, chiefly from the United Kingdom and the United States"—a curious definition of Americans as of 1981—that totaled 859,800.[4]

This "absent-mindedness" among historians about American immigration to Canada is one reflection, probably unconscious, of a long tradition of anti-Americanism among Anglo-Canadian nationalist intellectuals. In a brilliant and witty essay written twenty-five years ago, the political scientist David V. J. Bell put his finger on the origin of this ideological construction when he discussed what he called the myth of the Loyalist past. Bell argued that "the American Revolution produced not one country but two: a nation and a non-nation." In opposing the Revolution, Loyalists "did not intend to sacrifice [their] homes, their beliefs, their hard-won identity," but "robbed" of their American homes and identity, they not only had to move but to invent a new persona. The substitute was inadequate and in some fundamental sense dishonest, as it denied the liberalism at the core of Loyalist beliefs. Thus came about the self-created "anti-American Yankee"—a mythic figure necessary for survival—who affirmed against reality that he was essentially British. From then on the Loyalist "builds an American society and calls it by British names."[5]

As long as the Loyalist never visited Britain, he could continue his legend unchallenged, Bell argues. But the average British visitor was not fooled. For example, the travel writer G. T. Borrett noted in 1865, on the eve of Confederation, that "the typical Canadian tells you that he is not, but he *is* a Yankee— a Yankee in the sense in which we use the term at home, as synonymous with everything that smacks of democracy." Even the staunchest Loyalist, who appeared American to an actual British Tory, was internally divided about the Yankee without and the even more threatening Yankee within. As Bell writes, the loyalist myth "featured agonizing ambivalence: hatred mixed with envious love, invidiousness tinged with pathetic admiration."[6]

In an attempt to expunge the attractive and dreaded Yankee ghost, this activist minority of Americans who were Loyalists helped give birth to Canadian Tory nationalism in conjunction with social conservatives among the flood of British immigration after 1815. Ensconced as the economic, political, and judicial barons of both Montreal and Toronto, again in Bell's words, Canadian Tories "tried desperately to convince the masses that democracy was synonymous with republicanism and annexation." In the 1820s and 1830s, aided of course by memories of two U.S. military invasions, this small dominating group created, as the legal historian Paul Romney wrote in 1989, that part of Canadian "political culture that was elitist and loyalist, anti-democratic and

MICHAEL FELLMAN

278

anti-American."[7] During the past thirty-five years it has become fashionable among both conservative and socialist historians to argue that this Toryism is connected directly to statism (which I think is inaccurate) and to a willingness to submit to a kind of British-like social control that is the very core political value distinguishing Canadian from wildly individualistic American culture. This argument underestimates the internal ambivalence of the Tories, however, and it fails to come to grips with the dominant political culture of modern Canada, which is neither conservative nor socialist but liberal, capitalist, democratic, federalist, and only reluctantly statist—in sum much more American than Canadians like to admit.

The Canadians' faith that they are a kinder, gentler society than the Americans—their cherished myth of collective tenderness—masks both their own rougher qualities and the degree to which they are caught up with America and American ideas. The Canadian bias against Americans colors their history books and their mythic self-constructions: projecting their nastier realities south, they also refuse to believe that they have learned anything progressive from Americans, claiming, often inaccurately, global civility for themselves via the route of frequently bigoted anti-Americanism.

If American-style liberal capitalism was always concealed in the agenda of Canadian Tories, it was explicit in the resistance to them that developed during the 1820s and 1830s and, suppressed by the anti-democratic elites, burst forth in the rebellions of 1837–38. The leaders of this upsurge took American democratic capitalism as, in the words of Louis-Joseph Papineau, leader of the Patriote Party in Lower Canada, "our model and our text." Indeed, later in his life Papineau argued that French Canada would be better off as an independent state in a broad American union than as a subject people in an elitist and authoritarian British-influenced and English-dominated Canada.

William Lyon Mackenzie, leader of the rebellion in Upper Canada and the founder of the Liberal Party (at first called the Reform Party), was equally explicit in his admiration of American society, especially the Jacksonian insurgency. Although he believed that a "luxurious and immoral aristocracy . . . would willingly concentrate the wealth and power of the republic in a few hands," in the United States as elsewhere, he marveled at Andrew Jackson, whose bank bill veto "stands forth a splendid and imperishable monument of his hatred to oppression under the form of a licensed monopoly." Mackenzie had in mind not annexation to the United States but a liberalized and democratized Canada modeled on U.S. society and freed from the strictures of its heavy-handed merchant elite that controlled both government and economy. He believed that Canadians were thus in the same position as "our brother colonists of old," and the July 19, 1837, draft constitution he wrote for a new Canada began: "We, the people of the state of Upper Canada." It went on to outline a decentralized, secularized, and democratized state.[8]

Militarily, the rebellion fizzled and both Papineau and Mackenzie repudiated union with the United States, but only out of desperation, as their revolt crumbled. Although there were nasty episodes of repression immediately following the outbreak, by 1841 the British crown pushed Lower and Upper Canada into a weak legislative and executive union that contained some of the trappings of parliamentary democracy. In the larger political sense, the Liberals did not lose but were able to invite themselves, however reluctantly they were received, into the political structures of an emerging nation. This state continued to be dominated by Toryism—conservative, slow-growth nationalism run in the interest of a fairly narrow established elite—until the end of the nineteenth century, when a rather more inclusive Liberalism became the dominant political force, which it has remained ever since. Until then, Liberal government was an intermission in Tory hegemony; after then liberalism has been dominant.

Curiously, not only the Liberals at home but often as not the British themselves wished to divest Canada of old forms for new. Indeed, as the British government moved to a free-trade posture at mid-century, the U.S. market loomed far larger than the Canadian one, and defending Canada militarily and economically seemed not worth the price. As Canada lost preferential treatment in Britain, the ensuing collapse in markets produced the first movement for annexation in 1848 and 1849, centered among the Anglo merchant elite of Montreal and the borderlands settlers of the eastern townships. This episode died rather quickly in 1850, when the United States began importing Canadian goods rather than flooding Canadian markets. In 1854, Britain negotiated a reciprocity treaty between the United States and Canada, which further opened up north-south trade. Canadian pine forests would build much of the American Midwest, as the U.S. market continued to displace the English one.

Conservative anti-Americans were aided not only by the strongly American-tinged liberal rebellion, but by the strident and restless expansionism of Americans themselves, which faced north as well as west and south. The epitome of Manifest Destiny designs on Canada was uttered by the journalist Parke Godwin, who wrote in 1854 that "the fruit will fall into our hands when it is ripe," and such sentiments continued to come from the mouths of American politicians and writers for the next sixty years.[9] Godwin's statement implied that military conquest would be unnecessary, as forces internal to Canada would sue for annexation. However, as long as Americans expressed even indirect annexationism, Canadian conservatives tarred liberalism, democracy, and free trade with charges of treason. Yet, by dint of economic geography, Canadians were compelled to come to fundamental accommodation with the United States, which an active minority of Canadians saw as the surest road to economic growth and democratic reform.

The U.S. Civil War may not have produced a new Confederation of southern states, but it did serve as the violent midwife to the birth of a northern Confederation of Canadian provinces. Canada proved to be the British way out of a potential war with the Union. When the war began, the first British impulse was to reinforce its tiny 4,300–man army garrison in Canada: in July 1861 the *Great Eastern* sailed with 2,144 officers and men of the Royal Artillery. The following spring, in response to the *Trent* crisis, when an American naval captain snatched two Confederate diplomats off a British vessel, the British issued a stern diplomatic note and sent 11,175 more men to Canada. Despite heated exchanges by both American and British politicians over the next few months, cooler heads prevailed and war did not ensue. The Americans had their hands full with the Confederates, and the British realized that Canada was hostage to the Americans after the war if not sooner.

During the *Trent* crisis the British government sent over a team of military experts who concluded that it would take 150,000 more men and an immense expenditure of money to defend Canada, an obviously unacceptable price. For their own defense the Canadian Tories in charge proposed a militia bill to raise and equip fifty thousand men, which would have cost a bundle, but during the parliamentary debates John A. MacDonald, the Canadian leader, whose heart was not in the bill and whose French-Canadian followers opposed it, stayed so drunk as to render him *hors du combat.* The result was that the bill went down to defeat and with it MacDonald's government. This led many in Britain to fume, as did the *Spectator,* for example: "It is, perhaps, our duty to defend the Empire at all hazards; it is no part of it to defend men who will not defend themselves."[10]

As the Civil War continued, U.S. Secretary of State William H. Seward made loud expansionist noises in the Canadian direction, the Union army became the most powerful in the world, and the Union navy surpassed the British in numbers and technology. In response, the British searched for, in the words of W. L. Morton, the shrewdest historian of this issue, "some honorable and dignified way of disengagement" militarily from Canada. Thus they provided quite keen support for a British North American union, when local elites began negotiations among themselves in earnest in 1864.

In effect, the British conceded unchallenged U.S. military supremacy in

North America, appealing for American respect of a new North American nation that would be so unrivalrous and so unhostile that the Americans would leave it be; a nation, in Morton's words, more "with a legal than a political sovereignty, a sovereignty conditioned by the supremacy of the United States."[11] To be sure, Canadian politicians drummed up support for Confederation as a means of warding off a U.S. invasion or piecemeal annexation,[12] but their constitution was passed as a British parliamentary act, upon which the Canadian people were not invited to vote, except in New Brunswick, where they rejected it the first time around. Canada would maintain both a British-style parliamentary system and an American-style federation of provinces, and their principal foreign concern would always be how to play their American card with maximum wittiness given their relative weakness.

In August 1865, no less a personage than Ulysses S. Grant paid a visit to Quebec City, ostensibly for a postwar holiday, where, according to Morton, he worked out an understanding that if the British would refrain from supporting the French adventure in Mexico, the United States would leave Canada alone. However explicit such an undertaking may have been, far more interesting to the Americans was access to British capital for their anticipated postwar push to open the West, something Canadians also desired, as did of course the City and hence the government of Britain.[13] Because of an accumulation of wartime grievances, the Americans abrogated the Canadian reciprocity treaty of 1854 to push the British toward settlement of U.S. wartime claims, which occurred in 1871, in part because the British did not want to jeopardize the United States as a rapidly developing field for investment. Canada was a useful and unthreatening secondary partner for both great powers.

Undercapitalized and underpopulated, Canada needed immigrant settlers as well as British capital to people the West in the late nineteenth and early twentieth centuries. Many settlers came from Great Britain and northern and eastern Europe, but by 1905, American immigrants outnumbered British immigrants in Alberta and Saskatchewan by a ratio of two to one: from 1896 to 1912, 785,000 U.S. farmers came north to settle on cheap land. Much of this settlement was impermanent, as farmers were often restless settlers who moved north or south of the border as well as east or west within both nations. In part, this agriculturist migration was the western expression of Reginald Stuart's definition of naturally occurring "borderlands culture," but as the historian Harold Martin Troper has demonstrated, much of it was vigorously recruited by the Canadian authorities. Clifford Sifton, the powerful minister of the Interior during the long (though interrupted) Laurier Liberal government, created a body of invitational propaganda and a system of recruiting agents in the states, mostly railroad officers and clerks, who were paid by the head: with only nominal checks at the border, as well as vast reaches of cheap land suitable for wheat farming, linked to eastern markets by the new Canadian Pacific Railroad, the hundreds of thousands of American immigrants came.[14]

Most of these Americans were the same farmers of Anglo-Saxon, German, and northern European stock who had also settled the northern American Great Plains. One reason they were so eagerly recruited is that they seemed so like Canadians, so readily assimilative. As the Lethbridge, Alberta, *Herald* expressed in 1905, "This class of immigration is of a top-notch order and every true Canadian should be proud to see it and encourage it. Thus shall our vast tracts of God's bountifulness . . . be peopled by an intelligent progressive race of our own kind, who will readily be developed into permanent, patriotic, solid citizens who will adhere to one flag . . . and whose posterity. . . will become . . . a part and parcel of and inseparable from our proud standards of Canadianism."[15]

As some Canadian historians on the left have been loath to admit, these American farmers brought their politics with them, and their vigorous populism formed much of the ideological basis for Canadian agrarian protest movements to come. Indeed, as late as the 1930s the Canadian Co-operative Commonwealth Federation, parent to the current social-democratic New Democratic Party, shared speakers and funding with the ideologically similar Farmer-Labor Party of Minnesota and the Non-Partisan League of North Dakota.[16] Bringing their populism with them, these American farmers unfortunately also imported their racism, which fitted comfortably with Canadian racism, as it did with the virulent racism accompanying and justifying the often brutal imperialism of all the European powers as they conquered and then dominated most of the nonwhite world in the late nineteenth and early twentieth centuries. Although Canadian border officials made only cursory checks of Americans crossing the border, these were sufficient to screen out African Americans. Indeed, when the civil rights leader W. E. B. DuBois complained of this practice, L. M. Fortier, the Canadian secretary in charge of immigration, replied that although nothing in Canadian law disbarred any settler on the grounds of color, "since coloured people are not considered as a class likely to do well in this country, all the regulations respecting health, money, etc., are strictly enforced, and it is quite possible that a number of your fellow countrymen may be rejected on such grounds." This letter was part of a kind of public panic that occurred when Canadians learned that fifteen hundred part-Cherokee, part-black farmers from Oklahoma had managed to cross the border and settle on the prairies, to the anger of white settlers and Canadians in general. The high Tory *Toronto Mail & Empire* was less indirect than Secretary Fortier on the matter, when it editorialized in a textbook demonstration of aversive racism: "If we freely admit black people from that country, we shall soon have the race troubles that are a blot on the civilization of our neighbors. Canada cannot be accused of narrowness if she refuses to open up her West to waves of negro immigrants. . . .The negro question is of the United States own making and Canada should not allow any of her territory to be used as a relief colony on that account."[17] This policy was in line with the nasty treatment afforded black refugees of the American Revolution and the War of 1812 who had settled in eastern Canada.

If African Americans long had been abhorred and excluded on racial grounds, in the late nineteenth century so were southern and eastern Europeans, who were widely viewed, as the *Dominion Illustrated* put it in 1891, as "wretchedly . . . poor settlers [who] bring with them many of their vices and socialistic tendencies." How much superior were the "hardy German and Norwegian races," the paper insisted. As the historian Carl Berger demonstrates, Canadian ideologues, mainly but not exclusively Tory (joined in particular by the socialist leader J. S. Woodsworth), argued with great energy for the potential creation of pure white Canadians, a "hardy northern race of a stern nature which makes us struggle for existence," one created by the blessedly harsh northern climate, the "True North Strong and Free." As early as 1869, Robert Grant Haliburton, one of the founders of the Canada First League, had adapted the Social Darwinism then becoming fashionable in transatlantic imperialist circles to his image of Canada in the making. What should arise was a "healthy, hardy, virtuous dominant race . . . a Northern country inhabited by descendants of Northern races," including Celtic, Teutonic, Scandinavian, Celt and Norman French, in short, the British or "Aryan family," scourged clean of racial weakness by the harsh Canadian climate.[18] In this formulation French-Canadians (as were white Americans) were certainly acceptable, a racial prioritizing that many Quebec opinion makers returned in kind. As late as 1944, the Abbé Arthur Maheux, professor of history at Laval University, wrote that "the Norman blood, at least, is a real link between our two groups." In certain sectors of the Quebec separatist movement even today one hears echoes of the doctrine of the racial superiority of the "two founding races," in a manner almost completely out of fashion in polite English Canada. Perhaps ironically, as Berger points out, Canadian white supremacists successfully put into practice far earlier than the U.S. government much of the argument of American immigration restrictionists, including Senator

Henry Cabot Lodge, who campaigned from the 1880s until an overtly racist immigration policy was adopted in 1924 that the "dregs of the old world population were increasing too rapidly for assimilation." When Canadians such as George Parkin looked south in this period, they saw that "the Anglo-Saxon element, the real strength of the nation," was in decline. The "Negro problem" weighed "like a troublesome nightmare" on American civilization, and American cities were cesspools collecting the "vagrant population of Italy" and other decadent southern places. How blessedly lucky was Canada, inhospitable naturally to the base races, but Canadian policy makers helped reinforce climatic natural selection. As in the case of those Cherokee–African American would-be settlers of 1905, Canadian immigration officials were far more successful, far earlier, in standing on guard against non-Nordics than were the Americans. At the cost of slower economic development, they sustained racial exclusionism through World War II, when they were even more thorough than Americans in keeping out Jews fleeing Hitler, a popular policy enforced quite consciously by political leaders of both Norman races.[19]

While dreading the "wrong" immigrants and welcoming the "right" types, white American farmers included, Canadian politicians continued to negotiate trade policy with the Americans from both fear and hope. The dominant Tories pushed their National Policy, which meant more trade with Britain than with the United States against whom Canada maintained significant tariffs, in part as retaliation for high U.S. tariffs. The Liberal opposition, although internally divided over just what form it should take, pushed a free trade line. Naturally enough, such an opposition led the Tories to remount anti-Americanism and sing for Albion, and although the rebellions of 1837 were in the past, the Liberals were always easy to smear on the loyalty question. In 1888 the liberal leader of the opposition, Wilfred Laurier tried to turn this argument around by insisting that subservience to Britain constricted Canadian economic development, which it probably did, and that the National Policy was in fact insufficiently independent and Canadian. "To pretend that our colonial allegiance demands from us that we should be deterred from the spirit of enterprise is not loyalty, but is mere flunkyism," he declared. And in a not very oblique reference to the British-born prime minister, Sir John A. MacDonald, he added, "This is not a question of sentiment. This is a question of duty, and if you put it in that light, that I have to choose between the duty I owe to England, and the duty I owe to my native land, I stand by my native land."[20]

During the terrible depression of the late 1880s and early 1890s, free trade was coupled to renewed calls for annexationism on both sides of the border,

a combination that placed the Liberals in a very uncomfortable minority position with the voters. In 1888 the two countries negotiated lower tariffs, and
the powerful John Sherman then carelessly announced on the Senate floor
that he favored any policy that would "tend to promote free commercial inter-
course between these countries, yes anything that will tend to produce a union
of Canada and the United States of America. . . . I want Canada to be part of
the United States." The Senate defeated this treaty, but not before Sherman
had frightened many Canadians.[21]

As the depression continued, talk of free trade only increased, as one obvious means to reinflate the economy. In this climate the spark for annexation
was Goldwin Smith, a British-Canadian-American historian and journalist
whose gloomy book, *Canada and the Canadian Question*, published in 1891,
argued that Canada was insufficient to make a go of it economically outside
of union with the Americans. Smith and businessmen on both sides of the
border had organized the Continental Union Association in 1887, which
pushed both free trade and political amalgamation. In part to pressure the
Canadians into begging admission, the Republican Party passed the drastic
McKinley Tariff in 1890. Writing privately, Secretary of State James G. Blaine
told President Benjamin Harrison that this tariff would be for the Canadians,
"a hard row to hoe and will ultimately I believe lead [Canada] to seek admission to the Union." In response to such badgering from the Americans over
trade, the Canadian Tories won the 1891 election on protectionism and then
passed a mini-McKinley tariff of their own, which redirected trade back in
a British direction, away from the United States. Subsequently, the Liberals
were forced to backtrack on free trade, and when they came into what proved
to be a century of political dominance, they had apparently recognized that
successful Canadian politicians had to withstand all talk of union with the
United States.[22]

Yet Laurier, for one, was convinced that a "powerful combination of capitalists" in Canada were misleading the Canadian people, hiding behind the
Union Jack and tariff barriers to pursue their narrow self-interest while retard-
ing Canadian development. Laurier was also under intense western agrarian
pressure. Therefore he negotiated a free-trade treaty for primary resources
(while continuing to protect manufacturing, perhaps as a first stage treaty
that would be more politically acceptable than full-out free trade), that the
Americans adopted on July 26, 1911. Unfortunately for the Liberals, President
William Howard Taft noted when discussing the treaty that "Canada stands
at the parting of the ways," by which he probably meant trade isolation or
free trade, but Conservative Canadians pounced on this statement, insisting

it meant that Canadians had to choose between the United States and Great Britain. When the Speaker of the U.S. House of Representatives, Champ Clark, suggested that he hoped to soon see the day "when the American flag will float over every square foot of the British North American possessions clear to the North Pole," the Tories had their emotionally charged nationalist campaign issue, and despite in fact having sponsored a carefully limited treaty, Laurier was thumped when he called an election over it.[23]

Free trade had been but one plank in the Liberal reform program of the Laurier administration, which included the beginnings of state regulation in social and economic life, in tune with the Progressive administrations in the United States from 1900 until World War I, and British Liberalism of the same period. Indeed, one may speak of a transatlantic culture of political reform at this time. Such an approach was carried forward by the dominant figure in Canadian politics, William Lyon Mackenzie King, who was prime minister for most of the period from 1920 through 1948, and whose brand of timidly reformist Liberalism long dominated Canadian national political life—and in a sense still does to this day.

Mackenzie King, grandson of the 1837 rebel, heir to Laurier, was in many respects the most explicitly U.S.- influenced political leader Canada has ever had. After graduating from the University of Toronto in 1895, he spent the next three years doing graduate work at Harvard and the brand-new University of Chicago, and he worked for a spell at Jane Addams's Hull House in Chicago. Following a stint in parliament beginning in 1908, where he served as minister of Labor, after the Laurier government fell and he was defeated for reelection, King returned to the United States to serve as a labor conciliator with the Rockefeller Foundation. During his two lengthy sojourns in the United States, King absorbed the sentiments of the Social Gospel movement and of American Progressivism, much of which he expressed in his book *Industry and Humanity* (1918).[24]

After Laurier's death in 1919, the Liberals chose King as their leader and adopted his ambitious reform platform, including unemployment insurance, old-age pensions, and the eight-hour day, all progressive ideas in the American sense. In and out of power during the following three decades, but mainly in, King proved to be a cautious waffler who did not push his reform proposals very hard. In the late 1930s, despite a theoretical engagement with the U.S. New Deal and an almost fawning admiration for Franklin Roosevelt, King and his Liberals were slow to adopt much of the massive governmental programming characteristic of the New Deal. Only in 1940 did the Liberals enact an unemployment insurance program, at a time of full employment when it was not really needed. Only the pressure of a steep wartime rise in the polls for the Co-Operative Commonwealth Federation led King to run as a reformer in 1945. Canadian popular beliefs to the contrary notwithstanding, Canada was far slower than the United States to adopt a social safety net. Many older Canadians recall the bold statist FDR as the beacon of hope during the Depression rather than the passive King.

By the 1920s the United States had passed Britain forever as Canada's chief trading partner. After World War II, fearful of a return to the Depression, aware that the British economy was in shambles, Canada turned to the United States for economic connection, and cashed in on the long postwar American boom—both sides lowered tariffs considerably in the late 1940s (moves that were more significant economically than the later 1988 free trade treaty). This turn to freer trade with the Americans, this open invitation for economic investment, often of the branch plant variety, was led by C. D. Howe, an American immigrant himself, who had come to dominate vast reaches of the Canadian economy as minister of munitions and supply during the statism of war, when he helped Canadian industrialists procure huge and profitable contracts. (At the same time, while maintaining an independent military command structure, Canada came to depend on the United States to protect British Columbia from Japanese attack, and the Americans financed and built the Alaska highway right through Canada.) After King resigned in 1948, Howe stayed in cabinet as Louis St. Laurent's minister of trade and commerce, and remained the real power behind Canada's economic opening. During the 1950s, while the proportion of trade with Britain and British investment declined markedly, Canadian exports to the United States more than doubled, American investment in Canada tripled, and the Canadian economy produced an unprecedented rise in the standard of living. Among Howe's rewards was to be named *Time* magazine's Man of the Year in 1952.[25]

Although they welcomed this newfound wealth, many Canadians continued to fear getting too close to the American colossus. Indeed in 1947, Howe's negotiations had gone so well with the Americans that they had produced a free trade treaty, but King, remembering the fall of his mentor, Laurier, in 1911, killed the proposal in cabinet as impolitic. In 1956, Walter L. Gordon, a Toronto accountant, chaired a royal commission, which, unexpectedly to the Liberal cabinet that had created it, produced a report sharply critical of the Howe policy as a sellout of Canada's resources to the Americans and as economic submissiveness at the expense of independence. In response, Howe asserted in a speech that "had it not been for the enterprise and capital from the United States . . . our development would have been slower and some of the spectacular projects of which we are so proud . . . would still be in the future." Gordon's report, Howe concluded, was "manure."[26]

The Canadian debate over the 1988 free trade treaty (by which time the Tories had become the only free traders, reversing historical roles with the Liberals), was based on these same ancient issues. It is this deep ideological and emotional division, this love-hate, attraction-repulsion feeling for the elephant that characterizes much of Canadian nationalism—an always contingent sense of both dependence and independence. And this "contingent sense" is colored by economics: today thirty-eight percent of Canada's GDP is produced for export, the highest dependency on exports of any of the developed Group of Seven, and more than 80 percent of those exports go to the United States, with which Canada maintains a sizable balance of trade. This is a high level of economic integration that would be difficult to argue has impoverished Canada the way renewed protectionism would have done following World War II. Canadians complain of American domination but do little to return to economic isolation, which would purchase greater independence with a much diminished standard of living.

In foreign policy as well, after 1945, Canada gravitated unequivocally to the U.S. side of the Cold War. One of the first postwar Communist spy scares, the Gouzenko affair, happened in Ottawa in 1945, and from then on Canadian foreign-affairs officials denounced what they considered to be Soviet aggression, and the Royal Canadian Mounted Police instituted a red-baiting surveillance of radicals in Canadian life. Canadians were among the first to push for what became NATO, and they concluded the North American Air Defense agreement that integrated the defense umbrella under effective American control. Canada also leased a base in Labrador to the Americans. Even when acting through the United Nations, which Canadians were integral in founding, when Canadians supplied peacekeeping troops, it was understood that they were acting as an acceptable American nominee, a nation firmly part of the Western alliance. Occasionally, from the 1960s into the 1990s, Liberals, Tories, and New Democrats ran their election campaigns in part on the stated premise that Canada's peacekeeping role was that of an essentially neutral power, and ought to stay that way, which, given Cold War politics, has been a ludicrous analysis.

Because the Americans would hardly have let the Russians invade Canada, the Cold War paid an enormous peace benefit to Canada, which stripped its armed forces and defense budgets to a minimum, providing the least number of troops allowable for NATO, building weapons for export to America, and spending much of this indirect American dividend on social programs. Unburdened by a direct role in enforcing the Cold War, Canadians felt guilt-free about their actual military alliances and often preached to the Americans about the stupidity of the war in Vietnam. Because of this limited supporting role in the forty-five-year-long Cold War, Canada avoided the long history of militarism that so corrupted American society. Militarism justifying the use of force is one reason for the much higher incidence of violence in American society, as are stricter Canadian gun-control laws.

Protected from the need for expensive armed forces, Canadians were able to use the boom economy from 1945 to 1960 to construct a somewhat stronger social safety net than the Americans, including a relatively effective national medical insurance policy. On the whole the American safety net is bigger than Canadians realize, and in certain instances, such as rights for the handicapped and affirmative action for ethnic minorities and women, more interventionist and effective than Canadian equivalents: Canadian programs are far more limited than European ones and far more like the American programs than Canadians believe. The long swing to right-wing anti-statism, budget slashing, and decentralization is as strong in Canada as in the United States. As King was to American progressivism, so the Canadian right is to the American right, and both are to the British Thatcherites, with Clinton Democrats, Chrétien/Martin Liberals, and for that matter Blair New Laborites all moving smartly to the right as well. In the twentieth century, rather than being a Tory or socialist alternative to the United States, Canada has swung through the vicissitudes of liberalism as have the Americans, often in near tandem. Even the New Democratic Party had its equivalent in the left wing of the Democratic Party, although these forces have collapsed in the national politics of both countries, many of their remnants turning curiously neoconservative.

Canada remained slow in separating from Britain in large part out of deep fear of engagement with the United States, and this lack of confidence has meant that, unlike Australia, for example, there has been little Canadian Pommie bashing. Canadian troops made huge sacrifices for the British in both world wars and were as badly mismanaged as were Australian soldiers, yet there is little Canadian historical outrage, even over the 1942 Dieppe raid, botched by Louis Mountbatten, where thirty-three hundred Canadian troops were killed, wounded, or captured in a morning. No Canadian film equals the bitterness of *Gallipoli* or *Breaker Morant*, markers of Australian anti-British nationalism. Indeed the outraged reaction to the McKenna brothers' Canadian film *The Valour and the Horror* resembled the fury of the American right over the Enola Gay exhibit at the Smithsonian Institution. Nor is there a strong anti-monarchist movement in Canada.

Indeed, Canadians were late in creating independent national symbols. Until 1947 there was no Canadian citizenship and Canadians remained British subjects carrying British passports. Until 1949 final Canadian judicial appeal was to the Privy Council in London, and until 1952 the governor-general was a British peer. Canadians replaced the Red Ensign with the Maple Leaf flag only in the mid-1960s, and until 1982 Canada's constitution was a legislative act of the British parliament. Anglo-Canadians long maintained an increasingly inaccurate sensibility that they were somehow British as well as "not-Americans."

In lieu of other convincing symbols and forms of nationalism, with the passing of the British identification, Anglo-Canadians are left with only the negative side of their zeitgeist, anti-Americanism. Unlike other immigrant groups, Americans in Canada have been encouraged to assimilate to the point of cultural self-silencing, as part of a package of Canadian denial of the Americanism in the core of their identity. Many relatively recent U.S. immigrants, thousands of whom were Vietnam War draft dodgers and deserters, in a kind of recapitulation of the bitterest of Loyalism, have been only too glad to join the anti-American chorus, although thousands more American-Canadians are ambivalent about their land of origins, and are somewhat offended by the sweepingly inclusive and in fact intolerant nature of the critique of their former, complex society. For their part, U.S. politicians have at long last learned restraint in their dealings with Canada, not even hinting at political annexation when negotiating trade treaties. Whatever they fear, Canadians do quite well in their relations with the United States.

Finally, anti-Americanism is the cowbird of the Canadian psychic and ideological nest. While they displace their fears and aggressions south, English-speaking intellectuals on the whole remain curiously passive in the face of Quebec nationalism. Annexation is not the greatest threat to such a distended society; separatism is. Canadian intellectuals would be better served by a vigorous and systematic attack on the separatist readings of Canadian history and the economy, which are certainly curious to say the least. Pierre Trudeau seemed to understand this. It was he who noted that it was difficult to sleep with the American elephant, but Canadians have learned to do so. Obsessive anti-Americanism is fiddling outwardly while the enemy lurks within.

NOTES

An earlier version of this chapter was presented at "The New Academic Free Trade Area: The Seventeenth Biennial Conference of the Australia and New Zealand American Studies Association," in Christchurch, New Zealand, on February 6, 1996. Subsequently, a condensed version appeared under the title "Sam, I Am," in *Saturday Night* 111 (October 1996): 43–46. Many thanks to Richard Waterhouse in Australia and to my Simon Fraser colleague J. M. Little for his scholarly skills and his support.

1. These figures come from *Migration between the United States and Canada*, a joint publication of the U.S. Bureau of the Census and Statistics Canada (Washington, D.C.: Government Printing Office, 1990), and from the map in John Herd Thompson and Steven J. Randall, *The United States and Canada: Ambivalent Allies* (Athens: University of Georgia Press, 1994), p. 58.

2. Marcus Lee Hansen, *The Mingling of the American and Canadian Peoples* (New Haven, Conn.: Yale University Press, 1940), pp. 89–90.

3. Reginald C. Stuart, *United States Expansion and British North America, 1775–1971* (Chapel Hill: University of North Carolina Press, 1988), p. 53.

4. Jean R. Burnet with Howard Palmer, *"Coming Canadians": An Introduction to a History of Canada's Peoples* (Toronto: McClelland and Stewart and the Multi-culturalism Directorate, 1988), pp. 45, 47.

5. David V. J. Bell, "The Loyalist Tradition in Canada," *Journal of Canadian Studies* 5 (May 1970): 22–33, reprinted in J. M. Bumsted, comp., *Canadian History before Confederation,* 2d ed. (Georgetown, Ont.: Irwin Dorsey, 1979), pp. 209–26.

6. Ibid.; G. T. Borrett, "The Leveling Principle in Canadian Life," in *Letters from Canada and the United States* (1865), reprinted in Bumsted, *Canadian History,* p. 213.

7. Bell, "Loyalist Tradition," p. 209; Paul Romney, "From Constitutionalism to Legalism: Trial by Jury, Responsible Government, and the Rule of Law in the Canadian Political Culture," *Law and History Review* 7 (spring 1989): 121–74, 126.

8. Two concise essays on the rebellions of 1837, from which these quotations are taken, are S. F. Wise, "Colonial Attitudes from the Era of the War of 1812 to the Rebellions of 1837," in Wise and Robert Craig Brown, *Canada Views the United States: Nineteenth-Century Political Attitudes* (Seattle: University of Washington, 1967), pp. 16–43; and J. E. Rea, "William Lyon Mackenzie—Jacksonian?" *Mid-America* 50 (July 1968): 223–35, reprinted in Bumsted, *Canadian History,* pp. 375–86. For Papineau's ideology, see Fernand Ouellete, ed., *Papineau: Text Choisis* (Quebec: Presses Universitaires Laval, 1958); and for Mackenzie, see his *Sketches of Canada and the United States* (London: E. Wilson, 1833).

9. Godwin is quoted in Stuart, *United States Expansion,* p. 98.

10. The *Spectator* is quoted in P. B. Waite, *The Life and Times of Confederation,*

MICHAEL FELLMAN

1864–1867: Politics, Newspapers, and the Union of British North America (Toronto: University of Toronto Press, 1962), p. 19. For this discussion of the impact of the U.S. Civil War, I am also indebted to Robin Winks, *Canada and the United States: The Civil War Years* (Baltimore, Md.: Johns Hopkins University Press, 1960), and W. L. Morton, *The Critical Years: The Union of British North America, 1857–1873* (Toronto: McClelland and Stewart, 1964). Also see Morton's pithy essay, "British North America and a Continent in Dissolution, 1861–1871," *History*, n.s., 47 (June 1962): 139–56, reprinted in Bumsted, *Canadian History*, pp. 389–405.

11. Morton, in Bumsted, *Canadian History*, pp. 392, 402.

12. Winks, *Canada and the United States*, pp. 338–48.

13. Morton, *Critical Years*, p. 288.

14. Harold Martin Troper, *Only Farmers Need Apply: Official Canadian Government Encouragement of Immigration from the United States, 1896–1911* (Toronto: Griffin House, 1972).

15. Quoted in R. Douglas Francis, Richard Jones, and Donald B. Smith, *Destinies: Canadian History since Confederation*, 2d ed. (Toronto: Holt, Rinehart and Winston, 1992), p. 133.

16. John Richards once made this connection, based on astute research, in an essay he ran by me that was subsequently cut out by his co-author and editors of the otherwise excellent *Prairie Capitalism: Power and Influence in the New West*, by Richards and Larry Pratt (Toronto: McClelland and Stewart, 1979). Any politically astute Canadian would recognize George McGovern as a first cousin New Democrat, which demonstrates the long life of cross-border prairie social democracy.

17. L. M. Fortier to W. E. B. DuBois, March 17, 1911, quoted in Troper, *Only Farmers Need Apply*, pp. 23–24; *Toronto Mail & Empire*, April 28, 1911, quoted in Troper, *Only Farmers Need Apply*, p. 138.

18. All these quotations from Canadian racist ideologues are from Carl Berger, "The True North Strong and Free," in Peter Russell, ed., *Nationalism in Canada* (1966), and reprinted in Bumsted, *Canadian History*, pp. 215–36.

19. Quotations from Berger, "True North Strong and Free," reprinted in Bumsted, *Canadian History*, pp. 215–36. For Canadian exclusion of Jewish refugees from the Nazis, see Irving Abella and Harold Troper, *None Is Too Many: Canada and the Jews of Europe, 1933–1938* (Toronto: Lester & Orpen Dennys, 1982).

20. Wilfred Laurier is quoted in Robert Craig Brown, *Canada's National Policy, 1883–1900: A Study in Canadian-American Relations* (Princeton, N.J.: Princeton University Press, 1964), p. 178. Brown is a sure-footed guide to this period.

21. John Sherman is quoted in the plodding *Canadian-American Relations, 1875–1911*, by Charles C. Tansill (New Haven, Conn.: Yale University Press, 1943), p. 409.

22. James G. Blaine to Benjamin Harrison in Brown, *Canada's National Policy,* p. 235.

23. Tansill, *Canadian-American Relations,* pp. 463–66.

24. There is a strong literature on the connections of the Social Gospel, progressivism, and politics, of which the most useful book is Ramsay Cook, *The Regenerators: Social Criticism in Late Victorian English Canada* (Toronto: University of Toronto Press, 1985).

25. Thompson and Randall, *United States and Canada,* pp. 202–206.

26. Quoted in R. Douglas Francis, Richard Jones, and Donald B. Smith, *Destinies,* p. 342.

CONTRIBUTORS

CARL ABBOTT is professor of urban studies and planning at Portland State University. His most recent book is *Greater Portland: Urban Life and Landscape in the Pacific Northwest* (University of Pennsylvania Press, 2001).

KEN S. COATES is professor of history and dean of the College of Arts and Science at the University of Saskatchewan. His most recent publication is *The Marshall Decision and Native Rights* (McGill-Queen's University Press, 2001).

MICHAEL FELLMAN is professor of history and director of the graduate liberal studies program at Simon Fraser University. His most recent book is *The Making of Robert E. Lee* (New York: Random House, 2000).

JOHN M. FINDLAY is professor of history at the University of Washington, Seattle. He serves as managing editor of *Pacific Northwest Quarterly*.

JOHN LUTZ is assistant professor of history at the University of Victoria, British Columbia. Recent publications include "Making 'Indians' in British Columbia: Power, Race and the Importance of Place," in *Power and Place in the North American West,* edited by John Findlay and Richard White (Seattle: University of Washington Press, 1999); "'Relating to the Country': The Lekwammen and the Extension of Settlement," in *Beyond the City Limits: Rural History in British Columbia,* edited by Ruth Sandwell (Vancouver: UBC Press, 1999); and "Gender and Work in Lekwammen Families, 1843–1970," in *Gendered Pasts: Historical Essays on Femininity and Masculinity in Canada,* edited by Kathryn McPherson, Cecilia Morgan, and Nancy M. Forestell (Toronto: Oxford University Press, 1999).

DANIEL MARSHALL is a principal at Pacific Reach Consulting Limited. He is the author of *Those Who Fell from the Sky: A History of the Cowichan Peoples* (Victoria, B.C.: Cowichan Tribes, 1999).

JEREMY MOUAT is associate professor of history at Athabasca University. His most recent book is *Metal Mining in Canada, 1840–1950* (Ottawa: National Museum of Science and Technology, 2000).

GALEN ROGER PERRAS is assistant professor of history at Bishop's University, Lennoxville, Quebec. His most recent major publication is *Franklin Roosevelt and the Origins of the Canadian-American Security Alliance, 1933–1945: Necessary But Not Necessary Enough* (Westport, Conn.: Praeger, 1998).

CHAD REIMER is a member of the history faculty at University College of the Fraser Valley in Abbotsford, British Columbia, where he teaches courses in Canadian and applied history.

JOSEPH E. TAYLOR III is associate professor of history at Iowa State University. In 1999 he published *Making Salmon: An Environmental History of the Northwest Fisheries Crisis* (Seattle: University of Washington Press).

PATRICIA K. WOOD is assistant professor of geography at York University. She is the coauthor, with Engin F. Isin, of *Citizenship and Identity* (London: Sage, 1999).

DONALD WORSTER is Hall Distinguished Professor of American history at the University of Kansas. His most recent publication is *A River Running West: The Life of John Wesley Powell* (Oxford University Press, 2001).

INDEX

and defense of Canada, 181–82, 184, 186, 188, 196; Royal Navy of, 93, 94; and salmon diplomacy, 163. *See also* Hudson's Bay Company

British Columbia, 4–5, 15, 17, 19–20, 155, 172, 182–84, 225; attitudes toward corporations in, 132–33; economic conditions in, 108–9, 123–41; gold rush to, 14, 31–66; historiography of, 233, 237–38; and Italian immigrants, 107–8; politics in, 125, 132–34; and salmon diplomacy, 163; similarity of to U.S., 253; wilderness in, 253–54; wilderness advocacy in, 253–54

Calgary, 111, 113, 114

California: influence of on American Northwest, 212–13; influence of on British Columbia gold rush, 33–34, 40–41

Canada: identity of in relation to U.S., 259, 260–61; identity and myths of, 124, 139–40, 255, 257, 259, 261, 278; migrants from, to U.S., 80–82, 207, 275; as prospective military enemy of U.S., 182. *See also* anti-Americanism in Canada; British Columbia; Canadian national policy; diplomacy; immigration across U.S.–Canada border; liberalism in Canadian politics; nation-states

Canada–United States Free Trade Agreement, 6, 19, 203. *See also* North American Free Trade Agreement

Canadian national policy, 141, 275; effects of on attitudes toward railroads in British Columbia, 125, 128–30

Canadian Pacific Railroad, 108, 109,

124–41, 164; attitudes toward in British Columbia, 130–31, 132–34, 138–39; as Canadian symbol, 139–40

capitalism, 141, 205–6, 274; and borders, 123–24; Native peoples' response to, 95–96; and salmon fishery, 158–61. *See also* British Columbia; commerce; extractive industry; labor; salmon fishery; unions

Carson, Rachel, 255, 263

Cascadia, x, 7, 19, 118, 203, 204–5, 209–13, 237

cities, and cross-border regionalism, 211–13

Civil War (U.S.), and Canadian confederation, 280–81

Clallam, 89, 91, 94

Cold War, and Canadian-American relations, 288–89

Coleman, Alberta, 112, 113, 115

Columbia River, 205, 225–26

Columbia River chinook, 166, 167–68, 169

commerce, 15; among Native peoples, 11; cross-border, 6, 203, 210–11, 279, 284–86, 287–88

Consolidated Mining and Smelting Company of Canada (Cominco), 110, 137, 139

Corbin, D. C., 127, 135

Crerar, H. D. G., 189–90

diplomacy: during Cold War, 288–89; and defense of West Coast (1934–42), 181–96; and disputes over salmon, 155–75

Douglas, James, 40, 41, 42, 49–50, 62–65

Duncan, William, 88, 90, 92–93

LIBRARY OF CONGRESS CATALOGING-IN-PUBLICATION DATA

Parallel destinies : Canadian-American relations west of the Rockies /
edited by John M Findlay and Ken S. Coates

p.   cm.

Includes index.

ISBN 0-295-89252-7 (alk. paper)—ISBN 0-295-98253-5 (pbk.: alk. paper)

1. United States—Relations—Canada.

2. Canada—Relations—United States.

3. United States—Boundaries—Canada.

4. Canada—Boundaries—United States.

5. Northern boundary of the United States—History.

6. Northwest, Pacific—History.

7. Canada, Western—History.

I. Findlay, John M.

II. Coates, Ken S.

E183.8C2P36 2002   979.5—dc21   2002022406

NATIONAL LIBRARY OF CANADA CATALOGUING IN PUBLICATION

Main entry under title:

Parallel destinies : Canadian-American relations west of the Rockies /
edited by John M. Findlay and Ken S. Coates.

(Emil and Kathleen Sick lecture-book series in western history and biography)

Includes index.

ISBN 0-7735-2458-4 (bound).—ISBN 0-7735-2459-2 (pbk.: alk. paper)

1. Canada—Relations—United States.

2. United States—Relations—Canada.

3. Canada—Boundaries—United States.

4. United States—Boundaries—Canada.

5. Northern boundary of the United States—History.

6. Northwest, Pacific—History.

I. Findlay, John M. 1955–

II. Coates, Kenneth, 1956–

III. Series.

FC249.P35 2002   979.5   C2002-901536-7

E183.8.C2P36   2002